The Excellent Wife

DAY BY DAY

Karen Eiler

The Excellent Wife
DAY BY DAY

by Karen Eiler

Based on *The Excellent Wife* by Martha Peace

The names of the people in this book, as well as many of the details
in the stories, have been changed to protect the identity
and privacy of the individuals involved.

Cover design by Dan Elkins
Book design by Melanie Schmidt

ISBN 978-1-885904-86-7

PRINTED IN THE UNITED STATES OF AMERICA
BY
FOCUS PUBLISHING
Bemidji, Minnesota

Dedication

To my husband Scott

Whose love gets us through life

Acknowledgements

This book would never have happened without the love, support, guidance, encouragement and enabling of my Father God; my Lord and Savior Jesus Christ, and the Holy Spirit. I am so very grateful God saved me through His Son, and that He gives me gifts through His Spirit not only to write, but to use His Word to encourage you, the reader. I am *uber* excited to see how They are going to use this book to strengthen marriages and work in ways that I am completely incapable of on my own. I love You, God, and pray that You would help me to love you more.

My husband Scott is truly my other half, and if he weren't the encouraging, understanding guy that he is, this book would have never gotten off the ground. The long-running joke in our family is, "Sorry, Honey, I can't pay attention to you right now. I'm writing a book about being an excellent wife!" I love you, Sweetheart! Thank you for putting up with this project for so long; for loving, believing in and praying for me; and for being the best husband any man could ever be.

Likewise, I have to thank my daughters Amy, Brittan and Ciara for their prayers, encouragement and understanding. I know this has been a long time in coming, but I love you girls and thank you for your patience.

Martha Peace has been so gracious to allow me, an unknown author, to produce a work with her name and blessing on it. Her wisdom, experience and Spirit-filled insights have been invaluable as we have worked on this project together. Most of all, I have to thank her for writing *The Excellent Wife*, which had such a huge impact on my life and is a large part of who I am today. Thanks also to Jan Haley of Focus Publishing, who truly has the gift of encouragement. Jan is such a cheerleader, and has kept me going to the finish line!

I'd also like to thank my dear friend, Stephen Estep, who challenged my theology, proofread many of the lessons, helped re-write some of the stickier paragraphs, diligently checked every Scripture verse and reference, kept me laughing when I wanted to cry, and most of all prayed for me.

Thanks to my brother, Dan Elkins, who designed the cover; and my siblings, Matt and Angela Elkins, Jim and Dede Roos, and Dan's wife, Barb, for their prayers, wisdom and encouragement. I'd also like to thank my mother-in-law, Shirley Eiler, who prays for me faithfully, is so outspoken in her praise, and who raised that wonderful man who makes me smile.

Thanks to the many excellent wives (and future wives!) who prayed for me and/or contributed "life material" to this book: Tracy Riggs, Janet DeVaul, Sue Beswick, Lisa Boles, Diane Walsh, Terri Burkett, Wendy Foster, Danice Doganeiro, Amanda Congleton, Michelle Jocelyn, and Kathy Sanson. I'd also like to thank the women who made up my first Excellent Wife class; each one of them tenaciously stuck with me for twenty-four weeks, even though I certainly wasn't what anyone would call a "gifted" teacher, and their faithfulness was so encouraging to me: Michele, Dixie, Jacee, Michelle, Mary, Bellekys, Stefanie, Tammy, June, Tiffany, Lisa, Kathy, Tracy, Candie, Trish, and Lynda. Also, Shari and Betty, who watched the little ones so their moms could learn. I love you guys!

A special thank you to Michele Adams for her unfailing friendship, consistent prayers, and for contributing *so much* to this book. Her life and spirit continue to inspire me every day. Thanks also to Cheryl McCoy who, as a young believer, introduced me to *The Excellent Wife* Bible study. I will be forever grateful to these two women who live their lives sacrificially.

Finally, a shout-out goes to the Starbucks in Feather Sound of Clearwater, Florida. They have the best writing chairs, they keep the temperature perfect, and of course, they kept me fueled during my most productive days. I would probably still be writing this book if it weren't for them.

Karen Eiler

Foreword

Twenty-one years ago I was trained as a biblical counselor by Lou Priolo, and he assigned me to find a book on the role of women that we could use for homework in the counseling sessions. I read several popular books and concluded that none of them were good for our purposes. They were either psychology-based or held an unbiblical view of submission. As a result, Lou then asked and helped me to prepare and teach an eight-week Sunday school class for ladies on the topic. The very first Sunday, the person taping the classes asked me the title of my series. I had not previously thought about a title but one of the Scriptures in the first lesson was "An excellent wife who can find? She is far more precious than jewels." (Proverbs 31:10) Therefore, the title of the class became *The Excellent Wife*.

As time went on, Lou and I began to see how God was powerfully using His Word and those tapes to help women mature as Christian wives. Then, it occurred to Lou to ask me to write a book. Several years went by and finally three men insisted that I write a book—Lou, Ed Sherwood (my pastor at that time), and Sanford (my husband). Since Sanford told me to write it, I saw it as a submission issue. (Really, I did!) Thus the journey began and my pastor graciously met with me over the course of a year and taught me the basics of how to write. Several people helped me during the three-year process—Lou Priolo, Ed Sherwood, Anna Maupin, John Crotts, Stuart Scott, Jay Adams, and Sanford Peace. Fifteen years ago, Jan and Stan Haley from Focus Publishing agreed to publish it, and the rest is, as they say, "History."

Over the years, God in His grace has continued to not only use *The Excellent Wife* book to help individual women but also raised up many faithful women to teach and disciple others through the material. One such faithful teacher is Karen Eiler. Karen has not only taught *The Excellent Wife* but she has also brought her own God-given creativity to this project. Thus, *The Excellent Wife Day by Day* was conceived.

The Excellent Wife Day by Day is a five-days-a-week, year-long devotional for wives to remind them of their "primary ministry" to their husbands—to give glory to God as they show love, respect, and biblical submission to their husbands. Each day there is a Scripture on which to meditate, a brief very engaging story, and a reminder of at least one biblical principle. Karen's devotional book is a convicting and a challenging blessing to her readers to help them see a high and proper view of God as well as how to respond to Him in a way that pleases Him.

For those of you who love the LORD and want to be reminded of the precious truths in the Scriptures so that you can be a God-honoring wife, this is the devotional book for you. It will convict you but you will love it. *The Excellent Wife Day by Day* caught and held my attention even after a year's worth of days! I thank God for Karen's ministry to her ladies in her *Excellent Wife* class and now to you.

Because of His Mercies,

Martha Peace
Peachtree City, Georgia

Introduction

There are a number of things wrong with me right now.

I'm writing a book which is supposed to help and inspire women to love their husbands. Yet I'm not living a lot of what I'm writing. My hypocrisy cripples me.

I'm living some of it, but there are major portions where I write what I know, *not what I* live. *Is it possible for anyone to write a book of this magnitude and actually live all of it? At what point do you say, "My obedience is good enough, NOW I am qualified to write this book"?*

If this is my standard, then the book becomes about me and not about Christ.

This book is about Christ.

I wrote the above in my prayer journal one day, because I had just completed several days of epic failure in my life and marriage, and truly felt I was not good enough to write this book.

This daily devotional is based on Martha Peace's groundbreaking work, *The Excellent Wife*, and it was my firm belief that Martha would never behave as I had just behaved. And honestly, I still believe that (sort of). But I think Martha will be first to tell you she is not perfect, either.

You, me, Martha—we're all in the same boat. We may be at different points in our own personal journey with Christ, but we're all human—full of human weaknesses—and none of us are perfectly obedient to everything God asks of us. As you read this book, there will be days when you will be very encouraged in your faith and motivated to love your husband more. But there will be other days when you may become so discouraged that you'll want to give up. I understand that feeling, because in these pages we are looking at the Perfect Standard (Jesus Christ) for what we should do and how we should live. When we compare ourselves to these perfect standards, it's easy at times to feel completely worthless and unable to ever achieve any respectable level of obedience.

I hope it will encourage you to know that the author felt this way when faced with the righteous standards of truth in God's Word. I will never be good enough, on my own, to speak for God. But thankfully, my sufficiency—my right and authority to speak truth to you—is in Christ, not in myself.

Your sufficiency is also found in Christ. Nothing naturally occurring in you makes obedience possible. "All we like sheep have gone astray; We have turned, every one, to his own way" (Isaiah 53:6a, KJV). But the good news is that "The LORD has laid on **Him** *[Jesus Christ] the iniquity of us all"* (Isaiah 53:6b, KJV). In other words, Jesus has taken on the debt and the guilt of your sin, making you clean and ready for service. You don't have to be burdened by the weight of sin anymore; you are now and always will be free to obey, because of Jesus!

This book came about as a result of a conversation with a friend of mine who had gone through much of *The Excellent Wife* Bible study a couple of years prior, but found herself in a desperate situation with her husband. After talking with my friend for a few minutes, it was clear she had forgotten much of what she learned from God's Word about how to be the wife God wants her to be. I had a very clear vision in my mind of the deceiver lying on the steps leading up to her front door, ready to pounce on this beautiful family and devour them. And I knew it was critical for her to fight back. It was then that the concept of this book was born.

Even if your marriage is strong, God warns us to be diligent because our "adversary, the devil, prowls about like a roaring lion, seeking someone to devour" (1 Peter 5:8). Satan's entire game plan is to destroy the kingdom of God here on earth, and your marriage is in his crosshairs.

The Excellent Wife Day-by-Day devotional has been designed to reinforce the lessons taught in *The Excellent Wife* by Martha Peace, but even if you've never been through that study, you'll find wisdom here to supplement your daily time in God's Word, particularly as it relates to your role as a godly wife. If you haven't taken *The Excellent Wife* Bible study, I encourage you to find one in your area or see about getting one started in your own church. I promise, it will change your life, as it did mine!

While writing this book, in most of the lessons I have assumed that you love your husband, even if you are currently experiencing some difficulties in your relationship. Few marriages can go very far without hitting some "bumps" along the way. However, I also realize that some readers may no longer respect or feel love for their husbands. It is my hope that by committing yourself to discovering God's truth in these pages, and by becoming "doers of the word, and not merely hearers" (James 1:22), you will rediscover the love that you once had for your husband.

Whether your marriage is good or struggling, you will benefit by going through this study, if you commit to faithfully doing the lessons and then acting on what you've learned. We will cover ten basic themes in this study: communication, submission, sanctification, love, respect, the home, helping, idolatry, humility, and conflict. But we won't take these themes one at a time, exhaustively. Rather, we will hit a different theme each day, and cover each theme several times throughout the year. I chose to organize the book this way because that is the way your life works: you don't get sanctification down and then start working on humility. You'll be working on each of these issues throughout your life, on some days one issue more than others. I hope that God will use these lessons to remind you of His truths every day, and that you will find something on most days to encourage you and keep you pressing on toward the goal of glorifying God in your life and marriage.

The names of the people in this book, as well as many of the details in the stories, have been changed to protect the identity and privacy of the individuals involved. I have counseled and discipled many women who share similar stories, so if a particular story seems to be about you and your marriage, chances are you're one of the many women whose stories I've weaved together to portray a representative scenario.

How to Use This Book

- I chose to write five lessons a week, because I know how difficult it is to keep up with a devotional every single day. If you faithfully do all five lessons, use those extra days of the week to review the material again, review all of the Scripture you've previously memorized, or spend more time on some of the application sections. You could also spend those "free" days in prayer, quieting yourself to meditate on God's Word and asking Him to show you the lessons you need to work on the most.

- I strongly recommend you purchase a prayer journal or find a notebook you can use along with these lessons. Some of the lessons call for you to write in your prayer journal, and you will get more out of the lesson if you do the journaling.

- Each lesson has a sidebar that is the application part of the lesson. Read the lesson first, then the application. If the application section asks you to actually *do* something, then do it! You'll get so much more out of the study if you put God's Word into action.

- At the bottom of each lesson is a Memorize It! section. God loves it when we memorize His Word, and this devotional makes it easy for you to do that. Each week you'll be learning one verse. After you've completed the first day's lesson, read over the verse in the Memorize It! section, repeating it five to ten times, until you feel it starting to stick in your mind. On day two, cover the verse and see how much of it you can say without looking, then read it out loud again several times. On day 5, the verse is missing, but by then you should be able to say it without looking. If you do this faithfully each day, by the end of the week you will have the verse memorized! If you've already memorized the selected verse of the week, find another verse from a previous lesson to memorize, and work on it in the same way, using your prayer journal to write it out each day.

- Look up all of the Scriptures referred to in each lesson and read God's Word for yourself. This devotional does not have a daily Scripture reading program, but it is filled with Scripture. I also encourage you to continue your regular daily Bible reading program while you're doing this study.

- Neither the publishers or I have altered the wording of any Scripture included in this work, but we have sometimes added explanatory words (these words will always be enclosed within brackets [ ]), or used italics and/or bolding to emphasize certain words within the verses. Typically, when authors alter a Scripture verse in any way, they do something like this:

  "For God so *loved* the world..." (John 3:16a, emphasis added).

  I have not followed that format in this book. The reader should understand that nowhere in the Bible are words italicized or bolded to add emphasis, so I will not be reminding you of this every time. Also, some Scriptre verses are not reprinted in their entirety. Anytime a verse is not reprinted in its entirety, explanatory words have been added, or certain words have been emphasized, the reference will be followed by this symbol: †

  "For God so loved [all of] the world" (John 3:16†).

- There are some lessons which you may feel don't apply to you, and you may be tempted to skip them. If you are behind in your reading, feel free to skim these lessons quickly and move on to the next one. However, there are truths to be discovered in every lesson, even if at first you feel you can't relate to the topic. If you're moving on schedule, read each lesson carefully and ask God to help you examine your heart and life to see what truths He wants to remind you of in that lesson.

When you are finished with this book, hopefully you'll be more Christlike than you are now. But do not be discouraged if you're not living this perfectly. God doesn't expect perfection, only a continued willingness to be obedient and yielded to Him in every area of your life.

God bless you and your husband as you read through this book for the next twelve months and commit yourself to Jesus Christ, allowing Him to make you the excellent wife God wants you to be.

Week 1, Day 1

An excellent wife, who can find?
For her worth is far above jewels.
The heart of her husband
trusts in her, and he will
have no lack of gain.
She does him good and not
evil all the days of her life.
PROVERBS 31:10-12

Application

This is the "Application" section referred to in the Introduction. Each day, this space will contain either further explanation of the lesson or else an "assignment" for you to put the lesson into action. Today's assignment is to read Proverbs 31:10-31, then answer the following questions, taking action if necessary:

- ☑ Did you write out your prayer?
- ☑ Have you secured some type of prayer journal?
- ☑ Are you ready to memorize God's Word?
- ☑ Are you committed to faithfully doing this study for the entire year?

If so, you're ready to begin this journey!

Now may the God of peace Himself sanctify you entirely; and may your spirit and soul and body be preserved complete, without blame at the coming of our L*ORD Jesus Christ* (1 Thessalonians 5:23).

Getting Started

Your assignment for today is to read the Introduction to this book.

I know most people skip this section, but it contains some very useful information that will guide you through this study, and I don't want you to miss it. After you read it, write in the space below your prayer for what you want God to do in your life over the next year, as you seek His presence and His will for you as a godly wife:

*See Appendix A for guidance on what to do if you aren't sure whether or not you are a true believer.

Memorize It!

But let all who take refuge in You be glad, let them ever sing for joy; and may You shelter them, that those who love Your name may exult in You.
(Psalm 5:11)

Fertile Ground

Week 1, Day 2

Do not be amazed that I said to you, "You must be born again."

John 3:7

A farmer went out to plant seed in his field. As he scattered, not all of the seeds actually made it into the fertile soil. Some of the seeds fell onto the road and were eaten by the crows. Some of the seeds landed in the rocky, uncultivated patches of ground, and the thorny places where nothing but weeds could thrive. But the rest of the seeds were successfully planted in the rich soil, where they grew up into healthy, fruitful plants.

You may recognize that story as a parable Jesus told (Luke 8:4-15). He went on to describe how the seed is the Word of God, and we are the soil. My question to you today is this: what kind of soil are you?

If you're a "rocky soil" person, you may have "accepted" Christ just a short time ago and for reasons other than a desire to love and serve Him. Perhaps you got "saved" because you wanted God to fix some things in your life, or because you're afraid *not* to be a Christian out of fear of what will happen when you die. In "time of temptation" (i.e., when their faith is tested) "rocky soil Christians" stop following Christ.

"Thorny soil" persons are those who "accept" Christ, but they are so wrapped up in their own stuff—worrying about their life, spending all of their time pursuing wealth and "the pleasures of this life" (vs. 14)—that they never mature in Christ and never do anything for the Kingdom.

The "road" soil describes those whose hearts are so hardened, they can't receive the Word of God at all. Our hearts can be hardened by many things: life, trouble, wealth, and especially *religion*. Many religious people think they can earn their way to heaven by living a good, honorable life. Or they *know* Christ is the only way to heaven and they *think* they're born again, but there is no spiritual growth or fruit for God in their life. They have only "accepted" Christ as their Savior, but not as their Lord. They retain their right to live as they please.

Memorize It!

But let all who take refuge in You be glad, let them ever sing for joy; and may You shelter them, that those who love Your name may exult in You.

(Psalm 5:11)

Application

My hope is that you are a "fertile soil" believer:

- You know you're God's child, based on your faith in the gospel (Ephesians 2:8-9; John 3:1-21).
- You desire to spend time with God.
- Christ has the final say on how you live your life.
- You study the Scriptures to know what God requires of you.
- You are producing spiritual fruits of love, joy, peace, patience, kindness, etc. (Galatians 5:22-23).

If you're not a fertile soil believer, you will never be able to meet the demands of becoming an excellent wife. So before you go any further in this study, be sure you have truly accepted Christ, not just as your Savior, but also as your Lord.

Week 1, Day 3

Husbands, love your wives, just as Christ also loved the church and gave Himself up for her, so that He might sanctify her, having cleansed her by the washing of water with the word, that He might present to Himself the church in all her glory, having no spot or wrinkle or any such thing; but that she would be holy and blameless.
EPHESIANS 5:25-27

Application

God's primary purpose in marriage is not to make you happy, but to make you holy. However, if you are a Christian, being holy is what brings the most happiness. *"Now to Him who is able to keep you from stumbling, and to make you stand in the presence of His glory blameless with great joy..."* (Jude 1:24†).

Some couples have a Mission Statement for their marriage and their family, defining the purpose of their marriage. If you haven't done that yet, ask your husband to help you come up with one, and include this concept of holiness. A simple mission statement for a godly marriage might sound something like this: "To help each other become more holy and more conformed to the image of Christ, to love God, and to make Him known."

The Purpose of Marriage

Have you ever thought about the *purpose* of your marriage?

One thing that causes us to falter in any of our commitments is when we lose sight of their purpose. When soldiers out on the battlefield don't know why they're fighting, they have a hard time achieving their objectives. But people who have a strong sense of purpose are usually successful in achieving their goals.

If you're going to be successful in marriage, you must understand the purpose of marriage. In particular, *God's purpose* in your marriage.

God created marriage for procreation; as a picture of the relationship of Christ and the Church; for the protection of His people; and for His glory. But He has another very important purpose, upon which all those other purposes hinge: *to make you holy.*

God has been working on your holiness since the moment of your salvation. This process is called *sanctification*, and your husband is one of the greatest tools God has for sanctifying you and purifying sin from your life. God uses your husband—either through his leadership or through conflict—to show you your sin and weaknesses. When you are faced with your true spiritual condition, you can either respond to the Holy Spirit and repent; or you can "quench" the Holy Spirit (1 Thessalonians 5:19), continuing to sin and hardening your heart.

It is difficult to hide in marriage. You may try to cover up who you are, but those "fig leaves" always fail (Genesis 3:7) and your true character will eventually reveal itself, showing just how far you are from the image of Christ. "*Today if you hear His voice, do not harden your hearts*" (Hebrews 4:7). God does not want you to harden your heart, but to submit to what He is doing in your life through your husband and your marriage. The question is, are you resisting His will and your husband's role in your sanctification? Or do you look at everything that happens in your life as an opportunity for God to purify you and make you more holy?

Memorize It!

But let all who take refuge in You be glad, let them ever sing for joy; and may You shelter them, that those who love Your name may exult in You.
(Psalm 5:11)

Humility for Two

Rich was finishing his breakfast when Caroline sat down, looking somewhat uncomfortable. He could tell something was up. "Can I ask you a question?" she started. "Sure..." he said. "When we were at the Smith's last night, did I do something to embarrass you in any way?"

Rich thought briefly about something she had said to his friend Jack, but quickly dismissed it. "I don't think so," he answered. "Are you sure?" she said. "Well..." Rich hesitated, then began, "When you told Jack he looked good in that shirt, I was pretty humiliated, actually." Caroline reddened, but let him continue. "I know you didn't mean anything by it, but it came across as...well, flirting. I don't think it's a very godly way to act around other men."

Caroline knew asking Rich to point out areas where she needed to change would sometimes be embarrassing. But she was taken aback by his response; she honestly was not flirting! Still, she could see why it had hurt her husband. Moreover, she was committed to Christ and wanted to change her heart and actions to reflect His LORDship over her life. "OK," she said, "I see what you're saying. I'm sorry, and I will do my best to never let it happen again!"

Yesterday we talked about beginning (or continuing) the process of mutual sanctification. But no discussion of sanctification is complete without a thorough understanding of the concept of *humility*. You cannot participate in mutual sanctification without humbly recognizing your need to change. If you're going to receive reproof, correction and instruction from your husband, you must be humble. If your heart is proud and you think "*more highly*" of yourself than you "*ought to think*" (Romans 12:3), you will resist reproof from your husband. Why should you receive correction if you're already fairly perfect?

Submitting to accountability will sometimes be embarrassing or even humiliating. But don't forget that God gives grace to the humble! He will give you the grace to receive what your husband has to say.

Memorize It!

But let all who take refuge in You be glad, let them ever sing for joy; and may You shelter them, that those who love Your name may exult in You.
(Psalm 5:11)

Husbands, love your wives, just as Christ also loved the church and gave Himself up for her, so that He might sanctify her, having cleansed her by the washing of water with the word, that He might present to Himself the church in all her glory...that she would be holy and blameless. So husbands ought also to love their own wives as their own bodies.
EPHESIANS 5:25-28

Application

When your husband corrects you, it is helpful to remember that he is actually showing you love by helping you live in a way that is pleasing to Christ. *"Better is an open rebuke than love that is concealed. Faithful are the wounds of a friend"* (Proverbs 27:5-6†). How willing you are to let your husband help you in this way will reflect your level of maturity and your commitment to the LORD Jesus.

You can begin working on your humility today by asking your husband to give you an example of some area of your life where he thinks you need to improve to be a better, more godly wife. Coming to him first will keep you from being taken by surprise, and give you practice in receiving reproof when it is unexpected.

Week 1, Day 5

A new commandment I give to you,
that you love one another,
even as I have loved you, that
you also love one another.
JOHN 13:34

Application

Love is a choice we make, not an emotion we feel. Throughout this book we'll be talking about those specific choices. For today, you can begin this journey by praying your desires to God. (Pray the prayer below, writing in your husband's name in the blank, or write out your own prayer in your prayer journal.)

LORD, I know I have not loved __________ as fully as You have commanded. Today, I am recommitting myself to loving him with my whole heart, soul, mind and strength. I trust that as I am obedient to You, You will renew our love for each other and give us a richer, more intimate love than we've ever known before. Thank you for my husband, and help me to love him righteously and unselfishly.

THE PURPOSE OF MARRIAGE

After fifteen years of marriage, Kyle and Jessie are finally calling it quits. Their marriage has had its ups and downs, but the bottom line is that Jessie just does not love Kyle any more. She justifies her impending divorce by saying, "God would not want me to be unhappy for the rest of my life, and there is no hope of happiness with Kyle. Once love is gone, can it possibly come back?"

June is in a similar position, but divorce has never been an option for her and Roger. "I don't love him," she says, "but it would be wrong to divorce, and it would be bad for the kids. So we've decided to just do the best we can and make it work."

What Jessie and June are both missing is that loving your husband is a command, not an option. When the Pharisees came to Jesus and asked him to define the greatest commandment, he answered: "*'And you shall love the LORD your God with all your heart, and with all your soul, and with all your mind, and with all your strength.' The second is this, 'You shall love your neighbor as yourself.' There is no other commandment greater than these"* (Mark 12:30-31†).

Most of us would never think of stealing a car, or murdering someone. But those commands are not as important to God as His command to love our husbands. If we really believed that, we would stop acting as though we have a choice in the matter! If you don't love your husband, you are disobeying God.

In case you're wondering if your husband is your neighbor, think about this: who is closer to you than your husband, your closest "neighbor"? In the parallel passage in Matthew 22, Jesus says, "*the second* [command] *is like* [the first]" (Matthew 22:39†). Meaning, the command to love your husband is a corresponding command to loving God. You are to love your husband with your whole heart (emotionally and passionately), soul (the very core of who you are) mind (every thought), and strength (every action). You are commanded to be "all in."

YOUR #1 MINISTRY

After Heidi accepted Christ as her LORD and Savior, she was eager to get involved in church as soon as possible. She was especially interested in the outreach ministry that was instrumental in bringing her to Christ. So she met with her pastor's wife to find out what her next step should be.

"I'm glad you're so excited about this," Mary Beth told her. "But you need to concentrate on your most important ministry first." Heidi looked puzzled. "My most important ministry?" she asked.

"That's right," Mary Beth said. "Your number one ministry is to your husband. We'll always have plenty for you to do around here," she laughed. "But I want to make sure you keep your spiritual priorities straight. After your own relationship with Christ, *nothing* is more important than your ministry to Jack."

Just as God created Eve and gave her a ministry to be Adam's suitable helper (Genesis 2:18), He has also determined your primary ministry and role in life: to love, help, and serve your husband. Since no other ministry, occupation or pursuit should have greater priority, your husband should be the primary benefactor of your time and energy, not the recipient of whatever is left over at the end of the day. Whether your guy is a faithful Christian or an unbeliever, God wants you to serve and submit to him. This has been His plan for you since before you were even born! *"For we are His workmanship, created in Christ Jesus for good works, which God prepared beforehand so that we would walk in them"* (Ephesians 2:10).

This ministry is not a "sub-ministry"; it's one of the most important ministries in all of God's Kingdom! Strong, godly families are one of the two primary means God has set up for perpetuating the gospel throughout the earth (the other being His Church). Accordingly, God promises eternal rewards for fulfilling this ministry in faith. Your ministry to your husband is *"profitable for all things, since it holds promise for the present life and also for the life to come"* (1 Timothy 4:8).

Memorize It!

Therefore if you have been raised up with Christ, keep seeking the things above, where Christ is, seated at the right hand of God. Set your mind on the things above, not on the things that are on earth. (Colossians 3:1-2)

Then the LORD God said, "It is not good for the man to be alone; I will make him a helper suitable for him."
GENESIS 2:18

Application

Aside from Christ Jesus, is your husband your main focus in life? Is he getting more time and attention from you than any other person or activity? Do you understand and appreciate the importance of this ministry?

If your husband has not been your most important ministry, take time today to reevaluate your life and recommit to being the kind of wife God wants you to be. You might want to pray a prayer like this:

LORD, I confess I've not had Your priorities as my priorities. I need your help to become the wife you want me to be. I now commit myself to making ministry to my husband the primary ministry of my life. Teach me what I need to know. I want my life and my relationship with my husband to glorify You. In Jesus' Name, Amen.

Week 2, Day 2

You will make known to me the path of life; In Your presence is fullness of joy; In Your right hand there are pleasures forever.
PSALM 16:11

Application

Our focus today has been on the joy that comes from submitting to your husband. However, if you're not used to experiencing joy, the threat of losing what you've never had is not going to be very motivating. Your primary motivation, therefore, should not be *joy*, but to please Christ, who died for you. Take time now to talk to God about your feelings about submission, and about what you hope to accomplish through this devotional over the next year. Take time to write out a summary of your thoughts and your prayer in your prayer journal.

SUBMISSION = JOY

If you studied logic in school, you may remember this equation: *If a = b, and b = c, then a = c.* For example: "If John is a Marine, and Marines are always brave, then John is always brave." See how that works? So let's do a similar logic exercise as it pertains to biblical submission:

IF God commands you to be submitted to your husband;
AND Obeying God's commands always brings you joy;
THEN Submitting to your husband will always bring you joy.

Logically, our THEN statement is true. The question is, do you believe the IF and AND statements?

- **God commands you to be submitted to your husband** – *"Wives, be subject to your own husbands, as to the LORD"* (Ephesians 5:22). It's not an option, or a suggestion. It's a command.
- **Obedience to God's commands brings joy** – *"Your testimonies...are the joy of my heart"* (Psalm 119:111). Most of us can admit intellectually that God's commands bring joy. But if obeying God is not a regular pattern for you, you may not have experienced with any great frequency how much joy comes from saying *yes* to God.
- **Submitting to your husband will always bring you joy** – If you've agreed to the first two principles, then logically, you must agree to this one. So why does it seem that submitting to our husbands is usually *not* a joyful thing? Why do we run from this command?

  The problem is not in God or in His command. The problem is us. We're so used to doing things *our* way, we're unfamiliar with what it means to live a joyful life. We haven't experienced the joy of obedience because we're not consistently obedient.

  The godly Christian life is a life of joyful delight in God's commands, not a life of resentment and struggle against them. God designed His commands to benefit and protect you. Submitting to your husband should also be seen as a delight and a joy, knowing that it is for your good and your protection. If you really believed that, you would have no trouble submitting to your husband.

Memorize It!

Therefore if you have been raised up with Christ, keep seeking the things above, where Christ is, seated at the right hand of God. Set your mind on the things above, not on the things that are on earth.
(Colossians 3:1-2)

Love is Patient

Mike and Amy have been married for seven years, and have finally been able to conceive a child. For years, Amy dreamed of the perfect nursery. She picked out the paint, bought the furniture, bed linens, and curtains, and was looking forward to stenciling a design on the freshly painted walls. Mike's job was to replace the worn-out carpeting, paint the walls and hang a new light fixture. He promised the nursery would be ready before the baby arrived. But now with less than a month to go, Mike has still not started on the room.

On Saturday afternoon, Amy walked down the stairs to find Mike watching a college football game. She felt her blood begin to boil, but instead of dwelling on her husband's failures, Amy began to pray 1 Corinthians 13:4, *"Love is patient."* As she surrendered to the Holy Spirit's plan for her in that moment, she chose to be thankful that her husband was home with her, even if he wasn't doing what she wanted him to do.

It is not unusual for you to get aggravated when things don't go your way, when something interferes with your plans, or when you're not feeling well. However, by an act of your will, you can be patient whether you feel like it or not. It is an active, humble, dependent choice to obey God in this way. If you do, the Holy Spirit will help you by pouring out a measure of God's grace.

Impatience and frustration are emotions we experience when our focus is on ourselves and our plans, rather than on Christ. We should confess this to God while it is at the mental attitude stage, before it works its way out into a sinful act.

So, as those who have been chosen of God, holy and beloved, put on a heart of compassion, kindness, humility, gentleness and patience; bearing with one another, and forgiving each other, whoever has a complaint against anyone; just as the Lord forgave you, so also should you. Beyond all these things put on love, which is the perfect bond of unity.
Colossians 3:12-14

Application

A good way to develop the character quality of patience is to memorize Scripture and quote it to yourself when you begin to feel the irritation beginning to build. Another way is to thank God for specific irritants, since Scripture commands us to be thankful *"in everything...for this is God's will for you in Christ Jesus"* (1 Thessalonians 5:18). Sometimes, simply saying to yourself, "Love is patient," helps tremendously when tension is mounting.

Memorize It!

Therefore if you have been raised up with Christ, keep seeking the things above, where Christ is, seated at the right hand of God. Set your mind on the things above, not on the things that are on earth.
(Colossians 3:1-2)

Nevertheless, each individual among you also is to love his own wife even as himself, and the wife must see to it that she respects her husband.
EPHESIANS 5:33

Application

What is more important to you, love or respect? For most women, there's no contest: love is more important than anything. If you consider how strongly you feel about this, it will help you appreciate just how strongly your husband feels about respect. Most men desire respect more than just about anything else in the world.

Throughout this year we'll be talking about what it means to respect your husband. If you love your husband and want to be obedient to Christ, you will pay careful attention to these lessons and prayerfully seek to apply them. For today, ask God to begin revealing the areas of respect where you need the most work, and renew your commitment to respecting your husband in a way that makes him feel most loved.

LOVE = RESPECT

My daughter's roommate was having lunch with some friends, and the discussion turned to relationships. Emily asked the guys this question: *Would you rather be loved or respected?* Her friend Malachi said, "I don't get it. What's the difference?"

It may surprise you to learn that your husband would be equally confused by this question. The truth is that, when it comes to their wives, guys have *love* and *respect* so inextricably linked in their minds, there is no real difference. If they separate the two concepts, they'll almost always choose respect over love. Yes, it's that important! Most men would rather be respected than loved by their wives. In fact, if your husband thinks you don't respect him, he is going to feel you don't love him.

There are many reasons to respect your husband and many benefits to the wife who consistently demonstrates respect. Of course you should do it because it's commanded, but let's just take the word *should* out of the equation. I'm assuming you love your husband and, because you love him, you want to do him "*good and not evil all the days of [your] life*" (Proverbs 31:12). If that is the case, then you need to understand that the best thing you can do for him is to respect him. That is the *how* of love; loving your guy the way he wants to be loved means making sure he knows, beyond all doubt, that you respect him.

In Ephesians 5:33, God commands you to respect your husband. He is the only One who knows how you can best show love to your husband by showing him respect. If you're struggling in your marriage, respect is likely one of the culprits. If you're struggling with loving your husband, then learning to respect him will help you grow in your love for him.

Memorize It!

Therefore if you have been raised up with Christ, keep seeking the things above, where Christ is, seated at the right hand of God. Set your mind on the things above, not on the things that are on earth. (Colossians 3:1-2)

The Power of the Tongue

But no one can tame the tongue; it is a restless evil and full of deadly poison. With it we bless our Lord and Father, and with it we curse men, who have been made in the likeness of God; from the same mouth come both blessing and cursing. My brethren, these things ought not to be this way.
James 3:8-10

Cameron and April were cleaning out the garage, but Cameron was about ready to send April into the house. He appreciated her help, but didn't appreciate how she viewed this as an opportunity to berate him for his lack of tidiness. "Seriously," she said, shaking her head, "how hard is it to just put things back where they belong?" She was a hard worker, but Cameron wished she would just work without commenting about everything.

Thankfully, just as the tension was starting to boil over, April's cell phone rang. Her friend Jill was calling about yet another church ministry his wife was involved in. Cameron welcomed the interruption, but was amazed at the change in his wife's tone. Suddenly she was all bright and happy, and saying things like "the Lord is so good" and "what a blessing!" He shook his head and thought, *What a hypocrite!*

The old saying, "Familiarity breeds contempt," is so true when it comes to marriage. Because we live with our husbands day in and day out, what is in our hearts is not likely to stay hidden very long. It always works its way out into our words. *"But the things that proceed out of the mouth come from the heart"* (Matthew 15:18). If what's in your heart is bitterness or unkind thoughts about your husband, then your words will reflect that.

What makes this especially painful for your husband is when he hears you talk to your friends, and compares it to how you talk to him. *"From the same mouth come both blessing and cursing"* (James 3:10). If you talk to others more sweetly than you talk to your husband, he will see that you have more disdain for him than you do for your friends.

The key to changing your speech is to change your heart. If you have *"anger, wrath, and malice"* in your heart toward your husband, then it will be impossible for you to clean up your *"slander, and abusive speech."* That's why we are told to *"put them **all** aside"* (Colossians 3:8)—you can't put aside the abusive speech if malice is still hanging around.

Application

You put them all aside by putting on *"the new self"* (Colossians 3:10) and putting on *"a heart of compassion, kindness, humility, gentleness and patience"* (verse 12).

Sounds so easy, doesn't it? Just put on the good and put off the bad! But it's *not* easy, and as soon as you make progress, there will be another situation in which you'll be tempted to become angry.

You fight this battle of the heart and mind with the *"sword of the Spirit, which is the Word of God"* (Ephesians 6:17). That's why it is so important to memorize Scripture (the verses in this study will help you get started) and that you repeat God's words to yourself throughout the day. *"Your word I have treasured in my heart, that I may not sin against You"* (Psalm 119:11).

Week 3, Day 1

Older women (should) encourage the young women to love their husbands, to love their children, to be sensible, pure, workers at home, kind, being subject to their own husbands, so that the word of God will not be dishonored.
Titus 2:3-5

Keeping Up With Your Homework

When we were young parents, my husband and I attended a Bible study class at my church made up of couples in our same place in life. Most were in their 20's with young children at home. Our teacher took a couple of Sundays to carefully go over the teaching that wives are to be "workers at home." I would imagine he spent several sleepless nights preparing for what turned out to be, even in our conservative, Bible-believing church, a very controversial topic. Several women in that class worked outside of the home, and at times the discussion got a little "uncomfortable," to say the least!

There should be nothing controversial about this command. Someone has to "keep" the home, and the Bible makes it clear this responsibility falls on the woman.

That's you.

It is *your* responsibility to work at keeping the home: cleaning and organizing the house, planning the meals, caring for the children, operating under your family's budget, etc. It's not your husband's job, it's *yours*. Roughly half of the verses in Proverbs 31:10-31 are about the excellent wife taking care of her home and family. Even if you work outside of the home, and you and your husband share (by mutual agreement) many of the home responsibilities, you are still the one who has the ultimate responsibility to make sure the home is in order.

Throughout the course of this book, we will look closer into what it means to be a keeper of the home. My intent here is not to guilt you into compliance or chain you to the house. My desire is that, more than anything, you would devote yourself to Christ. If you are walking in obedience to Him, you will come to see your work at home as a joyful ministry—not a cross to bear or a drudgery to be endured.

Application

Let's take an assessment of how "plugged in" you are to your responsibility as the keeper of the home. Put a dot on the line that indicates where you believe you are in each area of home responsibility:

1. My home is:

10-----9-----8-----7-----6-----5-----4-----3-----2-----1

Immaculate — *Clean* — *A little grungy* — *Disaster!*

2. Frequency of dinners prepared or planned by me, and eaten at home:

10-----9-----8-----7-----6-----5-----4-----3-----2-----1

Every night — *Most nights* — *Sporadic* — *Almost Never*

3. Who does all the work around the house?

10-----9-----8-----7-----6-----5-----4-----3-----2-----1

I do Everything — *We all chip in* — *My husband runs the show* — *I do nothing*

4. Atmosphere in the home:

10-----9-----8-----7-----6-----5-----4-----3-----2-----1

Complete peace — *Generally calm* — *Up & Down* — *Utter chaos*

5. My attitude about being a keeper at home:

10-----9-----8-----7-----6-----5-----4-----3-----2-----1

Love it! — *It's a responsibility I keep up with* — *I do it, ok?* — *Loathe it!*

Memorize It!

For you have died and your life is hidden with Christ in God. When Christ, who is our life, is revealed, then you also will be revealed with Him in glory.
(Colossians 3:3-4)

Words of Grace

Let no unwholesome word proceed from your mouth, but only such a word as is good for edification according to the need of the moment, so that it will give grace to those who hear.
Ephesians 4:29

Alexa sat trembling, holding the letter her husband had received that day. The anonymous writer claimed to have seen Alexa with another man. Alexa knew it was a lie, but Andy had a jealous nature and did not trust easily. He refused to believe she was innocent. "How can you sit there and lie to me?" he snapped. "People don't just make up stuff like this!"

Alexa could feel tears starting to surface, but she refused to let her emotions control the situation. "I understand you're angry," she said gently, "but anger is not going to help us get to the bottom of this. I've never given you reason to doubt me, but even if I had, you still need to love me. No matter what we go through, we have to be patient, kind and not jealous. And we have to 'believe all things.'[1] I love you! You know I would never do anything to knowingly hurt you."

Someone once said, "Trouble is only opportunity in work clothes." Every conflict in your marriage is an opportunity for God to work, for you to glorify God, and for you and your husband to grow closer together in the Lord. When you're in the midst of a crisis, it's difficult to see it as an opportunity, but you make it an opportunity for good when you have the proper response.

There are a number of godly ways to respond to crisis; the first is to communicate biblically. This means training the tongue to speak the truth of God's Word in a calm, loving tone—not snapping back in a vindictive or harsh way, but gently speaking biblical principles into the situation. Our natural response when threatened is to return "evil for evil" (1 Peter 3:9) by matching our husband's anger and defending ourselves. Responding this way is disobedience and will only make matters worse. Communicating biblically means that we inject God's truth into the situation at the very start, to establish a biblical foundation for working through the crisis.

Application

You can't speak God's truth into the midst of your conflict if you don't know what God's Word says. That's why it is *so* important to memorize Scripture. If you've gotten this far in this study and have skipped the memorization exercises, it's time to start doing that today. You will find that, as you hide God's Word in your heart (Psalm 119:11), virtually every day will present opportunities for you to use those truths.

If your husband is not a Christian, it is best not to quote Scripture directly, but you can still speak God's principles to him in love. I don't usually quote whole passages to my husband, but I often pull short phrases from the Scripture that I've memorized, as a way to keep our conversation grounded in God's truth.

Memorize It!

For you have died and your life is hidden with Christ in God. When Christ, who is our life, is revealed, then you also will be revealed with Him in glory.
(Colossians 3:3-4)

Week 3, Day 3

You turn things around! Shall the potter be considered as equal with the clay, that what is made would say to its maker, "He did not make me"; or what is formed say to him who formed it, "He has no understanding"?
ISAIAH 29:16

Application

Knowing *about* God is no substitute for *knowing* God. I may know a lot about Buzz Aldrin, but I don't know him. The difference is relationship. No one can have an intimate relationship with God the Father and remain self-centered. He is Almighty God! Being in His presence always drives one to humility. Like Isaiah, we will say, *"Woe is me, for I am ruined! Because I am a man of unclean lips...for my eyes have seen the King, the LORD of hosts"* (Isaiah 6:5†).

Focusing on God every day and entering His presence through prayer will humble you. Take time right now to focus on who God is by meditating on Psalm 103. Then ask God to give you an appropriate reverential fear of Him that leads to humility.

A God-Centered View

No discussion of becoming an excellent wife is complete without a thorough understanding of *humility*. You cannot be a good wife, mother, friend or Christian if your heart is full of pride. We start on this path of humility by understanding who God is and gaining a proper fear and reverence of Him.

In Psalm 50:21 God says, *"You thought that I was just like you."* And that's our problem, isn't it? We tend to behave as though God is a lot like us: that His memory is short, that He is tolerant of sin, or that He is limited in His knowledge or power. We assume He must be so preoccupied with the Middle East or what's going on in mission fields and churches that we forget He is with us at all times (Jeremiah 23:23-24). He knows every thought you have and every tiny detail of your life. He knows more about you and what is going on with you than you do!

God is patient and loving, but He is also the sovereign, just, and righteous Creator and Ruler of the Universe. He is neither a jovial old grandfather who loves everyone and winks at sin, nor a crotchety old man who seems to always be angry about something. Nor is He a heavenly Santa Claus whose only concern is your personal comfort and happiness. He is God Most High (Psalm 57:2). You are here to serve Him, rather than Him being here to serve you.

Job 11:7 asks, *"Can you discover the depths of God? Can you discover the limits of the Almighty?"* The answer is *No*: You cannot fully know God, and He has no limits! You need to bow in humble submission and adoration before Him. He is the Potter, and you are the clay (Romans 9:20-22). His "*thoughts are not your thoughts, nor are your ways [His] ways*" (Isaiah 55:8†). Therefore, your view of life is to be God-centered, not self-centered. He alone is worthy to be praised. Understanding your proper position as a creature serving the Creator is the beginning of humility.

Memorize It!

For you have died and your life is hidden with Christ in God. When Christ, who is our life, is revealed, then you also will be revealed with Him in glory.
(Colossians 3:3-4)

If It Walks Like An Idol...

Courtney fingered her engagement ring nervously as she listened to Jennifer, the wedding coordinator, talk about the changes to their wedding plans. Courtney knew they were over budget, but she was determined to have the wedding she'd always dreamed of. As Jennifer handed the contract to Seth, Courtney watched his face carefully. She prayed he would accept it without a fight. Seth didn't say anything right away, but as soon as they left Jennifer's office, he turned to Courtney. "You're kidding me, right?" he said. "We can't afford this!" For the next several days, they argued over every detail. Finally, Courtney put her foot down: "If you want to marry me," she said, thrusting the new contract in Seth's face, "you'll sign this." She was sad and angry that many of the things she wanted in her wedding were gone, but at least the main things were still intact.

It's obvious the perfect wedding had become an idol in Courtney's heart. Anything you want so badly that you're willing to sin to obtain, or you react in sinful anger or frustration if you don't get it, is an idol. This usually happens because we are so focused on obtaining what we want, that we lose sight of what is really important.

As a believer, you have a God-given capacity to have a pure devotion to the LORD Jesus Christ. But in order to be wholly devoted to Him, you will have to deal with the other "gods" that are competing for your affections—those things which are really important to you, that you desire, spend your money on or sacrifice for. In other words, what you have your heart set on. God says we are to set our minds *"on the things above, not on the things that are on earth"* (Colossians 3:2). If you spend more of your thoughts, time and energy on anything other than Christ, if your heart is set on material possessions, a dream, your family, whatever, then that thing is an idol.

What is your heart set on? Is anything more important to you than knowing Christ and making Him known?

Memorize It!

For you have died and your life is hidden with Christ in God.
When Christ, who is our life, is revealed, then you
also will be revealed with Him in glory.
(Colossians 3:3-4)

Do not love the world nor the things in the world. If anyone loves the world, the love of the Father is not in him. For all that is in the world, the lust of the flesh and the lust of the eyes and the boastful pride of life, is not from the Father, but is from the world. The world is passing away, and also its lusts; but the one who does the will of God lives forever.
1 JOHN 2:15-17

Application

Throughout this study, we will be looking at several possible idols. Go through the following list and underline those which may be competing with Christ for your affections:

Good health
Material things/Money/Success
Children
Physical attractiveness
Friends/Relationships
Perfect home
Good, Christian,
or intimate marriage
Approval/Recognition
Worldly pleasures
Control/Autonomy/"Me"Time

None of these things can bring you the peace and joy that Christ offers. Take a moment to ask God to forgive you for allowing idols to take His place in your heart, and ask Him to give you new heart desires. Then commit yourself today to seeking Him with the same passion and energy that you are currently expending on the lusts of your flesh. (Jeremiah 29:13).

Week 3, Day 5

Seeing that His divine power has granted to us everything pertaining to life and godliness, through the true knowledge of Him who called us by His own glory and excellence. For by these He has granted to us His precious and magnificent promises, so that by them you may become partakers of the divine nature.
2 Peter 1:3-4†

Application

Being an excellent wife is not about being a perfect wife. The question is, do you desire to be the wife God wants you to be? One of the many purposes in this book is to show you the benefits of obedience in order to increase your desire. If you greatly desire obedience, God will do the rest.

He will give you the power to obey. He will give you strength, grace, mercy and forgiveness. He freely gives you wisdom (James 1:5). He gives you everything you need to be righteous and godly (2 Peter 1:3). How *much* He gives is in proportion to your faith and your hunger for it. But everything He has is yours for the asking.

It's All On Me?

Several months ago, I ran into a woman who had taken *The Excellent Wife* Bible study with me years earlier. I hadn't seen or talked to her in ages, and while we got caught up on each other's lives, I was heartbroken to learn that she and her husband were divorced.

As we talked more, I asked her if what she had learned about being an excellent wife had helped at all. She struggled to find the right words, but finally expressed her chief complaint: "While I was going through that study, I was also dealing with a husband who was unfaithful and abusive. And I think my heart was hardened, because I just kept thinking, 'What about *him*?' It just seemed like God was putting all of this responsibility on *me*, as though the success of our marriage was completely dependent on me doing all the right things."

I understand why Claudia felt that way. As you go through this study, you will be challenged to evaluate how obedient you are to God's Word, and you will be reminded of many of God's promises that are dependent upon your obedience. For example, Ephesians 6:11† promises that when we *"put on the full armor of God (we) will be able to stand firm against the schemes of the devil."* Many of God's promises are conditional: the supernatural consequences of living life His way.

However, even if you were able to do everything perfectly, the success of your marriage is not dependent on you. Your husband must also do his part and take responsibility for his share of the work God has called you to do as husband and wife.

But the success of your marriage does not rest on your husband's shoulders either. *God* is the one who does the real work. He is the only One capable of changing your heart and the heart of your husband, and conforming both of you to the image of His Son. He is the one who gets all the glory because He is the one who gives you the capacity for love and the ability to obey. *"With [you and your husband] this is impossible, but with God all things are possible"* (Matthew 19:26†). Your responsibility is to learn to put your confidence in the faithfulness of God and His Word.

Gold, Clearly

It's interesting how often *gold* comes up in Scripture. We see it in the Old Testament in the construction of the tabernacle and the temple. We see it throughout the books of Psalms and Proverbs as a picture of great value, and in Revelation 21 the New Jerusalem is described as having streets of gold.

I don't know how effective ancient goldsmiths were at purifying gold, but I know that God's requirement was for the gold in the tabernacle to be pure. (See Exodus 25.) However, we don't really know what pure gold is, because the gold in heaven is so completely free of impurities that John describes it as *"like clear glass"*(Revelation 21:18).

If you can grasp the importance of the gold metaphor in Scripture, then you can understand the concept of sanctification.

The word *sanctification* comes from the root word *hagios,* which simply means to be "holy." In other words, sinless. God is called holy because God is sinless. You gained a *positional* holiness at salvation: God declared you to be His holy child when you were sanctified by the blood of Christ through faith (1 John 1:7, Galatians 3:26). When you die you will gain *practical* holiness, free of all sin, just as the gold in heaven is 100% free of all impurities.

In between positional holiness and practical holiness is this earthly existence as a sinful believer. This is where God's grace enables you to work on your *progressive sanctification* by identifying and eliminating sin from your life. We tend to complicate the concept of sanctification by talking about "growing in faith" and "maturing as a Christian," but progressive sanctification is really just the progress you make on purifying your life and becoming more holy and sinless...and thus, more like Christ.

The question is, are you working on your progressive sanctification? Or are you content with the sin in your life? You and your husband are to help each other purify your hearts and lives from sin. The more sanctified and sinless you are, the more effective you will be for Christ.

Memorize It!

Therefore consider the members of your earthly body as dead to immorality, impurity, passion, evil desire, and greed, which amounts to idolatry. For it is because of these things that the wrath of God will come upon the sons of disobedience.
(Colossians 3:5-6)

For God has not called us for the purpose of impurity, but in sanctification.
1 Thessalonians 4:7

Application

If your husband is not a Christian you still have Christ, your "spiritual husband," to help you in this process of progressive sanctification. Your job is to submit to what He is doing in your life.

Think about what is going on in your life right now, particularly if you're going through a trial or very difficult circumstances. Remembering that God *"causes all things to work together for good"* (Romans 8:28) for your sanctification and His glory, see if you can identify any sins He may be trying to purify out of your life through this trial. Then ask God to help you remove that sin from your life. Not all trials are the result of sin, but many are. This is a good exercise to do every time you go through a trial in your life.

Week 4, Day 2

The eyes of the LORD are toward the righteous, and His ears attend to their prayer.
1 PETER 3:12

Application

If you are being physically abused, you need to remove yourself from that situation and seek help immediately from a pastor, crisis counselor or health care professional. But even as you are taking the necessary steps to protect yourself, *you can still do that without sinning*. No matter what your situation, the Bible has clear, specific answers for you. Don't let anyone tell you God's commands don't apply to your situation. His way is perfect, no matter what you're going through.

1 Peter 3 is rich with instructions on how to be a godly wife. Read this passage, then write out ways it applies to *your* life. For example: Vs. 9 "I don't have to return evil for evil when my husband mistreats me. I can always return a blessing instead."

SUBMISSION: WHAT IT'S NOT

Audrey thought she would never love again after her husband died, but then she met Jay. He was caring, great with her kids, and they spent many long hours talking about their love for Christ. She didn't hesitate when he asked her to marry him, less than a year after their first date.

Unfortunately, Jay was a different man after the honeymoon. He became verbally abusive, often reducing her to tears with his angry tirades. If she questioned any of his decisions, he accused her of not being submissive. He kept her from attending her old church, moving her and the kids to a church in another part of town. Jay was controlling, angry, and grossly lacking in his role as a loving, godly husband.

According to the Lake County (Illinois) Crisis Center, over 20 million American women are physically, verbally or emotionally abused by their partners every year. If you're a woman in America, there is a 37% chance you are one of those abused women. If so, you need to understand: submitting to your husband does not mean that you submit to physical or emotional abuse. It does not mean that you "suffer in silence," become a "doormat," or that you shut your mouth and turn off your brain.

God's plan is for the man to love and protect his wife, and for the woman to lovingly submit to her husband's leadership and protection. You are called to be your husband's lifelong helper, doing all you can to be an "agent of sanctification" in his life. If your husband is abusing you, he is obviously missing God's plan for his life. There may be nothing you can do for your husband at this point, but you can still do *"what is right without being frightened by any fear"* (1 Peter 3:6). For instance, no matter how he treats you, you can still show love to your husband through the power of the Holy Spirit. *Your* obedience is never dependent upon what anyone else—including your husband—is doing.

Memorize It!

Therefore consider the members of your earthly body as dead to immorality, impurity, passion, evil desire, and greed, which amounts to idolatry. For it is because of these things that the wrath of God will come upon the sons of disobedience.
(Colossians 3:5-6)

Love is Kind

Paige has been married to Jess for almost ten years. About three years into their marriage, Paige accepted Christ as her Savior, but Jess has not shown any interest in learning about Christ or exploring his wife's new faith. He has, in fact, flatly refused to go to church with her or even to listen to her talk about Jesus.

One weekend, Jess was putting up a new fence in their back yard. Paige could tell things weren't going well when Jess threw his hammer into the dirt, let out a string of swear words and stormed off. She looked quickly to see if their four-year-old son had witnessed his dad's tirade, and sure enough, Riley was standing just a few feet away and had heard everything. Her initial response was to reprimand her husband for losing his temper in front of their son. But then she remembered I Corinthians 13:4, *"Love is kind."* In that moment, Paige chose to be kind to her husband instead. She poured him a glass of iced tea, and brought it to him. "I'm sorry the fence is such a problem," she said sympathetically. "Is there anything I can do to help?"

Being kind is a key to creating a Christ-honoring atmosphere in the home. Kindness is shown in a gentle tone of voice and in kind acts. Kindness draws people to us (hence, to Christ), whereas criticism and harsh words push them away. Remember: *"The kindness of God leads to repentance"* (Romans 2:4).

This truth was even more important for Paige, who used an act of kindness to demonstrate Christ's love to her husband.

For by these He has granted to us His precious and magnificent promises, so that by them you may become partakers of the divine nature, having escaped the corruption that is in the world by lust. Now for this very reason also, applying all diligence, in your faith supply moral excellence, and in your moral excellence, knowledge, and in your knowledge, self-control, and in your self-control, perseverance, and in your perseverance, godliness, and in your godliness, brotherly kindness, and in your brotherly kindness, love. For if these qualities are yours and are increasing, they render you neither useless nor unfruitful in the true knowledge of our Lord Jesus Christ.
2 Peter 1:4-8

Application

Think of ways to express kindness to your husband. For example, your husband is aggravated with a project he is trying to complete because the instructions are not clear. You can speak soft words of encouragement to him, such as "I'm sorry you're so upset. What do you need me to do for you?" Even if your husband's anger gets directed toward you, by the grace of God and in His strength, you can still speak in a kind voice and offer to serve.

So, as those who have been chosen of God, holy and beloved, put on a heart of compassion, kindness, humility, gentleness and patience; bearing with one another, and forgiving each other, whoever has a complaint against anyone; just as the Lord forgave you, so also should you. Beyond all these things put on love, which is the perfect bond of unity (Colossians 3:12-14).

Memorize It!

Therefore consider the members of your earthly body as dead to immorality, impurity, passion, evil desire, and greed, which amounts to idolatry. For it is because of these things that the wrath of God will come upon the sons of disobedience.
(Colossians 3:5-6)

Week 4, Day 4

Older women likewise are to be reverent in their behavior . . . so that they may encourage the young women to love their husbands, to love their children, to be sensible, pure, workers at home, kind, being subject to their own husbands, so that the word of God will not be dishonored.
TITUS 2:3-5

Application

You may be looking at respect as an emotion you can't control. If this were true, God would not have commanded you to respect your husband. There *is* an emotional aspect to respect, but the emotion comes *as a result of* your respectful acts. And respectful acts result from submitting yourself to God's will.

If you have behaved disrespectfully toward your husband, or if your overall attitude is disrespectful, you need to recognize this is a SIN you need to confess today. Then purposefully commit an act of respect toward your husband today. Praise him for something he's done, or ask for his opinion on something you wouldn't normally ask his opinion on. Find some way today to communicate to your husband, "I respect you."

RESPECT IS A COMMAND

Early on in their marriage, Kevin failed his wife in many ways. Lois repeatedly forgave him, but with each failure her respect for him died a little, until one day she realized it was gone for good. Since then, they have lived in a sort of "workable" arrangement where he does what he wants and she does what she wants, but there's no real intimacy between them. She still loves him, but she gave up the idea of romantic love a long time ago.

As a result of her lack of respect, Lois is often critical of her husband—not outwardly, but in her heart she nurses the pain of his failures and continually judges him as unworthy of her respect. She's dismissive; in fact, she avoids him because she knows it's not right to fight in front of the children. They're still together because they know it's a sin to divorce, and she wants to do what's right. She even "submits" to him, doing everything he asks without complaint. Thankfully, Kevin doesn't ask for much! "No, I don't respect him," she says. "I've lived with him too long, and I know the kind of man he is. I take care of his physical needs, raise his children. I'm doing the best I can. But don't ask me to respect him. That ship sailed a long time ago!"

Lois is under the mistaken assumption that she can live righteously without respecting her husband. But the Bible is very clear: *"The wife **must** see to it that she respects her husband"* (Ephesians 5:33†). Since she is not obedient to that command, she is missing the righteous standard God has set for her and is, therefore, living in sin.

You may be in a similar position, where you have moved "respect" over into the OPTIONS column in your life. Perhaps your husband has done something that caused you to lose respect for him. Maybe it's a character flaw or aspects of his personality that rub you the wrong way. Or maybe you've just been together so long that you take him for granted. Whatever the reason, you need to understand that respecting your husband is not an option.

Memorize It!

Therefore consider the members of your earthly body as dead to immorality, impurity, passion, evil desire, and greed, which amounts to idolatry. For it is because of these things that the wrath of God will come upon the sons of disobedience.
(Colossians 3:5-6)

UNDERSTANDING YOUR PURPOSE

Allison spent years in community theatre, but her dream is to act in films. Her husband Aaron is very supportive and wants to give her every opportunity to make it in "show business." So when he lost his job, they decided it must be the LORD leading them to move to Hollywood to pursue Allison's dream.

As time wore on, however, Allison made little progress in acting and Aaron struggled to find a job that would pay the bills. Then one day he got a great job offer from a company in Minneapolis. "I know this probably means the end of your dreams," he said, "but I think we should take it." For the next several hours they argued, but Allison would not be moved. "God gave me a passion for acting," she cried. "I *know* He's going to honor that. He wouldn't have given me this dream if He didn't want me to do something about it!"

Allison thinks that because she feels so strongly about her dream, it must be of God. And we often do the same thing: we allow our dreams to occupy so much of our thoughts until they become idols we're not willing to give up. We then attach God to them in an attempt to get "divine approval" on what *we* want to do. We put our dreams first, before God's plans and before our husband's desires. It's a complete reversal of how we should act. It is assuming God is here to serve us, rather than humbly acknowledging that we are here to serve Him.

God does not bow to your plans for your life, and He is not obligated to fulfill your dreams for the future. *"I know the plans I have for you,"* God says in Jeremiah 29:11, but, *"my thoughts are not your thoughts"* (Isaiah 55:8). In other words, God has plans for you, but they're probably not what you're thinking. Your purpose on earth is to serve God and proclaim His excellencies (1 Peter 2:9), not to fulfill your own dreams. I'm not saying it's wrong to pursue a dream, but if that dream is your greatest passion, then you need to humble yourself to God and submit your will to *His* will for you.

But you are a chosen race, a royal priesthood, a holy nation, a people for God's own possession, so that you may proclaim the excellencies of Him who has called you out of darkness into His marvelous light.
1 PETER 2:9

Application

Too often our dreams are simply products of our own lusts (James 4:3). It's interesting how so many of us pursue our passions first, and promise God we'll serve Him *after* we've accomplished what we set out to do. "I'm going to make a lot of money, and then I'll have more to give God." "After my children are raised, *then* I'll get involved in ministry." This is the very definition of pride: believing that our plans are more important than God's plans for us.

Write in your prayer journal what dreams you have been pursuing to the exclusion of serving Christ. Then write down what work He's asked you to do that you've been putting off. Now, switch those two in your future plans, making His priorities your top priority.

Week 5, Day 1

By this we know that we have come to know Him, if we keep His commandments. But whoever keeps His word, in him the love of God has truly been perfected.
1 John 2:3, 5†

Application

The problem is, most people try to take the obeying part out of the love/obedience cycle. They learn about Him through His Word, and they think they trust Him, but they leave out that one element and expect that love will just happen. You can't do that! Love will not grow without obedience. And if you're not obeying Him, then you're revealing that you don't really trust Him.

Ask yourself: do you know God through His Word, and do you trust Him? If so, are you obeying Him? Are you daily presenting your body in service to Him for kingdom work? Or are you just trying to love Him without obedience? You might be able to manufacture a fuzzy emotion for a short time, but your love for Him will not grow until you consistently obey Him.

Loving God More

You know that the key to being an excellent wife is to obey the Greatest Commandment: *"You shall love the Lord your God with all your heart, and with all your soul, and with all your strength, and with all your mind; and your neighbor as yourself"* (Luke 10:27). One of our problems in obeying that command is this: we think love is a passive emotion, rather than an action. If we don't "feel" it, then we think nothing we do will create it. So we live our lives the way we want, and hope that God will do something amazing so that we will fall more in love with Him. We test God, thinking that once He does that miraculous thing in our lives—fixes our husband, heals that loved one, changes our kids' hearts, improves our financial situation—well, if He would just do *that*, then we would love and obey Him more.

Here's the problem with that thinking: God has already done something amazing. He created you and saved you. He gave you the power of the Holy Spirit and grace to live every day. If all of that doesn't make you love Him, what makes you think the "next big thing" will?

The truth is, God wants to do more amazing things in and through your life, but those amazing things are dependent upon your obedience to Him. As you obey Him, your love for Him will grow. Love comes out of *our* obedience to God; not as He obeys *us* and fixes the messes in our lives.

So what is stopping you from beginning (or persevering in) the cycle of love and obedience? For most people, it's a trust issue. You will obey someone if you trust them, and you only trust someone if you know them. God has revealed Himself to us in His Word, so we can know Him. Then if we can know Him, then we can trust Him. And if we can trust Him, then we can obey Him. When we know Him through His Word, trust Him to take care of us no matter what, *and obey His commands*, we will love Him. *"But whoever keeps His word, in him the love of God has truly been perfected"* (1 John 2:5).

Memorize It!

And in them you also once walked, when you were living in them. But now you also, put them all aside: anger, wrath, malice, slander, and abusive speech from your mouth.
(Colossians 3:7-8)

Lost In Translation

Then the Lord *God said, "It is not good for the man to be alone; I will make him a helper suitable for him."*
Genesis 2:18

If you come from a Christian background, you may have been taught that the wife is to be her husband's "help-meet." In its unhyphenated form, that is a scriptural term (based on the King James Version of Genesis 2:18), but it has always rubbed me the wrong way. Whenever I hear it, I get this mental picture of a side of beef called "help meat."

Genesis 2:18 actually reads, *"It is not good that the man should be alone; I will make him an help meet for him"* (KJV). The word *meet* here means "fit" or "suitable," and it was never meant to be attached to the word *help*. Rather, it is a modifier of the words *for him*. One of the reasons why I believe women resist the traditional roles of husband as head of the home and the wife as his "helpmeet" is because we really don't like being referred to as meat—no matter how it is spelled. However, it's helpful to focus on the rest of the verse: *"It is not good for the man to be alone; I will make him a helper [that is] suitable for him."*

In other words, God knew that this "alone" thing Adam had going on was not good, so He brought him Eve, a woman who would come alongside him and be his helper, lover, companion and friend. Your husband is no different. It's not good for our guys to be alone; they need us to help them. That's one of the main reasons God created marriage: so that you and your husband would be a picture to the world of Christ and the Church, and so you could be your husband's helper. And not just a halfway decent helper, but one who is "well suited" to help your husband.

That is one of your chief roles as a Christian wife: to help your husband. Help him around the house, help him raise your children, help him with whatever he needs. But most of all, help him become more like Christ. You can't help your husband if you're resisting him, working against him, or just living life your own way. You help him become more like Christ as you model submission for him, as an example of how he should submit himself to the Lord.

Application

This concept of "suitable" sometimes gets lost in translation, but take time now to focus on that aspect of your relationship to your husband. God knows that you are the one person on earth best suited to be your husband's helper. Perhaps your focus has been on yourself, and you've fallen down on your job to help your husband. Or perhaps you've come to believe that your guy would have been better off if he'd married someone else. Neither of these extremes is healthy. Remember: You are the salt to his pepper, the wheels to his car, the glove to his hand. God knows you're the perfect woman for your man. Today might be a good day to remind yourself of that truth.

Memorize It!

And in them you also once walked, when you were living in them. But now you also, put them all aside: anger, wrath, malice, slander, and abusive speech from your mouth.
(Colossians 3:7-8)

Week 5, Day 3

Let no unwholesome word proceed from your mouth, but only such a word as is good for edification according to the need of the moment, so that it will give grace to those who hear.
EPHESIANS 4:29

Application

There are several ways to learn to control your tongue. One is to work diligently on memorizing Scripture. Another is to identify attitudes that lead to hurtful words. Remember that wrong words come from wrong thoughts which come from wrong attitudes. Once those attitudes are identified, ask God to help you get rid of them with the truth of His Word.

A third way to control your tongue is to practice the right ways to respond whenever something stressful happens or whenever someone does something to make you angry. Instead of getting angry, *"be quick to hear, slow to speak and slow to anger"* (James 1:19). You know what your "triggers" are. Ask God to give you a Christ-honoring response whenever those situations arise.

CONTROLLING YOUR TONGUE

Chandler and Alana are a busy couple with three teenagers. Evenings can be absolute chaos in their home, and at times Alana feels like she doesn't know which end is up. One night, they were cleaning up after dinner when Chandler dropped a plate on the floor—and on Alana's last nerve, smashing it, and the plate, into a thousand pieces.

"What are you doing?!" she yelled. Alana grabbed the towel from his hands and turned her back on him, leaving him to clean up the shattered dish and his hurt feelings. He felt like leaving and letting her do it all herself, but then suddenly she was next to him, helping him pick up the broken pieces. He looked at her and she smiled weakly. "I'm sorry," she said. "I know it was an accident, and I should not have snapped at you like that."

Alana has been working on controlling her tongue. She, like many of us, has a habit of engaging the mouth before the brain. Add to that a quick temper, and you have a recipe for disaster. See what great power the uncontrolled tongue can have:

> *So also the tongue is a small part of the body, and yet it boasts of great things. See how great a forest is set aflame by such a small fire! And the tongue is a fire, the very world of iniquity; (it) sets on fire the course of our life, and is set on fire by hell.* (James 3:5-6)

Given our tongue's great potential, we *must* learn to control it, even when we're under stress. We often think being stressed gives us an excuse to say whatever we want. But stress is an opportunity for us to either glorify God with our correct responses, or to dishonor Him with our ungodly responses.

God often uses stressful situations to reveal our true character. It's like making tea: when you put a tea bag into hot water, what's inside the bag comes out. The hot water brings out the contents of the bag. Stress is like hot water: it doesn't *cause* wrong words or actions; it brings out the wrong attitudes that are inside. If we have righteous attitudes, loving words will leak out into the "hot water" of our lives.

Memorize It!

And in them you also once walked, when you were living in them. But now you also, put them all aside: anger, wrath, malice, slander, and abusive speech from your mouth.
(Colossians 3:7-8)

Overcoming Evil

Do not be overcome by evil,
but overcome evil with good.
Romans 12:21

Shortly before the holidays, Brett told Anita he was leaving her. "We don't love each other anymore," he said. "It's ridiculous to keep pretending." He promised to wait until after Christmas, for the kids' sake, but had already leased an apartment beginning January 1st. This gave Anita approximately a month to fight for her marriage.

Rather than sulking, plotting revenge, or exercising "tough love," Anita decided instead to obey the truths in Romans 12 and *"overcome evil with good"* (verse 21). She smiled at Brett each morning and told him she loved him. Every day before he left for work, she made him breakfast and packed him a lunch. She praised him in front of their children, initiated intimacy frequently, and bought tickets for them to go to a basketball game together.

At first, Brett didn't respond to his wife's overtures; in fact, he claimed she was being the "perfect wife" only because she was scared. If they stayed together, no doubt she would go right back to being the neglectful wife she was before. "You know what?" Anita replied. "A month ago I might have agreed with you. But I've learned something through this. I *like* being a good wife! I like serving you, and even though I struggle with fear, I am actually happier doing what's right. I love you and want you to stay. But even if you don't, I have peace knowing I've done everything God requires of me."

When you face a major crisis in your marriage, you must respond with the right actions, not just the right words. You must continue to do what is right no matter how difficult it is or how long it takes. God often brings a conflict into our life to make us more obedient—and He expects us to continue in obedience even after the crisis has passed. While you are fighting back biblically, you can be assured that even if your conflict is not resolved the way you would like, God will give you His peace (Psalm 119:165).

Memorize It!

And in them you also once walked, when you were living in them.
But now you also, put them all aside: anger, wrath, malice,
slander, and abusive speech from your mouth.
(Colossians 3:7-8)

Application

Giving your husband a blessing in the midst of conflict is especially difficult if you are struggling with hurt or bitterness. You certainly won't feel he deserves to be blessed in any way. But if your husband needs to be punished, you must get out of the way and "leave room for the wrath of God" (Romans 12:19). *Your* responsibility is to bless him with kindness. This is one of God's most gracious and powerful ways to *"heap burning coals upon his head"* (Romans 12:20).

Conflict is not overwhelming when you fight it God's way, with His grace. Romans 12:14-20 gives great insight on how to deal with conflict God's way. Read this passage over today, and then write down specific ways you can apply these commandments to conflict in your marriage.

Week 5, Day 5

Little children, guard yourselves from idols.
1 JOHN 5:21

Application

How would your husband feel if you loved other men more than him? If you spent more time with other men than you do with him? That is how God feels when you give the lusts of your heart first priority over Him. By your idol worship, you're demonstrating that you love something more than you love God. You're willing to sin against God in order to obtain the lusts of your heart. How that must break God's heart! Especially when He sees how much it harms you to be this way.

God wants to be your only heart's desire. He loves you passionately, and wants that intimacy with you. Guarding yourself against idols is a constant vigilance we must keep if we're going to love God with all of our heart, soul, mind and strength (Mark 12:30).

THE EFFECTS OF IDOLATRY

Usually we're not aware until it's too late that something has become an idol. If what we desire is not sinful, we might even ask God for it. ("LORD, I really want a baby." "LORD, You know how badly we need a new house.") And as long as everything goes smoothly, we will feel all right. The problem comes when: 1) our desires consume more of our thoughts, time and energy than we're giving to God; 2) we're willing to sin to obtain them; or 3) we react in sinful anger if we're denied them.

After the birth of our twins, I was driving a 1986 Honda Accord, which was a little tight for a family of five. I felt we needed a new car, but we couldn't afford one, and that irritated me. Then, when our friends who had *no* children bought a brand new SUV, I reacted with sinful envy, resenting them for having something *I* needed more than they did. Getting a new car had become an idol in my heart.

"But each one is tempted when he is carried away and enticed by his own lust. Then when lust has conceived, it gives birth to sin; and when sin is accomplished, it brings forth death" (James 1:14-15). In the case of my idolatrous vehicle worship, I lusted after a new car, which gave birth to envy, bitterness, ingratitude, and self-pity.

Rather than lusting after the things of this world, our hearts should be set on Christ and doing the will of God (1 John 2:15-17). How much further along would the kingdom of heaven be on earth if God's people were to pursue holiness with the same passion with which we pursue the lusts of our flesh? Instead, we are like the young man in Mark 10, who was technically a "good Christian." But Jesus knew that this man's heart was given to idols. *"Looking at him, Jesus felt a love for him and said to him, 'One thing you lack: go and sell all you possess and give to the poor, and you will have treasure in heaven; and come, follow Me.' But at these words he was saddened, and he went away grieving, for he was one who owned much property" (Mark 10:21-22).*

The Necessity of Humility

Kara woke up at 2:30 a.m. and reached for her husband, but he was not there, which could only mean one thing: he was on the computer, looking at pornography. For months she had pretended not to know Brad had a problem, but these late nights out of the bed were starting to affect his job. Too often he had trouble getting up for work because he'd stayed up late the night before.

Kara knew she had to confront Brad about this activity, so she spent the next several days studying Scripture and asking God to reveal her own sins that were equally affecting her marriage. Immediately, God convicted her about her favorite TV show. While it wasn't "pornography" *per se*, it certainly crossed the boundaries of appropriate entertainment for a committed Christ follower. "You're right, God," she prayed. "Why is my sin any less serious than Brad's?"

Humility means you are willing to examine your own sin with the same critical eye with which you judge your husband's sins. You cannot look at the "specks" in your husband's eye until you have properly dealt with the "logs" in your own eyes (Matthew 7:3-5). The problem with many of us is that even after we have examined ourselves, we still don't want to admit our sin is as serious as our husbands'. This is a result of thinking *"more highly of (ourselves) than (we) ought to think"* (Romans 12:3).

Achieving God's purpose in marriage begins with dealing with your own sin before you confront your husband with his (Matthew 7:1-5). This ensures that when you do confront your husband, you will not be coming to him in pride and self-righteousness, but in humility, *"looking to yourself, so that you too will not be tempted"* (Galatians 6:1†).

God wants you to confront your husband's sin, but you must first make sure your life is in order. Then, you will be able to talk to your husband about the sin in his life with a clear conscience. And your husband will have less reason to turn the tables and say, "But what about you?"

Why do you look at the speck that is in your brother's eye, but do not notice the log that is in your own eye? Or how can you say to your brother, "Let me take the speck out of your eye," and behold, the log is in your own eye? You hypocrite, first take the log out of your own eye, and then you will see clearly to take the speck out of your brother's eye.

Matthew 7:3-5

Application

When you pray, "Lord, help me to see the 'logs' in my own eyes by clearly showing me my sin," God will answer that prayer. It is a prayer of humility, and therefore glorifies Him.

Think about the sins your husband commits that most bother you. Then, take time to examine your heart to see what sins you commit that are equally egregious to God. Have you confessed those sins, or do you think they are not as serious as your husband's? Record your thoughts on these questions in your prayer journal, then ask God to help you be more biblical in your response to your husband's sin.

Memorize It!

Do not lie to one another, since you laid aside the old self with its evil practices, and have put on the new self who is being renewed to a true knowledge according to the image of the One who created him.

(Colossians 3:9-10)

Week 6, Day 2

But if your enemy is hungry, feed him, and if he is thirsty, give him a drink; for in so doing you will heap burning coals on his head. Do not be overcome by evil, but overcome evil with good.
ROMANS 12:20-21

Application

Revenge sounds like such a harsh word that it's hard for us to think of our actions as being vengeful. But anytime you try to even the score with your husband, or give yourself a pass on sinning because of your husband's sin, you are repaying the evil done to you with evil of your own, and that is the definition of revenge. Withholding sex, giving the silent treatment, getting angry, using sarcasm, or becoming apathetic toward your husband are all ways you could seek revenge.

Examine your actions and attitudes in the last day, week, or month—or however long it has been since your husband last did something to hurt you or make you angry. Have you been seeking revenge? Or have you been trying to overwhelm evil with good?

REVENGE: NOT SO SWEET

Annette could hardly believe where she was: in a restaurant, having dinner with a man who was not her husband. And after dinner, if he wanted to go to a hotel, she was OK with that. She wasn't in love with this guy; she actually still loved her husband. But Bryce had cheated on her—not once, but three times. She was tired of it, and had vowed to get back at him. *Now he will understand how I feel,* she thought. She didn't care how much damage she did to their marriage. She just wanted to hurt Bryce as much as he had hurt her.

The quickest way to ensure that conflict in your marriage has a satanic result is to seek revenge. Romans 12:19 says "***Never*** *take your own revenge, beloved, but leave room for the wrath of God, for it is written, 'Vengeance is mine, I will repay,' says the LORD.*"† Notice that word *never*; no matter what your husband has done to you, God never gives you the right to take revenge by returning "evil for evil" (1 Peter 3:9). "Evil" includes any ungracious, bitter or vindictive act—even if it pales in comparison to what he has done. For example, if a wife punishes her husband's anger by giving him the cold shoulder, she is paying back evil for evil.

"*The wise woman builds her house, but the foolish tears it down with her own hands*" (Proverbs 14:1). Seeking revenge against your husband is one way to tear down your house with your own hands. Consider this: when you try to hurt your husband, who are you really hurting? You're hurting yourself, because you and your husband are one flesh (Mark 10:8). You're helping tear down the "house" of your marriage. Even if your husband executed the first demolition blow, you do not have to take up the hammer also. You are responsible to continue doing what is right, no matter how he acts.

God wants you to be forbearing and patient when your husband sins against you. It is your responsibility to trust God to execute His justice for your husband's sin. In the meantime, you must overwhelm evil with good (Romans 12:21).

Memorize It!

Do not lie to one another, since you laid aside the old self with its evil practices, and have put on the new self who is being renewed to a true knowledge according to the image of the One who created him.
(Colossians 3:9-10)

In All Things

Bethany and Brian sat at the kitchen table, poring over their tax return. Prior to accepting Christ as her Savior, Bethany had agreed with Brian that it was sometimes necessary to "fudge" the figures a little to keep from having to pay more taxes. But now, she knew that a disciple of Christ is always honest. She also knew Brian was watching her—and sometimes testing her faith in Christ. "What about your Saturday income?" she asked. "I know Gary pays you 'under the table,' but we still need to report it."

Brian narrowed his eyes at the figures she'd totaled up from his income receipts. "Wow, did I make that much last year? Yeah, let's just not mention this!" He took the paper from her hands, wadded it up into a ball and shot it toward the waste can. Bethany shook her head, smiling, then retrieved the paper. "Look, honey," she said, entering the dollar amount into the tax return program on her laptop, then hitting the 'Recalculate' button. "It only increases our tax by forty-seven dollars. Is your integrity really for sale for forty-seven dollars?"

A godly wife is submissive to her husband in all things *unless he asks her to sin*. Only God has absolute authority over you; His authority is higher than your husband's. So if your husband asks you to sin, you must *"obey God rather than men"* (Acts 5:29). Even then, however, your response to your husband can still be one of submission. In those instances where you cannot obey him, be sure to prayerfully and respectfully let him know why.

Wives, be subject to your own husbands, as to the Lord. But as the church is subject to Christ, so also the wives ought to be to their husbands in everything.
Ephesians 5:22, 24

Application

Sometimes we claim our husbands are asking us to sin, when actually the only "law" violated is our own intelligence, preferences, or convictions. If you must go against your husband's wishes based on God's higher commands, make sure you meet the following criteria:

- Is what he is asking really a sin?
- Can you find a specific biblical principle to support your refusal to obey?
- Have you respectfully explained your reasons for not obeying?
- Can you find a way to meet his goals without sinning?
- Is your top priority obedience to Christ or getting your own way?

Scripture teaches us that we are called to obey God rather than men, and sometimes "men" includes your own husband. You can continue to respect him and have a submissive attitude, even when standing your ground on the truth of God's Word.

Memorize It!

Do not lie to one another, since you laid aside the old self with its evil practices, and have put on the new self who is being renewed to a true knowledge according to the image of the One who created him.
(Colossians 3:9-10)

Week 6, Day 4

In the same way, you wives, be submissive to your own husbands so that even if any of them are disobedient to the word, they may be won without a word by the behavior of their wives, as they observe your chaste and respectful behavior.
1 PETER 3:1-2

Application

One reason you may have trouble with respect is because you're focused on everything he's doing wrong and how he falls short. You may also believe you are outperforming him in terms of your contributions to your marriage and family. This is thinking *"more highly of (yourself) than you ought to think"* (Romans 12:3†) and is a form of pride.

Even if your husband messes up, it is wrong for you to withhold respect until he "gets it right." The Bible is clear that our respect to our husbands is to be without conditions. Just as you want your husband to love you unconditionally, guys want—and more importantly, *God demands*—unconditional respect.

UNCONDITIONAL RESPECT

Sharon's life with Neal has not been easy. For the 19 years they've been married, she has had to work long hours because Neal has never earned enough money to provide for them. Whenever they start to get a little bit ahead financially, he will usually buy something that puts them farther into debt. What's worse, now he has taken up gambling, and spends more and more time at the casino when he should be trying to find work. With the gambling came drinking; more than once, Neal has come home late and obviously inebriated.

What makes things especially painful is that when Sharon first met Neal, he was an ardent follower of Christ. But now, the life she thought she was signing up for has faded to a vague memory, while her husband is consumed by materialism and pleasure-seeking. Understandably, Sharon struggles to respect her husband the way God commands. "He knows better than this," she says. "How can I respect a man who makes such poor decisions?"

A popular sentiment these days is that love should be unconditional but respect must be earned. While this might sound reasonable, it is not biblical. God did not say, "If he loves you, and if he behaves well, then you should respect your husband." And when you think about it, what standards would you use to gauge whether or not your husband is worthy of your respect? Would he need to be perfect? Almost perfect? Perfect more often than not?

You always want your husband's love, even when you fail to meet his expectations or on days when you're not being very lovable. You want nothing to affect his love for you, right? It's the same way for him and respect. Continuing to demonstrate respect for him, apart from how he behaves, is a powerful way to demonstrate your love for him and for Christ. Don't be concerned that he will interpret your respect as a pass for him to continue messing up; there are respectful ways to reprove his sinful behavior. But withholding respect should never be part of your arsenal for expressing disapproval.

Memorize It!

Do not lie to one another, since you laid aside the old self with its evil practices, and have put on the new self who is being renewed to a true knowledge according to the image of the One who created him.
(Colossians 3:9-10)

Anger = Death

Julie wasn't feeling well, so Stephen and the kids started on the Saturday chores without her. When she finally got out of bed, she found her daughter sorting clean clothes. "Who did the laundry?" she asked, surprised. Kelsey rolled her eyes. "Dad," she said, and held up a blouse Julie bought just last week. It was supposed to be black, but Stephen had bleached it to a sickly brown.

"What??!!" Julie snatched the blouse from Kelsey's hands and went to find Stephen, who was mowing the lawn. "Look at my blouse!" she said, holding it in his face. "Why would you use bleach on this?" Stephen couldn't understand why she was so angry. The blouse looked fine; didn't she appreciate that he had done the laundry for her?

Julie is angry because in that moment, something she *wants* is more important to her than her relationship with her husband. She has not trained herself to control her anger, or to treasure her husband more than her things.

Anger is the heart attitude that leads to death. Jesus very closely linked anger with murder (Matthew 5:21-24). The first murder in human history happened as a result of Cain's anger against his brother (Genesis 4:1-13). It is unlikely that your anger will result in physical death, but every time you are angry with your husband, you kill intimacy, unity, and harmony in your marriage.

Anger is a manipulative tool we pull out in order to accomplish something. For instance, your husband does something you don't like, so you get angry to try to steer his future actions in the right direction. But using anger to motivate others is rarely effective, and is displeasing to God. *"The anger of man does not achieve the righteousness of God"* (James 1:20). You should want to influence your husband toward righteousness, and using something sinful to do that is counter-productive. Remember that anger is a love and unity killer. Whenever you are angry with your husband, ask yourself, "Is what I am angry about worth bringing *death* into my marriage?"

Be angry, and yet do not sin; do not let the sun go down on your anger, and do not give the devil an opportunity.
Ephesians 4:26-27

Application

Whenever you are angry, ask yourself what you are trying to achieve with your anger. If you want your husband to change his behavior to be more pleasing to God, then a little righteous anger may be necessary. But if you just want him to change his behavior to please *you* more, then your anger is sinful.

Righteous anger in marriage is always directed at the sin, not at the sinner. In other words, you should be angry at the effect sin has in your husband's life, but this anger toward sin should cause you to love your husband more, not less. *"Be angry, and yet do not sin"* (Ephesians 4:26). Sinful anger will always cause you to love your husband less. If your anger is not righteous, then ask God to help you let go of whatever is making you angry.

Week 7, Day 1

For you are still fleshly. For since there is jealousy and strife among you, are you not fleshly, and are you not walking like mere men?
1 Corinthians 3:3

Application

Instead of reacting to perceived threats with jealousy, learn to show love by taking an active interest in your husband's friends and activities. Be happy with him when he has the opportunity to hang out with his pals or participate in the things that interest him. When he works long hours, be cheerful and glad when he finally comes home. If you react jealously when he spends time away from you, your husband will dread coming home and will find more reasons to spend time away.

When you start to feel jealous, realize that you are focusing on yourself and not on what is best for your husband. Truly loving your husband means that you are never jealous; because true love seeks benefit and joy for your spouse, not yourself.

Love is Not Jealous

Ryan and Stephanie graduated from college, got married, moved to a new city, and started new jobs—all in the same month. Ryan's job sometimes requires him to work long hours, while Stephanie's job at the bank has her home by five. She often finds herself sitting alone, with dinner on hold in the oven, waiting for Ryan to come home.

To make matters worse, Ryan joined his company's softball team, and two nights a week he's either practicing or pitching his team to victory. At first Stephanie enjoyed going to the games, but soon she found herself resenting how much fun Ryan had while he was out on the field. "I don't get it," she complained to her mom on the phone one day. "He manages to leave work on time to play softball, but if there's no game then suddenly he has all this work to do!" "You sound like you're jealous," her mom pointed out. "That can't be good for your marriage."

Job 5:2 says, *"For anger slays the foolish man, and jealousy kills the simple."* Jealousy is the fear of being displaced by another person or thing. The fear may or may not be valid, but either way, it is self-focused and self-concerned. Jealousy is not a minor sin. It is one of the reasons Christ was nailed to a cross: the Pharisees and religious leaders were jealous of how popular He had become among the people, and were afraid more people would listen to Him than to them. (See Matthew 27:18.)

Even if your fears are justified, and your husband is in fact replacing you with work, hobbies, even an illicit affair, you can approach his sin in a way that focuses on what is best for him —not on what will make you happy or exact revenge. While Ryan may have been feeding Stephanie's jealous nature, it was up to Stephanie to confess her sin of jealousy and keep her mind focused on loving her husband and trusting God with her own insecurities.

Memorize It!

A renewal in which there is no distinction between Greek and Jew, circumcised and uncircumcised, barbarian, Scythian, slave and freeman, but Christ is all, and in all.
(Colossians 3:11)

Dying to Self

For just as you presented your members as slaves to impurity and to lawlessness, resulting in further lawlessness, so now present your members as slaves to righteousness, resulting in sanctification.
ROMANS 6:19†

On her way out the door to go grocery shopping, Alice stopped to look at her calendar for the upcoming weekend: baseball and football games, a "mani/pedi" with her sister, possibly a trip to the mall, then a camping trip Saturday night and Sunday. *Another crazy weekend,* she thought, as she headed out.

On her way to the store, she tuned the radio to a Christian station. She was searching for some Christian music, but was stopped by what the preacher was saying. "What do you do with your free time?" he asked. *What free time!?* She thought. "Do you use it entertaining yourself, pursuing wealth or comfort? Do you and your family do things to profit yourselves or the Kingdom? Are you dying to yourself to serve Him?"

Alice thought about that for a moment but decided, *You know what? I don't do that much for myself—it's all for my family. So don't talk to me about dying to self!*

Let's look at Alice's life. All of her days revolve around her kids' activities, keeping up with the house, taking care of her family, and pleasing her husband. If there is any free time or energy left, she fills it with self-indulgent activities like watching TV, going to the movies, shopping, or hanging out with her friends. She is like so many of us: very busy, but doing virtually nothing for Christ. She thinks she's dying to her own desires, but she really isn't. She still clings to her right to be rewarded for her hours of sacrifice for her family, and there is nothing left over for Christ, the One she claims is her LORD.

God wants us to stop living for ourselves and start living for Him. Paul wrote to the church at Corinth that *"they who live might no longer live for themselves, but for Him who died and rose again on their behalf"* (2 Corinthians 5:15†). That means that your life revolves around Christ, not yourself: loving and serving Him first, rather than trying to fit Him into the leftover spaces in your life.

Application

How do you prioritize your responsibilities in life? Is serving Christ one of your top priorities? What do you do with your free time? Do you use it to entertain yourself and pursue comfort? Or do you see it as more time to serve Him? Your life does not belong to you; it belongs to *"Him who died and rose again on [your] behalf"* (2 Corinthians 5:15†). It's time to stop living as though your life is yours to do with as you please.

We've talked throughout this study about how your husband is your number one ministry, but that does not mean he is your *only* ministry. Serving Christ by serving others, especially lost people, is one of the things you, your husband and your children should be doing together.

Memorize It!

A renewal in which there is no distinction between Greek and Jew, circumcised and uncircumcised, barbarian, Scythian, slave and freeman, but Christ is all, and in all.
(Colossians 3:11)

Week 7, Day 3

She looks well to the ways of her household.
PROVERBS 31:27

Application

If you are so busy outside the home that you're not keeping up with your home responsibilities, it's possible that you are one of those women who just can't say no. You may be a people-pleaser, who is more concerned about the opinions of other people than you are about God's opinion.

God's opinion is the only one that matters, and His desire is that your home and family are your top priority. Look at your schedule and see if you are over-extended outside the home, to the point where your home, husband and children are getting leftovers. If that's the case, talk to your husband and prayerfully consider which outside responsibilities you should cut out.

THE KINGDOM WORK OF HOUSEWORK

When Marissa was able to stop working after having her baby, she happily embraced the extra time as opportunity to get more involved at church and in charity work. She signed up to lead the nursery ministry, enrolled in a Bible study one morning a week, joined the missionary committee, and volunteered to cook meals for the homeless once a month. When her son started kindergarten, Marissa added to her already full schedule by offering to serve as a homeroom mom and teacher's assistant once a week.

Her husband has asked her to slow down and cut some things out of her schedule. "The house is being neglected," he complains, "and I can't believe you're spending any quality time with Micah. You guys are never home!" Marissa counters, "I'm in his classroom, and he's with me while I'm serving the LORD. I think that's just as important as keeping the house clean!"

It is the rare husband who is pleased with a wife who neglects her home and family for the sake of helping others outside the home. God seems to have given men this innate sense that the home should take top priority over things outside the home. In our desire to please ourselves, others, and even (in a misguided way) God, we often don't look at the time we spend at home as "kingdom" work.

If that's your attitude, you need to adjust your thinking. Your work at home is your kingdom ministry—it should take precedence over all other ministries and activities. As you work at home, you are creating a home environment that honors God and equips your family to serve Him better. But if you are never home or you're letting your responsibilities at home slide, that is dishonoring to both your husband and to Christ.

God has a very high opinion of the woman who is submissive to her husband and who attends to her home responsibilities as her most important ministry. According to Proverbs 31:10, *"her worth is far above jewels."*

Memorize It!

A renewal in which there is no distinction between Greek and Jew, circumcised and uncircumcised, barbarian, Scythian, slave and freeman, but Christ is all, and in all.
(Colossians 3:11)

Learn to Communicate Biblically

Aileen's 12-year-old daughter Bentley was talking about the current teenage obsession in her school: yet another pop star "sensation" whose face was everywhere and whose concerts were sold out. "Everyone has his picture on their folders and his songs as their ringtones," Bentley said. "I don't get what's the big deal. His music is not that great."

Aileen smiled at her daughter's wisdom. "We need to be very careful who we make our idols, don't we" she said. *'Our God is a jealous god.'*[2] He doesn't like to share His glory with anyone!" Even though she was speaking to her daughter, she hoped her husband was listening. Parker had just spent the last hour glued to ESPN, watching the NFL draft. She thanked God for the opportunity to give him a gentle reminder not to idolize professional athletes, which is something he could be tempted to do very easily.

Aileen is really good at working God and His Word into normal, everyday conversation. In this way, she is constantly speaking truth into the lives of her husband and children. If *"faith comes from hearing, and hearing by the Word of Christ"* (Romans 10:17) then the faith of her family is being encouraged by her constant reminders to involve God in every aspect of their lives.

Learning to communicate biblically is necessary if we're going to help our husbands, and ourselves, be conformed to the image of Christ. And not just communicating biblically when there's a conflict, but speaking God's truth into every situation. The Word of God is applicable to every part of our lives, not just the problem areas. God has very specific "kingdom principles" for living as believers in an unbelieving world. If we learn to make these principles part of our normal life, we will live in a way that is pleasing to Him, and we'll be less inclined to separate the "secular" from the "sacred." All of life is sacred for the believer: *"Whether, then, you eat or drink or whatever you do, do all to the glory of God"*(1 Corinthians 10:31).

Memorize It!

A renewal in which there is no distinction between Greek and Jew, circumcised and uncircumcised, barbarian, Scythian, slave and freeman, but Christ is all, and in all.
(Colossians 3:11)

Let the word of Christ richly dwell within you, with all wisdom teaching and admonishing one another with psalms and hymns and spiritual songs, singing with thankfulness in your hearts to God. Whatever you do in word or deed, do all in the name of the Lord Jesus, giving thanks through Him to God the Father.
Colossians 3:16-17

Application

Inserting God's Word into everyday conversation is a difficult habit to get into, if you're not used to doing it. It's something you must learn to do, just as you would learn to speak another language and start working it into your speech.

Start by identifying three or four key areas of your marriage where God's truth is really needed. Memorize a verse of Scripture that applies to that situation. Then ask God to set off some alarms in your mind when that situation comes up. When it does, quote the verse in a normal tone of voice, as you would anything else you would speak. *"Conduct yourselves with wisdom...making the most of the opportunity. Let your speech always be with grace...so that you will know how you should respond"* (Colossians 4:5-6).

Week 7, Day 5

For they exchanged the truth of God for a lie, and worshiped and served the creature rather than the Creator, who is blessed forever. Amen.
ROMANS 1:25

Application

There are as many false saviors as there are potential idols. A few of these include:

- An unbiblical view of God ("genie in a bottle," obligated to grant your wishes)
- Sex (immorality, pornography, masturbation)
- Relaxation (sleep, television, reading, hobbies, entertainment, etc.)
- Work, ministry, volunteer activities, or just staying busy
- Clinging to people (friends, your children) for comfort
- Food, shopping (indulging yourself)
- Withdrawing, running away
- Sports, exercise
- Drugs, alcohol

Not all of these things are bad, but if they take the place of Christ, it is likely that you are pursuing a "false savior" as a remedy for your frustrated idol worship. In your prayer time today, ask God to reveal to you any false saviors you may be leaning on.

FALSE SAVIORS

Gabe and Deahna have been married for seven years, and have started to experience symptoms of the "Seven Year Itch." Gabe feels frustrated that he's not making more money and not able to give Deahna the things he'd promised when they were dating. Because of his guilt and frustration, he's withdrawn emotionally, so Deahna looks for other ways to have her desires met. She works full-time to be able to pay for the many things she wants. She spends a lot of time with her friend Lora as a substitute for the companionship she and Gabe once shared, and she's become addicted to romance novels, including erotic literature. She often asks God to change her husband's job situation, but she never asks God to make her more content.

Deahna's desire for a good marriage and a certain lifestyle has become an idol in her life. God may be frustrating her idol worship to bring her closer to Him, but she won't recognize His hand in her heart as long as she continues to pursue her earthly desires. When she doesn't get her heart's desires, she turns to "false saviors," like romance novels, a career, or a friendship, instead of turning to the true Savior, Jesus Christ.

Pursuing a "false savior" only compounds sin and makes matters worse. As our sin increases, the stress and emotional pain of not getting what we want also increase. What may start out as a temporary relief measure could very well become an idol in itself. The righteousness, blessing and spiritual maturity God wants to accomplish in and through you is sacrificed on the altar of temporal things. Like the idol worshippers of Romans 1:23, you trade "*the glory of the incorruptible God*" for things that are "*corruptible*"—things that can never satisfy and will pass away. And you waste the opportunity God has given you to glorify Him in your marriage and in your life.

The Red Thread

A clean house is very important to my husband. Thankfully, I'm one of those women who thinks tidying and organizing is a fun way to spend the weekend. However, I'm not quite up to his level of perfectionism when it comes to the clean part. I love to organize, but keeping the house as clean as he likes it is an area of submission I've sometimes struggled with over the years.

In teaching *The Excellent Wife* class at my church, we talked about "submitting to your husband in all things," and I became convicted about the sometimes half-hearted way I follow this command. Then one day I was cleaning the house and after the vacuum cleaner was put away, I found a piece of red thread on our bedroom floor. I was about to throw it behind the headboard when the Holy Spirit said to me, "Would you be doing that if Scott were watching?" I almost laughed, "No!" and dutifully marched it to the trash basket.

Submission is not submission if it is not "in all things." If you're not submitted to your husband in all things at all times (even when he's not looking!) then you're not truly submitted. I don't mean to say you never fail, and you're perfectly obedient at all times. But a truly submitted wife is wholeheartedly behind her husband in everything, joyfully looking for ways to accomplish his goals. She does not regard his requests as odious, but rather opportunities to serve him selflessly.

My problem with the red thread was that I thought it was silly to have to walk that thread *all the way* to the trash can. (A whole ten feet!) But God used that little thread to show me that I had come to regard many of my husband's requests as ridiculous. I was not really submissive, was not really in his camp with the whole super-clean thing. I call it my "red thread turning point." Not that I always do everything his way—in fact, I've failed in much larger things since! But my attitude has changed and I no longer see his requests as inane. I'm much more committed to pleasing him in this area.

Memorize It!

So, as those who have been chosen of God, holy and beloved, put on a heart of compassion, kindness, humility, gentleness and patience; bearing with one another, and forgiving each other, whoever has a complaint against anyone; just as the Lord forgave you, so also should you. (Colossians 3:12-13)

Wives, be subject to your husbands, as is fitting in the Lord. Whatever you do, do your work heartily, as for the Lord rather than for men, knowing that from the Lord you will receive the reward of the inheritance. It is the Lord Christ whom you serve.

Colossians 3:18, 23-24

Application

Are the following statements true of you?

- My husband has a reason for everything he asks me to do, even if I don't always know what that reason is.
- I try to see what he's hoping to accomplish in everything, and I'm happy to do my part to help him realize his goals.
- I submit to my husband's requests because I love him, and am committed to being the best wife to him that I can be.
- I submit to my husband's requests because this is what honors God.

God knows if you're taking shortcuts, or obeying on the outside but scoffing on the inside. He sees every small act, every "red thread" that crosses your path. He deserves total submission, even when your husband doesn't.

Week 8, Day 2

Praise the Lord*! How blessed is the man who fears the* Lord*, who greatly delights in His commandments.*
Psalm 112:1

Application

We all want a happy life where we get most of the desires of our heart. But notice what is necessary for that to happen: "**Trust** *in the* Lord *and* **do good**; *dwell in the land and* **cultivate faithfulness. Delight yourself in the Lord**; *and He will give you the desires of your heart.* **Commit your way** *to the* Lord, *trust also in Him, and He will do it*" (Psalm 37:3-5†). This passage very closely ties the blessings of life with our obedience and TOTAL commitment to God.

Stop trying to give God just parts of yourself, and expecting His blessings in return. Remember that you are not entitled to anything in this life, but God does promise peace, joy, and eternal pleasures when your delight is in Him.

Delight in the Lord

What is your greatest joy in life—that one thing that brings you more happiness than anything else?

Take a moment to think about that, then write your answer here. It might be your kids, your husband, reading, watching TV, hiking, scrapbooking. Don't write down what you think your answer *should* be, but the most honest answer you can think of:

You probably know what your answer should be, but very few of us can honestly say that our greatest delight is Christ. And why is that? Because we never totally immerse ourselves—heart, body, mind and soul—in Him.

Let's say you wrote "running" in the space, and let's walk through the process whereby that became your greatest passion. You probably ran some as a kid, but at some point you got serious about it and began to run not as a game or to get from point A to point B, but as an end to itself. You may have researched or been coached on how to run better, and you equipped yourself with decent running shoes. When you ran, you ran with all of you: your body was in it (of course), as well as your emotions and your intellect. At some point, you may have experienced a "runner's high," which came right after you thought running was going to kill you, but you pushed through it and once you did, you experienced a euphoria that was amazing. After that point running was no longer a chore, but something you had come to love.

This is how you came to delight in your greatest passion: you experienced it with all of you. And that is exactly why we don't fall in love with Christ: because we don't immerse ourselves totally in Him. We keep Him up in that "mental" part of us, never engaging our heart, soul, mind AND strength in loving Him.

The promise of Scripture, however, is that when you engage all of yourself in God, He rewards you with a "servant's high" that is the greatest thing you can ever experience in this life. *"In Your presence is fullness of joy; In Your right hand there are pleasures forever"* (Psalm 16:11).

Memorize It!

So, as those who have been chosen of God, holy and beloved, put on a heart of compassion, kindness, humility, gentleness and patience; bearing with one another, and forgiving each other, whoever has a complaint against anyone; just as the Lord *forgave you, so also should you.*
(Colossians 3:12-13)

Respect His Position

You are to respect your husband because God has given him authority over you and your family. It wasn't a Divine accident, or an unavoidable consequence of your marriage. The very moment that the preacher said, "I now pronounce you husband and wife," God in His perfect wisdom purposefully and deliberately gave your husband authority over you. And this is not only OK, it is very good.

Take a moment to just consider that truth: *GOD gave your husband his authority over you and your family*.

Did you stop and think, or are you just continuing to read? If you haven't, do that now.

God has appointed positions of authority in human institutions: the home, the church, even in government. Respect from those who are under authority is required in order for any of these institutions to run properly. Because of your husband's position in the biblical chain-of-command, your responsibility is to respect him as your leader and God-appointed authority. You can do this because of your trust in God, not in your husband. "And in [Christ] *you have been made complete, and* ***He is the head over all rule and authority***" (Colossians 2:10†). In other words, Jesus is the head over your husband, even if your hubby is not saved. This is why you are to "*be subject to your husbands, as is fitting in the LORD…knowing that from the LORD you will receive the reward of the inheritance. It is the LORD Christ whom you serve*" (Colossians 3:18, 24†).

This is such a simple truth, but oftentimes we work around it by saying, "Well, I respect the position, but not the person in the position." That's like saying you respect the throne the king is sitting on, but not the king. What value is there in a throne? None whatsoever; it's the person who sits on the throne that gives the throne its value. If you don't respect your husband as a person, your attitude will come out in your speech and your behavior toward him. No matter what kind of man your husband is, you must ALWAYS respond to him respectfully.

Memorize It!

So, as those who have been chosen of God, holy and beloved, put on a heart of compassion, kindness, humility, gentleness and patience; bearing with one another, and forgiving each other, whoever has a complaint against anyone; just as the LORD forgave you, so also should you.
(Colossians 3:12-13)

But I want you to understand that Christ is the head of every man, and the man is the head of a woman, and God is the head of Christ.
1 Corinthians 11:3

Application

If you are not respecting your husband properly, it is likely that you have forgotten the Source of your husband's authority. When you fail to respect your husband, you are essentially telling God that He made a mistake in putting your husband over you in authority, and God never makes mistakes.

You may be more intelligent, wiser, or more gifted than your husband, but that does not give you the right to usurp your husband's God-given authority. To help you remember the importance of respecting your husband, write your husband's name in the blank below and then read it to out loud:

Because GOD has given ________________ authority over me, I *will*, with God's help, give my husband the respect God demands!

Week 8, Day 4

She opens her mouth in wisdom,
and the teaching of kindness
is on her tongue.
PROVERBS 31:26

Application

I have found it useful to preface my appeals with the statement, "I am committed to doing whatever you decide. However..." and then stating my position. No matter how you say it, your husband needs to know that you are willing to submit to his decision (as long as he is not asking you to sin), and that you want to accomplish his goals.

As your husband's helper, you should be ready to give your husband wise counsel and advice. *"A wise man will hear and increase in learning, and a man of understanding will acquire wise counsel"* (Proverbs 1:5). Who knows him better than you, and who has God placed next to him who is better able to give him wise counsel than you, his "suitable helper"?

Making a Biblical Appeal (Part 1)

When Eli's company relocated him to Seattle, Daphne was excited about living in a new city. They found a great apartment that was close to a good school for their daughter. But finding a new church proved to be much more difficult. After months of searching, Eli grew tired of the process. "I'm done looking," he said. "The last church we went to is my choice, so I hope you liked it too!"

Daphne wanted to submit to her husband's decision, but she knew they had not yet found the place where God wanted them to worship and serve. "I understand why you want to go there," she said. "But the pastor seems to be a little weak on the inerrancy of Scripture. Why don't I do some on-line and phone research? I can even visit some of these churches during the week and get more information *before* we visit them."

The godly wife should always do what her husband wants her to do unless he asks her to sin. Sometimes our husbands ask us to do things that might not be sins, but they're not the best ideas either. Or they reject our requests without fully considering what we've asked. In times like these, it may be wise to make a biblical appeal.

An appeal is a request or plea to a person in authority for the purpose of asking them to reconsider a directive or command. If you need to make a biblical appeal to your husband, make sure you are seeking to achieve his goals or desires, not your own. The appeal should not be just a manipulative attempt to get your own way. Always make the appeal in a respectful manner, at a time when your husband is relaxed and ready to hear it, if at all possible. Also, an appeal should be made only once. Serious circumstances may require you to repeat it, to ensure that he understands fully what you're asking. But frequent or repeated appeals are actually nagging, which defeats the effectiveness of a biblical appeal.

Making an appeal is one of the ways God has provided for you, and when done in a spirit of submission, is a great tool for handling conflict in marriage.

Memorize It!

So, as those who have been chosen of God, holy and beloved, put on a heart of compassion, kindness, humility, gentleness and patience; bearing with one another, and forgiving each other, whoever has a complaint against anyone; just as the LORD forgave you, so also should you.
(Colossians 3:12-13)

Making a Biblical Appeal (Part 2)

She opens her mouth in wisdom,
and the teaching of kindness
is on her tongue.
Proverbs 31:26

Most of the time it's fairly easy for Elena to submit to her husband, even though he is not a believer. But this time they are in sharp disagreement. Their daughter wants to go on a missions trip to Haiti. Carlos sees only the dangers; he cannot appreciate the chance to share the gospel or how it will grow Michele's faith. And since he tends to be a little over-protective, his answer was a firm "no."

Elena knows this trip could be a great experience for Michele, but she can't appeal to Carlos using Scripture. Instead, she must base her appeal on satisfying his concerns. "I have more information about the trip," she says. "They'll be staying in a dormitory at the Christian school, and the kids will always be in groups, with a chaperone. There is one adult for every three kids going, and I have asked that Michele be assigned to a male chaperone when they're off campus. I know that will help you feel better about her safety."

When an appeal is made to a believing husband it should be based on biblical principles. But if the appeal is to an unbelieving husband, the use of Scripture or referring to God may only provoke him. *"The mind set on the flesh is hostile toward God, for it does not subject itself to the law of God"* (Romans 8:7†). Instead, she must appeal to his conscience to do what is reasonable or right.

While Elena is not able to use Scripture, she can still use godly wisdom to appeal to her husband to reconsider his decision. She is being wise by looking to accomplish her husband's objectives, yet still getting what she and her daughter want. And what she is asking is not a selfish desire, but is something that will help her daughter grow in faith. What will hurt her daughter, however, is if Elena disrespects her husband by nagging him or by getting angry if he still rejects her request. If he still says *no*, she must accept his decision as God's will for her and her daughter at the moment, and trust God to change her husband's heart if that is His desire.

Application

Saved or unsaved, if your husband rejects your appeal you must accept his decision as God's will for you at that time (unless he is asking you to sin). If you're trying to prevent him from doing something unwise and he rejects your counsel, you must trust God to work things out for your good and His glory. It may be that He is disciplining your husband by allowing him to suffer the natural consequences of a foolish decision or a proud heart.

If your husband wants you to sin and does not listen to your appeal, you must respectfully refuse and prepare to suffer the consequences of being obedient to God. *"For it is better, if God should will it so, that you suffer for doing what is right rather than for doing what is wrong"* (1 Peter 3:17).

Week 9, Day 1

And let us consider how we may spur one another on toward love and good deeds.
HEBREWS 10:24, NIV

Application

What are some ways you can help your husband mature in Christ?

- Pray for him daily.
- Clear his home schedule if too many responsibilities keep him from spending time reading the Word and in prayer.
- Ask if the two of you can have a regular time of prayer and Bible study together.
- Look for opportunities to encourage him to use his gifts and abilities in ministry.
- Do whatever you can to support his ministry with specific help and prayer.

THE PURPOSE OF HELPING

Barb was looking at the church bulletin, waiting for the service to begin, when she saw that the fifth grade boys' class needed a teacher. It was just the type of ministry her husband Dan was made for. However, it would be a huge time commitment, and not just on Sundays. He'd have to prepare during the week, taking time away from her and the kids, and they'd have to discipline themselves to get to church early.

On the way home, Barb mentioned the position to Dan. "Well," he said. "I've been praying about getting more involved. You think I could do this?" "Are you kidding?" Barb laughed. "You'd be great! You're so good with kids, and they all love you. They need someone like you who has a heart for God to lead those boys."

The purpose of being your husband's helper is not to make his life easier, but to encourage him to live a godly life of obedience to Christ. Sometimes this means rebuking him for sin—which we are often quick to do. But it also means encouraging him to "love and good deeds" (Hebrews 10:24).

Helping each other become more like Christ involves a lot of work on God's part, your part, and your husband's part. God's part is to convict, discipline, guide and enable. Your part is not only to work on your own sanctification, but to remind and encourage your husband to *"grow in the grace and knowledge of our LORD and Savior Jesus Christ"* (2 Peter 3:18), and to *"discipline yourself for the purpose of godliness"* (1 Timothy 4:7).

Your husband is your "home team." When he takes the field of life, he needs you by his side helping him win. Sometimes men get so absorbed in their jobs, they forget the things of the Kingdom. Even if he doesn't respond well to your involvement in this area of his life, that doesn't exempt you from doing what is right. If your husband is lacking spiritually in any area, it is your responsibility to help him grow. This is God's design in making you your husband's "suitable helper."

Memorize It!

Beyond all these things put on love, which is the perfect bond of unity. Let the peace of Christ rule in your hearts, to which indeed you were called in one body; and be thankful.
(Colossians 3:14-15)

Love Does Not Brag

But he who boasts is to boast in the LORD. *For it is not he who commends himself that is approved, but he whom the* LORD *commends.*
2 CORINTHIANS 10:17

It's time for a pop quiz! Answer the following TRUE/FALSE questions as honestly as you can.

1. My world pretty much revolves around keeping my family going.
2. I'm the one who does the majority of the work around here.
3. My husband is spiritually less mature than I am.
4. I probably have a higher IQ than my husband.
5. My husband is blessed to have me in his life. No other woman could live with him!
6. My family would collapse without me.
7. For all that I do for this family, I deserve to be treated well.

If you answered with an emphatic YES to at least three of those questions, you may be guilty of boasting–even if some of those things are true! To boast or brag means to "talk conceitedly" with "an excessive appreciation of one's own worth." Boasting is focused on self rather than others, and it works against love in your relationship to your husband. *"For through the grace given to me I say to everyone among you not to think more highly of himself than he ought to think; but to think so as to have sound judgment, as God has allotted to each a measure of faith"* (Romans 12:3).

Many wives get in the habit of boasting about themselves and their value to the marriage. "The only reason this relationship works is because I..." The boastful wife takes her husband for granted, thinking she deserves the nice things he does for her, and in fact, she deserves more. Sometimes we don't boast out loud, because we know it sounds bad. But we can have a boastful attitude in our hearts, and even if it never works its way into our speech, it affects who we are and how well we're able to love.

Application

If you find yourself having a boastful attitude, ask God to forgive you and teach you humility. Think about how you would feel if your husband had your heart attitude; if he overvalued his importance to your marriage and undervalued your contributions. Then make a mental (or written) list of all the good things your husband brings to your marriage and family. Memorize Scripture that will help you keep a godly perspective on your own worth, such as Isaiah 53:6; 64:6; Jeremiah 17:9; or Ephesians 2:8-9. Finally, give God the credit for any good that is present in your life. Remember that without God, you can do nothing!

Memorize It!

Beyond all these things put on love, which is the perfect bond of unity. Let the peace of Christ rule in your hearts, to which indeed you were called in one body; and be thankful.
(Colossians 3:14-15)

Week 9, Day 3

So, as those who have been chosen of God, holy and beloved, put on a heart of compassion, kindness, humility, gentleness and patience.
COLOSSIANS 3:12

Application

How should you respond when faced with a similar situation? First, acknowledge that you are just as capable as your husband of doing something sinful and "stupid." Second, examine your heart to see what sins you may now be committing that are equally as dishonest or as selfish as your husband's. Third, regard your husband as more important than yourself (Philippians 2:3) and think about his desires first, above your own. Fourth, ask God to show you how to respond biblically to your husband's actions. Fifth, show your husband respect, even if you don't agree with his decisions, and learn to communicate your feelings humbly, without getting angry.

Humility's Part in Conflict Resolution

Ashley sat in the chair in her bedroom, fuming. Paul had done some dumb things, but this latest stunt excelled all others in rank stupidity. The money they were saving for a down payment on a house? He had taken several thousand dollars of it and bought a *motorcycle*. A money-sucking death bike. Ashley couldn't decide if she was more angry or incredulous. How in the world could he have thought this was a good idea?

What is making Ashley's anger worse is her belief that she would never do anything as stupid as what her husband did. She sees herself as more intelligent than her husband and therefore incapable of committing such sins. She is thinking of herself more highly than she ought to think (Romans 12:3). But in God's eyes, Ashley is just as sinful as her husband. True, Paul behaved selfishly, but Ashley is full of pride and unrighteous anger.

We often react to our husbands' sin by putting ourselves on a pedestal, glorifying ourselves rather than Christ by ascribing to ourselves some inner goodness or character quality that would not allow us to fall as horribly as our husbands have. This is pride, and an abomination in God's eyes. *"Everyone who is proud in heart is an abomination to the LORD; assuredly, he will not be unpunished"* (Proverbs 16:5).

Humility means "lowliness of mind." In other words, a humble woman views herself in proper perspective to God (the LORD is God, she is not) and her husband (they are both sinners, equally). Resolving conflict in marriage means you must continually humble yourself and seek what's best for your husband over what your own desires may be. As you seek God's will and not your own way, God will be glorified (rather than yourself) and any conflict you and your husband have will be well on its way to being solved.

Memorize It!

Beyond all these things put on love, which is the perfect bond of unity. Let the peace of Christ rule in your hearts, to which indeed you were called in one body; and be thankful.
(Colossians 3:14-15)

Your Heart's Desire

And you will seek Me and find Me, when you search for Me with all your heart.
Jeremiah 29:13

One of the most misused and misunderstood verses in the Bible is Psalm 37:4—*"Delight yourself in the Lord; and He will give you the desires of your heart."* Many people interpret this verse to mean that if they delight themselves in God, He will give them whatever they want (as long as what they want is not sinful). In life and in their interpretation of Scripture, their focus is not on God, but on the "desires of their heart." They don't turn to this verse when pursuing God; they turn to this verse to try to figure out why they're not getting what they want out of life.

We get so blinded and confused by our idol worship, we can't even see what God is aiming for in this passage. He's not giving a prescription for idol acquisition; He's saying, "As you delight yourself in Me, *I* will become your most passionate desire. And I will never withhold myself from those who love me and seek me with their whole heart." *"You will seek Me and find Me when you search for Me with all your heart"* (Jeremiah 29:13).

Most of us see God as a heavenly vending machine. If we put in enough money and press the right buttons, He is obligated to give us the things we want. We try using the currency of good works: if we do enough things for Him and follow His laws, that will get us what we want. As we come to understand that our works will get us nowhere (Ephesians 2:8-9; Romans 11:6), we then try to use the currency of love and devotion. If we love Him enough and are devoted to Him, He will give us our heart's desire. But guess what? This latter thinking is just as flawed as the first. The goal of knowing and loving God is never to get us what we want. Rather, our goal should be like Paul's: *"I count all things to be loss in view of the surpassing value of knowing Christ Jesus my Lord, for whom I have suffered the loss of all things, and count them but rubbish so that I may gain Christ"* (Philippians 3:8). Christ and Christ alone was Paul's greatest desire, and *nothing* was better than knowing Him.

Application

As you seek God, you begin to better understand who He is and what His will is. You lose the view of Him as the "heavenly vending machine" and begin to see Him as the sovereign God whose *"thoughts are not your thoughts, nor are your ways [His] ways"* (Isaiah 55:8†). He wants you to have joy, but He knows that this is only possible as you give Him your undivided worship and devotion. He wants your thoughts, motives, and choices to be focused on glorifying Him, not on achieving your heart's desire. *He* should be your greatest longing, desire and refuge, not some earthly thing. You should want what God wants, no matter what. If you're going to be obsessed about anything, let it be Him.

Memorize It!

Beyond all these things put on love, which is the perfect bond of unity. Let the peace of Christ rule in your hearts, to which indeed you were called in one body; and be thankful.
(Colossians 3:14-15)

Week 9, Day 5

The wise in heart will be called understanding, and sweetness of speech increases persuasiveness.
PROVERBS 16:21

Application

Proverbs 16:21 gives some very helpful advice on managing your tone: *"The wise in heart will be called understanding, and sweetness of speech increases persuasiveness."* If you are seeking to be understanding and patient with your husband, then your tone will reflect that.

Many of the petty arguments we get into as married couples could be avoided if everyone were to just be conscious of their tone. Think about the last time you and your husband got into a "heated discussion." If you can remember the details about the argument, try to replay it again in your mind, but this time, imagine saying everything in a softer, more gentle tone. Can you see the effect this would have had on your husband?

Watch Your Tone

My co-teacher and I were out on the church playground, watching twenty-six preschoolers running around enjoying the spring air and sunshine. Standing nearby were Chet and Dawn, a husband and wife team who taught the other class. Chet had as much energy as those kids, and was trying to engage them in a game of "freeze tag." The kids just weren't getting the concept, however; they would "freeze" until the tagger came near them, and then they would run off. When Chet called the kids to "huddle up" so he could explain the rules again, Dawn called out to him, "Forget it, Chet! They're too young to play this game!"

Now that wasn't a horrible thing to say, but the way she said it made it sound like, "You dummy! Don't you know anything about child development?" It didn't sound like a helpful suggestion; it sounded like a condemnation of his knowledge and his efforts. And it very quickly deflated his enthusiasm.

Tone is everything. You can say to your husband, "Do you need help?" and sound like you're genuinely offering to help, or you can say "You need help!" and sound like you think he's completely incompetent at whatever he's doing.

Proverbs 16:24 says, *"Pleasant words are a honeycomb, sweet to the soul and healing to the bones."* If your tone of voice is always respectful, kind and loving, then your husband will be more likely to hear the things you say. But if your tone is harsh or disapproving, your husband may misinterpret what you're trying to say because he is trying to process multiple messages: the message of your words, and the message of your tone.

Even if you need to question something your husband has done that was perhaps sinful or foolish, it is never right to do it in a condescending, angry, or sarcastic manner. Your husband should never feel like you are attacking him. Your tone should always communicate that you love and respect him, and that you are genuinely trying to help.

Giving a Biblical Reproof (Part 1)

Alicia was putting groceries away when she heard her husband yelling, then heard the slam of her daughter's bedroom door. Her heart sank to realize they were having yet another argument. She didn't know what had started this one, but most of the time it was because of her husband's anger and unreasonable demands on Jessica.

An hour later she and Austin were sitting on the front porch, talking about the situation. Alicia had been praying about Austin's anger, and she knew she had to be truthful with him. "Sweetheart, I know you love Jessie," she began. "But you're still trying to use anger to manipulate her into doing what you want. The only thing you're doing is frustrating and alienating her. The Bible says *"the anger of man does not achieve the righteousness of God."*[3] It also says fathers should not provoke their children to anger[4], but that's exactly what you've been doing. Do you realize we only have three years left with her before she goes off to college? Is this really how you want her to remember you?"

What Alicia is doing is giving her husband a *biblical reproof*. Alicia is motivated not just by her desire to protect her daughter, but also to help her husband overcome his anger. She knows that as long as he continues in this sin, he will not have a good relationship with his daughter or with God.

A biblical reproof is telling someone that what they are doing is contrary to God's Word. If you have children, you would use a biblical reproof to *"bring them up in the discipline and instruction of the Lord"* (Ephesians 6:4). But sometimes it may be necessary for you to reprove your husband. Pointing out his sin, and how to correct it, is one of the ways you love him and help him become more like Christ. Your motivation *must* be to restore him to a right relationship with God—not to punish him, to prove yourself more righteous, or to get your way. The focus should always be on your husband's walk with Christ.

Memorize It!

Let the word of Christ richly dwell within you, with all wisdom teaching and admonishing one another with psalms and hymns and spiritual songs, singing with thankfulness in your hearts to God. Whatever you do in word or deed, do all in the name of the Lord Jesus, giving thanks through Him to God the Father.
(Colossians 3:16-17)

Be on your guard! If your brother sins, rebuke him; and if he repents, forgive him.
Luke 17:3

Application

Giving a biblical reproof can be effective if done properly, yet disastrous if done carelessly. It is important for you to understand this tool in the light of Scripture so you can use it effectively. We will go over different aspects of this concept throughout the year. By the end of this study, you should be better equipped to give a biblical reproof for your husband's good and for God's glory.

Right now, say a prayer of commitment to always speak the truth in love to your husband (Ephesians 4:15). Then ask God to help you stay in His Word and be more diligent to memorize Scripture, so that you will be able to use it to both encourage and reprove your husband whenever necessary.

Week 10, Day 2

Above all, keep fervent in your love for one another, because love covers a multitude of sins.
1 Peter 4:8

Application

A word of caution about follow-through: If your husband will not admit he has a sin problem, or refuses to talk to a pastor or biblical counselor, do not keep bringing up the same occurrence. Remember that it is God who will change your husband's heart, not you (1 Corinthians 3:7, Philippians 2:13).

If your husband truly has a sin problem, it will reveal itself again in a different scenario. You should wait for that to happen before reproving him again. It is possible that each recurrence will grow progressively worse as God "turns up the heat" on your husband's sin. Then you may be more effective in getting through to him. If, after a reasonable time and repeated reproofs, he still does not repent, you may have to proceed with the steps in Matthew 18:15-18. (For more information, see pp. 166-167).

Giving a Biblical Reproof (Part 2)

Yesterday, we met Austin, who had an anger problem that he was taking out on his daughter Jessica. His wife, Alicia, reproved him biblically, but what if he didn't receive her reproof? Let's imagine the scenario…

Austin briefly considered what his wife had to say, but a thousand thoughts were flooding his mind. "I have to disagree. The fact that we have less than three years is exactly why I'm so hard on her," he answered. "And I can't help it if I get angry. *You* baby her, so I have to compensate for that."

Alicia could see that she was not going to get very far with him while he was still somewhat angry. So she waited for a better time to bring up the discussion again. A week later, while the two of them were having dinner, Alicia said, "I've been thinking about what you said last week, and you're right. I do tend to baby Jessica. I think both of us could use a little help in knowing how to better parent a teenager. Would you be willing to go with me to talk to Pastor about this?"

When giving a biblical reproof, it's also important to follow up on it. The temptation is to say, "I reproved him, so my job is done!" If you are truly seeking to restore your husband to proper fellowship with God, then you will see the reproof through to the end—to the point where he sees his sin and changes his behavior. This is one of the ways you *"keep fervent in your love"* for your husband (1 Peter 4:8). Bringing in a biblical counselor should be one of the first steps in follow-through. When a husband and wife cannot agree about what is and what is not a pattern of sinful behavior, the counsel of other mature believers is often necessary to help shine the light of Scripture on a difficult issue. Involving others also establishes accountability and ensures that you are seeing the situation accurately.

You may have to keep at it for a long time, but keep in mind the goal, which is to see your husband become more like Christ.

Memorize It!

Let the word of Christ richly dwell within you, with all wisdom teaching and admonishing one another with psalms and hymns and spiritual songs, singing with thankfulness in your hearts to God. Whatever you do in word or deed, do all in the name of the Lord Jesus, giving thanks through Him to God the Father.
(Colossians 3:16-17)

Die Before You Begin

We will be talking throughout this book about progressive sanctification, which is the process of purifying your life of sin and becoming more and more like the Lord Jesus Christ. God begins this process at the moment of your salvation, and uses your husband, other people, trials, and His Word in your life, for *"teaching... reproof... correction (and) training in righteousness"* (2 Timothy 3:16).

But *you* don't begin participating in the process until you do one simple, yet difficult, thing. You must first die to yourself.

A popular misconception is that "dying to self" is something you attain after you have reached a certain level of spiritual maturity. But dying to yourself is the *beginning* of your walk with Christ, not the culmination. (See Colossians 3:3, Galatians 2:20.)

Whenever God gives you an opportunity to obey, you have two choices: what will please Him, and what will please yourself. When you choose what He wants rather than what you want, you have in essence killed your desires for the sake of His. This is something you must do repeatedly, every day (1 Corinthians 15:31), if you are going to achieve any level of spiritual maturity at all.

My fear is that many of you reading this book feel about dying to self the way I once did: that it's a nice goal to hope for, someday, but "no way am I spiritual enough for that right now." If that is your attitude, you will be spiritually stagnant for as long as that opinion persists. Spiritual growth cannot begin until you *"have crucified the flesh with its passions and desires"* (Galatians 5:24). As long as your flesh and your desires are still living and thriving in your life, you will make no progress in your sanctification.

Jesus said, *"Unless a grain of wheat falls into the earth and dies, it remains alone; but if it dies, it bears much fruit"* (John 12:24†). No death? No fruit.

Memorize It!

Let the word of Christ richly dwell within you, with all wisdom teaching and admonishing one another with psalms and hymns and spiritual songs, singing with thankfulness in your hearts to God. Whatever you do in word or deed, do all in the name of the Lord Jesus, giving thanks through Him to God the Father.
(Colossians 3:16-17)

Therefore if you have been raised up with Christ, keep seeking the things above, where Christ is, seated at the right hand of God. Set your mind on the things above, not on the things that are on earth. For you have died and your life is hidden with Christ in God.
Colossians 3:1-3

Application

God wants us to stop living for ourselves, and to start living for Him. Paul wrote to the church at Corinth that *"they who live might no longer live for themselves, but for Him who died and rose again on their behalf"* (2 Corinthians 5:15). God wants us to glorify and serve Him now, to think and act like the Lord Jesus Christ would, and to actively participate in the process of becoming *"conformed to the image of His Son"* (Romans 8:29).

What keeps us from dying to self is a fear of not having the kind of life we want. But if you continually choose your own way, Christ warns that you are not a disciple of His: *"He who loves his life loses it, and he who hates his life in this world will keep it to life eternal"* (John 12:25).

Week 10, Day 4

He who is faithful in a very little thing is faithful also in much; and he who is unrighteous in a very little thing is unrighteous also in much.
LUKE 16:10

Application

Any time you encounter conflict or a difference of opinion with your husband over an issue, ask yourself: Is this a major decision or a minor decision? If it's a major decision, it may be that you and your husband need to discuss it further and work out a resolution together (keeping in mind that he still has the final say). If it's a minor issue, you can certainly make your desires known. But if he still insists on having his way, think of it as a chance to work those spiritual muscles of submission, and just say *yes* to your husband without arguing or reservation. Remember that love *"does not seek its own (way)"* (1 Corinthians 13:5). Thank God for the little things in life which give you the opportunity to show love to your husband in this way, by being obedient in the small as well as the big.

In All Things, Little and Big

Alyssa did not have the best role model of submission in her mom. Even though she came from a Christian family, her mom was strong-willed and often openly critical of her dad. Alyssa knew going into marriage that submission was going to be an uphill battle for her, as she had inherited much of her mother's temperament. As the years went by, Alyssa learned more and more about obedience to Christ and to her husband, and she tried to be the best wife she could be. When Adam made the decision to take their kids out of Christian school, Alyssa accepted his decision, trusting God to care for her children in public school. When Adam vetoed her idea to finish the basement, opting instead to use the money for a family vacation, she went along and had a great time.

However, there was one area where Alyssa would not submit: where to set the thermostat. Adam wanted to save money, so he set it at 79 degrees during the summer. But once he left for work in the morning, she would bump it down to 76. "I've sacrificed a lot for him," she reasoned. "I am NOT going to sweat in my own house!"

Sometimes we get into a similar pattern of thinking. We applaud ourselves for those victories of submission in the "big" things, like child-rearing or major financial decisions, but think that entitles us to having our own way in the little things—like where to set the thermostat. But as we've seen previously, submission is an attitude that affects how we respond to everything, no matter how seemingly insignificant.

Submitting to your husband in those small, everyday decisions reveals your true heart and character, and is good practice for when the stakes are higher and your emotions are more likely to be cranked up. Saying *yes* to his desires in the little things will help you develop a habit of submission that will help when major decisions come along. Remember too, that in God's eyes, there's no such thing as a "minor" issue of disobedience. Usually it is the *"little foxes that are ruining the vineyards"* (Song of Solomon 2:15).

Memorize It!

Let the word of Christ richly dwell within you, with all wisdom teaching and admonishing one another with psalms and hymns and spiritual songs, singing with thankfulness in your hearts to God. Whatever you do in word or deed, do all in the name of the LORD Jesus, giving thanks through Him to God the Father.
(Colossians 3:16-17)

Recognizing God's Sovereignty

Week 10, Day 5

Ephesians 5:33 makes it pretty clear that you're supposed to respect your husband: *"The wife must see to it that she respects her husband."* But perhaps you are still struggling to live out that command. Many of us struggle with respect because, face it, husbands are human, they make mistakes, and they don't always demonstrate that they are worthy of the level of respect God requires.

If anyone in the history of the world could understand that struggle, it would be King David. God hand-picked David to become the next king of Israel, yet in his *sovereignty*, He chose to keep the current king in place. As long as Saul remained on the throne, David had to respect him as his LORD and king—even when Saul tried to kill him! Several times, David had an opportunity to take the throne from Saul. Yet he refused. *"I will not stretch out my hand against my LORD* [Saul], *for he is the LORD's anointed"* (1 Samuel 24:10).

David respected Saul because he trusted in God's sovereignty. His faith was strong enough to wait on God and, in the meantime, be obedient to God's commands. And that's the lesson for you as a godly wife. It is not always easy to respect your husband, but a firm reliance on God's sovereignty—*knowing that God is in control and is actively working all things together for good* (Romans 8:28)—will keep you obedient. It is also helpful to remember that Christ is the Sovereign LORD whether you accept His LORDship over you or not. He's not waiting for you to make Him LORD or give Him that title; He *is* LORD. If you accept His LORDship and walk in step with His program, He promises to bless you.

So [David] said to his men, "Far be it from me because of the LORD that I should do this thing to my LORD, the LORD's anointed, to stretch out my hand against him, since he is the LORD's anointed." Now afterward David arose and...called after Saul, saying, "My LORD the king!" And when Saul looked behind him, David bowed with his face to the ground and prostrated himself.

1 Samuel 24:6, 8

Application

David was a superstar of faith, but remember that he was only human; he had weaknesses and experienced failure just like you. But in the end, he demonstrated that God can be trusted. Your husband may not deserve your respect; in fact, sometimes it may feel like he is actually working against you. Can you trust in God's sovereignty enough to respect him anyway?

Read 1 Samuel chapters 16—26 and focus on David's love and respect for King Saul. If David can respect the man who tried to kill him and made his life miserable, you can certainly respect your husband. He may be wonderful, or he may need a lot of work, but he is still the man God chose to lead you.

Week 11, Day 1

She looks well to the ways of her household, and does not eat the bread of idleness.
PROVERBS 31:27

Application

How well are you ruling your house? Does your husband get too involved in the things you should be doing? Do you get irritated when you're working and he's taking it easy? If you're keeping up with things and he still wants to be involved, you can graciously accept his help. But have a conversation with him, reminding him that this is your responsibility, and make sure he's not helping because of your lack of discipline in this area.

Remember that your home is your domain, but even as the house "ruler," you are still under your husband's and God's authority, *"so that the word of God will not be dishonored"* (Titus 2:5†).

YOUR HOME, YOUR DOMAIN

In a recent advice column, a woman wrote in to complain that her husband wasn't doing his share of the chores around their home. She estimated that he did only 40% of the work around the house, yet she excluded the chores he "enjoys," such as lawn care, finances, and cooking! She ended her letter by asking, "Short of threatening divorce, how do I convince him he's wrong?"

Now, I might be living in a Christian "bubble," but that woman sounds ridiculous even by the world's standards! God divides the authority for the many things that have to be done in a home between the husband and wife so that the family runs smoothly and everyone's needs are met. Your husband's main responsibility is to lead the family spiritually (Deuteronomy 6:7) and provide an income (1 Timothy 5:8). Your job is the care and keeping of the house and children.

In 1 Timothy 5:14, Paul encourages women[5] to *"bear children, keep house, and give the enemy no occasion for reproach."* The Greek word translated "keep house" is *oikodespoteo* which means "house ruler." This is your own little kingdom; if your husband wants to be involved, graciously accept his help, but do not get in the habit of expecting him to do the things that fall under your job description. This adds to his burden, and is not in keeping with being your husband's suitable helper. Instead, he becomes *your* helper as he carries both his load and yours.

I understand that in many homes, the lines between the husband's and the wife's responsibilities are somewhat blurred. Perhaps the wife has to work outside of the home, or because of illness, injury, a new baby, or caring for an elderly parent, she may be physically unable to keep up with the house. However, even under those circumstances, keep in mind that the home is still your domain, and ask God to give you the strength to do your job as well as possible. Ask Him to help you see your work in the home not as a burden, and thank Him for the privilege of being a "house ruler."

Memorize It!

The fear of the LORD is the instruction for wisdom,
and before honor comes humility.
(Proverbs 15:33)

Through the Heart and Out the Mouth

You brood of vipers, how can you, being evil, speak what is good? For the mouth speaks out of that which fills the heart. The good man brings out of his good treasure what is good; and the evil man brings out of his evil treasure what is evil.
MATTHEW 12:34-35

Pete, Gina and their five children have a dinnertime ritual where everyone gets a chance to talk about something that happened to them that day. The last one to share is Pete, but by then Gina is tired and ready to begin cleaning up. She often finds herself getting impatient with Pete's tales and can feel her irritation rising as he talks.

Tonight Pete's story is about meeting a well-known football player at the public relations firm where he works. Gina thinks he often exaggerates his stories to add "color" and make himself look good in the eyes of his children, which annoys her. In the past, she would have cut him short by saying, "Is that *really* what happened?" But she has been convicted about showing him disrespect, especially in front of the kids, so she has begun training herself with God's Word. Now when he talks, she reminds herself to listen attentively by thinking, *"Love is patient"* (1 Corinthians 13:4). If she doubts something he says, she reminds herself that *"Love believes all things"* (1 Corinthians 13:7).

In this way, Gina is not only training her speech to have Christ-honoring responses to her husband, but she is also changing her mind about many of the wrong attitudes she once held toward him.

Jesus said, *"For the mouth speaks out of that which fills the heart"* (Matthew 12:34). He made clear the connection between what you think and what you say. Wrong words always begin with wrong thoughts and attitudes.

If you are saying the wrong things, take time to identify the thoughts behind your wrong words. God's standard of holiness is not just outward conformity but inward transformation of your heart. He not only wants you to *"let your speech always be with grace"* (Colossians 4:6) but also to *"be transformed by the renewing of your mind"* (Romans 12:2) by meditating on Scripture which deals directly with the areas in which you are struggling.

Memorize It!

The fear of the LORD is the instruction for wisdom, and before honor comes humility.
(Proverbs 15:33)

Application

Make a list today of areas where you know you struggle, then over the next week, look for specific Scriptures that deal with that particular sin. (You may need a more mature Christian to help you with this, or use an online study Bible, searching by topic.)

For example, if you tend to remind your husband of his past failings, meditate on 1 Corinthians 13:5, *"Love does not take into account a wrong suffered."* If you have a habit of being condescending to your husband, memorize Philippians 2:3 and remind yourself to *"regard one another as more important than yourselves."* Doing this regularly and consistently will help you change your thoughts, attitudes, and speech to be more respectful to your husband and more honoring to Christ.

Week 11, Day 3

That He might present to Himself the church in all her glory, having no spot or wrinkle or any such thing; but that she would be holy and blameless.
EPHESIANS 5:27

Application

You can replace your idolatrous desire for a better life with a passionate heart's desire for God as you:

- Focus your thoughts on God, not yourself.
- Diligently seek Him through His Word.
- Cultivate a grateful attitude regardless of your circumstances.
- Take small steps of obedience every day, continuously moving forward in obedience to Christ.
- Ask God to give you a heart of passion for Him.

God will do the rest, because that is consistent with His character and His promises. *"This is the confidence which we have before Him, that, if we ask anything according to His will, He hears us. And if we know that He hears us in whatever we ask, we know that we have the requests which we have asked from Him"* (1 John 5:14-15).

ULTERIOR MOTIVES

Ava and I sat amidst piles of dirty laundry, sorting weeks' worth of clothes that she "just didn't have time to get to." She admitted that she had let slide many of her duties as a wife, but blamed it on her husband Charles: his apathy, lack of affection, and unwillingness to help her around the house. But most of all, she blamed it on poor spiritual leadership. "I don't have any joy in the LORD anymore," she said. "Charles never encourages me spiritually. I feel like so many things in our marriage would improve if he would just get engaged spiritually."

One of the most consistent complaints I hear from women is how their husbands fail to lead them spiritually. It is very rare for me to meet a woman who feels that her husband is doing a good job in this department.

Sadly, many women have ulterior motives in desiring change in this area. It's not because they want their husbands to lead them spiritually; in fact, they don't want to be led at all. But they believe they will be treated better and life will be easier if their husbands are doing what God tells them to do. They want their husbands to love them sacrificially, *"as Christ also loved the church and gave Himself up for her"* (Ephesians 5:25); but they don't really want their husbands to *"sanctify her...that she would be holy and blameless"* (Ephesians 5:26-27). They don't want to change themselves; they just want their husbands to change so that life gets better.

If that is your secret heart's desire, you are shortchanging yourself.

God wants your husband to be saved and to lead you spiritually both for your good and for His glory, to bring both of you into fuller obedience to Himself. His goal is not that your life gets better or that you are treated as you desire, but that you would know Him better and find your greatest joy and delight in Him.

This is the purpose of your husband's spiritual leadership: to increase your holiness, obedience, and love for Christ. Not to satisfy your desire for personal happiness.

Memorize It!

The fear of the LORD is the instruction for wisdom,
and before honor comes humility.
(Proverbs 15:33)

Love is Not Arrogant

For through the grace given to me I say to everyone among you not to think more highly of himself than he ought to think; but to think so as to have sound judgment, as God has allotted to each a measure of faith.
Romans 12:3

Growing up, my family's chief complaint about the person I was becoming was, "She thinks she's always right," to which I would reply, "Of course I think I'm right. Why would I hold an opinion if I thought it was wrong?"

While that kind of reasoning may sound logical, it betrays the truth that I had, in fact, become quite arrogant as a young woman. My arrogance led to many arguments with my husband, and had a devastating effect on love in our marriage. It took many years of God's humbling work in my life to heal the wounds I inflicted with my arrogant words and attitudes.

An arrogant woman is opinionated and full of self-importance. She's quick to offer her wisdom and insight on every situation—yet it's difficult to tell her anything because she is so sure she's right about most things. She's proud and therefore does not react humbly when reproved, corrected, or even disagreed with. *"An arrogant man stirs up strife, but he who trusts in the Lord will prosper"* (Proverbs 28:25).

Jeremiah 17:9 says *"The heart is more deceitful than all else."* Since your heart can deceive you, how can you tell if you're an arrogant wife? One way is to think about the last time someone disagreed with you, or tried to reprove or correct you. If you reacted defensively, arguing your way through the conflict until it passed, then most likely you are arrogant.

Application

A wife who is arrogant and prideful can hurt her husband deeply; therefore, do all you can to root arrogance out of your heart, life, and marriage. Ask God to reveal to you specific ways in which you may be arrogant. When your husband's opinions differ from yours, or if he is correcting or reproving you, listen carefully to him, and keep yourself open to the possibility that he may be right or have information you don't have. If you've been arrogant in the past, your husband will immediately recognize the change in you, and a deeper love between the two of you will likely result.

Memorize It!

The fear of the Lord is the instruction for wisdom,
and before honor comes humility.
(Proverbs 15:33)

Week 11, Day 5

Pride goes before destruction,
and a haughty spirit
before a fall.
PROVERBS 16:18, NKJV

Application

Brittan's story has a miraculous ending, as God lovingly spared her life. Despite falling three stories, she ended up with only a broken arm and a new respect for my commands. God's grace worked in every detail that day, to the praise of His glory!

In a similar way, God may allow your pride to have its natural consequence, resulting in a fall that threatens the life of your marriage. If you're experiencing difficulties in your marriage, ask God what part your *pride* plays in what is going on. *"(If) My people… humble themselves and pray and seek My face and turn from their wicked ways, then I will hear from heaven, will forgive their sin and will heal their land"* (2 Chronicles 7:14†). Humility may be what leads to healing for your marriage.

PRIDE: IT'S A LONG WAY DOWN

Pride brings all kinds of trouble, because pride always leads to disobedience. When we behave as though we are smarter than God, we will seek our own way rather than obeying Him. This proud thinking starts very young, as illustrated by my five-year-old daughter, whose pride and disobedience almost led to her death.

My girls and I were attending a summer camp at a Christian university, and were staying in one of the dorms. We were on the third floor, and the morning we were packing up to leave was a beautiful summer day, with a cool breeze coming in through the window. As I was moving our suitcases into the hallway, Brittan complained about the temperature in the room. "Can I close the window?" she pleaded. "I'm cold!" I told her to put on a sweater and leave the window alone, and I kept working. A couple of minutes later, I was out in the hallway when my older daughter screamed. "Brittan fell out the window!" I rushed into the room and saw the open window, now missing its screen. When I got to the window, I saw her little body lying on the ground below. In trying to close the window against my specific command, my precious daughter had fallen three stories. I didn't know if she was dead or alive.

Proverbs 16:18 says *"Pride goes before destruction, and a haughty spirit before a fall."* I often use Brittan's story to illustrate what happens when we think we know better than God. She thought she knew what was best for her, which led literally to her downfall! What moves us to act in opposition to God is our own pride; thinking that our way is best. This pride often manifests itself in our marriages. We know God wants us to submit to our husbands, but we often think we have a better idea. If we never deal with our pride, it will eventually lead to the destruction and fall of our marriages. Instead, we should seek God's favor in our marriages by humbling ourselves to His will. *"God is opposed to the proud, but gives grace to the humble"* (James 4:6).

The Exceptional Husband

Wives, be subject to your husbands, as is fitting in the Lord.
Colossians 3:18

I was talking to a friend of mine one day, and I mentioned how, in researching my book, I was learning that men value respect more than anything else their wives could give or do for them. Robin looked at me doubtfully, but when I said, "a man would rather be respected than loved," she laughed out loud. "My husband couldn't care less about respect," she said, "as long as things are good in the bedroom!"

Robin and Troy had not been married for very long, and I'm sure it seemed to her as though sex was about the only thing on her husband's mind. But she came back to me later, expressing surprise. "I asked Troy about the respect thing. I had no idea it was that important to him!"

I understood where Robin was coming from, because I'm often guilty of thinking my husband is the exception, rather than the rule. All too often when I read descriptions of male and female characteristics, my husband appears to have many female traits while I have co-opted a lot of the male traits: I'm more logical, I love football, and I hate shopping. Scott is more emotional, he detests all sports, and you'll find him at a mall sooner than you'll find me there. So like Robin, I tend to think my husband is an exception to the rule.

As you read through this book, you may find yourself thinking at times, "This doesn't apply to us." I'm sure it's true that you won't be able to relate to every scenario, but when it comes to love, submission, respect and obedience, you cannot claim an exemption. I have heard women say that they don't submit to their husbands because "he doesn't want a doormat." Such a statement betrays a lack of understanding of submission, but more importantly, your duty is to "*obey God rather than men*" (Acts 5:29). Even if your husband seems to have given you a pass on certain godly requirements, God hasn't. (See Colossians 3:18.) You are required by God to respect and submit to your husband whether he says he wants you to or not.

Memorize It!

Therefore if there is any encouragement in Christ, if there is any consolation of love, if there is any fellowship of the Spirit, if any affection and compassion, make my joy complete by being of the same mind, maintaining the same love, united in spirit, intent on one purpose. (Philippians 2:1-2)

Application

No matter what your husband is like, he is still your husband, and you are required to treat him as God wants you to treat him—not even, necessarily, the way he says he wants to be treated. The truth is, your husband will likely respond very positively as you become more obedient to God's way, because God's way, not man's, is perfect (Deuteronomy 32:4).

If you're guilty of not respecting your husband because you thought this was what he wanted, make it a point to go to him at the first opportunity and confess this as the sin it truly is. Even if he tries to argue with you, remind him that God's ways are better than yours and his ways, and that you are making a new commitment to honor him the way God wants you to.

Week 12, Day 2

Brethren, even if anyone is caught in any trespass, you who are spiritual, restore such a one in a spirit of gentleness; each one looking to yourself, so that you too will not be tempted.
GALATIANS 6:1

Application

The steps of a biblical reproof are as follows:

1. Keep your life pure before God; make sure your conscience is clean and there are no "*logs in your own eye*" before pointing out your husband's sins (Matthew 7:3-5).
2. Pray first, then plan what you're going to say. Make sure you have relevant Scripture to back up your point (Proverbs 15:28).
3. Come to him in a spirit of gentleness, at a time when he is most likely to receive what you have to say (Galatians 6:1).
4. Explain what he did, why it was wrong (using specific Scripture), and how he can biblically fix what he did or do better next time (2 Timothy 3:16-17).
5. Reassure him of your love; give him some genuine praise and encouragement (1 Peter 3:8).

Reproving a Christian Husband

Anna's mom never questioned her dad on anything. Even if her dad was clearly in the wrong, her mom never opened her mouth. When Anna was preparing for her marriage, she asked her mom about this. "The Bible says that if our husbands are '*disobedient to the word*,'" her mom explained, "then we are to win them by our behavior, not our words. I could never disrespect your father by telling him he's wrong!"

Anna's fiancé Braden grew up in the opposite home. His mom criticized his dad about virtually everything, and as a result, there was a great deal of stress in their family. Braden admired Anna's parents greatly, and hoped she would follow her mom's example of "total" submission. He did not want his home to be like his parents'! But Anna believed her mom was not correct in her approach to her husband's sin. One night, she and Braden got into a discussion about that very subject. "Your mom is right," Braden argued. "The Bible says that even if I'm being disobedient to Scripture, you still have to be submissive. That's how you help me change: by being a good example."

"I agree," Anna said. "Your sin does not give me the right to stop submitting to you. However, you're taking 1 Peter 3:1 out of context. The previous chapter is clear that those who are '*disobedient to the word*' are those who are not saved. Since you *are* a believer, I have a responsibility as your wife to help you grow to maturity in Christ."

The admonition in 1 Peter 3:1-2 is for Christian wives to win their unbelieving husbands to Christ by their "*chaste and respectful behavior*" without nagging them or trying to badger them into believing. But Christian spouses are responsible for helping each other become more like the LORD Jesus Christ; therefore, either one may reprove the other of sin. They are to "*be subject to one another in the fear of Christ*" (Ephesians 5:21). That doesn't mean that he submits to her authority, but he does respect her and listens when she speaks the truth of God's Word to him.

Memorize It!

Therefore if there is any encouragement in Christ, if there is any consolation of love, if there is any fellowship of the Spirit, if any affection and compassion, make my joy complete by being of the same mind, maintaining the same love, united in spirit, intent on one purpose. (Philippians 2:1-2)

Idolatrous vs. Godly Desires

We've talked several times so far about how being obsessed with anything other than God is idolatry. Today I'd like to go over some ungodly desires that are not so obvious. We will discuss sinful or ungodly idols further in this study, but today's focus is on things that you might not ordinarily think of as sinful. Remember that even if what you want is not inherently ungodly, your attention to it can be ungodly if it replaces God in your heart and on the throne of your life. If you desire *anything at all* more than you desire to know and please Christ, you can bet you are an idol worshipper.

Potentially Idolatrous Desires—"Lord, here's what I want":

- An affectionate husband who loves me as Christ loves the church
- An intimate marriage that fulfills all of my physical and emotional needs
- Well-behaved, godly children
- A good church that meets all of my family's needs
- Successful ministry

Surprised? If you're incredulous at this list, just remember that *nothing*—not even those things God wants you to have—should be more desirable to you than being obedient to and glorifying Christ.

Godly Desires—That I may:

- Know God's Word and obey it (James 1:22)
- Delight in Him (Psalm 37:4)
- Seek Him with all my heart (Deuteronomy 4:29)
- Be pleasing to Him regardless of my circumstances (2 Corinthians 12:10)
- Cultivate an attitude of joy and gratitude in what God is doing in my life no matter what my husband or children do or don't do (1 Thessalonians 5:18)
- Have joy in letting God decide how my life and circumstances can glorify Him the most (2 Thessalonians 1:11-12)

As you can see, this latter list requires a heart that is fully devoted to God. You can't live halfway for Christ; He wants all of you. Let your ambition be like Paul's, which was "*to be pleasing to Him*" (2 Corinthians 5:9). In fact, Paul felt so strongly about pleasing God that he described his entire purpose in life with the words "*to live is Christ*" (Philippians 1:21). That should be our desire and life purpose as well.

Memorize It!

Therefore if there is any encouragement in Christ, if there is any consolation of love, if there is any fellowship of the Spirit, if any affection and compassion, make my joy complete by being of the same mind, maintaining the same love, united in spirit, intent on one purpose. (Philippians 2:1-2)

If anyone comes to Me, and does not hate his own father and mother and wife and children and brothers and sisters, yes, and even his own life, he cannot be My disciple.
Luke 14:26

Application

Here's one big clue that you're not delighting in God as you should: If you look at your time with God as a "checklist" item, happy once it's done so you can move on to "bigger and better" things, then He is not your heart's desire. There are several ways to change your heart's desire to fall more in love with Him:

- Think about and deliberately delight in the Lord.
- Build contentment in your life. Frequently thank Him for your circumstances.
- Ask God to replace your idolatrous desires with righteous desires.
- Invest more time throughout your day reading, memorizing, and meditating on Scripture.
- Make pleasing the Lord, not personal happiness, your top priority.

Week 12, Day 4

But everyone must be quick to hear, slow to speak and slow to anger; for the anger of man does not achieve the righteousness of God.
James 1:19-20†

Application

Many wives use anger to manipulate their husbands, claiming, "If I didn't get angry, he'd never do anything I ask him to." But even if that were true, *"it is better to live in a desert land"*—or in a house in need of repair—*"than with a contentious and vexing woman"* (Proverbs 21:19).

You might think your anger is getting you what you want, but your husband may be giving in just for the sake of peace. You're actually subverting God's righteous plans for your marriage, which is to learn to humbly confront your man with gentleness. It would be better to be wronged by your husband's lack of concern than to grieve God with your sin. Seeing yourself as a "vexing woman" can sometimes help you calm down and seek a Christ-like response to frustration.

Impatience and Frustration

The first time Eva told Dwight that her car was leaking oil, she thought he would get right on it. Her dad was always very good at taking care of their cars, and she had no reason to believe her new husband wouldn't do the same. When a week went by and he did nothing about it, she reminded him again. "I'll take care of that this weekend," he promised. But he never got around to it, and the longer he continued to ignore the problem, the angrier she got. Three weeks later, she backed out of the garage and saw a huge oil slick on the garage floor. Eva was furious!

When Dwight got home from work that night, he found the house was a mess and Eva had not even started dinner. "What's going on?" he asked. "Well," Eva replied, "I figured since *you* don't have to take care of *your* responsibilities, then neither do I." Of course that just started an argument which lasted for the next two hours. Eva was upset and frustrated that Dwight didn't seem to care about her safety. She was also fearful that if she let him get away with being lazy, he would only get worse.

Anger is a powerful emotion that begins in the heart with what we think, usually as the result of frustration at not getting what we want. If we don't learn to handle our anger biblically, and the cause of the anger does not go away, then anger will continue to build until it gives birth to sinful actions such as yelling and screaming at our husbands or seeking revenge. Anger NEVER has a good result, and will always result in the death of peace and unity in your marriage.

Whenever you are tempted to get angry at your husband, take time to recognize the choice you must make. You can either please yourself by getting angry and trying to manipulate your husband into obeying you; or you can please God by responding to your husband *"with all humility and gentleness, with patience, showing tolerance for one another in love"* (Ephesians 4:2). Remember that *"the anger of man does not achieve the righteousness of God"* (James 1:20).

Memorize It!

Therefore if there is any encouragement in Christ, if there is any consolation of love, if there is any fellowship of the Spirit, if any affection and compassion, make my joy complete by being of the same mind, maintaining the same love, united in spirit, intent on one purpose. (Philippians 2:1-2)

Obedience Undeserved

Whatever you do, do your work heartily, as for the Lord rather than for men, knowing that from the Lord you will receive the reward of the inheritance. It is the Lord Christ whom you serve.
Colossians 3:23-24

Allen and Becky were having their church Life group over on Sunday evening, and had set aside all day Saturday for getting the yard whipped into shape. Bright and early, they stood facing a mound of mulch, lawn furniture to clean, grass to cut, and several other projects that needed to be done. "Well," Becky said, "there's nothing like a party to get us moving on this stuff!"

Allen frowned and rubbed his eyes. He had a sinus headache and her cheery attitude wasn't helping. Becky grabbed a shovel and started in on the mulch. "Don't worry about that," he said. "I need you to help me with the lawn." For the next two hours, she trimmed and edged while he cut the grass. Just as she finished, Allen sent her back to the flower beds. "You need to edge these also," he said. "I thought we were putting mulch there," she explained. "Just do it, ok?" he snapped. Becky looked at her husband, then picked up the edger. As she worked, she repeated Colossians 3:23, *"Heartily, as unto the Lord and not unto men."*

At times you may find it difficult to submit to your husband because of his sin, anger, or poor attitude. Remember, however, that you are not just obeying your husband, but the Lord. God's will for every Christian woman is that she love and submit to her husband. So when you submit to your husband, you're submitting to the will of God.

That's not always easy. If your hubby is crabby, unreasonable, or demanding, the natural response is to withhold obedience based on what he "deserves." Thankfully, God doesn't treat us that way! We don't deserve any of the blessings He gives, yet He loves and blesses us anyway. Therefore, you should not decide whether or not your husband is "worthy" before blessing him with your respect and obedience. Your submission is not based on what *he* deserves, but on what God deserves, which is our 100% faithfulness. Instead of obeying with an angry or bitter attitude, you can do it joyfully, knowing that God will recognize and reward your obedience, even if your husband never does.

Application

Sometimes, being submissive to your husband may require an extra measure of God's grace. At those times when you feel your husband doesn't deserve your obedience, it is often helpful to repeat Colossians 3:23 to yourself. Remind yourself that your submission to your husband is never based on his conduct, but on the truth of God's Word. Then intentionally look for something in your present circumstance for which you can be thankful, and express your gratitude for God for whatever it may be.

Week 13, Day 1

For I am confident of this very thing, that He who began a good work in you will perfect it until the day of Christ Jesus.
PHILIPPIANS 1:6

Application

No matter what is going on in your life, remember that God is working all things together for good (Romans 8:28). Your job is to do just as God challenged the children of Israel: *"I am going to send an angel before you...to bring you into the place which I have prepared... If you truly obey his voice and do all that I say, then I will be an enemy to your enemies"* (Exodus 23:20-22†).

Many believe this angel was Christ Himself. Whether he was or not, our responsibility is the same: to obey God's voice. When you're facing a real problem in your life, among other acts of obedience you can do, the most important is to *"trust in the LORD...in all your ways acknowledge Him: and He shall direct your paths"* (Proverbs 3:5-6, NKJV).

LITTLE BY LITTLE

When the children of Israel arrived at the land God had promised them, they discovered a BIG problem. The Promised Land was already occupied, and the people living there didn't seem too anxious to leave. These were not small people either, but *"men of great size"* (Numbers 13:32). You know the story: all of Israel *"lifted up their voices and cried, and the people wept that night"* (Numbers 14:1). It seemed all was lost.

The Israelites were despondent because they had forgotten God's promises to remove the inhabitants of the land for them. They looked at those giants and thought, "God wants us to do *what?*" Yet months earlier, God had told them He would take care of this problem for them: *"I will drive them out before you little by little, until you become fruitful and take possession of the land"* (Exodus 23:30).

Maybe you can relate to how the Israelites were feeling. Perhaps you're facing a very difficult trial in your marriage, and, so far, your prayers for help have gone unanswered. Like Joshua and Caleb tried to encourage the Israelites, other people are telling you that God will give you victory, but from where you stand right now, defeat seems both sure and imminent.

If this is how you're feeling, look again at Exodus 23:30. God promised to take care of this problem for His people, but He did not say it would happen overnight. Rather, victory would come "little by little."

Some trials are for the purpose of revealing sin. (Example: God allows your husband to lose his job to show you your sin of not trusting Him to provide.) Other trials are *because* of your sin. (Example: Your family suffers financially because you overspend your budget.) Whatever is going on in your life, it most likely did not come on suddenly and it's not going to resolve in an instant, either. Your problems will take time to resolve. But you can take comfort, knowing that God is faithful and He will either remove this trial or else use it to accomplish a greater purpose in your life.

Memorize It!

Do nothing from selfishness or empty conceit, but with humility of mind regard one another as more important than yourselves; do not merely look out for your own personal interests, but also for the interests of others.
(Philippians 2:3-4)

God's Part In Your Sanctification

In a previous lesson (see page 16), we talked about the concept of sanctification, and how God sanctified you *positionally* at the moment of your salvation, and will sanctify you *completely* when you go to be with Him in heaven. We said that in between those two works of sanctification is a process called "progressive sanctification," where, by God's grace, you work on identifying and eliminating sin from your life. The emphasis in that lesson was on *your* part: the progress you make on purifying your life and becoming more holy and sinless. Today we're going to focus on *God's* part in your progressive sanctification.

What part does God play, and what has He promised to perform in you? Let's look at Ephesians 1 for some answers to these questions:

- Through Christ, God blesses you *"with every spiritual blessing in the heavenly places"* (vs. 3);
- He chose you *"before the foundation of the world, that [you] would be holy and blameless before Him"* (vs. 4);
- In love, He *"predestined [you] to adoption as [a child] through Jesus Christ to Himself, according to the kind intention of His will"* (vs. 5);
- He freely gives you His grace (vs. 6);
- He redeemed you *"through His blood"* and forgave your sins, *"according to the riches of His grace which He lavished on [you]"* (vss. 7-8);
- *"In all wisdom and insight"* He revealed His divine will to you (vss. 8-9);
- He sealed you in Christ *"with the Holy Spirit of promise, who is given as a pledge of [your] inheritance"* (vss. 13-14);
- He gives you *"a spirit of wisdom and of revelation,"* enlightening your heart (vss. 17-18);
- He gives you knowledge of *"the riches of the glory of His inheritance... (and) the surpassing greatness of His power toward [you]"* (vss. 18-19);
- He gives you the full *"strength of His might"* (vs. 19).

You have all of this in Christ! Moreover, God has given you His own Holy Spirit to aid in your sanctification. Therefore, you should be diligent in your obedience—not to gain God's favor, but because you already *have* God's favor in Christ.

Memorize It!

Do nothing from selfishness or empty conceit, but with humility of mind regard one another as more important than yourselves; do not merely look out for your own personal interests, but also for the interests of others.
(Philippians 2:3-4)

Now may the God of peace Himself sanctify you entirely; and may your spirit and soul and body be preserved complete, without blame at the coming of our Lord Jesus Christ.
1 Thessalonians 5:23

Application

How does knowing God's part actually help you to become a more excellent wife?

- Focusing on God's part helps you to love God more. The more you love God, the more you will keep His commandments—not to gain the results you want, but because the Father you love expects it of you.
- Knowing you have all of God's strength and blessings at your disposal should give you more power to do the things He calls you to do.

God wants you to be diligent in working on your sanctification, yet realize that the results of your obedience are entirely up to Him. Your joy and reward should come from the pleasure you bring to God (Colossians 1:10), not the blessings He gives in return.

Week 13, Day 3

Then the LORD God said, "It is not good for the man to be alone; I will make him a helper suitable for him."
GENESIS 2:18

Application

It is easy to become consumed with your own plans. You have your own work to do, goals to meet and dreams to achieve. You might even be ambitious by nature. But it is important to remember that your purpose on earth is not to do what *you* want or to accomplish your own agenda. Your purpose is the same as Eve's: to glorify God by being a helper to your husband. Remember that Eve was created to be Adam's helper *before* the fall. It's not because of the curse of sin that you are called to serve your husband; this has always been God's perfect design for marriage.

How much of your day is spent on things that have nothing to do with helping your husband? Are *his* needs or your own agenda at the top of today's To Do list?

MADAM, I'M ADAM

Adam woke up and rubbed his eyes. The grass was soft and cool beneath him, and the air was warm and dry. The sun shone brightly in a deep blue sky, and birds were singing all around him. Another perfect day in paradise. But Adam felt something was different. He turned around and was startled to find a person, much like himself, sitting on the grass behind him. "Hello," he said tentatively.

"Hi!" The person flashed a beautiful smile at him, and Adam felt something burn inside him, a feeling he'd never felt before. Beside him, he heard God's warm laughter. "LORD, who is this?" he motioned toward the human.

"This, my son, is your wife Eve. I've made her for you." Adam looked at God in amazement. He was used to God doing the most wonderful things, but *this* was probably His crowning achievement. God interrupted Adam's thoughts: "I made everything on earth for you, but still, you are so very alone. You need someone to share your life with. So I created her to help you and to love you. You, in turn, will love her and provide for her."

Of course no one but God, Adam, and Eve were there when God performed this first wedding ceremony, so we don't know exactly how the whole "Hey, Adam, here's your wife!" conversation went down. But we do know that God created Eve for a specific purpose: to be Adam's helper, uniquely suited to Adam's needs and personality. (See Genesis 2:18-25). Eve was the perfect person to help Adam with whatever task God gave him to do.

God has similarly given your husband several things to do while here on earth. He must work, provide for your family, lead spiritually, immerse himself in ministry, and glorify God in all that he does. Even if your husband is not a believer, God has set up the family to function so that needs are met and goals are accomplished. Ultimately, His goal for the family is that each member be saved and conformed to the image of His Son. Your husband is called by God for that work, and as his wife, you are called to help him.

Memorize It!

Do nothing from selfishness or empty conceit, but with humility of mind regard one another as more important than yourselves; do not merely look out for your own personal interests, but also for the interests of others.
(Philippians 2:3-4)

Learning to Communicate

Let your speech always be with grace, as though seasoned with salt, so that you will know how you should respond to each person.
Colossians 4:6

Two weeks ago, Leah and Nigel had the fight of their lives. The gloves were off as they delivered blow after blow to each other's spirit, wounding with their words and trying their hardest to deliver that one victorious knock-out punch.

That was only two weeks ago, but so much has changed since then. That argument drove them to seek biblical counseling; they knew if they didn't, the marriage would not survive. After talking to a counselor, Leah realized how failing to control her tongue was making matters worse in her marriage. *"So also the tongue is a small part of the body, and yet it boasts of great things. See how great a forest is set aflame by such a small fire!"* (James 3:5). She is now working on learning to communicate biblically, rather than out of her own fear, hurt or frustration.

No skill will help a wife more in conflict with her husband than the ability to communicate based on biblical principles given in a God-honoring way. Even if you have a relatively healthy marriage, God desires that you train your tongue to respond properly in every situation. Getting control of your tongue is one of the first steps in biblically submitting to God and your husband.

This takes a lot of prayer and practice. What makes it difficult is that when everything is going well, we don't often remember to communicate biblically. But when we're scared, frustrated, or angry, it is more difficult to think straight about what we should say or do. We're too upset to bring those things to mind that need to be said in love and gentleness; the tools are just not there.

God-honoring responses are gentle, loving in tone, and they incorporate God's truth and principles. But you have to practice this when you are calm and there is relative peace in your home. It's like a soldier training for battle: he learns to carry the gun and use the tools of warfare while he is in friendly territory. If he doesn't develop the skills on base, he'll never be able to use them in the heat of the battle.

Application

A critical skill in biblical communication is learning to be *"quick to hear, slow to speak and slow to anger"* (James 1:19). Instead of "snapping" at your husband, think first about what you need to say and how you are going to say it. Then, respond with great care. That is God-honoring speech.

Failure to communicate biblically is sin, and your sin will always make your situation worse. But you can honor God with your obedience by allowing God to make your tongue an instrument of His grace (Ephesians 4:29), rather than *"a restless evil and full of deadly poison"* (James 3:8).

Memorize It!

Do nothing from selfishness or empty conceit, but with humility of mind regard one another as more important than yourselves; do not merely look out for your own personal interests, but also for the interests of others.
(Philippians 2:3-4)

Week 13, Day 5

Have this attitude in yourselves which was also in Christ Jesus, who, although He existed in the form of God, did not regard equality with God a thing to be grasped, but emptied Himself, taking the form of a bond-servant, and being made in the likeness of men. Being found in appearance as a man, He humbled Himself by becoming obedient to the point of death, even death on a cross.
PHILIPPIANS 2:5-8

Application

Even if your marriage is not as bad as Liz and Wayne's, it is likely that pride plays a role in any strife between you and your husband. God's goal is for you to be humble, as Christ was humble. Even though He was equal with God, He voluntarily submitted Himself to the wrath of sinful men. Even though He was 100% right and they were 100% wrong, He did not retaliate when they spit on Him, beat Him and crucified Him.

Yet in our pride, we think we have a right to "stand up" for ourselves, to disallow any mistreatment we think we don't deserve. Meditate on 1 Peter 2:19-25 today, and ask God how you can better follow Christ's example of humility in your marriage.

JESUS, THE EXAMPLE OF HUMILITY

Liz married an angry man, and for years she and Wayne argued about pretty much everything. Their kids were used to it, but Liz could see the effect anger was having on their kids—which only increased *her* anger. She was convinced it was her husband's fault the kids were rebelling against their parents' authority.

Liz and Wayne were both Christians, but consumed with their own selfish concerns. Then one Sunday the pastor preached about the humility of Christ, and Liz came face-to-face with her own pride. She learned how Christ humbled Himself to men and to God in order to do God's will. She thought about how important it was to her to get her way whenever she and Wayne were arguing; she'd never realized how her own lack of humility was a major factor in the chaos in their home.

After that sermon, it took less than a day for Wayne to find something to argue with Liz about. But this time, Liz turned to the Word and began reciting what she could remember of 1 Peter 2:21-24:

> *For you have been called for this purpose, since Christ also suffered for you, leaving you an example for you to follow in His steps, who committed no sin, nor was any deceit found in His mouth; and while being reviled, He did not revile in return; while suffering, He uttered no threats, but kept entrusting Himself to Him who judges righteously; and He Himself bore our sins in His body on the cross, so that we might die to sin and live to righteousness; for by His wounds you were healed.*

It took many months of Liz memorizing and practicing these verses for Wayne to see how much his wife had changed. Whenever he "reviled" (spoke angry words to) her, she would not return his anger, but would trust God to judge who was right in each situation. She prayed for God to humble her and make her willing to suffer without threatening in return. At first, her calm made Wayne angrier, as he realized he was the only one who was yelling. But after a while, her "soft words" turned away his wrath (Proverbs 15:1).

Joyful Obedience? Or Mere Compliance?

Anne looked through the phone book at the endless pages of attorney ads. Brody had asked her to find an attorney to help him incorporate his new home-based business, but there were so many, she hardly knew where to begin. Besides, she was not very happy about his decision to quit his job and go out on his own. "This is ridiculous!" she fumed. Finally, she made a few phone calls and got a couple of estimates. She scribbled the figures on a piece of paper and dropped it on his desk. "Is that the best we can do?" he asked. Anne rolled her eyes. "Yes. What did I tell you? It's expensive!"

Many times we think we're submitting to our husbands when all we're doing is going through the motions. We comply out of obligation, but our hearts aren't committed to what they're trying to accomplish. We're like the little boy whose mom put him into "time out." After a lot of fuss, the boy stomped over to his chair and sat down. But as he did, he said, "I may be sitting on the outside, but I'm standing on the inside!"

If you are obeying on the "outside" but still resisting on the inside, you're not submitting, you're *complying*. *Compliance* is doing what you're told to do with no real commitment to the task. You're like the hypocrites of Matthew 15:8—*"These people honor me with their lips, but their hearts are far from me."* Compliance is reflected in a poor attitude, which can grow into bitterness and resentment.

Obedience submits both inside and out, with a joyful attitude. When you immediately and cheerfully *obey* your husband, you are working to accomplish *his* goals, not your own. Even if you don't agree with what he's asked, you can still obey with the right attitude, knowing that your obedience pleases the Lord. You are keeping God's command to *"Do nothing from selfishness...but with humility of mind regard one another as more important than yourselves; do not merely look out for your own personal interests, but also for the interests of others"* (Philippians 2:3-4).

Memorize It!

Have this attitude in yourselves which was also in Christ Jesus, who, although He existed in the form of God, did not regard equality with God a thing to be grasped, but emptied Himself, taking the form of a bond-servant, and being made in the likeness of men. (Philippians 2:5-7)

Whatever you do in word or deed, do all in the name of the Lord Jesus, giving thanks through Him to God the Father.
Colossians 3:17

Application

God doesn't want you to do anything out of duty or obligation, but out of desire. He wants you to voluntarily submit yourself to your husband's authority out of love. The next time your husband asks you to do something you aren't wholly in favor of, do a quick check on your attitude by asking the following questions:

- If I don't agree with what he's asked me to do, can I at least accept his decision without bitterness?
- Do I have a joyful attitude in my obedience, or am I angry or pouting that I have to submit?
- Am I humbly regarding my husband's desires as more important than my own?
- Have I thanked God for my husband and for this opportunity to serve him?

Week 14, Day 2

Therefore if there is any encouragement in Christ, if there is any consolation of love, if there is any fellowship of the Spirit, if any affection and compassion, make my joy complete by being of the same mind, maintaining the same love, united in spirit, intent on one purpose. Do nothing from selfishness or empty conceit, but with humility of mind regard one another as more important than yourselves.
PHILIPPIANS 2:1-3

Application

If you've shown disrespect to your husband by questioning his decisions, there is only one thing you can do: acknowledge your fault and humbly ask him for forgiveness. You can say something like, "I'm sorry I disrespected you by doubting your judgment. That was wrong; I know I can trust you." With God's help, you can purpose to do better in the future, but actually confessing your faults to your husband will help keep you accountable.

It may also be helpful to remember that your ideas and opinions are not made of gold either. Keeping in mind your own capacity for failure, as well as the sheer number of decisions your husband has to make every day, will help you gain a new appreciation for your husband, making it easier to give him the respect he deserves.

Questioning His Decisions

Eric plopped down on the couch and let out an exasperated sigh. "What's wrong?" Melanie asked. "Oh, it's Jim at work. The man continually questions everything I do. '*Why are we using that program? Why don't we move the ship dates? What did you do that for?*' The guy is driving me crazy!" Melanie's jaw dropped open. "Hold it," she said. "Aren't you his boss? Where does he get off questioning you? That is unbelievable! If I were you, I'd fire him!"

Eric smiled and took Melanie's hands in his. "Forgive me, sweetie," he said, "but I just made all that stuff up. Jim is fine. But I wish I could say the same about you." At first Melanie was hurt, but as they talked, she realized that she had gotten into a very bad habit of questioning her husband's judgment about virtually everything. The next day during her quiet time with God, she prayed about it, and realized that she had unknowingly tried to put herself into the driver's seat in their marriage. It was true that Eric had made some bad decisions, and he wasn't exactly an expert in all things. But overall, he had proven himself to be trustworthy. She knew that the real reason she questioned his judgment was simply her own desire to be in control.

Melanie had fallen into the trap set up for Eve by Satan, when God declared *"Your desire* (to control) *will be for your husband"* (Genesis 3:16†). Our lust for control often makes us question our husband's judgment, knowledge, opinions and decisions. When you question him, what you're really saying is, "I don't respect you enough to trust your decision-making abilities." This will make your husband not only feel you don't respect him, but that you think he's stupid.

If you truly don't understand why he's made a particular decision, it's not wrong to ask for clarification. But you should question your own motives first: Do you have a different idea of how the situation should be handled? Is asking for more information simply a way to introduce *your* opinions into your husband's decisions?

Memorize It!

Have this attitude in yourselves which was also in Christ Jesus, who, although He existed in the form of God, did not regard equality with God a thing to be grasped, but emptied Himself, taking the form of a bond-servant, and being made in the likeness of men.
(Philippians 2:5-7)

Excuses, Excuses!

If your brother sins, go and show him his fault in private; if he listens to you, you have won your brother.
Matthew 18:15

We wives can come up with a lot of creative reasons for *not* confronting our husbands when they sin, and many of our excuses come straight from the Bible—taken out of context, of course. Which one(s) have you used?

- "If I loved him unconditionally, I wouldn't expect him to change."
- "Who am I to point out his sin? I have too many logs in my own eyes!"
- "The Bible says to 'judge not, that you be not judged.' I have no right to judge my husband's sin."
- "I don't know the Bible well enough to tell my husband how to live by it."
- "The Bible says 'you who are spiritual…' I don't think I'm spiritual enough to reprove my husband."
- "I'm afraid I won't do it properly, which will just make matters worse."

What's really interesting is that most of us have *no problem* pointing out when our husbands do something that offends us. All he has to do is track mud in the house, and we'll complain or demand corrective action. Yet we often neglect to point out when our husbands have offended *God*. And that's the real reason we don't biblically reprove our husbands: we're only offended if what he's doing hurts us. As long as it doesn't hurt us, we're willing to overlook it.

Throughout the Bible, we are commanded to *"bear one another's burdens,"* (Galatians 6:2) and one of the ways we do that is to lovingly confront each other when we sin. Your husband's sin is a burden to him and an offense to God. It works against unity in your marriage and cripples his ability to lead spiritually. If you refrain from *"speaking the truth in love"* (Ephesians 4:15), you are depriving your husband of one of God's greatest provisions for his own spiritual growth: words of encouragement and exhortation from his own wife.

True biblical love *"rejoices with the truth"* (1 Corinthians 13:6). This is not only an act of love, but if done properly and he humbly receives it, it will strengthen his love for you (Proverbs 9:8).

Memorize It!

Have this attitude in yourselves which was also in Christ Jesus, who, although He existed in the form of God, did not regard equality with God a thing to be grasped, but emptied Himself, taking the form of a bond-servant, and being made in the likeness of men.
(Philippians 2:5-7)

Application

Perhaps you have tried to reprove your husband, but your effort failed in some way (e.g., you weren't able to communicate biblically, he refused to listen, he repented for awhile but keeps going back to the same sin, etc.). Whatever the reason, don't give up! Giving a proper biblical reproof is a skill you will get better at with practice.

Think about something your husband did that was clearly a sin. Now, write out a proper biblical reproof, including a Scriptural principle as to how he should have behaved. Next, pray to see if God would have you communicate this particular reproof to him. If not, at least you have gained some practice in how to put together a proper reproof, so the next time one is required, you'll be better prepared.

Week 14, Day 4

Brethren, even if anyone is caught in any trespass, you who are spiritual, restore such a one in a spirit of gentleness; each one looking to yourself, so that you too will not be tempted. For if anyone thinks he is something when he is nothing, he deceives himself.
GALATIANS 6:1, 3

Application

Even if your husband is a good spiritual leader, you can still have differences of opinion as to the best way to guide your children. The sad truth is that few couples are on the same page early enough in their marriage to be able to raise their children in total unity.

Even if you don't have children, you may have unsaved friends or family who you fear will get the wrong idea of Christ when they see your husband's lack of spiritual maturity. What you cannot and must not do is constantly correct or apologize for your husband in front of your children or others. God has given you the responsibility of biblically reproving your husband, but that reproof must almost always be done in private. In front of others, your love and respect must be indisputable.

A House Divided

Brenda has a problem. Both she and her husband are professing Christians, but while she is trying to be a "good" Christian, Darryl doesn't have much of a spiritual life and rarely reacts to things in a Christ-like manner. Brenda fears that his lack of respect for God's Word seriously hampers their ability to bring their children up *"in the discipline and instruction of the LORD"*(Ephesians 6:4).

Coupled with her fears for her children is her spiritual pride. As her fear and pride grow, so does her frustration toward her husband, leading her to be angry and disrespectful. But she doesn't notice her children picking up *those* character qualities. She only notices when they say a cuss word, and thinks their short tempers are her husband's fault, not her own.

One night their son Jeff was talking about a kid at school who was starting to bully him. "If he does it again," Darryl said, "Just pop him."

"Darryl!" Brenda chided, "What is wrong with you? Not only would he get in trouble, but that is NOT what Jesus would do!"

Not all husbands are great spiritual leaders, and it's particularly distressing if you have children who are suffering as a result. But your children are just as affected by *your* sin as they are by their father's. Brenda could have very sweetly said something like, "Well, that's certainly one alternative. However, why don't we see if the Bible can tell us what would be the best thing to do, that would also keep you out of the principal's office?" In this way, she can lead her son as well as gently admonish her husband, without showing him disrespect.

If your trust is in God, your children will be protected in many ways (1 Corinthians 7:14). As they see you always responding in love and obedience to Christ, they will see a contrast between the joyful life Christ offers versus the life of an unbeliever or a "believer" in name only. The *last* thing you want to communicate to your children is that true followers of Christ are mean and judgmental.

Memorize It!

Have this attitude in yourselves which was also in Christ Jesus, who, although He existed in the form of God, did not regard equality with God a thing to be grasped, but emptied Himself, taking the form of a bond-servant, and being made in the likeness of men.
(Philippians 2:5-7)

Love is not Rude

So, as those who have been chosen of God, holy and beloved, put on a heart of compassion, kindness, humility, gentleness and patience; bearing with one another, and forgiving each other, whoever has a complaint against anyone; just as the Lord forgave you, so also should you. Beyond all these things put on love, which is the perfect bond of unity. Let the peace of Christ rule in your hearts, to which indeed you were called in one body; and be thankful.
Colossians 3:12-15

John and Melissa each come from large families and have always made an effort to spend time with both sides, especially during the holidays. Christmas Eve is usually spent on her parent's farm with all of the siblings and their families, while Christmas Day finds them at his sister's house, with an equal number of family surrounding them and adding to the happy chaos.

While Melissa loves her in-laws, she does not have a great relationship with John's three brothers, whom she finds crass and immature. To make matters worse, she fears that when John is with his brothers, he turns into one of them. One Christmas Eve, the guys went outside wearing just their undershirts and basketball shorts and started shooting hoops in the snow. Melissa was livid. "John, you idiot!" she yelled at him. "Get back in here before you catch pneumonia!"

Melissa had fallen into the habit many of us fall into: speaking or behaving rudely to our husbands. 1 Corinthians 13:5 says that love *"does not act unbecomingly."* Or, as the NIV translates it, love *"is not rude."* A wife acts unbecomingly when she is rude or disrespectful to her husband.

Different circumstances might tempt us to be rude. Sometimes our husbands do things that embarrass or make no sense to us; or perhaps we're just feeling moody or hormonal. At those times it is easy to treat our husbands rudely, in a way that is not "becoming" to an excellent wife. Perhaps this has become such a pattern in your marriage that your husband is used to it, so you're not aware you're causing him shame and embarrassment. However, that does not mean he does not feel the shame deeply—particularly if you act this way in front of his friends or family.

Application

Ask your husband if there has ever been a time when you've embarrassed him by your words or behavior. If so, ask his forgiveness, then pray with him that God will help you to always show love to him by treating him with honor and respect. When the two of you are in a public place or in a social gathering, keep in mind how your words, facial expressions, and actions reflect on him. Purpose in your heart to do everything you can to lift your husband up in the eyes of others.

Week 15, Day 1

Whatever you do, do your work heartily, as for the LORD rather than for men, knowing that from the LORD you will receive the reward of the inheritance. It is the LORD Christ whom you serve.
COLOSSIANS 3:23-24

Application

If you think of your work at home as your ministry, you may find it easier to be consistent in your work and find more pleasure in accomplishing the same tasks day after day, week after week, year after year. *"Therefore, my beloved brethren, be steadfast, immovable, always abounding in the work of the LORD, knowing that your toil is not in vain in the LORD"* (1 Corinthians 15:58). Your work at home is not in vain, so even if your family barely notices how much work you put into the home, God sees. Always keep in mind that you're working for Him more than for anyone else, and He will reward your faithfulness.

UNTO THE LORD, NOT UNTO MEN

As president of the local chamber of commerce, Carolyn's husband, Stan, had invited the governor and his wife over for dinner the next evening—giving Carolyn less than 24 hours to get ready. She immediately went to work cleaning the house and poring through her recipes, looking for the perfect meal to serve her honored guests. She was amazed at how much energy she had, and how work that was usually a burden seemed much lighter.

That evening, she opened her Bible and read, *"Do your work heartily, as for the LORD"* (Colossians 3:23). She thought about how happily energetic she'd been all day, and was rebuked at how she didn't usually have that attitude, even though her family deserved as much and more. And certainly, Christ deserved her best. "LORD," she prayed, "thank you for this lesson today. Help me to always work with the same joy and energy I had today, knowing that every day I work for you, not for men."

It's difficult, day in and day out, to have the same kind of energy for maintaining the home that we have when company is coming over. I understand that, and am certainly not saying you need to make your house perfect every single day. However, we too often forget Who it is we're actually working for. If Christ were coming to your house, most likely you would spend less time on the phone, in front of the television, on the computer, or in bed, and put more energy into your work.

The truth is, Christ is not "coming" to your house—He is already there! If you know Christ as your Savior, He lives inside you and is everywhere you are. *"I have been crucified with Christ; and it is no longer I who live, but Christ lives in me"* (Galatians 2:20). Every day He sees you work, He sees how you manage your time, and He understands you need to rest after your work is done. If you keep that truth in mind as you work, and ask for His help in doing all things well, then He will give you the strength and energy you need to complete your work well and to do it with a good attitude.

Memorize It!

Being found in appearance as a man, He humbled Himself by becoming obedient to the point of death, even death on a cross. For this reason also, God highly exalted Him, and bestowed on Him the name which is above every name.
(Philippians 2:8-9)

Health Nuts

For this reason I say to you, do not be worried about your life, as to what you will eat or what you will drink; nor for your body, as to what you will put on. Is not life more than food, and the body more than clothing?
Matthew 6:25

A couple of years before my first child was born, my mother was diagnosed with cancer. She went through several months of chemotherapy and radiation, beating the disease into remission. For a time she enjoyed good health, but unfortunately, the cancer came back with a vengeance, and mom went to be with the Lord a week after my daughter's second birthday.

I've always been healthy, but following my mom's death I became obsessed with diet and exercise. I read extensively about foods that contribute to cancer, determined not to fall victim to the same illness. The more I researched, the more anxious I became about my health. Before too long, there was little I could eat with thanksgiving: it seemed everything caused cancer! I was rabid about exercise too, hoping I could keep myself strong and sweat out any carcinogens that may have made their way into my system.

My obsession with diet and exercise was clearly an idol in my heart that led to anxiety lasting several years. Eventually, God used His Word, a loving husband, and some godly people to bring me out of that bondage and back to Him. But how much better would it have been if I had not wasted all those years being consumed with things that "profit little" (1 Timothy 4:8) but had put my trust in God instead? *"And who of you by being worried can add a single hour to his life?"* (Matthew 6:27).

American women are obsessed with health, beauty, and body image, as evidenced by the billions of dollars we spend every year on beauty products, cosmetic surgery, hair coloring, and gym memberships. And yet, even after all that time and money, we rarely look as good or are as healthy and pain-free as we'd like. Like all idols, it is never satisfied.

"For what will it profit a man if he gains the whole world"—a great body and perfect health—*"and forfeits his soul?"* (Matthew 16:26). God wants you to love Him with all you have (Mark 12:30). There's no room in that command for you to funnel off some of your energy toward self obsession.

Memorize It!

Being found in appearance as a man, He humbled Himself by becoming obedient to the point of death, even death on a cross. For this reason also, God highly exalted Him, and bestowed on Him the name which is above every name.
(Philippians 2:8-9)

Application

Estimate how many hours per week you spend in personal beautification, exercise, or physical activity. Write the number of hours here: ______ Now think about how much time you spend reading God's Word and focusing completely on Him. Write that number here: ______

If you're spending more time focused on your body than you are worshipping Christ, then you have an idol problem. Your love for God should crowd out all other idols and concerns. If you're anxious about your life, your health, or your appearance, you are not trusting and glorifying God. It's time today to repent of this obsession that we're all prone to, and ask God to give you an obsession for Him and His beauty (Proverbs 31:30).

Week 15, Day 3

She opens her mouth in wisdom,
and the teaching of kindness
is on her tongue.
Proverbs 31:26

Application

God's desires for your speech are spelled out in Ephesians 4:29-32. Read this carefully, examining each phrase to see how they all work together to promote grace-filled speech in us:

Let no unwholesome word proceed from your mouth | but only such a word as is good for edification | according to the need of the moment | so that it will give grace to those who hear. | Do not grieve the Holy Spirit of God, | by whom you were sealed for the day of redemption. | Let all bitterness | and wrath and anger | and clamor and slander | be put away from you, | along with all malice. | Be kind to one another, | tender-hearted, | forgiving each other, | just as God in Christ also has forgiven you.

Careless Words

When we were first married, I was young and rather naïve, and sometimes I would say things that meant nothing to me, but were very hurtful to my husband. For example, I had a habit of saying "You're crazy!" whenever I disagreed with what someone was saying. My husband would get very irritated whenever I said it, and even called me out on it several times. My response? "You're crazy!" *It's just an expression,* I thought. *What's the big deal?*

Evidently, there were some borderline "crazy" people in my husband's family, so to him, saying that he was "crazy" was a big deal. As soon as I fully grasped how much this hurt him, I stopped saying it.

We sometimes think that words are just words; they come and go and who remembers them? If that's your attitude, that wrong speech does not need to be repented of, then think again. Jesus obviously has a very different perspective on the words we say: *"But I tell you that every careless word that people speak, they shall give an accounting for it in the day of judgment"* (Matthew 12:36). This is a sobering thought when we consider how many "careless" words we probably speak every day.

Why are your words so important to Jesus? Because *"God sees not as man sees, for man looks at the outward appearance, but the Lord looks at the heart"* (1 Samuel 16:7). You just see a bunch of words, but God sees where those words came from (your heart attitudes), and He sees the impact they have on your husband's spirit. He knows the words you say can wound deeply, even when you don't intend for them to. And they don't just wound your husband; they "defile" *you*, the speaker (Matthew 15:18), and they grieve the Holy Spirit (Ephesians 4:30).

All of your sins are paid for at the cross. But you are still accountable to God for the things you say. As a Christian you are to be careful with your words. As a wife you must be especially careful if you are going to demonstrate love, respect, and submission to your husband. God desires for you to be holy at all times and in every way, even in the way you talk. His desire is that you *"let your speech always be with grace"* (Colossians 4:6).

Memorize It!

Being found in appearance as a man, He humbled Himself by becoming obedient to the point of death, even death on a cross. For this reason also, God highly exalted Him, and bestowed on Him the name which is above every name.
(Philippians 2:8-9)

Pride & Humility: An Inverse Relationship

But He gives a greater grace. Therefore it says, "God is opposed to the proud, but gives grace to the humble."
James 4:6

Throughout this book, we talk frequently about *dying* to yourself, *submitting* to your husband, *yielding* to the will of God, and *suffering* for the sake of righteousness (2 Corinthians 5:15, Colossians 3:18, James 4:7, and 1 Peter 3:17, respectively). Look at the verbs in those phrases, and ask yourself: what is the key character trait required to be able to do any of these things? If you're going to die, submit, yield and suffer, you must be *humble*.

The opposite of humility is *pride*, which is the natural, lack-of-character quality we're born with in our sin nature. Today we're going to focus on some of the many Scripture passages which show the inverse relationship between pride and humility; how pride and humility cannot coexist in the heart of the believer. Stop right now and ask God to pierce your *"soul and spirit"* and *"judge the thoughts and intentions of the heart"* (Hebrews 4:12). Then read each of these verses carefully and allow the Holy Spirit to use His Word to mold your heart to be more like the Lord Jesus.

Proverbs 29:23
A man's pride will bring him low, but a humble spirit will obtain honor.

James 4:10
Humble yourselves in the presence of the Lord, and He will exalt you.

Matthew 18:4
Whoever then humbles himself as this child, he is the greatest in the kingdom of heaven.

Matthew 23:12
Whoever exalts himself shall be humbled; and whoever humbles himself shall be exalted.

Proverbs 15:33
The fear of the Lord is the instruction for wisdom, and before honor comes humility.

Proverbs 18:12
Before destruction the heart of man is haughty, but humility goes before honor.

Proverbs 16:19
It is better to be humble in spirit with the lowly, than to divide the spoil with the proud.

Psalm 138:6
For though the Lord is exalted, yet He regards the lowly; but the haughty He knows from afar.

Application

If any of those verses jumped out at you, the Holy Spirit may be leading you to focus on those truths in particular. Memorize that passage today, and in your prayer journal, ask yourself the following questions about this verse:

- How is *pride* described or referred to in this passage?
- How is *humility* described or referred to in this passage?
- Can I think of a recent incident where remembering this passage would have helped me to respond humbly, as Christ would have responded?
- Can I think of a possible future incident where following this passage will help me respond humbly, as Christ would respond?

Memorize It!

Being found in appearance as a man, He humbled Himself by becoming obedient to the point of death, even death on a cross. For this reason also, God highly exalted Him, and bestowed on Him the name which is above every name.
(Philippians 2:8-9)

Week 15, Day 5

But as the church is subject to Christ, so also the wives ought to be to their husbands in everything.
EPHESIANS 5:24

Application

The next time your husband stubbornly drives in the wrong direction or spends hours trying to build a bookcase, ask yourself what is more important: accomplishing the task in your timeframe, or making your man feel trusted and respected? If you must question what he's doing or see that he genuinely needs your help, ask God to remove any traces of disrespect from your mind and your voice before asking questions or offering assistance. Make sure you are sincerely trying to help, and not just trying to have things done your way.

THE BACK-SEAT CARPENTER

It is generally agreed that I have a greater mechanical aptitude than my husband. Scott is a genius at all things electrical, but when it comes to putting stuff together or light carpentry duties, I usually rely on him for muscle, but I can quickly figure out the *how* and the *where* on my own.

Our various strengths work well as long as he is helping me with my projects. But if I'm trying to help him, look out! We will almost always clash, as my way of doing things differs wildly from his. As I watch him struggle, I want to jump in and take over. But I have learned over the years that this desire to "rescue" him is really just another form of disrespect. When I give my unsolicited guidance and suggestions, what I'm really saying is, "You're incapable of doing this correctly. Let me show you how it's done."

If I actually said something like that out loud to my husband, my disrespect would be so obvious I would deserve to get the stare-down of my life. Certainly God would not be pleased with me. Scott may not be mechanically inclined, but he is quite capable of figuring it out. Men thrive on their ability to learn and to conquer new challenges. What they want from us is to cheer them on and praise their efforts. Our encouragement gives them the strength they need to keep going, even when the task is difficult. Our job is to "*encourage one another and build up one another*"(1 Thessalonians 5:11†).

If your husband is tackling something that is a challenge to his normal skill set, you can show him a great amount of respect by letting him work it out on his own. Offering helpful "suggestions" and advice only demonstrates that you have little confidence in his abilities. If you don't respect him in small things like putting together a bike or finding his way without asking for directions, he finds it difficult to believe that you can trust him in the big things, like providing for your family or being a good father.

Love Does Not Seek Its Own Way

Week 16, Day 1

Every man's way is right in his own eyes, but the LORD weighs the hearts.
PROVERBS 21:2

One of the chief faults of man is his continual attempt to seek his own way. *"All we like sheep have gone astray; we have turned every one to his own way"* (Isaiah 53:6a). As a young child, my firstborn was a classic example of this "own way" kind of mentality. Amy was not difficult or openly rebellious; she just had a knack for taking every directive we gave her and putting her own spin on it. I often had to say to her, "This is what I want you to do, and the way I want you to do it!" Many of her methods were just attempts to do it quicker, but the bottom line was that she was always seeking to serve herself and not her parents.

Wives have a very strong tendency to act this way, and we need to just call it for what it is: Selfishness. Selfishness is a love killer in marriage. Love tries to do what is best for the other person. But selfishness asks, "How will this benefit me? How will this make me happy?" When we do whatever we want, trying to meet our own needs rather than our husband's, we are acting selfishly.

We often hide our selfishness with other acts of kindness; for instance, a wife who has spent the entire day goofing off, surfing the internet and yakking on the phone may suddenly kick it into high gear an hour before her husband gets home. She frantically tidies the house and makes dinner...but she has wasted hours on selfish pleasure. As a result, she is guilty, tired, and has missed hours of opportunity to serve her husband and Christ.

If you zealously guard your "me" time, always cater to yourself, and try to work some personal benefit into everything your husband asks you to do—you are not loving him biblically. *"Love does not seek its own [way]"* (1 Corinthians 13:5†). Seeking your own way is a sin you need to confess and turn from by seizing every opportunity you can to show love to your husband, without regard for yourself.

Memorize It!

So that at the name of Jesus every knee will bow, of those who are in heaven and on earth and under the earth, and that every tongue will confess that Jesus Christ is LORD, to the glory of God the Father. (Philippians 2:10-11)

Application

To determine if you're habitually seeking your own way in your marriage, ask yourself the following questions, using A – Almost Always; O – Often; S – Sometimes; R – Rarely; or N – Never. Then use this as a guide to help you remember not to seek your own way:

____ Do I obey my husband with a cheerful heart, even if it brings no immediate benefit to me personally?

____ Do I submit to him in everything, even when he's not there to see it?

____ Do I seek to accomplish his goals, rather than stubbornly working my own will into every situation or decision?

____ Do I put his needs above mine?

____ Do I use my time wisely, serving my husband and Christ before myself?

____ Do I do what he asks me to do, the way he asks me to do it?

Week 16, Day 2

Therefore, putting aside all filthiness and all that remains of wickedness, in humility receive the word implanted, which is able to save your souls. But prove yourselves doers of the word, and not merely hearers who delude themselves.
JAMES 1:21-22

Application

Throughout the New Testament, God gives many instructions that, if we follow them, contribute to our progressive sanctification. Following is a list of just a few of these commands. Look up each reference, and then write in your prayer journal the command you are to obey. The first one is done for you:

1 Corinthians 14:1 *Pursue love, desire spiritual gifts*
1 Corinthians 6:18
Luke 9:23
Romans 12:1
Ephesians 5:1
1 Peter 1:15
Colossians 3:2
Colossians 3:12

For a more extensive study, go through Ephesians 4-5 and 1 Peter 1-3 and write out all of the positive commands listed in these chapters (e.g., "lay aside the old self," "speak truth," "be kind"). Try to fit them on a half sheet of paper, then keep them as a reference in your Bible.

YOUR PART IN GOD'S PLAN

Rex walked through the living room on his way out to the garage, and found his wife Ginger watching television. He looked at his watch, and at the pile of laundry sitting on the dining room table. "Ginger," he said, "Is this the best use of your time right now?" Ginger rolled her eyes, then brought the laundry basket over to the couch so she could fold and watch at the same time.

A few hours later Rex brought up the midday TV viewing. "We've talked about being more disciplined in our work," he said. "I know," Ginger said, "and I've really been praying about it. It just seems that if God were answering that prayer, He would make it easier for me to do what I'm supposed to do!"

God is doing His part in Ginger's sanctification: He is using her husband to point out her sin, convicting her about what she should be doing, and giving her every opportunity to obey. But Ginger is not willing to work or to obey the Holy Spirit's leading in her life. Truth be told, she is lazy and only does what is easy or convenient for her.

Your progressive sanctification is a work of God as He convicts you of sin, enables you to obey, and disciplines you for your disobedience. But you also have a great amount of responsibility for your own growth. 2 Peter 3:18 says you are to *"grow in the grace and knowledge of our LORD and Savior Jesus Christ."* That word "grow" is an imperative verb; in other words, it's a command for you to follow. And that's just one command. The Bible is filled with commands that you are to learn and then obey.

As you consistently obey God's commands, you will gradually start to see real, measureable progress in your life and your marriage. Old sinful habits such as anger, deceitfulness, laziness, and immorality will disappear, replaced by love, truth, perseverance, and faithfulness. But these things take time, and you must work at them. You must *"discipline yourself for the purpose of godliness"* (1 Timothy 4:7).

Memorize It!

So that at the name of Jesus every knee will bow, of those who are in heaven and on earth and under the earth, and that every tongue will confess that Jesus Christ is LORD, to the glory of God the Father.
(Philippians 2:10-11)

A Sacrificial Spirit

I have never had a pedicure. I hear it's relaxing, although I can't imagine that, because I'm extremely ticklish and would probably fly wildly out of the chair the first time the pedicurist touched my foot. However, that's not the main reason I've never had a pedicure. The main reason is that I cannot imagine a more demeaning task than washing someone else's feet. And even though it's her job, I can't imagine hiring someone to do that for me.

Yet that's pretty much what Christ did just before He went to the cross. After the LORD's Supper, Jesus knelt before each of His disciples and washed their feet. He then taught them the meaning of what he'd done: *"If I then, the LORD and the Teacher, washed your feet, you also ought to wash one another's feet. For I gave you an example that you also should do as I did to you"* (John 13:14-15).

It would be humbling to have to wash your husband's feet, just as it is humbling to have to sacrifice your will to your husband's will. Yet that is the most loving thing you can do. It shows your love not only for your husband, but also for Christ.

It doesn't take much for us to feel the pain of sacrifice, particularly if our husbands are involved. When your husband asks you to do something that feels like a sacrifice, it is important to humble yourself and think of what Christ sacrificed for you. He didn't just give up a weekend, or that trip He'd always wanted to take, or a little cash that He'd been saving for something special. He gave up His position in heaven, His form as God, and equality with the Father, in order to become a helpless human baby. He humbly sacrificed His entire earthly life, not fulfilling any personal pleasure, but living His entire 33 years on earth for you. Doing things like washing people's feet. Then, He went to the cross and gave up life itself.

Memorize It!

So that at the name of Jesus every knee will bow, of those who are in heaven and on earth and under the earth, and that every tongue will confess that Jesus Christ is LORD, to the glory of God the Father. (Philippians 2:10-11)

Have this attitude in yourselves which was also in Christ Jesus, who, although He existed in the form of God, did not regard equality with God a thing to be grasped, but emptied Himself, taking the form of a bond-servant, and being made in the likeness of men. Being found in appearance as a man, He humbled Himself by becoming obedient to the point of death, even death on a cross.
PHILIPPIANS 2:5-8

Application

Is there something you've been clinging to—some sacrifice that God (through your husband) has been asking you to make? If so, write it here:

Now compare your "sacrifice" to what Jesus sacrificed. I don't care what you wrote in that space, there is nothing in the world that can compare to what Christ gave up for you. He gave up *equality with God* in order to humbly serve you. Take a moment to pray right now that God would help you to be willing to make that sacrifice, and any sacrifice He requires, in order for you to follow the example of Christ Jesus, the servant.

Week 16, Day 4

Do not answer a fool according to his folly, or you will also be like him.
PROVERBS 26:4

Application

Even the best husbands can sometimes abuse their God-given authority by being unkind, insensitive, thoughtless, manipulative, or overly critical of their wives. So how do you protect yourself from your husband's foolishness, yet remain submissive?

First, you should carefully consider what he is saying, even if he is saying it sinfully. If you were wrong in any way, acknowledge your responsibility before you point out his failures. In demonstrating such humility, you set a good example for him to follow when you later point out his responsibility to act in a biblical manner.

Tomorrow we'll talk about how to use God's Word to respond to your husband with grace, no matter how he is behaving towards you. So stay tuned!

FOOLISH DEMANDS (PART 1)

Ella was nervous but excited, waiting for Chase to come home. She had cleaned the house thoroughly, made one of his favorite meals using recipes his mom had given her, and had soft music playing on the stereo. Chase had been in such a foul mood lately, she really wanted to give him a good evening tonight.

As soon as he walked in the door, however, she saw that her efforts were in vain. Chase barely noticed the clean house, the nice music, or the aroma of pot roast wafting from the kitchen. What he did notice was that she was wearing a blouse he'd never seen before. "When did you get that?" he asked. "Last week..." she answered, her face getting flushed. "Last week? *After* I told you to reign in your spending?!"

Ella has two choices at this point. She can *"return evil for evil"* (1 Peter 3:9) and in so doing, become as foolish as her husband. Or she can *"give the fool the answer he deserves"* (Proverbs 26:5). In other words, his foolish behavior deserves a biblical rebuke from his wife, and she should not be afraid to answer him with a gentle reproof.

Biblically, a foolish man is one who rejects the Word of God and does what is right in his own eyes (Proverbs 1:7; 12:15). Even Christian men may sometimes act foolishly (contrary to Scripture) by making unreasonable demands or harsh accusations against their wives. Rather than leading their wives in a loving way, they use anger or intimidation to accomplish their objectives. Such behavior is not only hurtful, but can be extremely provoking, even to a wife who is committed to biblical submission. The natural response might be to get angry, cry, become fearful, clam up, run away—in short, respond *to* a fool *like* a fool (Proverbs 26:4). None of those responses are God-honoring, nor will they help resolve the conflict.

You should respond to foolish behavior with the wisdom of Scripture. That's difficult to do in the heat of the moment, but with God's grace, you *can* use His Word to give your husband "the answer he deserves."

Memorize It!

So that at the name of Jesus every knee will bow, of those who are in heaven and on earth and under the earth, and that every tongue will confess that Jesus Christ is LORD, to the glory of God the Father.
(Philippians 2:10-11)

Foolish Demands (Part 2)

When husbands use intimidation, harsh criticism or hostile teasing to manipulate their wives into submission, they are abusing their God-given authority and acting foolishly, rather than leading their wives in love.

The natural tendency when this happens is to get angry: to storm off, pout, clam up, cry, or "go home to mother"; then to slander, gossip, and plot revenge—in short, to return "evil for evil" by responding "to a fool like a fool" (1 Peter 3:9, Proverbs 26:4). None of these vindictive responses are pleasing to God, and they do nothing to resolve the conflict.

If and when this happens to you, your first response should be to humbly acknowledge any responsibility you have in the conflict. (See yesterday's lesson.) The second step is to gently remind your spouse of his responsibilities as your husband and as a disciple of Christ (if he is a Christian). These responsibilities include leading you in love, sacrificing himself for you, and speaking to you in a tenderhearted way. This step is the same as giving a biblical reproof, and you should not be afraid to use Scripture if your husband is a believer. *"The Word of God is living and active and sharper than any two-edged sword... and able to judge the thoughts and intentions of the heart"* (Hebrews 4:12†). It is your most effective weapon, and to *not* use it is like bringing a knife to a gun fight: you'll be defenseless and less effective in making any real change in your husband's heart.

In our story from yesterday, Ella could have responded, "I'm so sorry I bought this blouse, especially since we're trying to save money, and you were absolutely right to remind me. However, there is no reason for you to be angry. We are supposed to 'put aside anger and abusive speech.'[6] I know you're supposed to correct me when I do something wrong, but could you please do it in a more loving way?" If he was particularly abusive, she could have gently said, "The way you are talking to me is wrong. I will be happy to listen to you, but only after you calm down."

Answer a fool as his folly deserves, that he not be wise in his own eyes.
Proverbs 26:5

Application

Responding in a godly way is hard to do in the heat of the moment. Remember that you don't *have* to respond immediately. *"The heart of the righteous ponders how to answer"* (Proverbs 15:28†). If your husband is making unreasonable demands, ask him for time to consider your response. You could say, "I need to think about this, but I promise I'll give you an answer as soon as possible."

It is also helpful to take a moment to 1) remind yourself that this is an opportunity for you to demonstrate grace and loving patience to your husband, and 2) praise God that you can bring His truth into your marriage by applying it to the current situation. When we see conflict as an opportunity, this makes it much easier to respond in a God-honoring way.

Week 17, Day 1

At the name of Jesus every knee will bow, of those who are in heaven and on earth and under the earth, and...every tongue will confess that Jesus Christ is LORD, *to the glory of God the Father.*
PHILIPPIANS 2:10-11†

Application

The truth is that whether you submit to His authority or not, Jesus *is* LORD, and He has the *right* to say how every person on earth should live their life. Your acceptance or denial of that fact does not change a thing about Who He is. If you're struggling to obey God's commands, it is most likely because you have accepted Christ's authority in theory, but in practice you're still challenging His authority over you.

If this is how you're living, let me ask: Why did you accept Christ in the first place? Was it just for the "fire insurance," to keep you from hell? If that was your primary motivation at the time, have you grown to earnestly desire a relationship with Him? If so, that love relationship will make it easier to submit to His authority.

OBEDIENCE TO CHRIST'S AUTHORITY

One of the most frequently cited biblical passages about marriage is found in Matthew 19:

> *Some Pharisees came to Jesus, testing Him and asking, "Is it lawful for a man to divorce his wife for any reason at all?" And He answered and said, "Have you not read that He who created them from the beginning made them male and female, and said, "For this reason a man shall leave his father and mother and be joined to his wife, and the two shall become one flesh"? So they are no longer two, but one flesh* (Matthew 19:3-6a).

Notice that the Pharisees were *testing* Jesus. They wanted to challenge His authority by proving that His teachings contradicted the Law. If they could prove that, then Jesus would have no authority to teach in the temple.

It's interesting that this challenge to Christ's authority was included in a discussion about marriage, because it is in the area of marriage where we often challenge His authority in our own lives. Sometimes we look at the Bible and say, "I know what it says, but is that *really* what it says? Do I really have to submit to my husband? He treats me so poorly; do I really have to consider him as more important than myself?"

When you accepted Christ as your Savior, you also accepted Him as LORD, and must submit to His ultimate authority over your life, as revealed in His Word. You have given up your rights to your life. *"For you have died and your life is hidden with Christ in God"* (Colossians 3:3).

This is the difference between you and a woman who is not a believer. God's biblical model for marriage works well for everyone, and any lost person can keep her marriage vows with enough character and commitment. What you need God for is the really hard stuff, like *"love your enemies... bless those who curse you, pray for those [even your husband] who mistreat you"* (Luke 6:27-28†). God's requirements call for a supernatural gift of grace that is only available to His children, and only accessible to those who are fully submitted to the authority of Christ in their daily lives.

Memorize It!

So then, my beloved, just as you have always obeyed, not as in my presence only, but now much more in my absence, work out your salvation with fear and trembling; for it is God who is at work in you, both to will and to work for His good pleasure.
(Philippians 2:12-13)

No More Vain Regrets

Kylie held onto Dylan's arm and took a deep breath as they waited for the doorbell to be answered. They had just started going to a new church, and a very sweet couple from their adult Bible study class had invited them over for dinner. Kylie was extremely nervous: at the last church they had gone to, people somehow discovered that Dylan was her second husband. Even when she explained the circumstances behind her divorce, she could feel their disapproval. She was determined not to let her secret slip out at this new church.

You can see Kylie is not going to have much success becoming united in spirit with the members of her new church. Her problem is not that she's been divorced, but that she is dwelling on the past and focusing only on herself, not on how she can serve others in this new body of believers.

All of us have things from the past that we regret, whether it was something stupid we said or something sinful we did. We've all made life choices that we would do differently, given the chance. The danger is when we dwell on the past, giving in to our own brooding guilt and the "vain regrets" that we can do nothing about—and when we allow our past sin to keep us from present obedience.

This is not honoring to the Lord and His grace. If you've already confessed and turned from your sin, it's time to graciously accept the forgiveness you have in Christ. If you are still in bondage to the past, you need to understand God's heart toward you. God is gracious and compassionate, and He loves you deeply. There is no sin He cannot forgive and no mistake He cannot redeem. No matter what your past, you should never feel like a second-class citizen of the Kingdom. We are all sinners, and we *all* come short of God's glory (Romans 3:23). God is so powerful that He can redeem every situation and work all things together for our good (Romans 8:28) and His glory.

Memorize It!

So then, my beloved, just as you have always obeyed, not as in my presence only, but now much more in my absence, work out your salvation with fear and trembling; for it is God who is at work in you, both to will and to work for His good pleasure.
(Philippians 2:12-13)

Forgetting what lies behind and reaching forward to what lies ahead, I press on toward the goal for the prize of the upward call of God in Christ Jesus.
Philippians 3:13-14†

Application

Being consumed with past regrets is one way we become very selfishly focused. Instead, we should be focused on the Lord Jesus and on selflessly serving others. Is there a past sin or mistake that is keeping you in bondage to the past? If so, write it in the space below. If you don't want to write it out, simply write these words: "My sin, not in part, but the whole."

You may recognize that phrase as a line from the song, "It Is Well With My Soul." Ask God today to help you forget the past, then praise Him for His forgiveness by singing the rest of this verse to yourself:

My sin—oh the bliss of this glorious thought—
My sin, not in part, but the whole Is nailed to the cross and I bear it no more Praise the Lord! Praise the Lord!
O, my soul!

Week 17, Day 3

But I want you to understand that Christ is the head of every man, and the man is the head of a woman, and God is the head of Christ. For a man…is the image and glory of God; but the woman is the glory of man…Man was not created for the woman's sake, but woman for the man's sake.
1 CORINTHIANS 11:3, 7, 9†

Application

Part of being your husband's companion and helper is to make him look better than he actually is on his own. How you behave is a direct reflection on him, so it is important to always view your actions in terms of what makes him look good to others.

Take time today to think about the many ways you make your husband look good, and identify anything you might be doing that makes him look bad. Write them in your prayer journal, then commit yourself to walking in a way that glorifies your husband and Christ.

MAKING YOUR HUSBAND MORE ATTRACTIVE

Your job, as a wife, is to glorify your husband. *You want me to do* what? Glorify *my husband? Ok, well when he comes home I'll have his throne all ready for him!*

Now before you get all freaked out about this, let me put it into our own language, because "glorify" is not a word you hear much outside the church. What *glorify* means is simply, "to cause something or someone to look more pleasant, important or desirable." In other words, your job is to make your husband look good.

That sounds a lot more doable than "glorify," doesn't it? And that's really all it is: making your husband look good. Picture it like this: when your husband wears a good-looking outfit, the clothes make him look more attractive. That is your job as well: to make him look his best. God has given us a lot of influence in this area, so it's essential we use that influence wisely.

There are many ways you can make your husband look good, and just as many ways to make him look bad. Your husband looks good to others when you honor, respect, praise and build him up in front of others—including your children. He looks like a good provider when you take care of the home and spend money wisely. He looks like a man who cherishes his wife when you do all you can to look your best. He looks smart and capable when you help him accomplish tasks and keep life simple and organized for him.

Conversely, you make him look bad when you: put him down in front of others, say things to your children that make them think less of him, don't take care of yourself or your home, and leave him to do everything for himself. If that is your normal pattern of behavior, then you are not glorifying your husband. Remember that when Christ was on earth, He was *"seeking the glory of the One who sent Him"* (John 7:18). As He was obedient, He made God attractive to others. That is your job as well: to make your husband attractive to others. Not for the purpose of his own glory, but to bring glory to God.

Memorize It!

So then, my beloved, just as you have always obeyed, not as in my presence only, but now much more in my absence, work out your salvation with fear and trembling; for it is God who is at work in you, both to will and to work for His good pleasure.
(Philippians 2:12-13)

Respect His Opinions

Week 17, Day 4

To sum up, all of you be harmonious, sympathetic, brotherly, kindhearted, and humble in spirit.
1 Peter 3:8

Samantha is a talk-radio junkie. After her morning quiet time, she usually turns on the radio and listens to talk shows while she takes care of the house or runs errands. She's passionate about politics and socio-economic issues, and spends a great deal of time keeping up with what's going on in the world.

Her husband Phil, however, has to work and doesn't have the luxury of listening to the radio or digesting internet newsfeeds all day. Dinner is often a time for Samantha to share everything she's learned that day listening to the news. While Phil agrees with Samantha on most issues, he just doesn't get as excited about it as she does—which Samantha sees as a sign of ignorance. If Phil has an opinion that differs from hers, Samantha just tunes him out. *He doesn't know what he's talking about*, she thinks to herself. *If he knew what I knew, he'd feel differently*. What's worse is when they discuss politics with their friends. If Phil tries to talk, Samantha will jump in and take control of the conversation before he has a chance to embarrass himself. In trying to "save" Phil from embarrassment, she is actually showing a deep lack of respect for her husband and his opinions, which is far more damaging than letting him talk and possibly say something wrong.

Perhaps your husband is well informed, or perhaps he doesn't have the time you have for learning every nuance of American politics or the ins and outs of the economy. Or maybe he is not as mature in his faith and biblical knowledge as you are. In working with women over the years, I have found this is often the case. Many of us have the luxury, *provided by our husbands*, of spending more time learning and growing in spiritual matters as well as in knowledge of the world around us. Meanwhile, our poor husbands are just focused on their jobs and providing for our families. This often results in us getting a puffed-up image of ourselves and our opinions, which can easily turn to disrespect toward our husbands.

Application

Think honestly about how you respond when your husband expresses his opinions. Do you listen attentively, giving his ideas as much merit as you do your own? Or do you become argumentative or embarrassed? It doesn't matter how smart or well informed you are. The Bible is clear that you are to respect your husband (Ephesians 5:33), and that means respecting his opinions and his ideas as well.

Even if you don't agree with him, you must still show respect by listening carefully, with an open mind, while he shares his thoughts on politics, faith, child-rearing, the economy, etc. In this way, you are putting on *"a heart of compassion, kindness, humility . . . and patience; bearing with"* your husband and putting on *"love"* (Colossians 3:12-14).

Memorize It!

So then, my beloved, just as you have always obeyed, not as in my presence only, but now much more in my absence, work out your salvation with fear and trembling; for it is God who is at work in you, both to will and to work for His good pleasure.
(Philippians 2:12-13)

Week 17, Day 5

You shall not steal, nor deal falsely, nor lie to one another.
LEVITICUS 19:11

Application

One problem with lying is that when you cover up your actions, you lose the motivation to change your behavior. Why go to the trouble of being blameless when you can just *pretend* to be blameless? Instead, God wants us to be able to say, like the Apostle Paul, that our husbands, friends and family *"are witnesses, and so is God, how devoutly and uprightly and blamelessly we behaved"* (1 Thessalonians 2:10).

Try going for one day without hiding the truth at all. If something happens where you would be tempted to lie, ask yourself *why* you were tempted. Were you doing something you don't want anyone to know about? If so, then change your actions and your character so that you no longer have to lie about who you really are.

THE LYING HABIT

In the 1997 movie, *Liar, Liar,* the main character, Fletcher, loses his ability to lie. No matter how hard he tries, he is completely unable to speak anything but the truth. Can you imagine what it would be like if you *had* to tell all the truth and nothing but the truth? When your husband asks, "What are you doing?" instead of saying, "Catching up on my email" you might have to say, "Well, I sent out one email, but now I've wasted an hour on Facebook." While "catching up on email" might have been partly true, it wasn't the whole truth. It was the answer that puts you in the best light possible, which is deceiving.

The Bible makes it crystal clear that God hates lying. *"Lying lips are an abomination to the LORD, but those who deal faithfully are His delight"* (Proverbs 12:22). One of the reasons He hates it so much is because lying identifies the speaker with Satan, who *"does not stand in the truth because there is no truth in him. Whenever he speaks a lie, he speaks from his own nature, for he is a liar and the father of lies.* (John 8:44). Lying is something we do out of our old, sinful nature. It is not part of a redeemed, new nature:

> *If indeed you have heard Him and have been taught in Him, just as* ***truth*** *is in Jesus, that, in reference to your former manner of life, you lay aside the old self, which is being corrupted in accordance with the lusts of* ***deceit****, and that you be renewed in the spirit of your mind, and put on the new self, which in the likeness of God has been created in righteousness and holiness of the* ***truth****. Therefore, laying aside* ***falsehood****, speak* ***truth*** *each one of you with his neighbor, for we are members of one another.* (Ephesians 4:21-25†)

Most of us cover or distort the truth because we fear the consequences of being 100 percent honest. We don't want people (especially our husbands) to see our faults, so we regularly practice deceit with our words. And we think that it's OK as long as no one is hurt by it. But all deceit is lying, which dishonors Christ.

Taking Every Thought Captive

Week 18, Day 1

For though we walk in the flesh, we do not war according to the flesh, for the weapons of our warfare are not of the flesh, but divinely powerful for the destruction of fortresses. We are destroying speculations and every lofty thing raised up against the knowledge of God, and we are taking every thought captive to the obedience of Christ.
2 Corinthians 10:3-5

I caught up with Angie just as she was pulling into her driveway. She had spent the night in a hotel, and was returning to her house to pick up more of her belongings. A mutual friend had alerted me to Angie's situation, and I spent the morning fasting and praying about what I was going to say to try to talk her out of leaving her husband. As soon as she saw me, she burst into tears. "I just can't do it anymore," she cried. "Our problems are way too big, and I can't take the pressure. He's never going to change. He knows what's right, but he's got so many issues. It would take a miracle to fix him!"

Angie's marriage is in real trouble, and she has given up. Now, all of her thoughts and conversation about their marriage are centered around justifying her decision to give up and leave. Over time, Angie's thinking has become very unbiblical.

It is important to realize how wrong thoughts powerfully influence your emotions and make it virtually impossible to resolve conflict in a rational manner. It is only with correct thinking that couples can work through conflict in a godly way. When we have unbiblical—and therefore, untrue—thoughts about our situation, we won't see how God is working through the conflict to bring glory to Himself and peace to our marriages. When we don't see God, we lose hope. With the loss of hope comes intense emotional pain that we feel completely unable to manage ourselves.

This is not God's way of dealing with conflict. Even if your marriage is not in serious risk of falling apart, you could still be guilty of unbiblical thinking that makes conflict resolution extremely difficult. Instead of unbiblical thinking, we must be *"transformed by the renewing of (our) minds"* (Romans 12:2†). When we see God's hand in our circumstances and think *"true, honorable, right, and pure"* thoughts (Philippians 4:8†), we give the Spirit control of our emotions so they don't overpower us. This puts us in a much better position to work on through conflict.

Memorize It!

This you know, my beloved brethren. But everyone must be quick to hear, slow to speak and slow to anger; for the anger of man does not achieve the righteousness of God.
(James 1:19-20)

Application

Having the *"mind of Christ,"* (1 Corinthians 2:16) makes it much easier to resolve conflict biblically. Instead of the sinful thoughts, how should we be thinking? Following are some biblical thoughts that enhance conflict solving:

- "What can I learn about God through this?" (Philippians 3:10)
- "God will help me endure this." (1 Corinthians 10:13)
- "If I have to suffer, I want it to be for doing what is right." (1 Peter 3:17, 1 Peter 4:19)
- "God can use everything that happens for our good." (Romans 8:28, Genesis 50:20)
- "What can I do to make it easier for us to solve this problem?" (Philippians 2:3)
- "Even this is an opportunity for me to glorify God." (1 Corinthians 10:31)

Week 18, Day 2

There is neither Jew nor Greek,
there is neither slave nor free man,
there is neither male nor female;
for you are all one in Christ Jesus.
And if you belong to Christ, then
you are Abraham's descendants,
heirs according to promise.
GALATIANS 3:28-29

Application

Even if you know intellectually that your husband is your authority, you may not have accepted that truth emotionally. To see where your heart is on this issue, ask yourself the following:

- Do I bristle at the terms *obedience* and *submission*?
- Do I prefer to focus on *mutual submission* or *equal partnership*?
- Am I afraid of how people view me when I say I am submissive to my husband?
- Do I become incensed at the thought that anyone would regard me as "lower" than my husband?

If you answered *yes* to any of these, pray that God would help you rest in the knowledge that He sees you and your husband as equals. Knowing this should help you relinquish any control you're clinging to, and bring more harmony to your marriage.

INFERIORITY COMPLEX

Kelly plopped down on the couch next to her fiancé, Jay. "Do you want to keep the word *obey* in our wedding vows?" she asked. "It just sounds so...Middle Ages!" Jay shrugged, "I don't see us having one of those traditional marriages where the wife is 'subservient' to the husband. We're a team, an equal partnership." Kelly wrapped her arms around his neck and kissed him. "That's why I'm marrying you," she smiled.

Five years later, Jay and Kelly are sitting on that same couch, both very upset. "I can't believe you would just buy a car without my approval!" Kelly said. Jay replied, "I told you: my car needs too much work. When we disagree, somebody has to make a decision. Right now, that someone is me." Kelly looked shocked. "Why should it be you?!" When he gave no answer, Kelly began tearing up. "You think you're better than me, don't you?" Jay replied, "No, but we can't both be in charge. It just doesn't work."

You can see the problem. With no Scriptural basis for authority in their marriage, they have no idea who should have the final say when conflicts arise. Then if Jay makes a decision against his wife's wishes, his "power grab" causes Kelly to feel inferior.

God has a design for marriage, and we can trust that His plan was not designed to make us feel inferior as women, but rather to bring order and harmony in the home. You have a different position in your marriage than your husband, but that doesn't make you inferior. God sees you and your husband as equals. In fact, He knows that we are *all* weak, sinful, and incapable of anything good outside of His grace. Your husband being "in charge" is not a matter of superiority; it's a matter of purpose and design.

If you struggle with this concept, remember that Christ subordinated Himself to His parents while He was on earth (Luke 2:51). Were Mary and Joseph better than Jesus? Of course not! But He willingly submitted himself to their authority in order to carry out God's plan of redemption.

Memorize It!

This you know, my beloved brethren. But everyone must be quick to hear, slow to speak and slow to anger; for the anger of man does not achieve the righteousness of God.
(James 1:19-20)

Anger: It's Your Choice

Shannon's father molested her from the time she was six years old until he was killed in a car accident when she was fifteen—the same year she and her mom both accepted Christ as their Savior. Shannon knew she needed to forgive her dad (and her mom) for what had happened to her, but unfortunately, she held on to her anger, bringing it into her marriage with Russ.

Everything was great for the first year, as Russ did everything he could to make his bride happy. But then things started to degrade. The tiniest little things would make Shannon explode in anger, and if she wasn't outwardly angry, she just seemed sad. After she gave birth to their son, she suffered from extreme post-partum depression, and would not leave the baby with anyone. The birth of their second son pushed her to the breaking point, and Russ sought biblical counseling for his wife.

If Shannon had not gotten counseling, their marriage most likely would not have survived. Sinful anger is one of the most common factors contributing to divorce. Anger leads to bitterness, depression, and abuse, and it usually replicates itself in the children of angry people. There is nothing good we can say about anger...and yet, even God's people often allow themselves to be controlled by it.

No matter what your reasons are for getting angry or for being an angry person, you need to understand that anger is *always* something you choose. You never have to be angry. *"No temptation has overtaken you but such as is common to man; and God is faithful, who will not allow you to be tempted beyond what you are able, but with the temptation will provide the way of escape also, so that you will be able to endure it"* (1 Corinthians 10:13). If you do give in to sinful anger, it is because you have decided to do so to accomplish your own agenda. But when you give the Holy Spirit control, He gives you a *"sound mind"* (2 Timothy 1:7, NKJV) which enables you to always choose to do the right thing, no matter how provoked you may become.

Memorize It!

This you know, my beloved brethren. But everyone must be quick to hear, slow to speak and slow to anger; for the anger of man does not achieve the righteousness of God.
(James 1:19-20)

But now you also, put them all aside: anger, wrath, malice, slander, and abusive speech from your mouth.
Colossians 3:8

Application

If you are given to anger, it will greatly help you to realize that anger is always a choice. You can also memorize the following Scripture passage, and quote it to yourself whenever you are tempted to react with anger:

> *Now the deeds of the flesh are evident, which are... idolatry...strife, jealousy,* ***outbursts of anger****, disputes...and things like these, of which I forewarn you...that those who practice such things will not inherit the kingdom of God.*
>
> *But the fruit of the Spirit is love, joy, peace, patience, kindness, goodness, faithfulness, gentleness, self-control; against such things there is no law* (Galatians 5:19-23†).

Week 18, Day 4

No temptation has overtaken you but such as is common to man; and God is faithful, who will not allow you to be tempted beyond what you are able, but with the temptation will provide the way of escape also, so that you will be able to endure it.
1 CORINTHIANS 10:13

Application

"STP" (Stop, Think and Pray) is a useful acronym to remember when you feel provoked to anger by your husband's words or actions.

- STOP: Don't react at all to the situation. Stop what you're doing, and stop your mouth from speaking.
- THINK: Think before you say another word. Think about what is really going on in this situation, or how your husband might possibly be right and you may be wrong. Think about how best to love your husband and glorify God at this time.
- PRAY: Pray that God would help you to love your husband by not being "easily provoked" to sinful anger. Pray for God's love to cover you and your husband, and that God would give you supernatural control over your emotions and allow you to respond with grace and love.

LOVE IS NOT EASILY PROVOKED

I don't have many success stories from my early days of marriage to illustrate the concept of godly self-control. I've always been even-tempered, so anger was never a huge issue in my life. During times of real conflict, however, I found that my natural coolness was grossly insufficient to meet the challenge. I'd never been extremely tested in this area, so my spiritual self-control muscles were very weak.

Many marriages are put to the test after children come along. This was especially true for Scott and me. One evening we had a major disagreement over some child-rearing issue. As we argued, I could feel anger rising inside me like a tsunami. However, I had been studying the fruits of the Spirit, and knew this was a situation where self-control was needed. I had to deliver something to a neighbor, which gave me a good excuse to take a walk and pray. By the time my errand was done, God had cooled me down and shown me a more loving way to talk to my husband when I returned. If I hadn't taken the time to STP—Stop, Think and Pray—our conflict would have risen to new levels due to my anger and lack of self-control.

Showing love means that a wife controls herself even under very difficult circumstances. The sad fact is that wives are sometimes provoked to anger even when the circumstances are not especially difficult. *"But the fruit of the Spirit is love, joy, peace, patience, kindness, goodness, faithfulness, gentleness, self-control"* (Galatians 5:22-23). A wife shows love by having the godly character quality of self-control. Instead of becoming irritated, she responds with patience and kindness.

It would be great if you could always naturally respond to your husband with kindness, even when he does or says things that provoke you to anger. But as you continue to practice self-control during times of conflict, it will become easier to recall that fruit of the Spirit in your life. Your natural temper will be replaced with God's "supernatural" control of your emotions.

Memorize It!

This you know, my beloved brethren. But everyone must be quick to hear, slow to speak and slow to anger; for the anger of man does not achieve the righteousness of God.
(James 1:19-20)

The Idol of a Christian Marriage

For the unbelieving husband is sanctified through his wife, and the unbelieving wife is sanctified through her believing husband; for otherwise your children are unclean, but now they are holy.
1 Corinthians 7:14

When Erin met Jason at Bible college, she was sure God had brought her the perfect man and they would have a great marriage. Six years later, however, she wonders how she could have been so blind. Sure, he professes to know Christ, but there is little evidence of spiritual maturity in his life. She is frustrated because Jason is not leading their family spiritually, and they frequently argue about the best way to discipline their two children. "I would be better off raising them alone," she says to herself. "At least then I could make sure they'll grow up to love Christ."

Maryann was not a Christian when she met Chad. However, a few years ago she trusted Christ as her Lord and Savior. Now her focus is completely different from Chad's, who has no concern for spiritual things. He's not a bad guy, but she can already see the effects of their opposing life philosophies on their son. Zachary would much rather go fishing with dad on Sunday mornings than go to church with mom, and last week she heard him repeat a swear word Chad uses frequently. She pleads for God to save her husband, but until then, she is convinced she will be miserable in this "unequally yoked" marriage.

Like Erin and Maryann, most of us want a good Christian marriage. How much better would life be if our husbands would lead us spiritually, love us as Christ loves the Church, and always react to us with Spirit-filled cheerfulness and grace? However, not all of us have that, and it's easy to get our eyes off of Christ and become angry, frustrated, or miserable that our husbands are not changing according to our time table. Of course we should earnestly desire and pray for our husbands' salvation and sanctification. But if you believe you cannot be happy unless your husband is saved and growing in faith, your desire for a good Christian marriage may have become an idol in your heart. Your frustration is the result of not getting what you want, more than it is about glorifying Christ and obeying His command to be joyful and content no matter what.

Application

You may have a deep desire for your husband to be saved or to mature in his faith. And certainly this is a good desire. However, if you are not content to wait for God to work in your husband's heart, if you are miserable and sin as a result of your husband's failures, then your heart's desire has become an idol.

God alone knows if and when your husband will become a devoted Christ follower. He also knows the best way for you to respond to your husband, and He can use you to affect change in your husband's heart and life—but only as you continue to love and obey Him. *"Let your light shine before men in such a way that they may see your good works, and glorify your Father who is in heaven"* (Matthew 5:16).

Week 19, Day 1

Your adornment must not be merely external—braiding the hair, and wearing gold jewelry, or putting on dresses; but let it be the hidden person of the heart, with the imperishable quality of a gentle and quiet spirit, which is precious in the sight of God.
1 PETER 3:3-4

Application

If God puts a high value on the attitude of respect, we who have *"the mind of Christ"* (1 Corinthians 2:16) should also. Cultivating an attitude of respect should be one of your top priorities. If you're finding it difficult to change your actions, it is most likely because you have not changed your heart's attitude toward your husband. As you read through the lessons on respect throughout this book, remember to evaluate not just your outward actions, but your heart's attitude as well. Remember that *"man looks at the outward appearance, but the LORD looks at the heart"* (1 Samuel 16:7).

RESPECT, INSIDE OUT

First Peter 3 gives a great deal of instruction to women on their behavior and attitude toward their husbands. We cover much of this material in the lessons on submission, but let's focus today on that phrase in verse 4, *"the hidden person of the heart."* You know from Ephesians 5:33 that you are to respect your husband, and throughout much of this book, we talk about what respect looks like in all of its outward manifestations. We discuss how to demonstrate and express respect to our husbands—respecting their opinions, their judgment, their abilities, etc.

But I don't want you to miss the point Peter makes in this passage. Respect is *an inward heart attitude that results in respectful behavior*. Your *"hidden person"* is who you are at your core: the sum total of your emotions, your conscience, your thoughts and attitudes. Peter drives this point even deeper when he uses the phrase, *"of the heart."* Not just your surface thoughts, but your deepest held beliefs.

Is your deepest held belief toward your husband one of unwavering respect? If so, the outward expressions of respect will occur naturally. However, if you harbor any disrespectful attitudes toward your husband, that will come through in your actions, your voice, and your body language.

Notice that Peter does not say it is wrong to change your outward appearance—and even though he's focusing on clothing and up-do's, "outward appearances" can also include your speech and actions. Your beauty does not *just* come from the way you talk and act, but also from your heart attitudes. The specific attitude Peter refers to in this passage is *"a gentle and quiet spirit"* which is *"precious in the sight of God."* When you are quiet in your heart and respectful to your husband, no matter what kind of a man he is, God sees your heart and considers it *"precious."* In other words, God places a very high value on the hidden quality of respect.

Memorize It!

By this we know that we have come to know Him, if we keep His commandments. The one who says, "I have come to know Him," and does not keep His commandments, is a liar, and the truth is not in him.
(1 John 2:3-4)

Work at Home? Or Just Stay at Home?

So that they may encourage the young women to love their husbands, to love their children, to be sensible, pure, workers at home, kind, being subject to their own husbands, so that the word of God will not be dishonored.
Titus 2:4-5

Clara loves being a stay-at-home mom. She enjoyed having a full-time job before she started her family, but staying at home is so much better. She likes having the freedom to sleep in if she needs to, set her own schedule, and do the things she wants to do. She had thought that once she was no longer working outside the home she would have plenty of time to take care of the house. But she finds the innumerable activities that fill her days leave little time for cooking and cleaning. When she does have a few spare hours at home, that is her "me" time for catching up with email, napping, reading a book or watching TV.

Clara didn't realize how bad things had gotten around the house until one evening her husband asked, "What have you been doing all day?" She was irritated that he would even ask such a question and immediately countered with a list of all the things she'd done that day. "Sweetheart, I'm not accusing you of goofing off," Kent answered. "I know you're busy. But this house? This is your job. It needs to take priority over all that other stuff."

There's a difference between a "stay-at-home" mom and a "work-at-home" mom. Only your furniture stays at home. You, on the other hand, are to be working at your job of keeping the home. Too many women have the attitude that they answer to no one for how they manage their time during the day. Since no one ever asks for an accounting, they do what they want. If they behaved that way in a paid position, they'd be fired!

God has entrusted you with just so many hours in a day. Are you using those hours wisely? Are you putting as much energy into your duties at home as you would if you were being paid? Are you being accountable to God for how you're spending your time? *"Therefore be careful how you walk, not as unwise men but as wise, making the most of your time, because the days are evil"* (Ephesians 5:15-16).

Memorize It!

By this we know that we have come to know Him, if we keep His commandments. The one who says, "I have come to know Him," and does not keep His commandments, is a liar, and the truth is not in him. (1 John 2:3-4)

Application

Read the parable of the talents in Matthew 25:14-30. Jesus used this story as an illustration of how we should be spending our time in preparation for His return. But we can also think of it as a daily illustration of how we should redeem the time we have at home until our husbands return at the end of the day. If you find that you are not being a good steward of the time God has entrusted to you, ask your husband to hold you accountable. Think of the end of each day as a time when the Master (God, through your husband) asks for an accounting. Then spend your time during the day so that when the Master reviews your work, he can say, *"Well done, good and faithful servant"* (Matthew 25:21, NKJV).

Do nothing from selfishness or empty conceit, but with humility of mind regard one another as more important than yourselves; do not merely look out for your own personal interests, but also for the interests of others.
PHILIPPIANS 2:3-4

Application

It's easy to give in to your husband from time to time, but to do it regularly and consistently is extremely difficult because the flesh always craves satisfaction. Even though you are a new creation in Christ, your flesh is still active and pushing its own agenda. Humbling yourself is not just an act of the mind, it is also an act whereby you discipline your flesh to bring it into subjection to Christ (1 Corinthians 9:27).

Practice disciplining your flesh and treating your husband as more important than yourself by doing something sacrificial for your husband *today*. See the last paragraph of the lesson for some ideas, or ask God to show you the best way to put your husband first.

WHO'S MORE IMPORTANT?

Philippians 2:3 says that your husband is more important than you are.

Um...okay. Well, if the Bible says it then...what?

I can see you scratching your head, but here's the thing: If your husband is reading Philippians 2:3, then the Holy Spirit is telling him that you are more important than he is.

This passage is written to every believer. We are all to *regard*—treat, think about, and consider—each other as more important than ourselves. That means everyone in your church, and every other believer, and every member of your family, and your husband: they are all more important than you are, and you are to treat them that way. It's not that they are more important to God, but God wants you to put them first. Can you imagine a church, or a family, where everyone treated everyone else as more important than themselves? It's just like that old song: *Jesus and others and you, what a wonderful way to spell JOY!*

Treating others as more important than yourself requires *"humility of mind"* (Philippians 2:3); pride will cause you to constantly put yourself first, and think of what you want as more important than what your husband wants or requires. But true humility trusts God to take care of you, thereby allowing you to disregard your own desires and seek the good of your husband as your greater priority.

What does this look like in marriage? It means if your husband wants to go to Chick-fil-A but you want to go to Olive Garden, you go to Chick-fil-A. It means if you are tired but your husband wants sex, you lovingly give it to him. It means if you're tempted to skip church but your husband has been lagging spiritually, you get up and go to church. It means if your husband argues with you, you let him win the argument (unless his "win" means you have to disagree with God's Word, or would result in you having to sin). In all things and at all times, you put your needs, wants and desires last, after those of your husband.

Memorize It!

By this we know that we have come to know Him, if we keep His commandments. The one who says, "I have come to know Him," and does not keep His commandments, is a liar, and the truth is not in him.
(1 John 2:3-4)

Saying All The Wrong Things

Recently I was in the housewares section at Wal-Mart when I noticed a couple with a pre-teen daughter looking at blenders. The wife was clearly very irritated with her husband, as he was taking his time looking over all of the different options. She didn't say much as he talked on for a couple of minutes about blenders, then finally she said angrily, "Just pick one. Stop being so stupid about this!"

Hopefully it horrifies you that any wife would talk to her husband that way, especially in front of their child. But you would be surprised how many Christian wives speak to their husbands using "abusive speech." Perhaps you are guilty of using the types of speech that Colossians 3:8 tells us to put aside:

Anger—The attitude that starts it all. The husband does something to make the wife angry and rather than take it to the LORD in prayer, she allows it to fester in her heart. Her speech is then angry—from having a slight edge to her voice, to arguing or cursing.

Wrath—Anger will eventually work its way out into behavior: taking vengeance, being destructive in speech and actions, etc. A wrathful wife will yell, scream and curse; or, if that's not her style, she might take vengeance in quieter ways, like giving him the cold shoulder or refusing to have sex with him.

Malice—Desiring that harm comes to him. She might fantasize about him being killed in a car accident, or that everyone would find out "just what kind of man he *really* is."

Slander—Her anger is so strong, she must tell others about it, and paint him in as bad a light as possible.

Abusive speech—Directing all of her anger, wrath, malice and slander toward him; bitter, derogatory speech intended to hurt him.

We like to think we're not guilty of these awful things. But read over those items again, looking at the "softer" options: a slight edge in the voice, the cold shoulder, speaking in a derogatory way about your husband. There are few wives who have not done some or all of these things out of anger.

Memorize It!

By this we know that we have come to know Him, if we keep His commandments. The one who says, "I have come to know Him," and does not keep His commandments, is a liar, and the truth is not in him.

(1 John 2:3-4)

But now you also, put them all aside: anger, wrath, malice, slander, and abusive speech from your mouth.
COLOSSIANS 3:8

Application

Sometimes we are tempted to use angry, abusive, or even malicious words during those emotional days just before our periods. Even though control is harder during that time, God will still give you the grace to do what is right (1 Corinthians 10:13).

If angry speech is a problem for you, you may have to work extra hard to think about what you are going to say and to say it in love, no matter how you feel. Any kind of wrong speech is sin. You can begin changing your speech patterns by confessing to God each and every time you speak in a wrong way. Then replace those wrong words with the truth spoken in love (Ephesians 4:15). When this becomes a habit for you, you will have laid the wrong speech aside.

Week 19, Day 5

And may be found in Him, not having a righteousness of my own derived from the Law, but that which is through faith in Christ, the righteousness which comes from God on the basis of faith.
PHILIPPIANS 3:9

Application

Preparing for this particular lesson was extremely uplifting, because I found so many verses on faith that greatly encouraged me. Below are just a few of these passages. Look up each one of these and read it carefully, focusing on how God works in you through your faith in Him. Afterwards, take time to praise Him for *the "unfathomable riches of Christ"* (Ephesians 3:8).

Romans 1:16-17
Philippians 3:7-14
Galatians 2:19-20
Hebrews 10:19-25
Ephesians 3:8-21
Hebrews 11:1-6
Ephesians 4:1-16
Jeremiah 9:23-24

SANCTIFICATION: THE ROLE OF FAITH

Throughout the rest of this book we'll be talking about engaging in the process of mutual sanctification with your husband, based on passages such as Galatians 6:1-2, Luke 6:42, and Matthew 18 *("If your brother sins, go and show him his fault in private"*—verse 15). You and your husband can take specific steps to continually uncover and remove sin from your life. But you need to be sure you understand the role that *faith* plays in your sanctification, because *"without faith it is impossible to please [God]"* (Hebrews 11:6†).

None of the things God asks us to do are possible without faith. Your salvation came by faith, and you continue in faith. *"The righteous man shall live by faith"* (Romans 1:17). You were not saved by removing sin from your life, and you don't continue your life after salvation that way either. *"The life which [you] now live in the flesh [you] live by* ***faith*** *in the Son of God"* (Galatians 2:20†. See also Galatians 3:3).

In other words, you can work every single day on your sanctification, identifying and turning from sin, but you must recognize that it is GOD who takes care of that sin and removes it from your life. Your self-control in turning from sin is a fruit of His Holy Spirit (Galatians 5:23). If you've successfully stopped committing a particular sin, it is only because God made it possible. He gets the credit, deserves your gratitude, and should get all of the glory. It does not come from your own strength, *"so that no one may boast"* (Ephesians 2:9).

As you are working on your sanctification, at times you may get discouraged or think, "I just can't do it!" And that is true, you CAN'T do it on your own. But you must *"believe that He is and that He is a rewarder of those who seek Him"* (Hebrews 11:6). If you're having trouble removing sin from your life, the answer is to "seek Him"—to turn to God in faith, acknowledge that you have no strength in your flesh to gain victory over sin, and then focus on the LORD Jesus, the *"author and perfecter of faith"* (Hebrews 12:2).

Hard Choices for God's Kingdom

Week 20, Day 1

Walk in a manner worthy of the God who calls you into His own kingdom and glory.
1 Thessalonians 2:12†

Mark and Beth were married less than a week before Beth saw Mark really lose his temper for the first time. She had accidentally locked the keys in the car at their hotel, and Mark was furious. Back in the room, he berated her for over thirty minutes on how stupid and irresponsible she was. She was shocked and confused, but thought perhaps he was just stressed. Thirteen years later, they are still together, but she feels like she is constantly walking on eggshells for fear of setting him off.

Beth is seeing a counselor who has encouraged her to seek a divorce. "He has no right to treat you that way," the counselor says. The problem with the counselor's advice, however, is that the emphasis is on what Beth deserves, not on what is most glorifying to Christ.

In Matthew 19, the Pharisees were questioning Jesus about the issue of divorce, when God's ideal was for couples to stay together in most circumstances. His disciples were shocked at this teaching, *"If the relationship of the man with his wife is like this, it is better not to marry"* (Matthew 19:10†). Jesus replied, *"Not all men can accept this statement, but only those to whom it has been given"* (Matthew 19:11). In other words, this teaching is for those who take the LORDship of Christ seriously, and who desire to live their lives sacrificially, for God's Kingdom.

Perhaps your marriage is really tough, and you have considered leaving your husband. However, sometimes you have to make hard choices for the sake of the Kingdom. For some people, that hard choice is to stay in a bad marriage and trust God to make it a good marriage. In the meantime, God may be calling you to suffer until He changes your circumstances, your husband, or your heart. When God changes your heart, He can make even your suffering joyful (James 1:2-4). Your job is to *"humble (yourself) under the mighty hand of God...casting all your anxiety on Him, because He cares for you"* (1 Peter 5:6-7).

Memorize It!

But whoever keeps His word, in him the love of God has truly been perfected. By this we know that we are in Him: the one who says he abides in Him ought himself to walk in the same manner as He walked.
(1 John 2:5-6)

Application

There are only two biblical grounds for divorce: infidelity (Matthew 19:9) and abandonment by an unbelieving spouse (1 Corinthians 7:15). Your marriage might be tough, but if it doesn't meet either of those standards, then your responsibility is to stay faithful to your husband and to obey God despite the difficulty it may bring in this life.

If you are suffering as a result of your husband's sin, God has provided other means (besides divorce) for your protection. These resources include biblical reproofs, church discipline, and giving your husband over to the governing authorities. (See the index in the back of this book for lessons on giving a biblical reproof.) Pursuing these resources is not only wise, but is a matter of obedience.

Week 20, Day 2

Therefore I, the prisoner of the LORD, *implore you to walk in a manner worthy of the calling with which you have been called, with all humility and gentleness, with patience, showing tolerance for one another in love, being diligent to preserve the unity of the Spirit in the bond of peace.*
EPHESIANS 4:1-3

Application

We often choose *not* to be tolerant or forbearing because we want our own way. But this stubbornness usually comes at a heavy price, and it is not pleasing to God.

Whenever you and your husband have a conflict over traditions, personal habits, how to spend free time or how to decorate the house—any conflict where the choice is not between right or wrong, sin or righteousness—you can change your thinking to be selfless and forbearing, or you can stubbornly insist on getting your own way. If something is really important to your husband, even if your choice or opinion is equally as important to you, then you should be willing to give in graciously for the sake of unity and for the sake of remaining under your husband's authority.

Opposites Attract

One of the biggest conflicts my husband and I have had in our marriage is over *differentness*. Not in our family traditions, because he came to the marriage with very few traditions and gladly deferred to how I was raised. But our personalities are very different when it comes to people. I am a people person, and I love to entertain—probably because I was raised in a home with a revolving front door, where friends felt free to just come and go as they please. My husband was raised by a single mom and they rarely had anyone visit or stay in their home. So he gets uncomfortable if there are too many people in one room.

This difference in our personalities has caused more than one argument in our marriage. When I am not yielded to the Holy Spirit, I can get very irritated that Scott is not more of a "people person." But the truth is that Scott does want to make me happy and allow me to entertain. *My* responsibility is to renew my mind with Scripture and be forbearing. The passage I use in this situation is Colossians 3:12-15. Listen to how practical the Word is when you apply it to conflict over "differentness":

- *"Put on a heart of compassion, kindness, humility, gentleness and patience"*—I need to be compassionate toward my husband and understanding that this is difficult for him. I need to wait patiently while God works on his heart.
- *"Bearing with one another, and forgiving each other, whoever has a complaint against anyone"*—Yes, I have a complaint against my husband right now, but I should be forgiving and understanding.
- *"Put on love, which is the perfect bond of unity"*—I can show my husband love by being patient with him. Unity in our marriage is much more important than me getting my own way!
- *"Let the peace of Christ rule in your hearts, to which indeed you were called in one body; and be thankful"*—I am thankful I have a husband who has provided so well for us that I can entertain from time to time. I am thankful that he loves me enough to work through our differences.

Memorize It!

But whoever keeps His word, in him the love of God has truly been perfected. By this we know that we are in Him: the one who says he abides in Him ought himself to walk in the same manner as He walked.
(1 John 2:5-6)

Mirror Images

The Lord *God fashioned into a woman the rib which He had taken from the man, and brought her to the man.*
Genesis 2:22

My daughters are a rare kind of identical twins. Identicals result when a single fertilized egg splits into two separate embryos. If the split occurs late, the twins will form "facing" each other, the one twin's left side corresponding genetically to the other twin's right side. This is what happened to Brittan and Ciara. As a result, Ciara is left handed and Brittan is right handed. Their teeth and other physical features have opposite patterns, and if they face each other, they appear to be exact reflections—thus the term "mirror image" identical twins.

I can't think of a more beautiful analogy to Eve, Adam's "suitable helper" (Genesis 2:20). The Hebrew words for "suitable helper" are *ezer* "helper" and *kÿnegdo* meaning "in front of" or "corresponding." Just as Brittan and Ciara were created "corresponding" to each other, Eve was created "in front of" and "corresponding" to Adam. Not as his superior or his inferior, but equal to and complementary to him.

We can all accept the idea of *suitable*. I think what trips us up is the word *helper*. Yet the same word is used to describe the help God provided Israel (Exodus 18:4, Psalm 33:20). Certainly, being Israel's helper does not demean God. Likewise, being Adam's helper is not demeaning, but a description of her unique role in marriage. The idea that, as Adam's helper, Eve was simply there to follow Adam's orders is a gross misinterpretation of God's design.

Many people believe that because Adam was created first, Eve was just an afterthought. However, this idea is a twisting of truth designed to make us discontent with God's plan. The truth is, it was always in His plan to create both man *and* woman. Eve was created in God's image just as Adam was. When God brought Eve to Adam, *He was walking His daughter down the aisle.* He was just as pleased with her as He was with Adam. The point of Genesis 2:20 is not superiority or inferiority, but rather the deep partnership that would exist between her and the man.

Application

I think one of the most poignant pictures in Genesis is when Adam names the animals. Imagine the tigers come before him, he names them, and then off they go, ready to be fruitful and multiply tigers on the earth. Over and over, different animals come to Adam, and they all have mates. *"But for Adam there was not found a helper suitable for him"* (Genesis 2:20). I think one of God's purposes in this was to demonstrate to Adam that he was alone, and that this was not God's plan.

I hope you appreciate how cherished you are in God's sight, and you understand that helping your husband was God's design for you from the beginning of time. I pray that you love being your husband's "mirror image" and *"fellow heir of the grace of life"* (1 Peter 3:7).

Memorize It!

But whoever keeps His word, in him the love of God has truly been perfected. By this we know that we are in Him: the one who says he abides in Him ought himself to walk in the same manner as He walked.
(1 John 2:5-6)

Week 20, Day 4

For those who are according to the flesh set their minds on the things of the flesh, but those who are according to the Spirit, the things of the Spirit.
ROMANS 8:5

Application

Having a loving marriage starts with having a pure devotion to Christ. As you free your husband from the need to meet all your desires in this area, he will likely respond positively. But even if he doesn't, God promises you the *"peace that surpasses all comprehension"* (Philippians 4:7) when you obediently take your requests to Him.

Do you trust that? Do you believe that even if your husband is not meeting your need for romance and intimacy, that God will make up for that? As you turn from your idols to God, He will continue to sanctify and conform you; the fruit of the Spirit (Galatians 5:22) and contentedness in all circumstances (Philippians 4:11) will make up for what is lacking, and may even draw your husband's affection back to you.

THE IDOL OF AN INTIMATE MARRIAGE

It took her awhile, but finally Carol got to the point of her phone call. "Vic doesn't love me anymore," she said. "There's no tenderness, no intimacy in our marriage. I can't remember the last time he said 'I love you.'" As we talked, Carol related other symptoms their marriage had grown cold. Vic was a good provider, but he was uncommunicative and self-absorbed. She missed the days when he had been attentive and affectionate. I tried to get her to focus on what was still good in their marriage, but it was clear she had made up her mind. "I don't want to live the rest of my life with a husband who doesn't love me. He doesn't care, so why should I?"

Carol's heart's desire is for an intimate, romantic marriage, where she feels loved, cherished and appreciated. Certainly this is not a sinful desire, as this is God's desire for marriage as well. However, often our desire for sweetness in our marriage can become an idol. We can *set our hearts* on how our husbands make us feel, instead of on serving and worshipping the LORD Jesus. If our desire for something good is more important to us than being obedient to God, it has become a lust or idol.

If we don't get what we want from our husbands, particularly in the area of intimacy, we often look elsewhere to give us those special feelings that are missing with our husbands. Many women turn to other relationships, masturbation, romance novels, soap operas, or romantic movies to meet this need. But none of those things can even come close to God's design for our marriage. Instead of setting your heart on your husband, your deepest desires should be the same as those of the Psalmist in Psalm 119, whose *"soul [was] crushed with longing after Thine ordinances at all times"* (Psalm 119:20†) He longed for and sought after God with all his heart, as all of us should. If you long for God above everything else, you will be fully satisfied by God's presence (Psalm 37:4), even if your desires for earthly things go unfulfilled.

Memorize It!

But whoever keeps His word, in him the love of God has truly been perfected. By this we know that we are in Him: the one who says he abides in Him ought himself to walk in the same manner as He walked.
(1 John 2:5-6)

Spiritual Pride

A man's pride will bring him low, but a humble spirit will obtain honor.
PROVERBS 29:23

Elaine grew up in a good church and was saved at an early age. She met her husband at the restaurant where she waitressed during college; Jacob was a new Christian, but he wanted to please Christ. After they were married, Jacob started his own restaurant, working long hours trying to make it a success. He was a good husband, but his church attendance was spotty and soon he stopped growing spiritually.

Meanwhile, Elaine stayed faithful to church and the Word, and even led a Bible study at their church. Jacob wanted to do right, but he knew very little about the Bible and usually did what was "right in his own eyes" (Proverbs 21:2). So Elaine became their family's spiritual leader, reasoning, *I'm clearly the only one qualified to lead this family spiritually. Jacob doesn't know Chronicles from Corinthians!*

Elaine believed she was more righteous than her husband. It's true she was more obedient, but she lacked humility, and you cannot have righteousness without humility.

Once Elaine became aware of her pride, she began asking God to humble her. Over time, God revealed to her how valuable Jacob was to their family, and how she was not as righteous as she thought—particularly when she was full of pride! Elaine realized that her spiritual "leadership" had actually worked against their family's spiritual well-being. She began submitting herself fully to Jacob's leadership, even in spiritual matters. As she did, God gave Jacob a hunger for His Word. On their tenth anniversary, he told her he was abandoning plans to open another restaurant. "From here on out," he said, "I want to be satisfied with Christ alone."

The only reason you should be the spiritual leader in your home is if your husband is not a Christian. If your husband is saved but disobedient to the Word, your responsibility is to reprove him biblically, not take over his position as the leader. But you must first humble yourself and deal with sin in your own life (Matthew 7:3-5)—including the sin of pride.

Application

It's easy to become proud of our spiritual maturity. The cure is to learn how black and sinful your heart truly is. God says that your heart is *"deceitful above all things and desperately wicked"* (Jeremiah 17:9, NKJV), and that all of your righteousness is as *"filthy rags"* (Isaiah 64:6). Everything good that comes out of you is from Christ, not from any ability of your own (Romans 7:18, 1 Corinthians 1:26-31).

Are you guilty of believing you are more "righteous" than your husband? Even if you are more obedient, spiritual pride will keep you from being righteous and fully submitted to Christ. If pride is a problem in your heart, begin praying daily for God to humble you. That's one prayer to which you will always get a "yes" answer!

Week 21, Day 1

So, as those who have been chosen of God, holy and beloved, put on a heart of compassion, kindness, humility, gentleness and patience; bearing with one another, and forgiving each other, whoever has a complaint against anyone; just as the Lord *forgave you, so also should you.*
Colossians 3:12-13

Application

If you find yourself replaying his sins over and over again in your mind, remember that this is a form of meditation: you are actually "meditating" on evil, rather than on God's Word. Instead, memorize and quote to yourself Philippians 4:8, *"Finally, brethren, whatever is true, whatever is honorable, whatever is right, whatever is pure, whatever is lovely, whatever is of good repute, if there is any excellence and if anything worthy of praise, dwell on these things."* Then take the time to meditate instead on the things your husband has done that are "worthy of praise."

Love Doesn't Keep the Books

A friend of mine was pulling out of his driveway one night when, suddenly, someone walking on the sidewalk stepped right into the path of the car. Fortunately, Jim was driving very slowly, so he was able to stop before hurting the pedestrian. He got out of his car and asked if the man was all right, and the man assured Jim he was fine and had suffered no injury.

Imagine Jim's shock when, six months later, he got a summons to appear in court. Evidently the pedestrian had changed his mind about the event, and was suing Jim for damages.

As awful as that sounds, we often do this to our husbands, don't we? Perhaps it's an annoying little habit of his, a careless word he said, or even an actual sin he committed against us. To keep the peace, we don't say anything about it, or we might even tell our husbands everything is fine. But when there's a conflict, we pull out the books and start reading off everything they've done "wrong" since the wedding!

Some wives keep track of virtually every sin their husbands have ever committed against them, and use that ammunition against him when the time is right. However, love *"does not take into account a wrong suffered"* (1 Corinthians 13:5). A loving wife shows love by not holding onto her bitterness, by forgiving, by not bringing up the past to her husband, and by not replaying bitter thoughts to herself in her mind. Catching herself and correcting her thoughts are a tremendous way to show love.

The time to catch bitter thoughts is when they're born. When your husband does something to irritate you, make you angry or even when he sins against you, take a moment to get alone with God and pray about what your husband did. Ask God to help you forgive. Then, do it! It helps greatly to remember that you are not perfect either. Even if he does something that you would never do, we are all sinners in need of grace.

Memorize It!

Even so consider yourselves to be dead to sin, but alive to God in Christ Jesus. Therefore do not let sin reign in your mortal body so that you obey its lusts. (Romans 6:11-12)

EXAMINE YOUR MOTIVES

For to me, to live is Christ and to die is gain.
PHILIPPIANS 1:21

Sue was walking to her car after the Bible study when she found Paula waiting for her. "I get the feeling you've got something on your mind," she said. Paula burst into tears. "I have learned so much in this study about being a good wife. I've changed the way I do everything! I really am trying to please God."

"So what's the problem?" Sue asked. "The problem is, I've made all these changes, but it's not working!" Paula cried. "My husband is not even close to what he should be." Paula had been encouraged to see how God used Sue's obedience to change her husband; she was sure that if she did the same things, her own husband would respond as Sue's husband had. "I have claimed 1 Peter 3:1, that my husband can be *'won without a word'* by my behavior," she said. "But I am tired of doing everything right, yet it has no effect on him whatsoever."

Paula needs to trust God to change her husband in His time. But the bigger problem is not her impatience or lack of faith; her problem is she is hoping that as she is faithful to His Word, God will transform her husband's life. She is obeying as a way to *earn* something from God.

We all do this. We "*delight (ourselves) in the LORD,*" hoping He will give us "*the desires of [our] heart*" (Psalm 37:4). But what should be our motivation for obedience? Christ said, *"If you love Me, you will keep My commandments"* (John 14:15). 1 Corinthians 10:31 says, "*Whether… you eat or drink or whatever you do, do all to the glory of God.*" Our motivation for obedience should always be a deep love for Christ and a desire to bring glory to God. No other motivation is pleasing to God.

Once you rid yourself of the need to change your husband, you are free to really love and trust Christ as your end goal. You will be a better helper to your husband as you seek God's best for him, rather than your own designs. If he doesn't respond as you would like, you can still have peace and joy in the LORD, knowing that what matters most is that you are pleasing Christ.

Memorize It!

Even so consider yourselves to be dead to sin, but alive to God in Christ Jesus. Therefore do not let sin reign in your mortal body so that you obey its lusts.
(Romans 6:11-12)

Application

Are you ever tempted to stop being obedient, since it's not accomplishing what you had hoped it would? Do you get upset or angry when your husband fails you? If so, your motivation for obedience is not a love for Christ, but attaining what you want. Even if what you want is good, it should not be your motivation.

Christ promises that we will walk with Him in love when we keep his commands (John 15:10). He is faithful, and will always give you everything you need when you follow Him. You won't always get what you want when you serve your husband, but if Christ is the desire of your heart, you will always be rewarded with His presence in your life. And seriously, what more could you want than that?

Week 21, Day 3

There is one who speaks rashly like the thrusts of a sword, but the tongue of the wise brings healing.
PROVERBS 12:18

Application

We most often use rash speech when we are striking back at our husbands for something they've done to hurt us. This is *"returning insult for insult"* (1 Peter 3:9†) and is not following the example of Christ, who *"while being reviled, He did not revile in return; while suffering, He uttered no threats, but kept entrusting Himself to Him who judges righteously"* (1 Peter 2:23†). Our LORD entrusted Himself to God. He did not fight back with evil.

Even while suffering an emotional battering from your husband, you are to look to the LORD Jesus Christ as your example. Instead of wounding your husband, use your tongue wisely, looking for a way to bring healing to the conversation, rather than pain (Proverbs 12:18).

Don't Be Rash

Whitney and Simon were having one of their heated arguments again; this time, it was about the long hours Simon has been putting in at work. "Well, maybe if you didn't *spend* so much, I wouldn't have to work so much!" he said. Whitney was flabbergasted. "Spend so much?! When was the last time I even went to the mall?" she countered.

Simon could see that argument wasn't going anywhere, so he tried another approach. "Besides, Jim really needs me right now, until he hires another salesman..." Whitney interrupted him, "Oh, he'll never hire another salesman as long as he has *you* to be his slave!"

Whitney's rash speech has just totally emasculated her husband. She thinks she's being persuasive, but she's doing exactly the opposite. By speaking rashly and in anger, she has disparaged her husband's intelligence, manhood, leadership, ability to provide—pretty much everything about him. The sad thing is that, being a woman, she has no idea the damage she's done to her husband's heart.

The Bible likens rash speech to *"the thrusts of a sword"* (Proverbs 12:18). Rash words are quick, painful, and deeply wounding to the person receiving them. They can be deadly to a person's spirit and to the relationship. When used in a vengeful way, rash words are often more painful than the original offense. For example, Simon accused Whitney of spending too much money, and in return, she obliterated his masculinity.

If you've ever hurt your husband with rash speech, you may have simply been careless and not realized what you were saying and the effect it would have. But if you were intentionally trying to cause your husband pain, it is likely that you use vengeful words as a way to control him. People who have a desire to be in control often communicate in hurtful ways in order to hamstring their "opponent" (the one threatening their control). It puts the other party at a disadvantage, so the speaker can gain control and get what they want.

Memorize It!

Even so consider yourselves to be dead to sin, but alive to God in Christ Jesus. Therefore do not let sin reign in your mortal body so that you obey its lusts.
(Romans 6:11-12)

The Lust For Fairness

Have this attitude in yourselves which was also in Christ Jesus, who, although He existed in the form of God, did not regard equality with God a thing to be grasped, but emptied Himself, taking the form of a bond-servant...
PHILIPPIANS 2:5-7†

Carly has a highly developed sense of justice. She wants to be treated fairly, and nothing sets her off quicker than feeling she is not being treated as an equal. She's very aware of how much she gives in to her husband and keeps track of her "sacrifices" so she can settle the score down the road. When she and Drew argue, she will not rest until he has heard her viewpoint. "I let you talk," she says. "Now it's my turn."

Carly's need to be treated equally and fairly is simply a fleshly resistance to being humbled in any way. You can imagine that submitting is not easy for her. "Why should he have all the power?" is her justification for frequently assuming control in the home.

Equality and fairness are *virtues* when we treat others fairly and respect them as equals. But these same traits become idols of the heart when we demand them for ourselves. The wife who has this idol in her heart will often sin by "getting even" with her husband. If he buys something he wants, she thinks she's entitled to something she wants. If he spends time with the guys one weekend, she demands equal time with her friends the next weekend. If he hurts her, she hurts him back in some way. She is never willing to suffer loss at the hand of her husband.

As a result of our fallen nature, we are all tempted to lust after equality in our marriages. But this is not God's way for the godly wife. He desires that we be conformed to the image of His Son, which means we must *"have this attitude in yourselves which was also in Christ Jesus"* (Philippians 2:5)—the attitude that equality was not a *"thing to be grasped"* (vs. 6). He did not cling to His right to be equal with God, but rather He *"emptied Himself, taking the form of a bond-servant"* (vs. 7). If Christ, who is equal to God and who *is* God, can humble Himself, surely we, who are humble creatures compared to the beauty and majesty of Christ, have no business trying to lift ourselves up in equality.

Memorize It!

Even so consider yourselves to be dead to sin, but alive to God in Christ Jesus. Therefore do not let sin reign in your mortal body so that you obey its lusts.
(Romans 6:11-12)

Application

Life is not fair to anyone, but it will be especially unfair to those who seek to have the mind of Christ. *"For Christ also died for sins once for all, the just for the unjust, so that He might bring us to God"* (1 Peter 3:18†). He was "just" (sinless), yet He died for the "unjust" (sinners like you and me). He was willing to suffer unjustly for the sake of *your* righteousness, sacrificing Himself without any thought for what was "fair." You, too, should be willing to "suffer for doing what is right" (1 Peter 3:17)—to love and serve your husband, putting his needs first, even if that means that you are not treated fairly.

Week 21, Day 5

For consider your calling, brethren, that there were not many wise according to the flesh, not many mighty, not many noble; but God has chosen the foolish things of the world to shame the wise, and God has chosen the weak things of the world to shame the things which are strong.
1 CORINTHIANS 1:26-27

Application

Does anything in Gloria's personality sound familiar to you? If you believe any of the following statements are true of yourself, you're probably guilty of pride:

- I have a keen ability to understand people and what motivates them.
- I have very good discernment and judgment in most situations.
- I am more intelligent than most people, including my husband.

If you are of measurably high intelligence, the question is, how often do you think about how much smarter you are than most? Do you treat people as though they are less intelligent than you?

"The fear of the LORD is the beginning of wisdom" (Psalm 111:10†). When we fear God, we realize that even our intelligence is a gift from Him to be used for His glory, not to serve ourselves.

You're Not as Think as You Smart You Are

Gloria has always prided herself on her ability to "read" people. Since she's been married to Sam for almost five years, she's certain she knows him like the back of her hand.

But Sam is much more complicated than she realizes, and he doesn't always react predictably. One afternoon, a co-worker came into Sam's office and talked for over an hour about problems in his marriage. Sam tried to encourage him and their talk went well past quitting time. Even though he was running late, Sam left with a new appreciation for his own wife, and he stopped at a florist to get her some flowers.

When he walked in the door forty-five minutes late with an armful of roses, Gloria immediately assumed the flowers were an apology. "They're nice" she said coolly. "But they don't get you off the hook." He was hurt—not only that she wasn't more enthusiastic about the beautiful bouquet he'd picked out, but also that she assumed he had done something wrong.

Gloria's problem is pride: she assumes she knows her husband's every thought and she judges his motives. She's argumentative, believing she is right about everything. Instead of always thinking the best of Sam, she is presumptuous and quick to jump to negative conclusions, and she is convinced she's right, because she's such a "good judge of character."

God wants you to assume the best of your husband at all times. Only He knows everything that is going on in your husband's life; He alone can read your husband's mind and judge the motives of your husband's heart. You are not omniscient, and your husband may surprise you. Even if you are very intelligent, you don't know everything. You can be wrong, and should always allow for that very real possibility.

If you want to be wise, then seek humility. *"When pride comes, then comes dishonor, but with the humble is wisdom"* (Proverbs 11:2). Wisdom is better than intelligence, because wisdom is rooted in humility, whereas intelligence and cunning are often fuel for a proud heart.

IDOLIZING YOUR KIDS

Nora and Peggy are both trying to raise successful children, but their approaches are quite different. Nora's four kids are excellent athletes, and their entire family life revolves around sports. They've spent a great deal of time and money fostering their kids' athleticism, and it's paid off: her oldest son has a full-ride basketball scholarship to an elite college, and they are sure the others will have some type of sports scholarship when their time comes.

Peggy's three kids are not at all athletic, but they excel in other ways. Their mom is very strict on their dress, behavior, and speech, and it's all "yes, ma'am" and "no, sir" at their house. When they come home from school, they do their homework immediately, and Peggy goes over every assignment. Their performance at church is of equal concern to her. They consistently win awards in Bible club for Scripture memorization and their Sunday school teachers all love them. All three kids are in the gifted program at school, and you will not find three more well-behaved children in your life.

Which of these women is an idol worshipper? You might think it's Nora, who has put athletic performance above godly concerns. However, neither of these women focus on their relationship with Christ nearly as much as they focus on how well their children are performing. Their lust for "perfect" children is based on the "pride of life" (1 John 2:16) and exceeds their love for God. Because they have their children on the throne of their hearts instead of God, both women are idol worshippers.

Just as we may lust after having a perfect marriage with a godly husband (p. 90), we can also desire well-behaved, perfect children more than we desire God. If we are investing more of ourselves in achieving a certain level of "success" for our children than we do in knowing and following Christ, then we are worshipping an idol—even if we are trying to mold them into what God wants them to be.

Memorize It!

And do not go on presenting the members of your body to sin as instruments of unrighteousness; but present yourselves to God as those alive from the dead, and your members as instruments of righteousness to God.
(Romans 6:13)

Do not love the world nor the things in the world. If anyone loves the world, the love of the Father is not in him. For all that is in the world, the lust of the flesh and the lust of the eyes and the boastful pride of life, is not from the Father, but is from the world. The world is passing away, and also its lusts; but the one who does the will of God lives forever.
1 JOHN 2:15-17

Application

See Appendix B for the Assessment, "How to tell if your desire for successful children is an idol."

It's easy for our kids to take over the throne of our hearts, because we are so wrapped up in raising them and making sure they succeed in life. You have a responsibility to raise your children up in the *"discipline and instruction of the LORD"* (Ephesians 6:4) and to teach them God's commands (Deuteronomy 6:6-7). But being obsessed with them is not the way to guarantee they "turn out well." What you should desire above all else is that they love the LORD with all their heart, soul, mind and strength. They are more likely to do this if they see you loving Him passionately, and if they know that Jesus Christ is mom's greatest heart's desire.

Week 22, Day 2

Do nothing from selfishness or empty conceit, but with humility of mind regard one another as more important than yourselves.
PHILIPPIANS 2:3

Application

Selfishly pushing to get your own way may get you what you want, but the cost to your relationship with your husband, and with God, will be high. Think back to a time when you won an argument and got what you wanted. Now ask yourself: Was that vacation/car/paint color, etc. worth the damage done to your marriage? Was it worth displeasing Christ?

If you believe you never get your own way, that your husband is so selfish that he always wins, then you need to pray about biblically reproving him for selfishness. But be very cautious: selfishness is so firmly rooted in our hearts, it is often difficult to recognize. Make sure that reproving him is not just your way of getting what you want.

NATURALLY SELFISH

I'm having a bit of a writer's block, because my task for the moment is to write about Selfishness as a Cause of Conflict. This is rather like saying, "Give a history of Russia in 500 words or less." Ridding our hearts of selfishness is really what this entire book is about. We wouldn't need a book like this if we were naturally selfless.

But we're not. We're naturally selfish, and most of the conflict in our marriages is due to our insistence on satisfying ourselves, getting what we want—our *own way*.

We wives frequently accuse our husbands of selfishness, but that's because *their* desires often interfere with *our* desires. Whoever wins (gets what they want) is thereafter called *selfish*, but the reality is that in most cases, both were being selfish. For instance, he wants a new grill, she wants a new kitchen table; she wants to go to a beach resort, he wants to go camping. If either party pushes their agenda to the point of getting angry, arguing, pouting, manipulating, nagging, or disregarding the other person, they've gone beyond *thinking* selfishly to *acting* selfishly. The attitude of their hearts has worked its way into sinful behavior. *"Then when lust has conceived, it gives birth to sin"* (James 1:15†).

Whenever you and your husband have a conflict, you must first determine whether or not selfishness—either yours or your husband's—is a root cause. If you are being selfish, your husband may react more to your attitude than to what you actually want. So it is important that you change your heart to *"put on love, which is the perfect bond of unity"* (Colossians 3:14†). If your husband is being selfish, you may have to reprove him biblically—in a spirit of gentleness, of course. Remind him that *"love...does not seek its own"* (1 Corinthians 13:5†). If your conflict is due to both of you wanting your own way, you can resolve the conflict peacefully when each decides that preserving unity, obeying Christ, and loving each other is more important than anything else.

Memorize It!

And do not go on presenting the members of your body to sin as instruments of unrighteousness; but present yourselves to God as those alive from the dead, and your members as instruments of righteousness to God.
(Romans 6:13)

Sanctification: Helping Each Other

Angela and Matt sat on the couch for their bi-weekly Bible study time. Today they were studying Romans 12, and after they discussed the passage, Matt asked Angela, "So how do you think I'm doing in obeying these truths?"

"Well, I think you are very devoted to me and the kids," she said. "So for us, you are definitely living out verse 10, *'Be devoted to one another in...love.'* However, sometimes you lack that same devotion when it comes to our church family." She went on to gently explain how he could sometimes be judgmental toward other believers, and did not *"give preference to one another in honor"* (verse 10). After they discussed how he could change, Angela asked Matt, "So how am I doing?" It always made her nervous to ask that question, because it was still hard to hear her husband reprove her for her sin. But she was definitely better at handling his reproof than she used to be.

Matt and Angela are actively involved in helping each other become more conformed to the image of Christ—in other words, mutual sanctification. Since they started this regular Bible study time together, their marriage has grown more intimate and satisfying. Angela feels that she is finally living in harmony with her husband and that their marriage glorifies the Lord Jesus. Both of them say they wish they'd started this a lot sooner.

Not only does God want you to be like His Son, but he wants you to help your husband become more like Christ as well. If you love God, you will obey His command to participate in and submit to the process of mutual sanctification. Hebrews 12:11 says that *"all discipline for the moment seems not to be joyful, but sorrowful; yet to those who have been trained by it, afterwards it yields the peaceful fruit of righteousness."* If you are not used to working on your sin with your husband this way, you may find it is not a pleasant thing at first. But it will get easier as you practice it, and God promises that it will yield peace and righteousness in your life.

Memorize It!

And do not go on presenting the members of your body to sin as instruments of unrighteousness; but present yourselves to God as those alive from the dead, and your members as instruments of righteousness to God.
(Romans 6:13)

Brethren, even if anyone is caught in any trespass, you who are spiritual, restore such a one in a spirit of gentleness; each one looking to yourself, so that you too will not be tempted. Bear one another's burdens, and thereby fulfill the law of Christ.
Galatians 6:1-2

Application

This is God's purpose in marriage: for you and your husband to help each other become more like Christ so that you can glorify Him more. If you do not have a regular time of studying God's Word together, you can ask your husband to consider doing a Bible study with you. You could then suggest the following simple steps:

- Prepare your heart in advance to both give and receive instruction in humility.
- Read a short passage together, then discuss what you each think it means. Use a study Bible or commentary for help if needed.
- Identify all of the commands in the passage.
- Ask your husband how he thinks you are doing in obeying those commands, and what sins are currently in your life that are contrary to this Scripture.
- Be ready to give him an answer to the same question.

Week 22, Day 4

An excellent wife, who can find? For her worth is far above jewels. The heart of her husband trusts in her, and he will have no lack of gain...She looks well to the ways of her household, and does not eat the bread of idleness.
PROVERBS 31:10-11, 27

Application

How are you doing in the house "keeping" department? Are you using submission as an excuse for laziness? When your husband comes home from work (or comes out of his home office), is your home peaceful and lacking in stress and chaos? Or do you keep piles of laundry around, dirty dishes in the sink, and dust so thick everyone can write on the furniture?

If you're feeling overwhelmed in this area, it may be because you haven't really "owned" the responsibility, and you're hoping someone will come to your rescue. Today is the day to renew your commitment to God and your husband that, no matter what your other responsibilities may be, *you* will keep your home clean, and create an environment where your family can relax and enjoy each other.

Submission: Not an Excuse

I know a woman who had taken the concept of *submission* to mean that her husband makes *all* the decisions—right down to what kind of laundry detergent they should use. Every time I asked for her thoughts on a decision facing their family, she claimed to have no opinion. He did all the grocery shopping, because she would not make food-buying decisions. She waited until he was home to clean the house, so that he could help and it would be done the way he liked it.

What my friend was doing was not submission; it was either laziness or else a gross misinterpretation of God's commands. At first her husband enjoyed the power trip, but eventually the weight of all these decisions began to drag him down. I encouraged her to work with her husband to make a list of those responsibilities he wanted to "hand down" to her. Then, she needed to accept them as her own, without the need to constantly check with him for approval.

Your husband is in charge of the family, but you are to be the "keeper" of the home (Titus 2:5, KJV), the one mainly responsible for cleaning, cooking and taking care of the children. If he wants to help, great! But make sure you are doing the lion's share of the work. If your man is controlling in that area, gently remind him that the home is your responsibility—then make sure you're doing it in a way that glorifies God and pleases your husband. Remember that your job is to be your husband's helper, making his load lighter, not heavier.

In Proverbs 31, we see the excellent wife taking charge of the home. She makes clothing; she plants, gathers and prepares food; she helps the poor and needy. She engages in commerce, and takes care of all of the people in her household. She stays in shape (vs. 17), and is a kind, spiritual mentor to her children and to others (vs. 26). She is not lazy: *"She looks well to the ways of her household, and does not eat the bread of idleness"* (vs. 27). Does this sound like the kind of woman who lets her husband make all the decisions and do everything?

Memorize It!

And do not go on presenting the members of your body to sin as instruments of unrighteousness; but present yourselves to God as those alive from the dead, and your members as instruments of righteousness to God.
(Romans 6:13)

Laziness vs. Self-Discipline

This is one lesson I was not looking forward to writing, because being self-disciplined has always been a struggle for me. I actually like creating a nice home, and my house usually looks good because I enjoy cleaning. But, I'm not disciplined at it. If I'm not in the mood, I'll find a thousand other things to do first. I don't do it out of discipline; I do it for my own pleasure.

Today's passage from Proverbs 6 paints a vivid picture contrasting the lazy person with the disciplined person. The truth is that if you are not disciplined, you are lazy. I've looked for another word to soften the blow, to make us all feel better about our lack of discipline and self-motivation, but *indolent, idle, sluggish* and *slothful* don't sound very appealing either! The Bible puts it this way: *"He also who is slack in his work is brother to him who destroys"* (Proverbs 18:9).

Staying on top of your responsibilities and keeping your home orderly takes discipline to do it consistently. The best illustration I can think of for a disciplined person is someone in the military. A soldier must be disciplined, and laziness is never tolerated in the armed forces. This is so that the unit can run smoothly and efficiently and operate at peak effectiveness in battle.

Your home and family are like a military unit, and if you, the Commanding Officer, are lazy and undisciplined, the unit will not be effective in battle for Christ. Your home may be in order in some areas, but other areas will suffer. No one can keep up with everything that needs to be done unless they are disciplined. My house is clean, but I know that other areas have suffered because of my lack of self discipline. I'm confessing this to you now, knowing that this is an area I am still working on, and trusting Christ that He will give me victory in this as I yield myself to Him day after day.

Go to the ant, O sluggard, observe her ways and be wise, which, having no chief, officer or ruler, prepares her food in the summer and gathers her provision in the harvest. How long will you lie down, O sluggard? When will you arise from your sleep? "A little sleep, a little slumber, a little folding of the hands to rest"—Your poverty will come in like a vagabond and your need like an armed man.

Proverbs 6:6-11

Application

I've taught my children this adage to help them manage their time during the day, and it's one that I have to remind myself of when I'm tempted to slack off on my responsibilities:

Do what you MUST
Then what you SHOULD
Then what you WANT.

If you were raised to be self-disciplined, take time now to thank God for parents who instilled this virtue in you. However, many of us have to work at becoming more disciplined. If the latter describes you, write out Proverbs 31:27—*"She looks well to the ways of her household, and does not eat the bread of idleness"*—and post it someplace where you will see it throughout the day to remind yourself to be disciplined in your work.

Week 23, Day 1

Nevertheless let every one of you in particular so love his wife even as himself; and the wife see that she reverence her husband.
EPHESIANS 5:33 KJV

Application

Are you so awestruck by your husband you almost *gasp* when you see him? That sounds a little ridiculous—especially if you've just looked up and found him asleep on the couch, his mouth hanging open and his belly peeking out from under his shirt! But a sense of awe is the idea behind the word *reverence*. Many of us start out that way when we're first married. Unfortunately, we can get so used to our husbands we forget God's admonition to treat our husbands as someone special.

Ask God today to help you see your husband with new eyes, through the lens of God's Word. *"Let…the wife see that she reverence her husband"* (Ephesians 5:33, KJV).

REVERENTIAL AWE

The crowd fidgeted in their chairs as the auctioneer held up the next item for bid: a dust-covered violin and bow. "How much will you bid for this old fiddle?" the auctioneer asked. Slowly, the bidding reached five dollars, then eight, then ten. "Going once!" the auctioneer cried as he raised his gavel.

Suddenly an old man appeared at his side, tugging on his sleeve. He whispered something in the auctioneer's ear, and the auctioneer smiled. The old man took the fiddle and wiped it down with a cloth as the curious crowd looked on. Then he raised the instrument to his chin and began playing the sweetest, most beautiful music they had ever heard. As he finished, the auctioneer stepped up to the microphone and announced, "Now how much will you bid for this magnificent violin?"

You may have heard that story before and know that the violin went on to be sold for a large sum of money. But what was the difference between the $10 fiddle and the $10,000 violin? As the story goes, the difference was the "touch of the Master's hand." But the bottom line is that the audience gained new respect for the instrument when they understood its true worth.

Respecting your husband is seeing him as a $10,000 violin, rather than a $10 fiddle. In Ephesians 5:33 the Holy Spirit says *"the wife must see to it that she respects her husband."* The King James version uses the word "reverence" here, and that might actually be a better translation. *Revere* comes from the Greek word *phobeo* which means "to be frightened or alarmed." It can also mean "to be in awe of, to treat as special." The idea is that you are in awe of your husband; that you see him as so special you are afraid to treat him as anything less than awe-inspiring.

Memorize It!

Be anxious for nothing, but in everything by prayer and supplication with thanksgiving let your requests be made known to God. And the peace of God, which surpasses all comprehension, will guard your hearts and your minds in Christ Jesus. (Philippians 4:6-7)

Love Doesn't Rejoice in Unrighteousness

(Love) does not rejoice in unrighteousness, but rejoices with the truth.
1 Corinthians 13:6

There are many ways a wife can rejoice in unrighteousness. When her husband hurts her, she can delight in punishing him with her words or giving him the cold shoulder. She can be secretly pleased when he fails in a spiritual issue, because his failure gives her an excuse to not submit to him. Or she can try to draw him into her own sinful life patterns so that she doesn't have to change her ways.

All of these are ways of "rejoicing in unrighteousness," and from time to time I have practiced each one.

For many years, I did not encourage my husband to grow spiritually because I was afraid that if he were walking the narrow path, I would have to as well. And frankly, I did not want to. I liked the way we were: each doing our own thing, with the freedom to live life the way I wanted to live it. I had so much unaddressed sin in my life that the thought of having to submit to a godly husband was frightening to me.

I have a feeling I am not alone. Over the years I've talked to many women who are running from righteousness. Today is a good day to examine whether this may be true in your life as well. Do you encourage your husband's relationship with Christ, or do you keep trying to drag him down to your level? Does your heart sing when he shows signs of spiritual maturity, or are you secretly a little disappointed or even scared?

A loving wife not only deals with the sin in her life, but also does not entice, influence, or provoke her husband to sin. She certainly does not rejoice when he fails! Hebrews 10:24 says that we are to *"spur one another on toward love and good deeds."* The most loving thing you can do as a wife is to pray for and encourage your husband to be righteous.

Application

Take time right now to pray for your husband's relationship with Christ, that he would be fully submitted to God's will. (Even if your husband is not a Christian, you can still pray this prayer, because being submitted starts at salvation.) If you don't already, ask your husband if the two of you can start praying together every day, either in the morning when you first get up or at night when you go to sleep. There is no better way to encourage each other toward righteousness than to pray with and for each other every day.

Memorize It!

Be anxious for nothing, but in everything by prayer and supplication
with thanksgiving let your requests be made known to God.
And the peace of God, which surpasses all comprehension,
will guard your hearts and your minds in Christ Jesus.
(Philippians 4:6-7)

Week 23, Day 3

Be anxious for nothing, but in everything by prayer and supplication with thanksgiving let your requests be made known to God.
PHILIPPIANS 4:6

Application

As someone who once struggled with anxiety, I am privileged by God, through this "thorn in the flesh," to have gained a deeper understanding of this crippling way of thinking. Tomorrow I will share with you what years of struggle and God's Word have taught me—and go over a game plan for ridding yourself of worry and anxiety.

For now, hold onto this truth: God asks you to fear Him, for He holds your life in His hands. But He is also the One who loves you more than anyone possibly can, and who has promised never to leave or forsake you. He alone has the power to quiet the storms, both without and within. *"Even though I walk through the valley of the shadow of death, I fear no evil, for You are with me"* (Psalm 23:4†).

Fear, Anxiety and Worry, Oh My! (Part 1)

Holly sat in the bathtub, watching the water rise. It was 3:30 a.m., and she had awakened feeling panicked and nauseated. She tried to pray her feelings away, but nothing calmed her nerves like a warm bath. Lost in her thoughts, she almost didn't notice when her husband walked into the bathroom.

"Another attack?" Evan asked. Holly gave him a weak smile and closed her eyes. The frustrating thing was she had no real reason to be anxious. Her life was stressful, but no worse than others. She had regular checkups and so far, she was healthy. But that didn't keep her from worrying. Her sister died of cancer when Holly was a teen, and even when she wasn't actively worrying about her health, the tiniest sign that something might be wrong would send her into an anxiety tailspin.

Panic and anxiety are physical responses to fear. We all have fears. Wives particularly fear a variety of possibilities: that something bad will happen to their husband or children, financial troubles and loss of security, natural disasters, their husbands leaving them, health issues, etc.

Fear is a God-given emotion that is vital to our protection. If you were completely fearless, you would not have the healthy respect you need to keep yourself and your family safe. But when normal fear is exaggerated, focusing on the negative potential of the future, anxiety results. It's an overreaction to life's uncertainties.

The Bible warns us not to fear the future or other men, but to channel our fear into the only Person we should ever fear, and that is God Almighty. *"Do not fear those who kill the body but are unable to kill the soul; but rather fear Him who is able to destroy both soul and body in hell"* (Matthew 10:28). When you fear God as you should, focusing all of your fears and anxieties into Him, you will find that He is more than capable of calming your fears and managing your future.

Memorize It!

Be anxious for nothing, but in everything by prayer and supplication with thanksgiving let your requests be made known to God. And the peace of God, which surpasses all comprehension, will guard your hearts and your minds in Christ Jesus.
(Philippians 4:6-7)

Fear, Anxiety and Worry, Oh My! (Part 2)

Week 23, Day 4

And the peace of God, which surpasses all comprehension, will guard your hearts and your minds in Christ Jesus.
Philippians 4:7

Take a moment to evaluate your anxiety level. Do you have panic attacks, phobias or suffer from hypochondria? Are you nervous, or does the fear of harm or failure keep you from doing what you want or need to do? Do you worry about the future, your children, your husband, financial security? Now give yourself a number from 1 to 10 that you feel matches your level of anxiety, with 1 being no worry at all and 10 being the maximum panic and anxiety. Write that number here: _____

If you wrote a 1 or 2 in that space, praise God that He has given you His peace...but keep reading, because you may find that even though you're a naturally calm and positive person, you're still not being obedient to those things which make for peace (Romans 14:19).

If you wrote a 3 or higher in that space, I want to assure you that you can get that number down to a 1. A life of fear is not the life God wants for you, and He has provided a "way of escape" from worry (1 Corinthians 10:13). But that way is not easy; it is often easier for us just to suffer with our anxiety, hoping that medication or a change in our circumstances will make it go away.

Ready? Let's get started on the **Steps to Overcoming Fear and Anxiety**:

Saturate yourself in God's Word. Read it daily, meditate on it, and memorize verses that remind you of God's power and His presence. If you struggle with anxiety, some recommended verses are Psalm 119:165; 2 Timothy 1:7; Psalm 23:4; Psalm 56:4; Psalm 34:4; Matthew 10:28; Proverbs 3:21-26; and 1 John 4:18.

Obey God's Word. It's not enough to quote verses to yourself if you are not living them out in your life.

Be diligent to meet your responsibilities. This is one of the biggest things that causes stress for women, resulting in fear and anxiety: the guilt that comes from not doing what we know we're supposed to do, such as keeping the house, being honest with our husbands, or guiding our children. The temptation when you're stressed is to kick back and pamper yourself, but that only leads to more guilt and more stress.

Memorize It!

Be anxious for nothing, but in everything by prayer and supplication with thanksgiving let your requests be made known to God. And the peace of God, which surpasses all comprehension, will guard your hearts and your minds in Christ Jesus. (Philippians 4:6-7)

Application

Give yourself time. I've covered less than half of the steps to living a worry-free life (we'll get to the rest tomorrow), but you can see already that these are not quick fixes. You most likely have struggled with fear and anxiety for years, so the problem will not be cured overnight. But I want to end with one more step:

Pray. Prayer alone will not help you overcome anxiety, but prayer keeps your thoughts focused on Christ, enlists God's help in overcoming worry, and reminds you of your responsibility to work on the other areas of your life that promote peace. *"Be anxious for nothing, but in everything by prayer and supplication with thanksgiving let your requests be made known to God"* (Philippians 4:6).

Week 23, Day 5

Finally, brethren, whatever is true, whatever is honorable, whatever is right, whatever is pure, whatever is lovely, whatever is of good repute, if there is any excellence and if anything worthy of praise, dwell on these things.
PHILIPPIANS 4:8

Application

Trust God to give you peace. Whether you are worried about a very small matter or experiencing an overwhelming crisis, if you faithfully follow all of these steps, God will give you peace. His peace is supernatural and not dependent on your circumstances. There is no way you can have fear, worry or anxiety if you are thinking, acting, and trusting God according to His Word. You will be able to say that, on the "Anxiety vs. Peace" scale (see yesterday's lesson), you are a 1!

One suggestion for overcoming fear with love is to find someone who struggles with fear and anxiety, and lovingly serve them by sharing these steps to overcoming fear. As you disciple them in this way, you will learn these truths better yourself.

Fear, Anxiety and Worry, Oh My! (Part 3)

Today we're continuing with the STEPS TO OVERCOMING FEAR AND ANXIETY.

Make wise decisions. Wisdom is the ability to apply God's truth to life situations. When you make wise decisions, your life will be easier, you will sleep better and you will not be afraid. The LORD will be your confidence. If you are not wise, you make life unnecessarily difficult for yourself.

Don't neglect your body. Eat a balanced diet, exercise regularly, lose weight if you need to. Turn off the TV, and get active. If you're worried about your health, get a checkup. If you have a current medical condition, be faithful in following the necessary treatment, and trust God to either heal you or give you the grace to praise Him no matter how serious your illness.

Think thoughts that are grateful, true, right, pure and honorable. When you "renew your mind" (Romans 12:2) with thoughts that please God, you will focus on what is true, rather than what is not true. Anxiety comes from worrying about the future, and you don't know what the future will bring. Here is an example of true thoughts that honor God when a wife is going through a conflict with her husband:

> *"This is scary, but I'm going to do the right thing and God will give me the grace to get through it. If I have to feel anxious, so be it; but I am going to obey God and show love to my husband no matter what. My responsibility is to do what is right. God will give me grace and wisdom when I need it."*

Overcome your fear with love. Concentrate on showing love to God by obeying His Word whether you feel like it or not; and to others by being patient, kind, etc. (1 Corinthians 13:4). Fear keeps an eye on the consequences to self, but love looks for opportunities to give. Love "believes all things" and "thinks no evil" (1 Corinthians 13:5-7, NKJV); fear is highly suspicious and thinks of nothing *but* evil. When you think about yourself, your fear escalates; but when you love and serve others, your fear will subside.

Submission Impossible

Caitlyn and Rob decided early on that they wanted to homeschool their children. However, when the time came for their son to start kindergarten, Rob's parents insisted on paying for him to go to an exclusive private school. Caitlyn worried about the influence the other kids would have on her son, and was convinced that giving her children a Bible-based education was the only right thing to do.

Rob, however, was not as committed to homeschooling as his wife was. After months of discussion, he finally decided to take his parents up on their offer. Caitlyn continued to argue with him, but he would not change his mind. "The only reason he's doing this," she cried to her friend one day, "is because he can't say no to his parents. But what he's doing is just *wrong*!"

Submitting to your husband is not always easy. Sometimes his desires may go against your own intelligence, personal standards, preferences, or convictions. In Caitlyn's case, she was convinced putting their kids in a non-Christian school was a sin. But she eventually realized that she was leaning more on the "commandments of men" (Matthew 15:9, NKJV) than on a direct command of God. She was using the "unless he asks you to sin" clause as an excuse to get what she wanted.

The Bible says "*it is better to live in a corner of a roof than in a house shared with a contentious woman*" (Proverbs 21:9). It's easy to become argumentative or whiny when things don't go our way. But sometimes we have to accept that everything is not going to be just as we like it, and when our kids are involved, it becomes especially difficult to submit. We often feel we know more about what's best for our kids than our husbands do. But of all the things you want to give your children, the best thing you can give them is a godly example of submission and a great marriage for them to model. Obedience to Christ, peace in the home, and peace between you and your husband should be your number one priority.

Memorize It!

Finally, brethren, whatever is true, whatever is honorable, whatever is right, whatever is pure, whatever is lovely, whatever is of good repute, if there is any excellence and if anything worthy of praise, dwell on these things. (Philippians 4:8)

Wives, be subject to your own husbands, as to the Lord. For the husband is the head of the wife, as Christ also is the head of the church, He Himself being the Savior of the body. But as the church is subject to Christ, so also the wives ought to be to their husbands in everything.
Ephesians 5:22-24

Application

Every conflict between you and your husband should be examined in the light of God's Word to determine what is really going on. If you're holding your ground based on what you believe is right, you must determine if what your husband wants is a *sin*—not just an unwise course of action. If you're unsure, search the Scriptures and get biblical advice from a pastor or godly woman.

If you are passionate about what you want, your passion may be clouding your judgment, and your desire may have become an idol in your heart. If sin is not an issue, then set aside your preferences and ask God to give you the grace to joyfully accept your husband's decision. Even if your idea was "better," your willful obedience is God's priority above everything else.

Week 24, Day 2

Come to Me, all who are weary and heavy-laden, and I will give you rest. Take My yoke upon you and learn from Me, for I am gentle and humble in heart, and you will find rest for your souls. For My yoke is easy and My burden is light.
MATTHEW 11:28-30

Application

Living righteously can be a tough, lonely road, but *God is always looking out for you*. Even if your husband is not living as he should, don't give up! *Giving up* is actually *giving in* to Satan, whose main objective is to get you to live separately from God.

Remember that Christ has made you certain promises. You can remind yourself of some of these promises by memorizing today's Scripture: "*Come to Me, all who are weary and heavy-laden, and I will give you rest. Take My yoke upon you and learn from Me, for I am gentle and humble in heart, and you will find rest for your souls. For My yoke is easy and My burden is light*" (Matthew 11:28-30).

His Part

When Valerie completed *The Excellent Wife* Bible study, she felt strong, full of hope, and ready to do all that she'd learned in the class. And for a few months, things went really well. She had a good attitude and was committed to putting her husband first before herself.

But as the months wore on, Valerie grew tired and discouraged. James was moody and often spoke to her rudely or impatiently. Things would go along fine for a few days, then suddenly they would be arguing again. The tension in their home was palpable, and their love life suffered. She knew it was selfish, but she was tired of being the only one trying to live righteously. She often prayed, "What about me, LORD? When do *my* needs get met?"

God has commanded your husband to live with you *"in an understanding way"* (1 Peter 3:7), and to love you sacrificially, as Christ loves the Church (Ephesians 5:25). If he's not doing that; if he's living selfishly and not considering your needs; if he's demanding, angry, or self-centered; then he is living in sin. As your husband's "suitable helper," how should you respond?

If you try to hold him accountable for loving you biblically, you can come across as self-centered and demanding. However, as your husband's helper, you must allow God to use you in the process of sanctification. In other words, you may have to *reprove* your husband if he is not living biblically—even if his sin is failing to sacrifice for you. But it is very important to remember that ***the purpose of reproving your husband is not to get your own way.*** The purpose is to help your husband be restored to a right relationship with God by helping him live in obedience to God's commands.

We have talked throughout this book about giving a biblical reproof. For now, I just want to remind you that God knows everything that is happening in your life, and He has made provisions for you. He has spelled out in His Word the steps you can take if your husband is falling down on the job.

Memorize It!

Finally, brethren, whatever is true, whatever is honorable, whatever is right, whatever is pure, whatever is lovely, whatever is of good repute, if there is any excellence and if anything worthy of praise, dwell on these things.
(Philippians 4:8)

Gentleness & Self-Control

But the wisdom from above is first pure, then peaceable, gentle, reasonable, full of mercy and good fruits, unwavering, without hypocrisy.
James 3:17

My friend Michelle was at our house one day with Riley, our neighbor's 18-month-old son whom she was babysitting. While we talked, Riley found a knick-knack that wasn't appropriate for him to play with. So Michelle seized the teachable moment. "Riley, let's put it back. *Gentle*," she said, as she guided him to gently set the breakable item back on the shelf. Riley looked at us, then set it down very carefully as Michelle repeated the word "gentle" to him. Both of us praised him excessively for being gentle, which of course made him want to pick it up and set it down several more times, as we repeated "gentle" and clapped excitedly each time he did it successfully.

Riley was learning *gentleness*, which requires *self-control*—both of which are essential for conflict resolution in marriage.

You've probably heard it said that gentleness is "strength under control." When you and your husband are in the heat of a conflict, you will likely feel strong emotions. A person who is controlled by their emotions may think they are demonstrating strength—that they're a "force to be reckoned with"—but they're actually proving they are too weak to control themselves. And sometimes we *choose* to be "out of control" in an attempt to manipulate our husbands with our emotions. We think we have to overreact; to put the hurricane force of our emotions behind our request in order to get his attention or make him give in to us.

Strong emotions are not innately sinful, but if we're using them sinfully to accomplish our own objectives, then we are not demonstrating gentleness. 1 Peter 3:4 says that we are to adorn ourselves with gentleness (meekness) which is *"precious in the sight of God."* When you're having a conflict with your husband, God will bless you in many ways if you demonstrate tenderness and compassion toward your man. Those blessings may not include getting what you want in the conflict, but your character will grow to be more like the Lord Jesus.

Application

Self-control is a discipline we need to practice, much as Riley practiced controlling his urge to slam that knick-knack down on the shelf. The opposite of being gentle is to be hard, harsh, sarcastic, or hysterical—as opposed to being careful, thoughtful, and calm under pressure.

Gentleness and self-control are both fruits of the Spirit (Galatians 5:23) that we are to pursue (1 Timothy 6:11). While you and your husband are in the midst of a conflict is not the time to start learning gentleness. It is much easier to call it up in the heat of battle if you are consistently working on being gentle and self-controlled every day of your life. Ask God to help you be more gentle in how you relate to your husband and to others today and every day.

Memorize It!

Finally, brethren, whatever is true, whatever is honorable, whatever is right, whatever is pure, whatever is lovely, whatever is of good repute, if there is any excellence and if anything worthy of praise, dwell on these things. (Philippians 4:8)

Week 24, Day 4

He who is slow to anger is better than the mighty, and he who rules his spirit, than he who captures a city.
PROVERBS 16:32

Application

We tell ourselves we're just being "honest" by saying what we're thinking and expressing our anger, but Scripture calls this what it is: foolishness. *"A fool does not delight in understanding, but only in revealing his own mind"* (Proverbs 18:2). Instead, we are to be wise and forgiving. *"He who is slow to anger has great understanding, but he who is quick-tempered exalts folly"* (Proverbs 14:29).

The following passages have great insight on the subject of anger. Look up each one of these and do a five-minute study on the effects of, and the godly alternatives to, anger: Psalm 37:8, Proverbs 15:18, Proverbs 16:32, Proverbs 19:11, Ephesians 4:26-32 and Colossians 3:8.

Ungodly Responses to Anger

Ruth stood staring at her husband in shocked disbelief. In his hand was a brochure and a receipt for a brand new 20-foot ski boat. "We talked about this!" she cried. "We agreed we don't have the money for this right now!"

"We did?" Vince said. "I don't remember that." Ruth could feel her anger rising, so she just turned and left the room. She knew if she didn't, she would end up yelling at him, and she was trying to work on not being so angry. Still, she had to vent to someone! She picked up the phone and called her friend Janet. As soon as Janet answered, Ruth launched into it. "Oh my word, you will never guess what my husband did!" For the next forty minutes, she ranted about her husband and his lack of responsibility. When they finally hung up, she turned around and found Vince looking at her. "Are you done gossiping about me?" he asked.

Because Ruth chose a sinful, rather than a God-honoring, expression for her anger, she has compounded her sin and guilt and hurt her husband deeply. She has also "defiled" her friend Janet with her bitterness (Hebrews 12:15). Venting is something we often choose to do because we think keeping our thoughts bottled up inside will just make things worse. But the exact opposite is the truth. Jesus said that *"the things that proceed out of the mouth come from the heart, and those defile the man"* (Matthew 15:18). If you have anger in your heart, and you let those angry thoughts come out of your mouth, you are not freeing yourself from those thoughts. You are, in fact, reinforcing them and "defiling" yourself with your words.

God's prescription for an angry heart is not to vent or give expression to the anger, but to "subdue" it by replacing bitter, angry thoughts with kind and forgiving thoughts. One of the fruits of the Spirit is self-control, not more expression. When you get angry with your husband, do you vent your frustration to him or to others, or do you give it to God and allow His Spirit to control your thoughts about the matter?

Memorize It!

Finally, brethren, whatever is true, whatever is honorable, whatever is right, whatever is pure, whatever is lovely, whatever is of good repute, if there is any excellence and if anything worthy of praise, dwell on these things. (Philippians 4:8)

GRACEFUL WORDS

Week 24, Day 5

The wise in heart will be called discerning, and sweetness of speech increases persuasiveness.
PROVERBS 16:21

My husband has a rule that has taken me about 25 years to get used to: we *never* wear shoes or go barefoot in the house. We have to have slippers or clean socks. (Foot oils = bad for carpets.) Now if it has taken me this long to get in step with the rule, I can only imagine what it is like for visitors.

Not too long ago, I decided that one of our Kingdom callings was to be more hospitable...which means, making people feel welcome in our home. I really felt like the no-shoes rule was a hindrance to this, as many people are uncomfortable taking their shoes off, and I'm uncomfortable asking them, "Hey, can I check out your socks?" So I approached my husband with the proposal that, for visitors only, we give them the choice of leaving their shoes on if they so desired.

I've tried this several times in the past—about once every five years, I would say. In fact, for the first five years of marriage I refused to wear socks or slippers in the house, as I was a barefoot kind of girl. Each successive time we discussed it, I took a different approach: guilt, manipulation, anger—you name it, I tried them all! It was only the last time I asked that I actually had a *godly* motive. And I found that when my motives were right, my speech was much more God-honoring. I was able to be forbearing (understanding) and sweet, and we had a good talk not just about shoes and foot oils, but also about how to use our possessions for the Kingdom of Christ.

Proverbs 25:15 says, "*By forbearance a ruler may be persuaded, and a soft tongue breaks the bone.*" The closest I've ever come to breaking my husband's iron will on the matter of shoes in the house has been this last time, when I used "*sweetness of speech*" (Proverbs 16:21) and my motives were pure. He's still not there, but I figure in another five years, he'll be able to welcome a shoed person into our home with open arms!

Application

Your husband will be much more likely to consider your requests if they are given sweetly. I'm not talking about a fake "sugary" sweetness, but genuine kindness. One word of caution, however: sweet words are not to be used as a manipulative ploy for you to have your way. Rather, we are commanded to speak in a way that gives "*grace to those who hear*" (Ephesians 4:29).

The next time you need to ask your husband for something, or tell him something that could be unpleasant, recite Proverbs 16:21 to yourself first. Practice using gentle, kind words with your husband, your children, salespeople—everyone you come into contact with should be the recipient of your *graceful* words.

Week 25, Day 1

For just as you presented your members as slaves to impurity and to lawlessness, resulting in further lawlessness, so now present your members as slaves to righteousness, resulting in sanctification.
ROMANS 6:19†

Application

The book of Romans is rich with guidance on how and why we should present ourselves for service to our King. Read Romans 6, and underline the words *present* (or *presenting*), *sanctification*, *obey* (or *obedience*), *death* (or *crucified*) and *live* (or *life*). Notice especially verses 3-4, which says that we have already been crucified with Christ, and we have already been resurrected with Him, so that "*we too might walk in newness of life.*" This new life is now!

But this new life is not done in our own strength. Read verse 4 to discover where the power of this new life comes from:

"Christ was raised from the dead through ______________________ ______________________."

PRESENTING YOURSELF

A king called together his servants and began to give them their assignments for the day. One by one, the servants presented themselves to the king: "Here I am, master, ready to do your bidding!" But one servant came to the throne and said, "Here I am, master, ready to do your bidding...just as soon as I take care of something." And off he ran to his own house.

An hour or so later, the servant returned. "OK, I'm back! Ready to do your bidding!" The king opened his mouth to give the servant instructions, but just then, the servant's cell phone rang. The servant looked apologetically at the king and said, "Excuse me, I need to take this." And he walked off, chatting on his cell phone. This went on throughout the day, and each time the servant was more apologetic, yet distracted by various things he had to do.

A major component of biblical sanctification is presenting yourself to the King. *"And do not go on presenting the members of your body to sin as instruments of unrighteousness; but present yourselves to God...and your members as instruments of righteousness"* (Romans 6:13†. See also Romans 12:1). God commands us to present ourselves to Him and be ready and willing to do whatever He asks. But just as the servant in our parable above, we are too often distracted by our own "stuff." We say, "Here I am, LORD" but then we run out and do our own thing. This only demonstrates that we have not *"crucified the flesh"* (Galatians 5:24).

The most effective servants are those who consider themselves dead to their own desires (Colossians 3:5). If you were enlisted in the military, you would have no life separate from your service. *"No soldier in active service entangles himself in the affairs of everyday life, so that he may please the one who enlisted him as a soldier"* (2 Timothy 2:4). This is the way we are to regard our lives. When we present ourselves to God and do what He asks us to do, this results in our further sanctification (Romans 6:19).

Memorize It!

Never pay back evil for evil to anyone. Respect what is right in the sight of all men. If possible, so far as it depends on you, be at peace with all men.
(Romans 12:17-18)

Not As Good As You Think You Are

I planted, Apollos watered, but God was causing the growth. So then neither the one who plants nor the one who waters is anything, but God who causes the growth.
1 Corinthians 3:6-7

As leader of a women's Bible study at church, Hope worked tirelessly on preparing her lessons and organizing the meetings. She had to ensure there were enough childcare workers for each meeting, and that someone was on board to bring the food. At least once a week, she met with one of the women in her group for coffee, to see how she was doing and if she had any issues Hope could pray about.

What Hope discovered in her Kingdom work was how difficult it was for her *not* to take pride in all of the good she was doing for Christ. "I'm amazed," she told her husband one evening, "at how easy it is for me to think I'm 'all that,' because of how well our Bible study group is going. My flesh really wants me to believe it's all because of me and my efforts."

Jim Berg, in his book, *Changed Into His Image*[7], tells the story of a young boy who wanted a new bicycle. He worked hard to earn money by doing extra chores, and he didn't spend any of his money on candy or comic books because he wanted that new bike more than anything. Finally, his dad said he could get the bike. They went to the store and the boy proudly put all of his money on the counter: a grand total of $5. The problem was that the bike cost $100. The dad told the boy to go pick out the bike he wanted, and while the boy was gone, the dad paid the remaining $95.

We are like that little boy. We believe that our $5 is what paid for the bike; that our good works are making a difference for the Kingdom. But the truth is that any good we do is just our *vote* for righteousness. The real work is done by God, according to His will and as He responds to our desire for righteousness. It is only as He moves in people's hearts that we are able to bear any fruit. Yet even as we are doing good, we still face the temptation to take pride in our efforts. This truth is evidence of just how evil our old nature truly is. Recognizing our bent toward evil should help keep us humble, even as we are doing "great" things for Christ.

Application

Probably few men did as much for the kingdom as the Apostle Paul, yet he was one of God's most humble servants. Paul's humility was the result of his awareness that he had a persistent, natural inclination toward evil. Remember that even if you are doing good works for Christ, all of your efforts are just a "vote" for righteousness, which only God can perform.

Paul wrote Romans 7:18-25 as he reflected on his natural bent toward evil. *"For I know that nothing good dwells in me, that is, in my flesh"* (Romans 7:18†). Look up and study this passage right now. Then ask God to remind you of the weakness of your own flesh, and to humble you for His purposes.

Memorize It!

Never pay back evil for evil to anyone. Respect what is right in the sight of all men. If possible, so far as it depends on you, be at peace with all men.
(Romans 12:17-18)

Week 25, Day 3

Do not lie to one another, since you laid aside the old self with its evil practices, and have put on the new self who is being renewed to a true knowledge according to the image of the One who created him.
COLOSSIANS 3:9-10

Application

Would you say that your marriage is characterized by complete honesty, or is there something in your life that you are hiding from your husband? If you are lying to him about anything (and remember, hiding the truth is the same thing as lying!) confess that sin to him today. Believe me, I know how difficult that is to do! But telling your husband the truth, even if it is difficult for him and embarrassing for you, is a direct command of God (Colossians 3:9), and one of the ways you show love to your husband.

LOVE REJOICES IN THE TRUTH

Dean and Michele were living the American dream. Dean owned a profitable business that allowed Michele to stay home with their children. They had a nice home which was probably a little more than they could afford, but somehow managed to make ends meet. Since Dean worked long hours, Michele managed the family's finances. She always had the ability to buy herself nice clothes and keep the kids in piano lessons and private school.

But then Dean's company lost a major contract, and his income dropped drastically. Michele knew they had to make big lifestyle changes, but some things she was just not willing to give up. Each month she would take a little money out of savings, telling herself that when things changed at Dean's company, she'd pay it all back. Dean frequently asked her, "Are we OK financially?" and Michele would assure him they were fine. "He has enough to worry about," she reasoned. "I don't want to put more stress on him!"

Obviously, that only worked for a short time before Dean discovered the truth. What hurt him most was not that their savings account had been cut almost in half, but that his wife had been lying to him for months.

Sometimes it's difficult to be completely truthful with our husbands. I'm not talking about the blunt honesty that says, "Oh honey, that shirt looks awful on you!" I'm talking about being honest even if the truth brings some pain. We often say we're protecting our husbands from the truth, when in reality, the person we're protecting is ourselves. We don't want to sacrifice or suffer the consequences of telling the truth.

You cannot say that you love your husband in a self-sacrificial way if you're not being 100% truthful with him in all things. When the truth brings unpleasant consequences, it is difficult to "rejoice with the truth" (1 Corinthians 13:6†). But God knows that truth brings redemption. God wants us to trust Him enough to always be truthful with our husbands, even when the truth hurts.

Memorize It!

Never pay back evil for evil to anyone. Respect what is right in the sight of all men. If possible, so far as it depends on you, be at peace with all men.
(Romans 12:17-18)

Respect Defined

If you skipped over the Amplified Bible's translation of Ephesians 5:33, take a moment now to read through it.

The editors of the Amplified Bible had a lot to say about those two little words *respect* and *reverence*, didn't they?! It's easy for us to gloss over the word *respect* without really thinking about what that looks like in our marriage. If we'll take the time to review each word in the Amplified Bible, we'll see just how awesome (yet practical) the concept of *respect* is.

- Do you *notice* your husband? When he walks into a room, comes home at the end of the day, talks at the dinner table, do you ignore him or do you visually and mentally take note of him?
- *Regard* goes beyond *noticing* to actually giving careful thought to what he is saying or doing at the moment.
- *Honor* encompasses many aspects of your relationship with your husband. Do your words and actions cause people to think well of your husband?
- *Venerate* kicks the concept of "honor" up a notch. It means to have *profound* respect, to treat him as something special or even sacred.

Getting heavy enough for you? If so, you're in good company! Let's keep going:

- *Esteem* speaks of value. You should put a high value on your husband and his many good qualities. Even if good qualities are hard to find, you should emphasize the positive qualities and discount the negatives.
- *Defers to him*. To *defer* means to give way, or yield, to him and his judgments. It implies giving his opinions and desires a far greater weight than your own or those of others.
- *Praises him* takes all of this head stuff we've been talking about (how you think about him) and makes it public so that he and others can hear your high opinion of your husband.
- *Admires him exceedingly. Honor, defer, venerate,* and *regard* are things that happen in the mind, but admiration comes from the heart. If you have fulfilled all of these other aspects of respect, then you will find it easy to admire him. And not just a little bit, but a LOT.

Memorize It!

Never pay back evil for evil to anyone. Respect what is right in the sight of all men. If possible, so far as it depends on you, be at peace with all men.
(Romans 12:17-18)

However, let each man of you [without exception] *love his wife as* [being in a sense] *his very own self; and let the wife see that she respects and reverences her husband* [that she notices him, regards him, honors him, prefers him, venerates, and esteems him; and that she defers to him, praises him, and loves and admires him exceedingly].

Ephesians 5:33
The Amplified Bible

Application

I left out one word from the Amplified Bible's translation of Ephesians 5:33 – *Love*. If you fulfill all of the other aspects of respect, you will find that your love for your husband will grow exponentially. Conversely, if you're failing in any one of them, then your love for your husband will suffer. Evaluate each of these eight aspects of respect, and see where you need to ask God to help you do better in respecting your husband.

Week 25, Day 5

For all that is in the world, the lust of the flesh and the lust of the eyes and the boastful pride of life, is not from the Father, but is from the world.
1 John 2:16

Application

"The fear of the Lord is the instruction for wisdom, and before honor comes humility" (Proverbs 15:33). Living in the fear of the Lord is the best way to avoid "my way" kind of thinking. Read the following verses, then make a list of things you do throughout the week which reflect "my way" kind of thinking, similar to the scenarios in today's lesson.

2 Chronicles

Proverbs 16:18

Proverbs 21:2-4

Isaiah 66:2

Proverbs 8:13

If you have trouble coming up with examples, ask God to show you how you are maintaining control of your life, rather than living in fear of Him and submitting to His ways. After you finish your list, ask God to forgive you and help you choose His ways rather than your own.

Pride Defined: "My Way" Kind of Thinking

Pride is defined by the dictionary as "a haughty attitude shown by someone who believes he or she is better than others." The Biblical definition of pride is a little more inclusive: *"Each of us has turned to his own way"* (Isaiah 53:6). It's a worldly way of thinking that says "I'm smart enough to be the boss of me." This "own way" kind of proud thinking causes us to prefer our way to God's way. Pride says we are capable of living our lives without God's help, or that God is obligated to help us even when we neglect His truth.

We don't always recognize pride in our life because it is such an integral part of who we are as fallen human beings. We think if we are not bragging, haughty, boastful people then we don't have a problem with pride. Remember, however, that any time you hold on to your right to be in "control," you are living in pride and not humbly submitting to God's way.

Following are some not-so-obvious scenarios of a wife who has a proud, "own way" kind of thinking:

- Sheri's husband wants her to stop working, but she knows they couldn't survive without her income.
- Rose spends most of her day talking on the phone, watching TV or scrapbooking.
- Laura has little time for God during the day; she is a beauty consultant who has to work hard to keep her business profitable.
- Jill knows she should "turn the other cheek," but she will NOT let her husband get away with being verbally abusive.
- Kelsey doesn't tithe, but she spends a great deal of money on clothes and things for her house.
- Stacy and her husband leave after the first church service because getting home at 1:00 p.m. really eats into their Sunday afternoons.
- Marsha only submits to her husband if what he's asking her to do makes sense.

None of these scenarios sound like horrible sins, but they are all "my way" kind of thinking: living every day with an eye to what will bring the most comfort to the flesh, rather than being obedient to God's Word.

By God's Standards, Not Yours

For we are not bold to class or compare ourselves with some of those who commend themselves; but when they measure themselves by themselves and compare themselves with themselves, they are without understanding.
2 Corinthians 10:12

Alex and Carrie were not Christians when they married, but a couple of years later they both accepted Christ as their Lord and Savior. One of the issues they immediately faced was re-orienting their marriage relationship to God's pattern and design. The concept of *submission* was foreign to Carrie; she knew it would take hard work to make it a reality in her life.

As Carrie grew in faith, she surprised herself at how well she submitted to her husband. It was against her nature to yield her will to anyone, so she considered every success a major victory. One day, however, she and Alex had a major disagreement. As Carrie resisted her husband, he gently reminded her she was not being submissive. "Give me a break!" she shot back at him. "I've come a long way from where I used to be. I think I'm doing just fine in that department."

The Bible says that if we compare ourselves to ourselves, we're making a big mistake (2 Corinthians 10:12). We often use our starting point as our reference, rather than the finish line. "Look how far I've come; I'm so much more submissive than I used to be." If you've come a long way, that's great and you should praise God for it. But that doesn't mean it's time to rest on your laurels, and it doesn't give you a pass to take occasional "breaks" from obedience.

The Apostle Paul said, "*I press on toward the goal for the prize of the upward call of God in Christ Jesus*" (Philippians 3:14). Your call from Christ is to be conformed to His image and to comply with *His* standards of submission, not your own. It won't come all at once, and you are not wrong to rejoice in the victories God gives you in this area. But if you're going to "grade" yourself in how well you're doing, don't use your past as your measuring stick. Christ is the measure: "*Until we all attain to the unity of the faith, and of the knowledge of the Son of God, to a mature man, to the measure of the stature which belongs to the fullness of Christ*" (Ephesians 4:13).

Memorize It!

Never take your own revenge, beloved, but leave room for the wrath of God, for it is written, "'Vengeance is Mine, I will repay,' says the Lord."
(Romans 12:19)

Application

Since what you're working toward is submitting to and pleasing your husband, then an easy way to measure your progress is just to ask your husband about it. The next time you and your husband have some time alone, ask him the following questions:

- How do you think I'm doing in submitting to you?
- What am I doing right in our marriage?
- Where do you think I can improve?"

Make sure you set aside anything you think he is doing wrong, and ask God to help you focus only on your responsibilities in the marriage. Getting a submission "checkup" from your husband should be a regular habit in building a healthy marriage.

Week 26, Day 2

I am my beloved's, and his desire is for me. Let us rise early and go to the vineyards; let us see whether the vine has budded and its blossoms have opened, and whether the pomegranates have bloomed. There I will give you my love.
Song of Solomon 7:10, 12

Application

Both you and your husband should find intimacy with each other to be satisfying and pleasurable. If your love life is sporadic or humdrum, the cure is to recommit yourself to making intimacy a priority in your life. Focus on pleasing your husband, not yourself—yet teach your husband what pleases you in lovemaking. The more pleasure you get from sex, the more pleasure *he* gets from sex. If you're not in the mood or you're too tired, do it anyway. In this way you are not selfishly depriving your husband, but instead looking out for what is best for him and for your marriage (Philippians 2:3-4).

Sex: The Happy Mandate

In many ways, sex is like going to church: sometimes it's hard to get going, but once you're there, it's always good. And like attending church, sex with your husband is a command of God: *"The husband must fulfill his duty to his wife, and likewise also the wife to her husband. The wife does not have authority over her own body, but the husband does; and likewise also the husband does not have authority over his own body, but the wife does"* (1 Corinthians 7:3-4).

Another way sex is like church is because sex is good, enjoyable, and one of the ways we worship God. Our loving Father is the author of sexual intimacy. He created it to be beautiful, perfect, and wonderful, and not just for makin' babies, but also for fun. It's one of the best ways to build unity in your marriage.

Many couples go for too long without satisfying each other in this way. This can be frustrating, especially for the man, and can lead to temptation to sin. If you're not enjoying frequent, happy sex in your marriage, then you need to not only figure out why you aren't, but also how to fix it. Following are just some of the possible reasons for a loss of sexual intimacy in marriage:

Sin—Perhaps something big happened, like an affair, or just plain selfishness, but sin is the #1 reason we don't enjoy sex as we should. Not having sex is a sin, so even if sin wasn't the cause, it is certainly the end result.

Busy-ness and Fatigue—The typical pattern for couples is to enjoy frequent sex at the beginning of the marriage, then life just starts crowding it out. Kids, activities, ministry, and careers all conspire to deprive the husband and wife of exclusive time and energy for each other. By the time their lives are less busy, they are out of the habit of regular intimacy.

Dissatisfaction—Some couples never quite get the hang of pleasing each other during sex. It's important to consistently communicate what brings you pleasure, and to ask your husband to guide you, rather than grade you.

Memorize It!

Never take your own revenge, beloved, but leave room for the wrath of God, for it is written, "'Vengeance is Mine, I will repay,' says the Lord."
(Romans 12:19)

God Can Be Trusted

After months of discipling Charlene about her lack of submission to her husband, I finally asked, "What is keeping you from obeying God in this? What is your biggest fear?" Her answer was very revealing: "I'm afraid that if I submit to my husband, that I'll lose myself. I won't be 'me' anymore, but just a shadow of who I really am. I really believe I'll become some miserable robot."

What Charlene was saying is this: I don't trust God to have my best interests in mind.

Many of us are like Charlene, choosing not to surrender to God because we are afraid if we do, He will mess up our lives and interfere with what we want to do. We don't trust God's promises. We think *our* ideas for a happy, fulfilling life are more to be trusted than God's ideas—thus, *we* are more trustworthy than *God*.

Some very good guidance on this subject comes from Jim Berg in his book, *Changed Into His Image*[8]:

> The fear that God would make life *miserable* is just the opposite of the truth. Stop and think about something for a moment. If God were really trying to find some way to "mess up" our lives, He would not need to wait until we finally surrendered to Him to go ahead with His plans for destruction. Since He is God, He could do it any time He wanted to. God doesn't need our permission to "mess up" our lives. In our wickedness, we believe that *God* is the biggest evil we could encounter and that it is *our* resistance to Him that keeps life from charging headlong into misery! What arrogance that is! What corruption within us it reveals!

Isn't this the truth behind Romans 1? *"Even though they knew God, they did not honor Him as God or give thanks...they exchanged the truth of God for a lie, and worshiped and served the creature [ourselves] rather than the Creator"* (Romans 1:21, 25†). We don't submit to God and our husbands because we worship and serve ourselves, rather than God.

If that describes your life, you need to recognize that evil within, and turn to the true and living God. The joy and happiness you seek can *only* be found in Him.

Memorize It!

Never take your own revenge, beloved, but leave room for the wrath of God, for it is written, "'Vengeance is Mine, I will repay,' says the Lord."
(Romans 12:19)

He who has found his life will lose it, and he who has lost his life for My sake will find it.
Matthew 10:39

Application

Those who have surrendered all to God can testify to the fallacy of this kind of evil thinking. No one who has left everything and followed Him to the end has ever regretted it (Luke 9:24). God promises to meet all your needs as you are obedient to Him (Matthew 6:32-33).

As your dreams become conformed to God's plans, you will find that your life is *more* fulfilling and satisfying, not less. You will be less frustrated and more likely to accomplish your dreams than if you go against God's call on your life. Remember these truths today about God:

- ☑ God is gracious, righteous, and compassionate.
- ☑ God's strength and understanding are unlimited.
- ☑ God is purposefully working in your life.
- ☑ God wants you to be a joyful, fulfilled wife.

Week 26, Day 4

Be devoted to one another in brotherly love; give preference to one another in honor; not lagging behind in diligence, fervent in spirit, serving the LORD; rejoicing in hope, persevering in tribulation, devoted to prayer, contributing to the needs of the saints, practicing hospitality.
ROMANS 12:10-13

Application

What is your home like? Is it a place where people feel comfortable, or do they feel they need to walk on eggshells when they visit? Or is it so messy, people feel uncomfortable in the chaos? Are you leveraging your possessions for the work of the Kingdom of God?

If you aren't regularly practicing hospitality in your home, then you are selfishly using your possessions strictly for your own pleasure, rather than for the purposes for which God gave them to you. Make this a matter of prayer, then talk to your husband about how you and your family can use everything God has given you for His glory.

People-Centered, Not Things-Centered

Jenny is a work-at-home mom who loves her children and enjoys working around the home. However, she's a bit of a perfectionist. Once the house is clean, she keeps the kids inside so they don't track in dirt. When friends come over, she entertains them in the basement. She rarely has guests over, because making the house perfect, and returning it to perfection after they leave, is too stressful for her.

Charity is also a work-at-home mom who sees the importance of being a good steward of the things God has given to her, but she is not obsessive about "stuff." Instead, her focus is on creating a home atmosphere where people feel comfortable. She often invites neighbors over for dinner or backyard barbeques; she and her husband have shared the gospel with almost everyone on their street. And her kids' friends love hanging out at their house. Charity's home is pretty much the neighborhood focal point for social activity.

The difference between Jenny and Charity is that while Jenny is taking good care of the things God has entrusted to her, she is using her possessions to make herself happy. Charity, on the other hand, is leveraging everything she has for the Kingdom. She understands that people are more important than possessions. "Nothing I have belongs to me," she says. "If something gets broken or dirty while we're serving Christ, I think God is OK with that."

Doing our work *"heartily as for the LORD"* (Colossians 3:23) is important, but a clean house is not the end game here. Bringing others to Christ should always be our ultimate goal. Why do we work to have solid marriages and peace in the home? Why do we teach our children to be submissive and self-disciplined? Are all of the things we're working for just for ourselves? Hopefully, our motivation is to magnify Christ by showing the world that His ways are perfect. In lifting up Christ, we draw people to Him. Everything we do should be for the glory of God (1 Corinthians 10:31) and for His Kingdom.

Memorize It!

Never take your own revenge, beloved, but leave room for the wrath of God, for it is written, "'Vengeance is Mine, I will repay,' says the LORD." (Romans 12:19)

Conflict Over Righteousness

Blake grew up in a fairly liberal household in terms of the freedoms his parents gave him. He was allowed to watch horror movies, listen to rock music, and wear whatever he wanted. Chelsea, on the other hand, came from a very conservative family. Her parents raised her to dress modestly and listen to only traditional gospel or classical music. They didn't even have a television, so when she and Blake were first married, she was shocked at many of his entertainment choices.

It took them a few years to get used to each other's preferences, but once children came into their home, their differing convictions became a source of contention. Blake saw no problem with letting their eight-year-old son watch a scary movie, and Chelsea was concerned that his music choices would adversely influence their children. Her fear was the catalyst for many arguments over the standards of righteousness they would uphold in their home.

Many couples have "conflicts of righteousness" when one partner believes the other is violating God's moral will. If you and your husband have such conflicts, you need to be careful to distinguish between your own interpretation of God's Word and God's absolute Law. Let's say your husband takes you to a restaurant that serves alcohol. You're not entirely comfortable, but you need to be submissive unless he asks you to sin. So you should go ahead and enjoy eating there, but you don't have to drink alcohol yourself. You should come as close as you can to what he wants, but not step over the line into violating your conscience before God (1 Corinthians 10:27-28).

Some conflicts are easily resolved when we show patience, gentleness and forbearance. But sometimes you may have to take a stand and as a result, *"suffer for doing what is right"* (1 Peter 3:17). Even then, you should never suffer because of your own sin. For example, if your husband asks you to sin and you get angry with him, part of your suffering is due to your anger, not because of what he's asked you to do.

But the wisdom from above is first pure, then peaceable, gentle, reasonable, full of mercy and good fruits, unwavering, without hypocrisy.
JAMES 3:17

Application

If something is clearly a sin according to the Bible, you must stand your ground. In everything else, God wants you to be flexible and reasonable (James 3:17). Regardless of the basis of the conflict, disagreement is not an excuse to sin. Your responsibility is to *"walk in a manner worthy of the calling with which you have been called, with all humility and gentleness, with patience, showing tolerance for one another in love"* (Ephesians 4:1-2).

Having the attitudes reflected in Ephesians 4 will, in many instances resolve the disagreement instantly. But even if you cannot come to an agreement quickly, these attitudes will help you work on and resolve the conflict without sinning.

Week 27, Day 1

[Hannah] made a vow and said, "O LORD of hosts, if You will indeed look on the affliction of Your maidservant and remember me, and not forget Your maidservant, but will give Your maidservant a son, then I will give him to the LORD all the days of his life."
1 SAMUEL 1:11†

Application

If you have been unable to have children, please know: I don't want to trivialize your pain. I can't imagine how difficult this is, and I'm not saying you should stop desiring children. But for you, it is perhaps even more critical to keep Christ as your main focus, and learn *"to be content in whatever circumstances"* you are in (Philippians 4:11). You *can* be content as you focus on Him and enjoy the spiritual blessings of the peace, love, joy, and grace He freely pours out on you.

Because this issue of becoming and being a mom is so important to so many of us, we're going to spend a couple of days on this subject. If you already have children and this is not an issue for you, you will definitely want to tune in to tomorrow's lesson!

THE IDOL OF A CHILD (PART 1)

Rachel sat staring out the window as her husband drove them home from the obstetrician's office. They'd just learned that her baby had passed away *in utero*. Now came the painful waiting for her body to naturally miscarry the baby's body. Rachel did not know how she was going to make it—the emotional pain was more than she could bear. As soon as they pulled into the driveway, Riley shut off the car and turned to her, tears in his eyes. But she rejected his outstretched hand and fled. Once inside the door, she dropped to her knees and began sobbing. "God, I don't understand!" she cried. "I've been faithful to You, I've done everything You've asked of me. Why isn't it good enough? Why are You withholding from me my greatest heart's desire?"

God designed us to want certain things, and getting married and having children are two of our most basic human desires. It sometimes stretches our understanding of God when we seem unable to attain or hold onto those things He designed us to have. Many single Christians begin to doubt God's love and care for them when they go for years without any prospect of marriage, or when the mate they thought they would have somehow disappears. Likewise, some of God's people find themselves questioning God when they are unable to conceive children or, even worse, lose a child in miscarriage or death.

If your dream of having children seems elusive, what you cannot do is doubt the LORD's love for you. (See Romans 8:38-39.) You might not understand all of His ways, but being devoted to God means you never question His character, His provision, or His care of you. God wants you to be happy. But *having a child is not the key to your happiness.* If you believe you cannot be happy unless you have a child, then being a mom has become an idol in your heart. You are rejecting the joy God provides by clinging to your right to be miserable until He answers this prayer.

Memorize It!

But if your enemy is hungry, feed him, and if he is thirsty, give him a drink; for in so doing you will heap burning coals on his head. Do not be overcome by evil, but overcome evil with good.
(Romans 12:20-21)

The Idol of a Child (Part 2)

If anyone comes to Me, and does not hate his own father and mother and wife and children and brothers and sisters, yes, and even his own life, he cannot be My disciple.
Luke 14:26

This is one lesson I wanted to throw out of this book. I've been reading blogs and articles by women who have suffered miscarriages or lost children, and I feel wholly inadequate to address that kind of pain. Many couples try desperately to bear children, and it feels calloused to refer to their pain as "idolatry." If you have suffered in this way, please understand that I'm not being flippant, and I don't want to add to your suffering. I hope, instead, to offer you a better way to deal with your pain.

Even if others can't relate to your suffering, Jesus can and does. He will comfort you, but His desire for you is that your passion for children not become an idol in your heart. There should only be one consuming passion in our hearts, and that is the Lord Jesus Christ. A passion for Christ enables us to mourn our losses with peace and hope. This is true for all of us, whether we have children or not, whether we've lost children, or whether we have no desire for children at all. In any and all circumstances, God is moving us toward Himself. He truly does cause *"all things to work together for good to those who love God, to those who are called according to His purpose"* (Romans 8:28†). Yes, He can cause *everything*—even the lack or loss of a child—to result in good for you, but only if His kingdom is your overarching concern. If having a child is your greatest passion, then you have "another god" before Him, and that is idolatry.

If you have children, this lesson is still for you, because many of us are more devoted to our kids than we are to Christ. But Jesus said, *"If anyone comes to Me, and does not hate his own father and mother and wife and* ***children*** *and brothers and sisters, yes, and even his own life, he cannot be My disciple"* (Luke 14:26†). In other words, our love for Christ should be so all-consuming that every other human relationship is as hatred in comparison. How many of us can say we love Christ more than we love our children?

Application

Lord, I know there are many women reading this book today who desperately want a child, or who are suffering because they have lost a child. God, I pray for them, that You would comfort them and give them peace. Help them to trust in Your faithfulness and to know how much You love them, and that You would never withhold something good from them out of cruelty or apathy. We don't always understand why certain things happen, but we know that above all else, You want our hearts. Our whole *hearts. In return, You have promised to give us* "peace that passes understanding" *(Philippians 4:7). Help us, Lord, to trust You and to desire intimacy with You above any earthly relationship, even that of a mother and child. In Jesus' name, Amen.*

Memorize It!

But if your enemy is hungry, feed him, and if he is thirsty, give him a drink; for in so doing you will heap burning coals on his head. Do not be overcome by evil, but overcome evil with good.
(Romans 12:20-21)

Week 27, Day 3

*She opens her mouth in wisdom,
and the teaching of kindness
is on her tongue.*
PROVERBS 31:26

Application

One way to change the way you speak to your husband is to think about how you would like *him* to speak to you (Matthew 7:12). If you were wrong about something, you would want him to be wise, kind, forgiving and understanding. You would want him to be helpful without being sarcastic or condescending, right? Then this is how you should treat him.

God's Word makes us wise; and His Spirit makes us kind. Therefore, you must stay in God's Word so you can gain God's wisdom, not the wisdom of the world, and so He can change your character. No matter what the issue is or how you are feeling, you can be wise in your words and kind in your tone.

WISDOM AND KINDNESS

"Yes, God, you know I'm ready to begin becoming a godly wife. And you know what has hindered me thus far ~ nothing but the flesh: my own carnal will and my fleshly fear of becoming a 'weirdo.' But I'm not going to worry about that. The picture I see in Scripture of the excellent wife is a woman of diverse interests, well-connected, happy and successful. That's what I want. But I'm torn between the flesh and the spirit: too spiritual for this world and too carnal for the church. I want to be fully ME, yet fully Christ's."

That's what I wrote in my prayer journal the first time I took *The Excellent Wife* Bible study. One of the things I was concerned about was becoming a robotic, "unreal" version of myself. As I sat looking over my notes for this lesson, those fears came back.

The godly wife *"opens her mouth in wisdom, and the teaching of kindness is on her tongue"* (Proverbs 31:26). I'll be honest with you: that kind of woman doesn't seem real to me. She's the kind of person I was once afraid of becoming: a plastic woman who has this smooth, gentle way of talking about everything. Kind of like the computer voice on Star Trek: *"The warp core will self-destruct in 10 seconds. Thank you and have a nice day!"*

I don't think that is exactly what God wants for us. He wants us to be wise, and our wisdom comes from His Word, which is passionate, relevant, and more "real" than anything. When you are saturated in the Word of God, you begin reacting to all of life with a wisdom that can only come from Him. When that wisdom comes out of your mouth, it looks a lot like James 3:17, *"But the wisdom from above is first pure, then peaceable, gentle, reasonable, full of mercy and good fruits, unwavering, without hypocrisy."*

If you had a recording of all of the things you said in a day, what would it sound like? Are your words rude, unforgiving, terse, or harsh? Or are they edifying, wise, helpful, and kind? How closely do your words match up to James 3:17?

Memorize It!

But if your enemy is hungry, feed him, and if he is thirsty, give him a drink; for in so doing you will heap burning coals on his head. Do not be overcome by evil, but overcome evil with good.
(Romans 12:20-21)

NOT A BURDEN

In the early days of marriage, Christina loved spending every minute with Eddie, and hated it when they had to spend time apart. However, over time (especially after the kids came along) she began looking forward to him going off to work and getting out of her hair. Once he left for the office, Christina could get busy on all she had to accomplish during the day. She had a routine that worked for her and even allowed a few hours a week for her to relax.

All of that came to a screeching halt when Eddie lost his job. Suddenly, in addition to all of her other responsibilities, *he* was there, and he had needs. Bologna sandwiches for lunch wouldn't cut it for him: he needed real food, and her time in the kitchen was now doubled. Plus, he needed help sending out résumés and answering emails from potential employers. When he finally decided to work from home, Christina felt disappointed. She had longed for the day when he got a new job and her life could get back to normal. Now, he would be home day after day. She really didn't know if she could take that!

I must confess I am a lot like Christina. I love my husband, but if he decided he was going to work from home or retire, it would be a difficult adjustment. Most of us, particularly those who have been married awhile or who have children, are very protective of our right to control our own schedule. If we have to stop what we're doing to focus time and energy on a needy husband, we can get pretty grumpy.

The fact that many women are like this doesn't mean it's right. First Corinthians 11:3-12 reminds us that, as Christians, we are not independent agents, but we are to live dependent upon each other and upon God. Woman was created *"for the man's sake"* (1 Corinthians 11:9). If you've been treating your husband as an imposition or burden, you need to bring your thinking back in line with Scripture. God has placed a high calling on your life—to love and serve your husband—and that is more important than anything else you have to do.

Memorize It!

But if your enemy is hungry, feed him, and if he is thirsty, give him a drink; for in so doing you will heap burning coals on his head. Do not be overcome by evil, but overcome evil with good.
(Romans 12:20-21)

However, in the LORD, neither is woman independent of man, nor is man independent of woman.
1 CORINTHIANS 11:11

Application

We often need reminders of what our true "job" is in the home and in our marriages. Your job is not to run your own schedule or attend to all other priorities, but your job is to help your husband. A good way to remind yourself of this priority is to get in the habit of asking him the following questions on a regular basis:

What can I do for you today?

What do you need me to accomplish for you this week?

What can I do differently that would make life easier for you?

When you ask, remember to display a loving and willing readiness to set aside your own priorities to help him achieve his goals.

Week 27, Day 5

An excellent wife, who can find? For her worth is far above jewels. The heart of her husband trusts in her, and he will have no lack of gain. She does him good and not evil all the days of her life.
PROVERBS 31:10-12

Application

Answer the questions below to see if you're passing The Respect Test. Use A for *Almost Always*, S for *Sometimes*, and N for *Almost Never:*

___ I consider my husband's needs before anyone else's, including me or the kids.

___ I don't interrupt or contradict him, especially in front of others.

___ I never roll my eyes or look disgusted or impatient when he's talking.

___ I respect his opinions, even if I don't always agree with him.

___ I never put him down, make him feel stupid, or speak to him in a condescending way.

Respect is one of those things you must constantly monitor to make sure you're being obedient. Mark this page and refer back to this test from time to time to see how you're doing in the area of respect.

RESPECT DEFINED: TREATING HIM DIFFERENTLY

I have three daughters, and no sons—yet. I do have the hope, however, that someday I'll get the sons I've always wanted when my daughters are married. Because I'm a "boys' mom" at heart, when my oldest daughter brought her first boyfriend home from college, I probably went a little overboard making him feel welcome. I asked about his favorite foods ahead of time so I would be sure to make things he liked. The guy could barely relax without me checking to see that he was happy and his needs were met. I rolled out the red carpet and pretty much elevated this 21-year-old kid to the status of royalty.

I treated Amy's boyfriend this way not just because he is my brother in Christ, but also because I was thrilled that, out of all the girls he could have dated, he chose my daughter. However, it was a great reminder for me as to how I should treat my husband. After all, out of all the girls *my husband* could have married, he chose me. Should I not be equally attentive to him and treat him with more respect than I do anyone else?

There is a level of respect you should give to all people, but the respect you give your husband should go beyond that. The sad fact is many of us treat our husbands *worse* than we treat others! We are quicker to talk down to them, use an angry tone of voice with them, ignore or disregard them. This is just wrong. You should treat your husband better than you treat anyone else. If Philippians 2:3 says to *"regard one another as more important than yourselves,"* how much more should you regard your husband as *the* most important person in your life? He is your top priority and your most important ministry; if you truly believed and lived that truth, you would give your husband the greatest respect you could possibly give.

Love Bears All Things

With all humility and gentleness, with patience, showing tolerance for one another in love, being diligent to preserve the unity of the Spirit in the bond of peace.
Ephesians 4:2-3

Life has not been easy for Jeff and Kellie. Shortly after the honeymoon, Jeff lost his job and has worked only low-paying, temporary jobs for years—sometimes going for many months without working at all. Their kids have never lacked for food or clothing, but only because of food stamps and their friends at church, who have kept them supplied with "hand-me-downs." To make matters worse, Jeff has become rude and selfish. When he does make a little extra money, he often buys something for himself to make him feel better.

Kellie knows Jeff is depressed and embarrassed about his failure to provide for their family. But there are days when she just wants to throw in the towel. Most of her friends have advised her to leave him and take care of herself and her children. But despite everything they've been through, Kellie truly loves her husband. Rarely a day goes by when she does not say to herself, *"Love bears all things."*

"Bearing all things" includes times when your husband is being selfish or unreasonable, or when he is having a tough time at work and money is tight. What often makes these circumstances difficult to bear is when we believe that we are owed so much more than what we've been given. "I deserve better than this" is an ungrateful attitude of self-love. But loving involves self-sacrifice.

If your situation seems unbearable, it is important to remember that this does not give you an excuse to sin. Sometimes wives compound their difficult circumstances by complaining or withholding love from their husbands. God's way, however, is to continue to love no matter what. This is what Christ did, and we are conformed to His image when we suffer as He suffered and love as He loved. If you must suffer, it should be for "doing what is right" (1 Peter 3:17).

Application

Not only are we called to "bear all things" when we love (1 Corinthians 13:7), but we're also called to give thanks "in everything" (1 Thessalonians 5:18). All things and everything means just that: EVERYTHING. Think about the trials you're having in your life and marriage. Then take a moment to thank God for each one. Even if it's a seemingly unbearable situation, God can use it to make you stronger, more dependent on Him, and more conformed to the image of His Son—and that is something to be grateful for! Cultivating this attitude of thankfulness will show your husband that you are committed to loving him, no matter what.

Memorize It!

But the fruit of the Spirit is love, joy, peace, patience, kindness, goodness, faithfulness, gentleness, self-control; against such things there is no law.
(Galatians 5:22-23)

Week 28, Day 2

Or do you think lightly of the riches of His kindness and tolerance and patience, not knowing that the kindness of God leads you to repentance?
ROMANS 2:4

Application

Conflict will often come to your marriage as a test of your faith. Are you going to trust in yourself, or in God? If you will trust in God, then that trial will produce patience in you. *"But let patience have its perfect work, that you may be perfect and complete, lacking nothing"* (James 1:4, NKJV).

The Bible has a lot to say about patience. Use a concordance or an online study Bible (such as biblegateway.com) and look up all of the verses you can find about patience. The verses listed in today's lesson are a start, but the Word of God is rich with teaching about this subject! See if you can find more verses about patience, then write out the principles you find in those verses.

Attitudes For Conflict Resolution: Patience

Before Chloe was saved, she used to go all *ninja* on her husband Amos whenever he did the slightest thing that hurt or offended her. Her personality type is very expressive, and without the Holy Spirit helping to guard her tongue, she really let Amos have it when he messed up.

Now that she has Christ and His Spirit working in and through her, she is cooperating in this process of changing her heart and renewing her mind to make her less contentious. Through biblical counseling, Chloe realized one of her problems: she lacks patience with her husband, and with people in general.

Chloe's counselor shared the following Scriptural principles with her to help her understand the concept of patience. Now, whenever she and Amos have a conflict and she can feel impatience starting to rise inside her heart, she reminds herself of one of these principles. Usually, she only has to remember the first one, *God is patient with me*, to make herself remember to have more patience with her husband.

I can be patient because:

- God is patient with me. (Romans 2:4)
- God is listening; He knows my struggles. (Psalm 40:1)
- God commands it. (Colossians 3:12-13)
- Being patient is how I demonstrate love. (1 Corinthians 13:4)
- Being patient is how I live out God's calling in my life. (Colossians 1:10-12)
- Patience shows humility. (Ecclesiastes 7:8)
- Patience builds unity in my marriage. (Ephesians 4:2-3)

Impatience is usually caused by two things: 1) **Fear**—we are afraid that if we wait patiently, we will miss an opportunity to say something we need to say or to do something we want to do; and 2) **Pride**—we believe we are smarter so we don't want to listen to what our husbands have to say; or we believe our time is too valuable to spend on things that don't matter to us as much as they matter to our husbands.

The cure for impatience, then, is humility and trust. As you work on becoming more humble and trusting God to work in your situation, you will find it easier to be patient.

Memorize It!

But the fruit of the Spirit is love, joy, peace, patience, kindness, goodness, faithfulness, gentleness, self-control; against such things there is no law.
(Galatians 5:22-23)

Even If He's Not A Christian

Lauren sat down at one end of a row of chairs and got out her Bible study materials. As she opened up her book, her heart sank. *Great,* she said to herself, *we're talking about submitting to our husbands this week.* She was tempted to pack up and slip out before too many other women arrived, but just then the leader of the study came into the room. "Hey, Lauren!" Marie said, "How are you?"

Lauren smiled back. "I'm ok, but I'm wondering if I'm going to get anything out of our study today. I know submission is a great concept, but my husband isn't a Christian. Honestly, I don't think God expects me to submit to him. He and God are rarely on the same page, you know." Marie laughed as she took her seat. "Oh, sweetie, I think today's study was written *especially* for you!"

If you have an unbelieving husband, you may think you're held to a different standard than women with believing husbands. Or perhaps you know you're supposed to submit, but that's not the way it plays out in your day-to-day life. Either way, it's good to remind yourself that God's command to *"be submissive to your own husbands"* (1 Peter 3:1) is for *all* wives, no matter who they're married to.

It's not that God is so unbending on His rules that He doesn't care about your situation. He knows what is best for you and your unbelieving husband, and all of His laws are designed to redeem mankind. Obedience to Christ in the area of submission is the best avenue for God to work in your husband's heart and redeem him to Himself, and redeem your marriage, making it a "vessel for honor" (2 Timothy 2:21).

Perhaps you married during a time of rebellion to God, and you believe God can never bless your marriage because of your sin. But holding this sin over your head would be cruel and vindictive, and that is not God's way. He is always ready to forgive (1 John 1:9) and can redeem any marriage for His glory.

Memorize It!

But the fruit of the Spirit is love, joy, peace, patience, kindness, goodness, faithfulness, gentleness, self-control; against such things there is no law.
(Galatians 5:22-23)

In the same way, you wives, be submissive to your own husbands so that even if any of them are disobedient to the word, they may be won without a word by the behavior of their wives.
1 Peter 3:1

Application

Husbands who are *"disobedient to the Word"* means a husband who is an unbeliever. The best way to reach your unsaved husband is to live truth out in your life. That means submitting to him in everything, unless he asks you to sin, so that he *"may be won...by your chaste and respectful behavior"* (1 Peter 3:1-2). If your husband has rejected Christ, ask God if your rebellious behavior might be one of the contributing factors. Ultimately, it is your husband's responsibility and he can't blame you for his sin. But loving him means doing all you can to show forth Christ into his life.

Week 28, Day 4

For I am confident of this very thing, that He who began a good work in you will perfect it until the day of Christ Jesus.
PHILIPPIANS 1:6

Application

If you knew you could never in a thousand years achieve something, would you stop trying? Of course! Well then, it's time to stop trying to be good enough for God, because the truth is, you aren't, and you never will be. You will always *"come short of the glory of God"* (Romans 3:23, KJV). But God sees you as holy, because His Son sanctified you with His blood. Your response to this should be to *"present yourself to God"* (Romans 6:13) in gratitude. In other words, set yourself apart and commit to doing God's will, no matter what your condition.

That doesn't mean it doesn't matter if you sin, because we are still commanded to stop sinning (Romans 6:12). But it's time to stop being defeated by something that no longer has a hold on you.

Positional Sanctification

If you've ever read through the Old Testament, you may have gotten a little weary reading about the various items used in the tabernacle. God was very specific about all of the bowls, candlesticks, curtain rods, dishes, etc. that His people were to make and use in their worship. It's difficult to wade through all of this information, because it just doesn't seem relevant.

However, this information could not be more relevant, because when God talks about instruments used in service and worship, He is also talking about us as believers. Like the items in the tabernacle, God wants to use us for His glory, but He cannot do that unless we are holy.

God commanded the priests to "consecrate" all of the tools used in the tabernacle. (See Exodus 40.) The word *consecrate* simply means "set apart," and is very close in meaning to the word *sanctify*. In order for us to be used by God in His service, we must first be consecrated, sanctified, made holy.

If you're like most Christians, you struggle with that knowledge, knowing that you just aren't as holy as you would like to be. Most Christians do so little for God because they are defeated by their many failures to live up to His righteous standards. If God were to say to you, "Child, you are good enough just as you are, and I want to use you *today*," how would you react to that news?

The truth is God has already told you that. *"By [God's] will* ***we have been sanctified*** *through the offering of the body of Jesus Christ once for all...For by one offering* ***He has perfected for all time*** *those who are sanctified"* (Hebrews 10:10, 14†). God sanctified and made you holy when He saved you.

In other words, "It is finished!" (John 19:30). Christ's sacrifice on the cross is not just sufficient to save you and get you to heaven, but it is sufficient to make you holy and fit for God's use. Not at some point in the future, when you are "good enough," but today, right now. *Nothing* is stopping you from presenting yourself to God for His service and glory!

Memorize It!

But the fruit of the Spirit is love, joy, peace, patience, kindness, goodness, faithfulness, gentleness, self-control; against such things there is no law.
(Galatians 5:22-23)

Positional Sanctification (Part 2)

Week 28, Day 5

Therefore, brethren, since we have confidence to enter the holy place by the blood of Jesus...let us draw near with a sincere heart in full assurance of faith, having our hearts sprinkled clean from an evil conscience and our bodies washed with pure water.
Hebrews 10:19, 22

If we were to interview every successful athlete, business entrepreneur, entertainer, artist...anyone who is successful at anything, we would find one common thread that runs through each of them: they all knew they would be successful. That belief gave them hope to keep trying until they achieved their dreams.

One of the problems we have in achieving success for Christ is that many of us don't believe we will ever be successful at it. Yesterday we talked about how you were sanctified and made holy at the moment of your salvation. (Another word for this is "justification," where God declares you to be "not guilty" of sin.) God sees you as holy, yet many of us don't believe that. We are held back from service because we don't believe we will ever be good enough to be used by God. Overcoming this feeling of guilt and unworthiness is essential to having a proper, loving relationship with God and for believing you can be effective for Christ.

Imagine you had a child who did some awful things, but he repented and you completely forgave him. Now imagine that every time he saw you, he looked the other way and avoided you; that he does nothing around the house and performs poorly in school because he thinks, "I'm such a loser, I'll never be able to do that." Not only would you grieve for that child, but it would also hurt that he doesn't believe in your forgiveness.

This is how we treat God. We really don't believe in His complete and total forgiveness.

"Yes, but I keep sinning!" God knows that, and He wants you to continue your "search and destroy" mission against sin in your heart. But He understands that this is a process, and He is not waiting for you to achieve a certain level before He declares you righteous and fit for service. At any point in time, you can *"present your [body] a living and holy sacrifice, acceptable to God"* (Romans 12:1). God has already declared you holy, so any time you present yourself to Him, your offering is "acceptable to God" and He *will* use you.

Application

Most of us wait too long to begin serving God, waiting to feel like we're good enough to be used. The funny thing about that is we would pick a point of "good enough" that *still* falls short of God's righteousness! What we don't realize is that serving Him is *how* we grow in righteousness. It's like learning any skill: you don't wait to be an expert before you begin practicing, right?

If you have kids, perhaps you let them help you with doing things around the house before they were old enough to do it well, because that helps their development. Serving God is the same way: start before you think you're ready, because God can always use you just as you are. He uses *"the weak things...to shame the things which are strong"* (1 Corinthians 1:27†).

Week 29, Day 1

Your adornment must not be merely external... but let it be the hidden person of the heart, with the imperishable quality of a gentle and quiet spirit, which is precious in the sight of God.
1 PETER 3:3-4

Application

How do you know if you have a meek and quiet spirit? Quiz yourself on the following questions:

- When my husband asks me to do something I don't want to do, I accept his decision without arguing.
- I don't spend a lot of time worrying about how my husband's decisions will affect me and my family.
- When we're around others, I am relaxed and pleasant, not uptight about my husband's speech or behavior.
- I'm not easily angered, and I usually treat others with gentleness.
- In my heart of hearts, I feel that I am at peace with my God and my husband.

If you can't check off all these questions, ask God to help you cultivate a "gentle and quiet spirit," which is the most incredible beauty any woman can have.

RESPECT DEFINED: A MEEK AND QUIET SPIRIT

If there is one concept more misunderstood, one verse more maligned than any other, it's 1 Peter 3:4. I can't tell you how many women have said to me, "I'm just not a meek and quiet person. Nor do I want to be!" I can understand that, because I'm naturally outgoing (not what one would call "meek") and in my younger days, I could be pretty loud. If you're anything like me, you know what I'm talking about.

So what does it mean to have a "gentle (or meek) and quiet spirit"? Let's look first at what it does *not* mean. It does not necessarily mean that you have a quiet *demeanor*. We all have different personalities, and God does not expect you to lose your unique personality in the shadow of your husband. It also does not mean that you are weak or a doormat. In 2 Corinthians 10:1, Paul describes Christ as *meek* and *gentle*. Psalm 35 describes Christ as a conquering King: *"Gird Your sword on your thigh, O Mighty One, in Your splendor and Your majesty! And in Your majesty ride on victoriously, for the cause of truth and* ***meekness*** *and righteousness"* (Psalm 45:3-4†). This is hardly a picture of Christ as a doormat!

Gentleness has been described as *strength under control*, which is a good definition. But it also speaks to the idea of *peace*; a woman who is meek or gentle is a woman who is at peace in her heart, no matter what the rest of her life is like. She has no need to fight for her agenda or to resist her husband's will. She finds a lasting, imperishable peace in Christ, which no circumstance can take away from her.

Memorize It!

Let me hear Your lovingkindness in the morning; for I trust in You;
Teach me the way in which I should walk; for to You I lift up my soul.
(Psalm 143:8)

Atmosphere Creator: The Fruit of the Spirit

Have you ever read the description of the Proverbs 31 woman and thought, "Yeah, right. That is so not me!"? I know I have. I don't sew, garden, or buy fields. Just the part about "rising while it is still night" is a challenge for me!

Even if you don't look exactly like the Superwoman of Proverbs, several verses in that passage can describe you, no matter what your personality, skills, or gifts may be:

> *An excellent wife, who can find? For her worth is far above jewels. She does (her husband)* ***good*** *and not evil all the days of her life. She...works with her hands in* ***delight***. ***Strength*** *and* ***dignity*** *are her clothing, and she* ***smiles*** *at the future. She opens her mouth in* ***wisdom***, *and the teaching of* ***kindness*** *is on her tongue. Her children rise up and* ***bless*** *her; her husband also, and he* ***praises*** *her, saying: "Many daughters have done nobly, but you* ***excel*** *them all."* (Proverbs 31:10, 12-13, 25-26, 28-29)

We can all work with joy, and be kind, strong and dignified. We can all respect our husbands, doing them good all our lives. When we are organized and diligent, we can look to the future with hope. We can all study the Scriptures to learn wisdom and teach it to our children.

As the keeper of the home, you set the tone and the altitude at which your family soars. If you're walking in the flesh, unhappy, complaining or bitter, your family will absorb that attitude from you. But if you're growing in Christ and manifesting the fruit of the Spirit, you will have a cheerful, optimistic attitude. You will be sowing the seeds of *"love, joy, peace, patience, kindness, gentleness (and) self-control"* (Galatians 5:22-23) in your home. Everyone has their own personality, so your good attitude is not a guarantee that the other members of your family will walk with Christ as well. But even if they're walking in disobedience, you can (with the Spirit's enabling) establish a godly atmosphere in your home. This attitude is what causes your husband and children to "rise up and bless" you in praise to your Father.

Memorize It!

Let me hear Your lovingkindness in the morning; for I trust in You;
Teach me the way in which I should walk; for to You I lift up my soul.
(Psalm 143:8)

But the fruit of the Spirit is love, joy, peace, patience, kindness, goodness, faithfulness, gentleness, self-control; against such things there is no law.
Galatians 5:22-23

Application

On my refrigerator is a "Code of Respect" which serves as a reminder of the kind of atmosphere I want to create in my family. You can use this one, or you and your family can come up with your own Code of Respect:

In This Family

- We don't use cut-downs, hurtful teasing, or mean-spirited humor.
- Everyone can share their opinions freely and honestly.
- Everyone gets encouragement and affection.
- Parents respect children.
- Children respect parents.
- There is a lot of love.
- The atmosphere is very positive and upbeat.
- Everyone is becoming more like Jesus Christ.[9]

Week 29, Day 3

The tongue of the righteous is as choice silver. The heart of the wicked is worth little.
PROVERBS 10:20

Application

Are you guilty of any of the impure speech listed in today's lesson? Do you use swear words, tell dirty jokes, insult your husband, gossip, lie? Do you use racial slurs or call people "idiots"? One of the ways you can purify your speech is to ask God to identify for you, instantly, whenever you use impure words or an ungracious tone in your voice. As soon as the words come out of your mouth, you need to stop, confess the impure speech immediately to the hearer, and ask God's forgiveness.

Purifying your speech involves disciplining yourself over and over until, with God's help, you get it right (1 Timothy 4:7). If you want to please God, you must be pure in both words and actions. Then, the value of your godly tongue will truly be like pure polished silver.

SILVER-TONGUED

Some time ago, a few ladies met to read the Scriptures. While reading Malachi they came upon a remarkable expression in the third chapter: *"And He shall sit as a refiner and purifier of silver"* (Malachi 3:3, KJV). One lady's opinion was that this was a picture of the sanctifying influence of Christ. So she visited a silversmith and asked about the process of refining silver, which he fully described to her. "How do you know when it is done?" she asked. "When I can see in the silver my own reflection," the silversmith replied.

That's an abbreviated version of a story preachers often tell when talking about Christ's work of sanctification in our lives. Unfortunately, like many of these stories, it's not accurate. When silver is in the fire, it's a white hot liquid. The silversmith will not see his reflection in the silver until it is *polished*.

This still makes silver a good metaphor for the tongue. Silver is a precious, treasured element. So is a righteous tongue. But both the silver and your speech must be purified if they're going to be useful and beautiful. Just as the refiner purifies the silver time and time again to make it pure, you need to purify your speech until it is more and more flawless. Part of that purification process is polishing: rubbing off the rough edges until the silver is so smooth and shiny you can see your own reflection in it.

Christ is involved in the process of sanctification in the lives of His people, but we can participate in this process by refining and polishing our speech—getting rid of the filthiness, silly talk, "coarse jesting" (Ephesians 5:4), cursing (James 3:10), insults (1 Peter 3:9), "gutter talk," unwholesome words (Ephesians 4:29), gossip (Titus 2:3), slander, abusive speech, and lies (Colossians 3:8-9), as well as foolishness (Proverbs 10:14). None of this speech has any place in the life of a committed Christ-follower.

When your mouth is "cleaned up"—purified and polished—then people will be able to see Christ's reflection in you.

Memorize It!

Let me hear Your lovingkindness in the morning; for I trust in You;
Teach me the way in which I should walk; for to You I lift up my soul.
(Psalm 143:8)

Responding in Humility

When Eva met Tony, she was attracted to his discipline, intelligence, and strong moral character. She knew he would be faithful and a good provider. What she didn't realize was how harsh and demanding he would be. He required a perfectly clean house, and treated their kids like military recruits. If Eva failed in any way, Tony would tell her she was "worthless" and make her write out Scripture that addressed her shortcomings. Eva found it ironic that her husband was oblivious to his own sins of anger and not living with her in an "understanding way" (1 Peter 3:7).

One day when Tony was yelling at her for spending too much on groceries, Eva snapped. She got in his face and said, "That's *enough!* I am not a child; I am perfectly capable of making these decisions. You will NOT talk to me this way ever again, do you understand?"

Most people looking at Eva's situation would say she is justified in standing up to her overly demanding husband. And it's true she is living in very difficult circumstances. However, God requires us to respond in love no matter how our husbands treat us. Eva is acting in arrogance and pride. She is giving herself glory, rather than glorifying Christ, and is making matters worse.

No matter what the situation, God will give you the power to resist temptation and to demonstrate love. As you respond humbly, He can turn even the most difficult circumstance into an opportunity for your good and for His glory. But if you react in pride and arrogance, you are "sowing to the flesh" and will reap destruction (Galatians 6:8). Pride and the flesh destroy love in your marriage, but humility makes love possible.

How should Eva respond to her husband? She should 1) demonstrate love by humbly and prayerfully considering what he has to say, and adjusting her behavior if necessary; 2) and biblically reprove her husband, (see pp. 50, 51 and 61 to review how to give a biblical reproof), but only after she has cleared her conscience, and always for the purpose of helping him live in obedience to Christ.

Memorize It!

Let me hear Your lovingkindness in the morning; for I trust in You;
Teach me the way in which I should walk; for to You I lift up my soul.
(Psalm 143:8)

Love is patient, love is kind and is not jealous; love does not brag and is not arrogant.
1 Corinthians 13:4

Application

God does not promise to deliver you from crises or painful circumstances, but He does promise to give you the power of the Holy Spirit to respond in love, no matter what is happening to you. *"For God has not given us a spirit of fear, but of power and of love and of a sound mind"* (2 Timothy 1:7, NKJV). You can look at every hardship as both an opportunity for you to glorify Christ and also to make positive changes in your marriage. But godly change is only possible as you humble yourself and seek God's glory above your own.

Are you enduring a difficult trial right now in your marriage? If so, ask God to help you begin (or continue) responding with humility, seeking His glory first above your own rights or personal comfort.

Week 29, Day 5

There is neither Jew nor Greek,
there is neither slave nor free man,
there is neither male nor female;
for you are all one in Christ Jesus.
GALATIANS 3:28

Application

The bottom line is that God has set limits in Scripture for both women *and* men, and we can trust that He values and has a purpose for the unique gifts of both genders. Women are not singled out as having all sorts of restrictions while men get to have all of the fun. If anything, your husband has more responsibility before God than you, and is answerable to Him for much more.

Unfortunately, rather than responding to that truth in gratitude to God and to our husbands, we often rebel and seek greater "equality." Take time today to thank God for your husband and for all he brings to the marriage; then be sure to express that gratitude to your husband as well.

GENDER-EQUAL

Many women resist obeying God's command to submit to their husbands because they reject biblical teachings on gender roles. Specifically, there is often a predisposition in American culture against Paul's teachings about the unique characteristics and corresponding biblical responsibilities of men versus women. I have often heard it said that Paul was a "chauvinist," based on passages such as 1 Timothy 2:9-14†:

> *Likewise, I want women to adorn themselves with proper clothing, modestly and discreetly, not with braided hair and...costly garments, but rather by means of good works, as is proper for women making a claim to godliness. A woman must quietly receive instruction with entire submissiveness. But I do not allow a woman to teach or exercise authority over a man, but to remain quiet. For it was Adam who was first created, and then Eve. And it was not Adam who was deceived, but the woman being deceived, fell into transgression.*

That kind of teaching certainly goes against our Western thinking, doesn't it? Even if you are in 100% concurrence with this passage, you need to understand what Paul is saying here.

First of all, this is not a blanket assertion that all men have authority over all women. The husband has authority over the wife, for her care and protection; and her job is to submit to his authority, as well as to the authority of the elders of the church, "with entire submissiveness."

Secondly, God is not saying that the woman has the greater fault, therefore she must suffer for all of human history because of it. Remember that Eve was deceived, but Adam is the one on whom the charge of original sin fell (Romans 5:12), because Adam willingly *rebelled* against God's command.

Third, the command by Paul that women should remain "quiet" doesn't mean that we have to keep our mouths shut. This word "quiet" is more accurately translated *tranquil* or *calm*. In other words, stop thrashing about, trying to overthrow your husband's authority over you.

Love Believes All Things

(Love) bears all things, believes all things, hopes all things, endures all things. Love never fails.
1 Corinthians 13:7-8†

A top-40 radio station in my area plays an annoying game show called "War of the Roses." A woman who believes her husband is cheating calls the station. After she tells her story, the DJ calls the suspected cheater and pretends to be a florist. "For no charge," says the pretend florist, "we will send a dozen roses to your wife or girlfriend." With the woman listening in, the DJ asks what name they should write on the card. If the husband says her name, everything is OK. But if he gives another woman's name, the DJ tells him he's busted, and the woman either starts crying or jumps all over his case. It's like Jerry Springer on the radio.

I loathe this game because it is everything that love is not. Not only are these women trapping their husbands, but they are subjecting them to public shame and embarrassment. Perhaps they have viable reasons for suspecting their guys, but they should approach them privately, not on a live broadcast!

Biblical love paints the person loved in the best possible light. If your husband does something that doesn't square up in your mind, you may be tempted to suspect him, question his motives, or accuse him of trying to hurt you. None of these reactions are God's will for you in any situation. God's will is for you to love your husband by believing the best instead of assuming the worst about what he says or does. When, at times, the "worst" is a fact, you can continue demonstrating biblical love to your husband because your trust is not in him, but in God's sovereign care over your marriage.

God has a purpose in every circumstance, and He can *"work all things together for good to those that love Him"* (Romans 8:28). Knowing this gives you the freedom to love your husband by believing in him. If he knows you always believe the best, he is more likely to be the man you think him to be. But if you always assume the worst, he'll lack motivation to keep trying, and your assumptions may become a self-fulfilling prophesy.

Application

Is something causing you to doubt your husband? Perhaps you suspect him of infidelity, or believe he's involved in illegal or unethical activities. Maybe he's done something hurtful, and you believe he did it intentionally. No matter what is causing you to doubt your husband, until you have evidence to the contrary, you need to assume the best.

Take time right now to pray over whatever is causing you doubt: that God would reveal to you a reasonable explanation for what he's done or a plausible scenario that sheds a more favorable light on his actions. If your doubts are serious and possibly founded, talk to your husband about it. Not in an accusing way, but express your fears in a way that lets him know you want to believe the best of him.

Memorize It!

He who is slow to anger is better than the mighty, and he who rules his spirit, than he who captures a city.
(Proverbs 16:32)

Week 30, Day 2

(Love) bears all things, believes all things, hopes all things, endures all things. Love never fails.
1 CORINTHIANS 13:7-8†

Application

It's easy to hope that God will work everything together for your good. Loving your husband transfers this hope to him as well. The unloving wife says, "My husband has sinned but God will take care of me. I don't really care what happens to him. In fact, if God wants to punish him, that would be fantastic." The loving wife says, "My husband has sinned, but I am not sinless either. God can redeem this situation for our good, conforming us to the image of his Son."

If you are going through a major disappointment in your marriage, take time right now to pray that God will help you continue loving your husband despite everything. Confess your own sins to God, and cling to the hope that God can, in His time, redeem your marriage for His glory.

LOVE HOPES

Bonnie sat at the kitchen table, her heart pounding out of her chest. In her hands was a letter from a woman who claimed to be having an affair with her husband. The woman's knowledge of Max and his whereabouts over the past year was indisputable, and confirmed what Bonnie already suspected.

Bonnie's first response was to throw dishes against the wall and watch them shatter—much as her marriage was now shattered. Instead, she fell to her knees. "Oh God," she cried, "You have promised to work all things together for good to those who love you. This affair is not good. But LORD, in me is the potential for this sin and much more. Help me not to think more highly of myself than I ought to think, but help me to forgive him. Help me not to sin in my response, but to glorify You in all I do. Help me to continue loving Max the way You love me, even though I am continually unfaithful to You."

If you think Bonnie's prayer was completely unnatural, you're right. However, I know a woman who prayed that very prayer after learning her husband had had an affair. It wasn't easy, but God gave her the strength and grace to humble herself and continue loving her husband, despite his unfaithfulness.

Sometimes, despite our desire to think the best of our husbands, our fears will turn out to be true. However, even then you can still love your husband by expressing hope to him. Your hope is found in Christ (not your spouse), and Christ can redeem even the most difficult circumstance. The hope here is that your husband will repent and become more godly if he is a Christian, or perhaps be saved if he is not.

Even if your husband has done nothing wrong and things are fine, love means clinging to the hope that God will continue to work in your hearts and make you and your husband more holy and useful for His kingdom. This hope is a confident expectation, not just wishful thinking, rooted in the all-powerful Creator of the Universe who will eventually "bring it to pass" (1 Thessalonians 5:24).

Memorize It!

He who is slow to anger is better than the mighty, and he who rules his spirit, than he who captures a city.
(Proverbs 16:32)

Giving Up Your Right To Be Angry

Week 30, Day 3

Do not be eager in your heart to be angry, for anger resides in the bosom of fools.
Ecclesiastes 7:9

Ivy sat in the bleachers at her son Andrew's soccer game, her eyes scanning the distant parking lot for any sign of her husband. Dustin had only made it to one game the entire season, but he promised he would make it tonight. Suddenly Ivy's cell phone buzzed; she opened it and found a text message from Dustin: *"Can't make it. I'll explain later. Tell Andy I'm sorry."*

For the rest of the game, Ivy struggled with two competing desires: to be angry at her husband, or to be obedient to Christ. She wanted to punish Dustin with her anger, and felt that overlooking this latest transgression was tantamount to stamping the word "approved" on his behavior. But she reminded herself to be *"quick to hear, slow to speak and slow to anger"* (James 1:19). After the game, Andy began complaining about his dad; but because she had subdued her anger, Ivy was able to calm him down. "I'm sure he has a good explanation," she told Andy. "But even if he doesn't, *you* still have to do what's right and respect your dad."

Giving up your right to be angry is how you show love to your husband and obedience to Christ. Instead of fueling the fire of your anger with condemning thoughts, you need to give your husband the benefit of the doubt until you know the full story. If it turns out that he has done something sinful or foolish, you can take appropriate action to reprove him of his sin or forgive him for his foolishness. But either way, there is never a reason to get angry.

If his actions require a reproof, you won't be able to do that if you have lost your temper. An angry reproof is not biblical or godly, but rather a selfish attempt at control. Remember that biblical reproof is always done *"in a spirit of gentleness"* (Galatians 6:1), not anger.

The Bible has much to say about anger, and rarely is our anger righteous. An angry person is described as a "fool," whereas *"He who is slow to anger is better than the mighty, and he who rules his spirit, than he who captures a city"* (Proverbs 16:32).

Application

How do you respond when your guy upsets, frustrates or annoys you? Do you lose your temper and react in anger? Or are you able to set aside your right to be angry and instead seek peace?

Anger is like fire: it is much easier to control when it is small. The point then is to keep it small by being "quick to hear" and "slow to speak." Don't jump right in with your opinions or accusations; instead, be eager to listen. After you have heard your husband's full explanation, think about how you're going to respond (Proverbs 15:28). Prayerfully choose words that are truthful, yet edifying, encouraging, and respectful—and say them in a gentle tone of voice. As you practice these techniques, you will become a woman who is "slow to anger."

Memorize It!

He who is slow to anger is better than the mighty, and he who rules his spirit, than he who captures a city.
(Proverbs 16:32)

Week 30, Day 4

To obey is better than sacrifice…
1 Samuel 15:22†

Application

Obedience to your husband "in all things, unless he asks you to sin" is one of those biblical commands that often takes precedence over other commands. But the greatest command is this: *"Love the Lord your God with all your heart, and with all your soul, and with all your strength, and with all your mind; and your neighbor* [including your husband] *as yourself"* (Luke 10:27†).

If your focus is on loving God and your husband, more than getting your own way, many of these apparent conflicts will take care of themselves. You and God will have such a close, Spirit-filled relationship that you'll know quite clearly what to do when the time comes.

Obedience: More Important Than Getting Your Own Way

Sometimes it's not real clear what God wants of us, and deciding what is right too often comes down to personal preferences or human wisdom. While there is no conflict in God's Law, we can sometimes run into an apparent conflict between two of His commands and where they intersect in our life.

For example, I was raised to tithe but my husband was not, and for years he did not want me to give ten percent of his income to the church. So my choice was between two commands: "Be subject to your husband" (Colossians 3:18) and be a "cheerful giver" (2 Corinthians 9:7). For a long time I ignored my husband's desires and did what I thought was the right thing to do.

In 1 Samuel 15, King Saul used one of God's laws as an excuse for disobeying the greater law of obedience. God had commanded him to completely destroy the Amalekites, yet Saul *"spared* [king] *Agag and the best of the sheep… but everything despised and worthless, that they utterly destroyed"* (1 Samuel 15:9). When he got caught, Saul immediately threw a spiritual spin on the situation: *"The people spared the best of the sheep and oxen,* ***to sacrifice to the Lord your God****; but the rest we have utterly destroyed"* (1 Samuel 15:15†). Saul used one of the sacrificial laws as an excuse to disobey God's direct command!

I was doing the same thing with my husband's income. I knew I should obey him in everything, but tithing was important to me. Rather than help my husband understand the importance of tithing or reprove him for his sin, I just went ahead and did what I thought was right. 1 Samuel 15:22-23† says, *"Has the Lord as much delight in burnt offerings and sacrifices as in obeying the voice of the Lord? Behold, to obey is better than sacrifice…For rebellion is as the sin of [witchcraft], and insubordination is as … idolatry."* I was using obedience to the Law as a cover for getting my own way. But God had no delight in my offerings. It was vastly more important to submit to my husband than to give God money He didn't need!

Memorize It!

He who is slow to anger is better than the mighty, and he who rules his spirit, than he who captures a city.
(Proverbs 16:32)

Attitudes For Conflict Resolution

We've talked throughout this study about resolving conflict biblically. In *The Excellent Wife* (the book this devotional is based upon), Martha Peace has an excellent summary of the attitudes necessary to resolve conflict within marriage. We've discussed each of these separately, but I'd like to briefly go over Martha's summary here, as a way of review.

Attitudes Needed to Solve Conflict

Humility—A humble person views himself in proper perspective to God and others. They do not *"think more highly of [themselves] than they ought to think"* (Romans 12:3†). We naturally think about ourselves first. God, however, commands us to *"regard one another as more important than himself"* (Philippians 2:3). Humble yourself by putting your husband first over yourself. Consider his desires as more important than your own (unless he is asking you to sin).

Gentleness—You are to have self-restraint and not overreact to conflict. If you are gentle, you will be tender, compassionate, and content in the circumstances God has given you. You do not try to manipulate circumstances to suit yourself. You are calm, careful, and thoughtful in how you respond when you and your husband disagree.

Patience—Our goal is to be *"strengthened with all power, according to His glorious might, for the attaining of all steadfastness and patience"* (Colossians 1:11). God teaches us patience through tribulation (Romans 5:3) and testing (James 1:3), both of which are common catalysts for conflict. Patience, like gentleness, is part of the fruit of the Holy Spirit (Galatians 5:22-23). You are to patiently listen and respond to your husband, *especially* when there is conflict.

Tolerance—Forbearance, or "putting up with" one another. In His forbearance, God *"passed over the sins previously committed"* (Romans 3:25). It is not through our sinful flesh that we forbear, but with God's enablement and in obedience to His Word. Tolerance means putting up with your husband. It goes a long way toward solving conflict and maintaining unity.

Week 30, Day 5

Therefore I, the prisoner of the Lord, implore you to walk in a manner worthy of the calling with which you have been called, with all humility and gentleness, with patience, showing tolerance for one another in love, being diligent to preserve the unity of the Spirit in the bond of peace.
Ephesians 4:1-3

Application

If there is conflict, look first to yourself to see if you are manifesting these four character qualities—humility, patience, gentleness and tolerance—in your life. If not, identify specific instances of times when you have failed, confess those sins to God, and ask your husband's forgiveness. Think through how you should have responded. Next time, respond the biblical way.

Through His enabling Spirit and obedience to His Word, you can achieve and maintain *"unity of the Spirit in the bond of peace"* (Ephesians 4:3). Regardless of the cause or even the outcome of the conflict, you can continue to be an excellent wife as you strive to solve conflict biblically.

Week 31, Day 1

For the love of Christ controls us, having concluded this, that one died for all, therefore all died; and He died for all, so that they who live might no longer live for themselves, but for Him who died and rose again on their behalf.
2 CORINTHIANS 5:14-15

Application

Read the Faith chapter of Hebrews 11 and note how people of great faith have been rewarded throughout human history. Some, like Rahab, were spared from danger (verse 31), or "received back their dead by resurrection" (verse 35). Yet others were tortured, imprisoned and put to death.

The truth is that, sometimes, being sanctified and fit for the Master's use brings *more* suffering, not less (1 Peter 4:12-19). If you are submitting to and serving Christ because you expect something in return, then you will lose faith in Him when you are rewarded with more suffering. *This life is not about you.* It is about God and His Son Jesus Christ. Ask God today to give you a pure love for Him that expects nothing in return.

The Motivation for Sanctification

When Laurel walked in the door after a really hard day at work, she was surprised by the smell of dinner wafting from the kitchen. She walked in and found the table set, and her husband Rob standing at the stove making stir-fried chicken. Pleased that he was doing something so sweet for her, she gave him a hug and asked, "What's this?" "Well," he answered, "I'd figured I'd have to make dinner if there was any chance of us making love tonight."

Niiice. That's just exactly what we want to hear from our husbands, right? "I'm only doing this for you so I can get something in return." Where is the love in that?

Yet that is exactly how we treat God. Many of you picked up this book because you needed something from God, and the path to getting what you want seems to be performance related: If I submit to my husband, serve God, and purify my life from sin, then surely God will:

- ☑ Accept me and see that I am good enough to enjoy His favor.
- ☑ Reward me with good things.
- ☑ Make life easier for me.
- ☑ Give me a happier marriage and ensure the salvation of my children.

We do not earn God's favor by being "sinless" and by doing good works for Him. *"Are you so foolish? Having begun by the Spirit, are you now being perfected by the flesh?"* (Galatians 3:3). So what is the purpose of doing good works if it doesn't earn us anything? Well, let me ask you: wouldn't you rather your husband do something for you out of love, and not because it's going to earn him something? This is what God wants: *"If you love Me, you will keep My commandments"* (John 14:15). He wants us to do our good works purely out of love for Him, not because it earns us anything.

You and your husband are to help each other in the process of mutual sanctification so that you will be better able to serve Christ and each other. God will reward you, but your reward may not be in this life (Hebrews 11:26). If you are motivated by love and devotion to Christ and a desire to please Him, then your obedience will be its own reward.

Memorize It!

For those who are according to the flesh set their minds on the things of the flesh, but those who are according to the Spirit, the things of the Spirit. For the mind set on the flesh is death, but the mind set on the Spirit is life and peace.
(Romans 8:5-6)

INFLUENTIAL RESPECT

She does him good and not evil all the days of her life... Her husband is known in the gates, when he sits among the elders of the land.
PROVERBS 31:12, 23

Austin and Nolan are best friends who grew up together, went to the same church and school, and now work for the same company. They both come from good Christian homes, have similar interests and education, and are both really great guys. They're good at what they do, and are fairly equal in their qualifications for their jobs. However, Nolan is much more successful in his career, and was recently promoted to management, while Austin seems to be constantly struggling. The difference?

Well, we're not quite sure, but it's interesting to note how different their wives are. Nolan's wife is loving, supportive, and respects her husband greatly. Austin's wife, on the other hand, criticizes him constantly. It seems that there is little he can do to please her, and the tension at home affects his emotions and consequently, his job performance.

The old adage, "Behind every successful man is a good woman" is one we don't hear very often any more, but it is still just as true as it ever was. Part of being a "good woman" is respecting, supporting, and believing in your man. As much as he may not want to admit it, your husband feeds off your approval and respect. Consequently, you have more influence in your marriage than you may have realized. Respecting your husband builds him up and helps give him the strength to face the challenges of the day. Your respect gives him confidence and energy, enabling him to be more productive at work and more effective as a leader in the home, church and community. Like the excellent wife of Proverbs 31, whose husband was *"known in the gates"* (vs. 23), you can have a profound effect on your husband's reputation, just by being respectful and supportive. But a lack of respect from you will tear him down and make him feel inadequate in every area of his life.

Application

To the best of your knowledge, examine the level of respect your husband has in the eyes of his family, friends, and co-workers. If he is not very well respected, it is highly probable that your lack of respect for him is a contributing factor. True, he may have done things to cause others to lose respect for him. But others look to you, the one who knows him best, as a measure of how worthy or unworthy he is of respect. If your husband is a hero in your eyes, he'll be a hero in his own eyes and is much more likely to act accordingly, thereby earning the respect of others.

Memorize It!

For those who are according to the flesh set their minds on the things of the flesh, but those who are according to the Spirit, the things of the Spirit. For the mind set on the flesh is death, but the mind set on the Spirit is life and peace.
(Romans 8:5-6)

Week 31, Day 3

But Martha was distracted with all her preparations; and she came up to Him and said, "Lord, do You not care that my sister has left me to do all the serving alone? Then tell her to help me.
Luke 10:40

Application

Don't be confused by the biblical injunctive to "do all to the glory of God" (1 Corinthians 10:31). God is glorified by how much we love others, not by how clean our house is or how perfect our kids are. Being a perfectionist is seeking to please your fleshly lust for perfection and your view of how things should be. The cure for perfectionism is to love Christ with all your heart, soul, mind and strength (Mark 12:30), and to put others first. We should try to glorify God in all we do, but we don't glorify Him by working to achieve our own goals. We glorify Him by accomplishing *His* goals. His goals are always to bring people to Himself, not to alienate them by holding them to impossibly perfect standards.

The Lust for Perfection

I am a perfectionist. I don't understand or care about all of the psychological influences that create a perfectionist. I just know that I am one and that it's not a good thing! For years, I believed God has a special affection for perfectionists more than for those who are sloppy or careless about life. After all, God is the ultimate perfectionist, right? Is there anything He does halfway?

Even if you're not a neat-freak, you can be a perfectionist in other areas. I have a friend whose house always looks like news footage of a tornado's aftermath, but she demands perfect performance from her kids. Some women are rigid in their schedules, and will overwork themselves and others to accomplish their goals. Other women lust after a perfectly clean home, and become nasty if anyone messes it up.

Martha was this type of housekeeper (Luke 10:38-42). While her sister Mary sat at Jesus' feet, Martha was frantically cooking and cleaning. In fact, she was so focused on this objective that she tried to tell Christ what *He* should do! She was likely concerned about impressing both Christ and their other guests by making sure everything was perfect. But Christ rebuked her and said, *"Martha, Martha, you are worried and bothered about so many things; but only one thing is necessary, for Mary has chosen the good part, which shall not be taken away from her."* The message is clear: our relationship with Christ should always take first priority over our rigid ideas about how things should be done.

While it is good to be disciplined, it is wrong to be intolerant or harsh if everything is not perfect. People are more important than clean houses and tight schedules, and if someone disrupts your routine or messes up your home, you should be *"easy to be entreated"* (James 3:17, KJV). If your heart is *set* on achieving perfection, you probably have made it an idol in your heart. Instead, you must set your heart on glorifying the Lord Jesus Christ and letting Him decide how you can best glorify Him.

Memorize It!

For those who are according to the flesh set their minds on the things of the flesh, but those who are according to the Spirit, the things of the Spirit. For the mind set on the flesh is death, but the mind set on the Spirit is life and peace.
(Romans 8:5-6)

Hands Off the Wheel!

By awesome deeds You answer us in righteousness, O God of our salvation, You who are the trust of all the ends of the earth and of the farthest sea.
Psalm 65:5

Throughout the long night, the little ship tossed on the waves like a toy. Gale-force winds blew hard against the sails, driving the ship miles off course. The captain yelled into the wind, "Lower the sails!" but no one answered. Finally, he jumped from the ship's helm and lowered the sails himself. A few men came to his aid, but it was too late, they had already taken on water.

Eventually the storm passed, but the ship was on its side and sinking fast. As the sailors clung to splintered pieces of the ship, the captain asked, "What were ye doin' during the storm?" "Aye, cap'n, I was balancing the cargo," one sailor said. "I be closin' the gunports," said another. The captain was speechless. No one had followed orders! But the third crewman was the worst of all. "I was at the helm, captain!" he said. "I've seen ye in the waves, and yer no match for the sea!"

What these sailors didn't realize was that by doing what they thought was right, the captain was unable to protect them. Because his authority was not regarded, he was unable to keep the ship on course.

Your marriage is like a ship at sea. Too often, we're off doing our own thing, with no regard for what our husbands need. Or we try to wrestle our husbands for control, when we should be doing all we can to help. *Helping* your husband gives him the freedom to do his job well—including his job to protect and love you.

Notice I said helping gives him the *freedom* to do his job well. That doesn't mean he *will* do his job well. Not all husbands are good at steering the ship of their family. Your husband may a good leader, or he may be the type who rules by intimidation or who lets the crew do all the work. However he steers, your job remains the same: to love and help him.

Your obedience in this area is not a guarantee, but it will keep you from being a hindrance to the work God is doing in your husband's life. Moreover, you should help your husband out of love for him and for the Lord (1 Corinthians 16:14).

Application

When the seas are rough, it takes a lot of trust in God to let your husband stay at the wheel, but you must remember that, ultimately, it is God who is steering the ship, not your husband. God knows what lies ahead in the ship's path, and He is in control of the waves. Your job is not to steer the ship; your job is to be your husband's "first mate"!

What kind of first mate are you? Do you trust God to let your husband steer, or do you try to take the wheel out of his hands? Using the sailor's analogy, write in your prayer journal what kind of "crewman" you think you are. Then write down specific ways you can be a better "first mate" to your husband.

Memorize It!

For those who are according to the flesh set their minds on the things of the flesh, but those who are according to the Spirit, the things of the Spirit. For the mind set on the flesh is death, but the mind set on the Spirit is life and peace.
(Romans 8:5-6)

Week 31, Day 5

But if your enemy is hungry, feed him, and if he is thirsty, give him a drink; for in so doing you will heap burning coals on his head. Do not be overcome by evil, but overcome evil with good.
ROMANS 12:20-21

Application

Instead of making things worse by saying the wrong thing, or returning evil for evil by saying nothing at all, what you must do in these circumstances is set aside your pride, anger, and self-righteousness, and look for a way to bless your husband (Romans 12:20). If you had any part in the conflict, confess that and ask for his forgiveness—even if you believe he was guiltier than you.

During a conflict, you may think the "dark cloud" you're living under—the one that keeps you from talking to your husband—is caused by your husband's sin, but it's not; it's the oppression of your *own* sin. You would be surprised how freeing it is to unload the burden of your sin and *"be at peace with all men"* (Romans 12:18), especially your husband.

THE SILENT TREATMENT

I can't believe he did that. I am so angry, I can't think straight! And then to blame it on me? OK, I admit my actions were not made of gold either. But they're NOTHING compared to what he did. And if he thinks I'm going to apologize first...? Absolutely not! I will not reward this behavior, and I am certainly not going to be the first to break the silence. He's the guilty party here. He *needs to apologize to* me*!*

Have you ever had that conversation with yourself? What was the result? I can tell you this: it wasn't God-honoring, and did nothing to promote peace and harmony in your marriage. The usual result of this kind of talk is the "silent treatment." Not all of us have a problem with yelling or abusive speech, but most of us are good at freezing out our husbands. He does or says something sinful or stupid, and we just clam up, give him the cold shoulder, and refuse to grace him with any words of kindness until he has apologized.

Some women can go for days without talking to their husbands. The problem is pride and anger: They feel they have been wronged, they are unforgiving (not stopping to think about how much Christ has forgiven them), and they refuse to "lower" themselves by even speaking to their husband until he humbles himself first.

When you are angry, it is very easy to give your husband the silent treatment. Often the justification for this is, "If I talk, I'll say something I'll regret." But this is not a humble or obedient way to respond to our husbands. This is nothing more than taking revenge by "paying back evil for evil" (Romans 12:17), rather than "overcoming evil with good" (Romans 12:21). If you're not ready to talk yet and need time to calm down, then use that calming time wisely by thinking righteous, God-honoring thoughts about your husband, and asking God to redeem this situation for His glory. Confess any part you had in the conflict, and ask God for the wisdom to respond lovingly, righteously, and *quickly* to your husband.

How To Know God's Will

Danielle has been praying for years that God would make it possible for her children to get a Christian education. Then one day she called me with incredible news: her parents had offered to pay for both of her children to go to a Christian school. There was just one problem: her husband wasn't happy about it.

"I don't know what to do," she said. "He hasn't said no, but I can tell he's not crazy about the idea. Yet God has clearly opened the door. I just know this is His will!" In Danielle's mind, this amazing opportunity for her children to go to Christian school was how God was "working all things together for good" (Romans 8:28) and providing "the desires of her heart" (Psalm 37:4).

When faced with a decision like this one, many wives struggle with the question, "What is God's will?" When you and your husband disagree about the best decision to make, God's will **every time** is that *you submit to your husband in all things, unless he asks you to sin*. As God's child, you have the Holy Spirit living in you, and you also have circumstances to navigate and interpret. But the primary way God speaks to you is through His Word. The Bible should be the final authority for the practice of your life. The Bible clearly says, *"As the church is subject to Christ, so also the wives ought to be to their husbands in everything"* (Ephesians 5:24).

I know that's probably not what you wanted to hear. But your responsibility is to submit to God, and submitting to your husband is the primary way you do that. This chain of command makes most decisions fairly simple.

What we often try to do is use "signs and wonders" as indications that God is moving in a particular direction. Amazingly, that is usually the direction that gets us what we want!) But any plan we come up with that contradicts His command to humbly submit to our husbands will be a very bad plan. Even if it's based on how we are *convinced* the Holy Spirit is leading.

Memorize It!

Therefore I, the prisoner of the Lord, implore you to walk in a manner worthy of the calling with which you have been called, with all humility and gentleness, with patience, showing tolerance for one another in love, being diligent to preserve the unity of the Spirit in the bond of peace.
(Ephesians 4:1-3)

Wives, be subject to your own husbands, as to the Lord. For the husband is the head of the wife, as Christ also is the head of the church, He Himself being the Savior of the body.
Ephesians 5:22-23

Application

God will never lead you to rebel against your husband, unless your husband is asking you to disobey God's commands. If you are tempted to disregard your husband and go your own way, thinking that you're following God, you need to remember that God will never tempt you to sin (James 1:13). If He were leading you to not submit to your husband, then He would be tempting you to sin and that is impossible.

It is much more likely that your own desires are speaking louder than the voice of His Spirit, and that you have asked things of God *"with wrong motives, so that you may spend it on your pleasures"* (James 4:3). Nothing is more important than yielding your will to God's will. Even if your will is for something good.

Week 32, Day 2

A wise man will hear and increase in learning, and a man of understanding will acquire wise counsel.
PROVERBS 1:5

Application

Are you facing a situation right now in which you need godly advice? Consider the following questions when seeking counsel:

- Is the counselor godly, humble, and submitted to Christ?
- Is the counselor biased in any way?
- Have I fairly presented both sides and portrayed my husband in the best light possible?
- Have they advised me to submit to my husband in all things, unless he's asking me to sin?
- Did they use Scripture to back up their advice, or just their own experience and human wisdom?

Above all, pray that God would: lead you to the best counselor; give you humility in telling your story; prepare you to receive His truth; and give you discernment and strength to act on the godly counsel you're given.

GOING AGAINST THE POPULAR VOTE

When Madison married Paul, she knew she'd found the love of her life. She loved him so much, submitting to him was easy and life was good—for a couple of years. But then the economy fell apart and Paul had to sell his business. Living in California was expensive, so they packed up and moved to Tennessee, near Madison's family. Once they got settled, Madison was anxious for her husband to find a job, but after more than a year Paul had still not found work, and the bills were piling up.

One day Madison's father told them about a duplex for sale that could provide a good income. He offered to loan them the down payment, which they could pay back from the rental income. It looked like a great opportunity, but Paul rejected it as too risky. For weeks Madison tried to convince him, but he would not change his mind. Finally, she talked to her pastor, who told her that if her husband was not going to provide for their family, then she needed to take matters into her own hands. His advice was exactly what everyone else had told her, so she wrongly went ahead and signed the papers—against her husband's wishes.

When faced with a tough decision, it is wise to seek advice from others. *"In abundance of counselors there is victory"* (Proverbs 24:6). However, you must choose counselors wisely, and any advice contrary to Scripture should be instantly discarded, no matter who gave you the advice. I have found that education on biblical submission is severely lacking in the church, so it does not surprise me when I hear bad advice in this area, even from pastors. Sometimes, you may have to go against conventional wisdom and the advice of all your friends and family in order to be subject to your husband. Remember, too, that sometimes we get the advice we "want" because we've so skewed the telling of the story that we're unlikely to get any advice other than what we've programmed others to give.

Memorize It!

Therefore I, the prisoner of the LORD, implore you to walk in a manner worthy of the calling with which you have been called, with all humility and gentleness, with patience, showing tolerance for one another in love, being diligent to preserve the unity of the Spirit in the bond of peace.
(Ephesians 4:1-3)

Love Endures

(Love) bears all things, believes all things, hopes all things, endures all things. Love never fails.
1 Corinthians 13:7-8†

In contemplating 1 Corinthians 13:7, I found myself wondering what the distinction was between "bearing all things" and "enduring all things." The picture God brought to mind was of two athletes: one a weight lifter, the other a runner. The lifter feels the weight pushing him down, and he must summon the strength not to buckle under the burden. The runner is on an obstacle course, but she is moving forward no matter what tries to stop her.

"Love endures all things" is a picture of that runner. Life throws many obstacles in our way, Satan seeks every opportunity to trip us up, and our own flesh works against us as we head toward the finish line. Unfortunately, our husbands can often be just as involved in the conspiracy as those other obstacles. Not that they're trying to; they just are, by nature of being human.

The challenge for us as women is to see all of life's pressures—every obstacle, every trial—as opportunities to become more like the Lord Jesus. Even when that trial comes in the form of your husband, you can still love him, knowing that Christ endured much more suffering for us than we will ever have to endure for Him. Why did He do it? Because of *"the joy that was set before Him"* (Hebrews 12:2).

It's not that we take joy in suffering or playing the role of a martyr. The joy comes in knowing that we are God's children, and therefore no trial or difficulty is wasted; God uses everything in our lives to humble us and make us more like His Son. Keeping this in mind will help you love your husband through all of life's obstacles.

Application

Following are some excellent verses you can quote to yourself when you're going through a difficult trial or circumstance. Read them and choose one to write out and post someplace where you will see it often:

Philippians 4:11-13
1 Peter 3:13-16
Hebrews 12:2
Acts 5:41
Romans 8:16-18
2 Corinthians 12:9

Endurance is what the grace of God promises, so picture yourself as a runner on an obstacle course, and visualize the finish line: Christ Jesus Himself. Keeping your eyes on Him will make all obstacles seem small in comparison, and free you to love your husband without regard to circumstances. Whatever the injustice or trial, you can endure *"all things through Christ who strengthens"* you (Philippians 4:13).

Memorize It!

Therefore I, the prisoner of the Lord, implore you to walk in a manner worthy of the calling with which you have been called, with all humility and gentleness, with patience, showing tolerance for one another in love, being diligent to preserve the unity of the Spirit in the bond of peace.
(Ephesians 4:1-3)

Week 32, Day 4

Now we have received, not the spirit of the world, but the Spirit who is from God, so that we might know the things freely given to us by God, which things we also speak, not in words taught by human wisdom, but in those taught by the Spirit, combining spiritual thoughts with spiritual words.
1 CORINTHIANS 2:12-13

Application

The Bible cannot lead people astray if it is properly understood and obeyed. It is *"profitable for teaching, for reproof, for correction, for training in righteousness"* (2 Timothy 3:16). Unfortunately, even Bible-teaching pastors sometimes rely on man's wisdom to give counsel. Using the guidelines above should help you determine if you're getting good, biblical advice. You can also look for a counselor who is certified by the National Association of Nouthetic Counselors (NANC)[10].

GODLY COUNSEL (PART 1)

Brea was talking to her friend, Jan, about the problems she and Darren were having." I know we should get counseling," she said, "but Darren would be livid if I told our pastor what was going on." Jan smiled and reached into her purse, and pulled out a business card that read *Meg Jacobsen, Christian Counseling*. "Call this woman," Jan said. "She's *wonderful*." Brea took the card and later that day called to set an appointment.

At their first meeting, Meg talked a lot about Brea's self-esteem, and how Darren probably suffered from "Narcissistic Personality Disorder." Meg seemed to understand exactly what Brea was going through, and while she didn't really open her Bible or offer specific Scripture, Brea trusted that the advice she was getting was biblically based.

Sadly, Brea has been duped into thinking she's getting Scriptural advice, when what she's really getting is a lot of human wisdom. Many "Christian" counselors offer advice based on worldly thinking, not on the truth of God's Word. That's exactly the kind of counselor Brea has found, and the advice she's getting will not lead her and her husband into a closer walk with Christ and each other.

If you and your husband are unable to work things out on your own, you will need to bring in outside help. Your first priority in seeking a counselor is to find a faithful, godly person who believes the Bible is true and without error, and that it contains practical guidance for every situation. They must believe that only God's Word can answer all of life's questions.

Once you've found a counselor who claims to believe those truths, examine carefully the advice they give. Is it supported by Scripture in both its major and minor points? Do they define the problem biblically (for example, what is each person doing that is violating the Word of God?) and offer a biblical solution, using appropriate Scripture references? Above all else, does their advice encourage greater understanding and obedience to God's Word?

Memorize It!

Therefore I, the prisoner of the LORD, implore you to walk in a manner worthy of the calling with which you have been called, with all humility and gentleness, with patience, showing tolerance for one another in love, being diligent to preserve the unity of the Spirit in the bond of peace.
(Ephesians 4:1-3)

Godly Counsel (Part 2)

The first to plead his case seems right, until another comes and examines him.
Proverbs 18:17

Cora has always depended on her mother for godly advice, so when she discovered her husband Bradley lost thousands of dollars playing online poker, she called her mom first. She expected her mom to give her wisdom from God's Word, as she'd always done in the past. She was startled, then, when her mom got angry. "I can't believe he would do this to you and the kids!"

Immediately, Cora felt the need to defend her husband. "Well, mom, I don't think he was planning on it going this far..." "He shouldn't be gambling in the first place," her mom cried.

Cora quickly realized their problem was beyond what her mom would be able to help her with. She talked to Bradley, and they both went to their pastor for counseling. Many months later, he was gambling-free... but his relationship with his mother-in-law actually took longer to heal than the addiction.

The first criteria when seeking a counselor is to find a godly person who knows God's Word and believes that only Scripture can answer all of life's questions. But after that, probably the second most important criteria is that the counselor be objective and eager to hear both sides (Proverbs 18:17). Your family and close friends may not be the best people to go to, especially if they are more loyal to you than to your husband. Because you are comfortable with them, you may be tempted to gossip freely about your husband, rather than genuinely seek biblical guidance. If you have bitterness against him, you could "defile" their attitude (Hebrews 12:15) and adversely affect their relationship with your husband, even after you and he have reconciled.

If you are truly seeking a biblical solution to your problems, and not just the opportunity to justify yourself to your friends, you will limit the number of people you tell about the problems in your marriage, and you will be careful not to slander your husband. Like biased, unbiblical counsel, speaking evil of your husband will only make the situation worse, not better.

Application

"In abundance of counselors there is victory" (Proverbs 11:14†); however, a wife who tells everyone about her husband's sin problems without making a serious effort to receive biblical counseling is merely gossiping. For this reason, you might consider going to a pastor or an older, godly woman in the church (Titus 2:3-4) for help initially.

Restoring your relationship with your husband and both of your relationships with God should be the goal of any biblical counseling. The counselor should help both of you identify your sin, and seek forgiveness from each other as well as God. If your husband refuses to go, you can go alone and work on your part. After you've made progress, your husband might be more inclined to seek counsel also.

Week 33, Day 1

Older women (should) encourage the young women to love their husbands, to love their children, to be sensible, pure, workers at home, kind, being subject to their own husbands, so that the word of God will not be dishonored.
Titus 2:3-5†

Application

I know it can be discouraging, day after day, reading about what you *should* do, how you should live as an excellent wife. Giving God and your husband the bulk of your strength and love every day can seem like a tall order. But know this: God's grace is what produces good results in your life, not your own righteous efforts. Your sufficiency is in *Christ*, not yourself, and His strength is made perfect in your weakness (2 Corinthians 12:9). Cling to that promise today, as your renew your commitment to give God and your family your very best.

Home Priorities

My mom was an amazing woman, but she wasn't necessarily a great cook. She kept us well fed, and we passionately loved certain dishes she made, like chicken and homemade noodles or pies made from the cherry tree in our front yard. But usually, it was the same thing week after week. Whenever she did make something out of the ordinary, you can be sure it wasn't meant for us, but for some event going on at church. I can remember her setting a special dish out on the counter, and when one of my brothers would go to sample it, my dad would say, "I wouldn't do that. It's probably not for us!"

A lot of us are like that when it comes to our families. We consume all of our energy, gifts and talents on our jobs, our work at church, or on other volunteer activities, and give our families the leftovers. We do this for several reasons: 1) They might come to expect our best every day and who has that kind of energy? 2) We work harder to please people outside of our families because we're still trying to win their love. 3) We usually default to what gives immediate gratification. Investing in the family is a long-term commitment that doesn't always yield immediate results.

I hesitate using my mom as an illustration because she was the best mom I could have asked for. She always had a cheerful attitude, and whatever she lacked in doing everything perfectly, Christ made up for in our family because she honored Him and my dad and put them first. The truth is, she did have her priorities straight.

You know what your priorities should be: God first, then Husband, Children, Home, and Ministry in that order. But do you actually live that way? Do you live as though God is Number 1—does He get your first and your best? Then, do your husband, kids and home get the bulk of your energies, or do you live for yourself, your job or your ministries, and give your family whatever is left of you at the end of the day?

Memorize It!

Your adornment must not be merely external—braiding the hair, and wearing gold jewelry, or putting on dresses; but let it be the hidden person of the heart, with the imperishable quality of a gentle and quiet spirit, which is precious in the sight of God.

(1 Peter 3:3-4)

No Submission Without Humility

Why is submission *so* hard for us? Few of us realized when we got married how extremely difficult it would be to submit to our husbands. We thought being in love would make everything easy. And sometimes it is easy, but much of the time it is really, really hard.

The reason submission is so hard is because of one little word: *Pride*. Pride says I have every right to be my own boss, make decisions for myself and determine what is best for me. Why should I have to ask whether or not I can buy that dress? Why can't my kids take those piano lessons or go to that school? Why does the thermostat have to be set at 65?? What makes *him* more qualified to make decisions than me?

As long as you allow pride and self to rule in your heart, you will continue to ask these kinds of questions, and will never know the joy and peace that comes from submitting your will completely to your husband. Instead, you are behaving just like Pharaoh in the book of Exodus.

Pharaoh was the supreme ruler of his people, and considered himself a god. It was his birthright and a manifestation of his extreme power, glory and majesty that he had absolute power over his people, to do with them whatever he wished. Then there was Moses, a puny little Hebrew *nobody*, telling him what to do. It was as though the ant had approached the mountain and said, "Out of my way!" Why in the world would Pharaoh submit his will to the will of someone who was not even an Egyptian, much less a god like himself? His pride would simply not allow it.

In refusing to submit his will to Moses, Pharaoh was actually refusing to submit to the God of the Universe. Pharaoh saw himself as this great and mighty ruler-god, but in comparison to God, he was nothing. God let Pharoah know exactly what his problem was: *"Thus says the Lord, the God of the Hebrews, 'How long will you refuse to humble yourself before Me? Let My people go, that they may serve Me"* (Exodus 10:3). Pharaoh was too proud to submit to anyone—including God.

Memorize It!

Your adornment must not be merely external—braiding the hair, and wearing gold jewelry, or putting on dresses; but let it be the hidden person of the heart, with the imperishable quality of a gentle and quiet spirit, which is precious in the sight of God.
(1 Peter 3:3-4)

All of you, clothe yourselves with humility toward one another, for God is opposed to the proud, but gives grace to the humble. Therefore humble yourselves under the mighty hand of God, that He may exalt you at the proper time.
1 Peter 5:5-6†

Application

Are you like Pharaoh, too proud to submit? Or are you more like Moses, who was *"very humble, more than any man who was on the face of the earth"* (Numbers 12:3)? Because Moses had such humility, he submitted to Pharaoh even though Pharaoh was harsh and unjust. Moses led the Hebrews from Egypt only after Pharaoh finally gave his begrudging permission.

If you're struggling to submit to your husband, then like Pharoah, you have a pride problem. The solution is to purposely work toward the opposite of pride, which is humility. We are humbled when we see ourselves as weak and sinful, and see God as the holy, omnipotent, loving and perfect God Most High. In your worship time today, focus on who God is, and ask Him to humble you, as Moses was humbled.

Week 33, Day 3

Therefore encourage one another and build up one another, just as you also are doing.
1 THESSALONIANS 5:11

Application

You might not normally be an expressive person, but with practice you can learn to speak words of praise to your husband. The next time you and your husband are together, look for an opportunity to praise him for something specific that he's done recently. Even better, praise him in front of his friends or family. You will be amazed at how encouraging words of praise can be to your husband!

HONEST PRAISE: RESPECT IN COMMUNICATION

Ken lifted the last of the heavy stones onto the hearth and cemented it into place. It had been a big job, but finally the fireplace in their family room was finished. As he stepped back to admire his work, Janet walked into the room. "You're done?" she asked. "Yep!" Ken answered, smiling broadly as he wiped the sweat from the back of his neck.

Option #1: Janet walked up to the fireplace and examined it closely. "Wow, honey, you did an amazing job. It's beautiful!" she cooed. "I can't wait to show this to everyone tonight!"

Option #2: "Finally!" Janet replied. "How long's it been, eight months? Well, at least you got it done before the party tonight!" She walked out of the room and called over her shoulder, "Don't leave those tools lying around!"

Which of these two options portrays the more godly response? Of course, it's the first one. The question is, which of these two scenarios is more likely to happen in your home? It is not likely that the husband in Scenario #2 will race to do anything more to help his wife get ready for their party. And why should he? His wife doesn't appreciate what he has done for her, and she has shown a great lack of respect for him and his abilities.

One of the ways you show respect for your husband is by genuinely praising him. He needs to hear *I'm proud of you—I trust you—You did a great job—You're such a good husband/father*. This tells him that you respect and value him, and appreciate his efforts. Yet for some reason, we often find it easier to criticize our husbands or point out their shortcomings. Instead of tracking your husband's failures, Peter commands us to *"keep fervent in your love for one another, because love covers a multitude of sins"* (1 Peter 4:8†). When you love and respect your husband, you will keep an account of the good things he has done, and praise him for those things at every opportunity.

Memorize It!

Your adornment must not be merely external—braiding the hair, and wearing gold jewelry, or putting on dresses; but let it be the hidden person of the heart, with the imperishable quality of a gentle and quiet spirit, which is precious in the sight of God.
(1 Peter 3:3-4)

Verbal Abuse and Miscommunication

Reid has been living with a terrible secret: for years, his wife Libby has been verbally abusing him. Sometimes she's just careless, saying matter-of-factly, "That's because you're stupid." But when she gets angry or moody, she can really lose control and give her husband a verbal beat-down. Libby suffers from terrible PMS, and when it's that time of the month, it's like she becomes another person—nothing like the sweet, beautiful, caring woman he married. She has always been aggressive and passionate, which Reid admired when they were dating. But he had no idea Dr. Jekyll was also "Mrs. Hyde."

We usually think of men being the abusers, but women can be just as guilty, especially when it comes to verbal abuse. The reason you don't hear much about husband abuse is because guys don't talk about it when it happens to them. It brings them great shame that they would let their wives treat them this way, so they're certainly not going to talk about it, much less seek help for it. But they are just as wounded by verbal abuse as a woman would be, and perhaps even more so, given how important it is for a man to look good in the eyes of his wife. If she talks down to him or tells him he is incompetent or stupid, that tears at the very fabric of a man's masculinity.

None of this kind of speech is good, but it crosses the line into being abusive when it is relentless, harsh or repetitive. A wife who is abusive may have other serious issues and should seek the help of a competent pastor or a biblical counselor to help her turn from this destructive habit, and purify her heart and her speech.

Even if you're not abusive, you can still be guilty of "abusive speech" if your objective is to hurt your husband or get revenge against him for something he said or did to you. This kind of talk has no place in the life of a godly woman. Rather, your speech should be *"pleasant...sweet to the soul and healing to the bones"* (Proverbs 16:24†).

Hide me from the secret counsel of evildoers, from the tumult of those who do iniquity, who have sharpened their tongue like a sword. They aimed bitter speech as their arrow.
Psalm 64:2-3

Application

Before you say, "I would never abuse my husband like this," look over the following examples and see if you ever use any type of this speech toward your husband:

- Have you ever attacked his character or abilities?
- Has he ever accused you of being *mean*?
- Do you ever make fun of him?
- Do you belittle or insult him?

If you have spoken to your husband in these ways and not asked him to forgive you, you need to do that *today*. Then ask God to help you remove *"all bitterness and wrath and anger and clamor and slander ... away from you, along with all malice."* Purpose that from this day forward, with God's help, you will *"be kind... tender-hearted [and] forgiving... just as God in Christ also has forgiven you"* (Ephesians 4:31-32).

Memorize It!

Your adornment must not be merely external—braiding the hair, and wearing gold jewelry, or putting on dresses; but let it be the hidden person of the heart, with the imperishable quality of a gentle and quiet spirit, which is precious in the sight of God.
(1 Peter 3:3-4)

Week 33, Day 5

For we also once were foolish ourselves, disobedient, deceived, enslaved to various lusts and pleasures.
Titus 3:3†

Application

When you received Christ as your Savior, you were sealed by the Spirit into God (Ephesians 1:13). But you must continually yield your life to the Spirit in order to have victory over any idols that would distract you from Him. This takes practice, and you have to continually remind yourself of the need for it. Otherwise, you will go right back to your old sinful habits and living in the flesh. Start each day with a prayer something like this:

Lord, I know that in my own strength, I am completely unable to control myself. Today, I want to die to myself and live to serve You and others. Fill me with your Holy Spirit; help me to remember to continually yield my body and my heart to the Spirit's control. In Christ's name I pray, Amen.

Addicted to Idols?

Summer had a hard life growing up, and turned to sex, drugs and alcohol to numb the pain of her childhood. But when she was 26, someone shared the gospel with her and she accepted Christ as her Lord and Savior. God turned her life around and she joined a good church, eventually marrying a godly man who knew all about her past but loved her anyway. She rarely thinks about her former life, until something happens that shakes her faith in God. Then she thinks about taking a drink of alcohol to escape her troubles. And if an attractive man catches her eye, she fantasizes about sleeping with him, remembering how much she used to enjoy casual sex.

Jeanne never struggled with the sins Summer did, but she has a hard time controlling her eating habits. She knows she should eat sensibly and avoid foods that aren't good for her, but if she's in line at the grocery store, it's impossible *not* to grab a candy bar. When she takes the kids through the drive-through, she'll resist ordering burgers and fries...and reward her "self-control" with a chocolate shake.

What the world often calls an "addiction" is actually just a lack of self control. A person "addicted" to alcohol has willingly relinquished their self control in order to drink. We can choose to be controlled by things that are clearly sinful—such as drugs, sex, or gambling—or things that are relatively benign, such as food, television, social networking sites (like Facebook, etc.), computer games, etc. Whatever you allow to control you is an idol in your life.

Self control is one of the fruits of the Holy Spirit (Galatians 5:23), so the key to controlling your idolatrous desires is to be filled with the Spirit. This occurs as we desire what *God* wants for our lives more than what *we* want. When you allow something other than the Holy Spirit to control you, the Bible says you are *foolish*, *disobedient*, *deceived*, and *enslaved* (Titus 3:3). And how true that is! Doesn't it seem terribly foolish to be controlled by anything other than Christ?

Family Meeting: Discipline in the Church (Part 1)

Amber has done everything she knows to do, but her marriage is not getting any better. Alec hasn't worked in over four years and is verbally abusive. She tried reproving him biblically about his unkindness and failure to provide for them, but Alec shifted the blame onto her: "If you wouldn't spend so much," he said, "We could survive while I concentrate on getting my realtor's license." He also tried to blame his anger on her. "You go out of your way to provoke me," he claimed.

After much prayer, Amber realized she had no choice but to take the next step in getting her husband to face his sin honestly. She waited until he was in a fairly good mood, then seized the opportunity. "I know deep down, you love me," she said gently. "But it has been a long time since you have loved me biblically as you should. Your sin is deeply affecting our family, as well as your relationship with God. I've tried to talk to you about this, but you refuse to listen. So I don't have any choice. I have to take this up with Pastor and the elders." Amber carefully explained to Alec how Matthew 18:15-17 requires her to follow through on her previous reproofs. "I don't want to do this," she cried, "but I can't let you continue to hurt us and yourself."

Matthew 18 details the steps God has provided to protect you if your husband refuses to repent of sin. Step 1 is to *"reprove him in private"* (verse 15). If he does not listen to your reproof, step 2 is to *"take one or two (witnesses) with you"* (verse 16). These witnesses should be godly men in your church or family who know and love your husband and are committed to seeing him restored to you and to Christ. When you meet, you and your husband should each give your side of the story. After hearing both sides, if the witnesses determine that he is indeed sinning, they should be prepared to confront him directly using specific Scriptures. They should then offer him a biblical course of corrective action.

Memorize It!

Servants, be submissive to your masters with all fear, not only to the good and gentle, but also to the harsh. For this is commendable, if because of conscience toward God one endures grief, suffering wrongfully.
(1 Peter 2:18-19, NKJV)

If your brother sins, go and show him his fault in private; if he listens to you, you have won your brother. But if he does not listen to you, take one or two more with you, so that by the mouth of two or three witnesses every fact may be confirmed.
Matthew 18:15-16

Application

In most cases, if your husband is truly a believer, he will likely respond to these first two steps and repent. If not, you'll have to move on to step three, which we'll discuss tomorrow.

For today, consider this: what sins are serious enough for you to address biblically? Too often, we only go through these steps for the "big" sins, such as abuse or infidelity. But *every* sin is serious to God, because every sin interferes with our fellowship with and our effectiveness for Him.

If we were serious about holiness, we would go through this process a lot more often. The result? Stronger marriages, and a more powerful church. Neglecting this process, and the resulting lack of holiness, is one of the reasons why we are so ineffective for Christ.

Week 34, Day 2

If he refuses to listen to them, tell it to the church; and if he refuses to listen even to the church, let him be to you as a Gentile and a tax collector.
MATTHEW 18:17

Application

It is humiliating to have to stand before the church and admit that the man you want others to think the best of is, in fact, an unrepentant sinner. Fearing that this is where confrontation will lead, many wives are reluctant to even do step one (the biblical reproof). We prefer instead to cover up, ignore, or give tacit approval to our husbands' sin. If this is your normal approach, know that you are not being helpful to him, and are being disobedient to Christ.

Confronting your husband with his sin is the loving thing to do. Love *"does not rejoice in unrighteousness, but rejoices with the truth"* (1 Corinthians 13:6). It is difficult, but God gives grace to the humble. He will always give you the grace to do what is right.

Family Meeting: Discipline in the Church (Part 2)

Amber said goodbye to the pastor and Mitch Howell, the two men who had come to confront her husband, and closed the door quietly behind them as they walked to their car. The meeting had not gone well: Alec refused to admit he had a problem with abusive speech, and had lied about looking for a job. The pastor promised he would bring Alec's situation up at the next deacons' meeting.

When she returned to the den, Alec was sitting in his chair watching TV. He glared at her, but didn't say a word. She knew he would be angry for a few days...just *how* angry remained to be seen. "Thank you for agreeing to see them," she said. "I'm sorry you still can't admit to your sin, but I love you and am committed to you." She smiled at him and could see him melt just a little. "Can I get you anything?" she added.

Even while you are reproving your husband, you can still bless him by being *"harmonious, sympathetic...kindhearted, and humble in spirit"* (1 Peter 3:8†) through the entire process. Remember the goal of pointing out his sin: to see him return to a right relationship with God. You are more likely to be successful in this if you continue showing him the love of Christ through your words and actions.

Step 3 of the discipline process is to *"tell [your husband's sin] to the church"* (Matthew 18:17†). If your husband is unrepentant, your pastors and church elders may decide to proceed with church discipline: to bring his name and sin before the congregation, so the church members may lovingly put pressure on him to repent. This is a difficult thing to do, but it is one of the most effective means we have for purifying the church, warning people against hardening their heart in willful sin, and restoring a sinning brother to a right relationship with God, his church, and his wife.

If he still refuses to repent, both you and the church are to consider him to be what he is proving himself to be: an unbeliever (*"a Gentile and a tax collector,"* Matthew 18:17).

Memorize It!

Servants, be submissive to your masters with all fear, not only to the good and gentle, but also to the harsh. For this is commendable, if because of conscience toward God one endures grief, suffering wrongfully.
(1 Peter 2:18-19, NKJV)

Intimacy vs. Immorality

For this is the will of God, your sanctification; that is, that you abstain from sexual immorality... For God has not called us for the purpose of impurity, but in sanctification.
1 Thessalonians 4:3, 7

Brooke opened up her mailbox and found the book she had ordered online: *Erotic Short Stories for the New Century.* It wasn't the type of book she was comfortable getting at the bookstore, and she probably needed to hide it from her husband. Nate had been working so much lately, and she needed to get her sexual thrills somewhere! She had looked at soft porn on the internet, but she was sure Nate would find out by looking at her web browsing history. A book was much easier to hide.

If we could fast forward a year, it would not be at all surprising to find Brooke involved in hardcore pornography or even an affair. By not seeking purity in her life, she is opening herself up to major failure in this area of her life.

A very important component of your progressive sanctification is learning how to *"possess [your] own vessel in sanctification and honor, not in lustful passion, like [those] who do not know God"*(1 Thessalonians 4:4-5†). It's difficult to know how to do this, because God created us as sexual creatures, and we are born as sinful creatures. Our sinful flesh craves the excitement of sex, and keeping that excitement with our husbands day after day, year after year can be a challenge. That's why it is important to learn sexual self-control; if you don't, you will be disobeying God and leaving the door to failure wide open.

Many Christians have been brought down by sexual sin, and no one was ever effective for Christ who did not first learn how to control themselves sexually. It is so important that Paul addresses it in all of his epistles. If your husband is falling short of his duty to you in this area, you may be tempted to look for sexual thrills in things such as pornography, sexual fantasizing, or masturbation. While these things don't always lead to extramarital affairs, they are "lusts of the flesh" (1 John 2:16) that are displeasing to God and work against your sanctification and purity.

Memorize It!

Servants, be submissive to your masters with all fear, not only to the good and gentle, but also to the harsh. For this is commendable, if because of conscience toward God one endures grief, suffering wrongfully.
(1 Peter 2:18-19, NKJV)

Application

Working on having a healthy intimacy with your husband is crucial to avoiding sexual temptation. What is helpful to that process is eliminating any sexual activity from your life that is outside your intimate relationship with your husband. Look up the following verses, and make notes in your prayer journal about God's attitude toward sexual impurity:

1 Thessalonians 4:1-7
Matthew 15:18-20
Romans 1:24-27
Romans 13:13-14
1 Corinthians 5:11 Galatians 5:16-21
Ephesians 5:3-7
Colossians 3:5-10

Even if you don't currently have a problem in this area, it's helpful to study what God has to say about it so that, when temptation comes, you are equipped to reject Satan's lies.

Week 34, Day 4

Through Him then, let us continually offer up a sacrifice of praise to God, that is, the fruit of lips that give thanks to His name.
HEBREWS 13:15

Application

Gratitude and joy go hand-in-hand. If you've gotten into the habit of complaining, either aloud or in your heart, it is likely that you're not thanking God for all He's done and therefore not motivated to be obedient by joyfully submitting to your husband. Examine your heart today to see if your attitude lately has been one of joyful gratitude, or ungrateful complaining. Make a list of all you have to be grateful for, starting with the LORD Jesus and his atoning work on the cross. Then spend time in prayer thanking God for each thing on your list.

ATTITUDE OF GRATITUDE

Christy sat across from me, tears pooling in her eyes. We had been talking about her marriage, and I knew she was near her breaking point. "When is it going to get better?" she asked. "I tried the whole 'excellent wife' thing, yet my life continues to go downhill. I can't do it anymore!" Admittedly, Christy had many obstacles to overcome, but her life was not nearly as hopeless as she made it out to be. "OK," I said, "Let's start here: You're saved, right?" She let out a huge sigh. "Yeah, I know. But so what? It's not getting me anywhere."

Christy's lack of gratitude for the things God had done for her extended to her husband as well: she did not see him as a gift from God, and was unable to see anything in her marriage to be thankful for. Yet in just a few minutes, I was able to list several things that she had not thought of or had dismissed as irrelevant. I knew God was not the only one who recognized her lack of gratitude; her husband was sensitive to it as well and it was seriously affecting their marriage.

An ungrateful wife is difficult to please, and her ingratitude keeps her from being properly submitted to her husband. Her attitude is, "Why should I submit? What has he done for me lately?" But things fall into proper perspective when we stop to remember what Jesus Christ has done for us. "*You were not redeemed with perishable things like silver or gold...but with precious blood, as of a lamb unblemished and spotless, the blood of Christ*" (1 Peter 1:18-19†). Jesus was scourged, mocked, despised, rejected, humiliated, and crucified for our sin.

If you have accepted Christ as your LORD and Savior, you can thank God that He has rescued you from sin; that He wants to have an intimate, conversational relationship with you; and that you will live with Him forever someday. If nothing else in your life is right, those three facts alone should cause you to be filled with gratitude, and being grateful is an important part of becoming biblically submissive to your husband.

Memorize It!

Servants, be submissive to your masters with all fear, not only to the good and gentle, but also to the harsh. For this is commendable, if because of conscience toward God one endures grief, suffering wrongfully.
(1 Peter 2:18-19, NKJV)

Where Your Treasure Is

Do not store up for yourselves treasures on earth, where moth and rust destroy, and where thieves break in and steal. But store up for yourselves treasures in heaven, where neither moth nor rust destroys, and where thieves do not break in or steal; for where your treasure is, there your heart will be also.
Matthew 6:19-21

Terri's husband has a good job, but they can't live as though money is no object. Her best friend, however, is very wealthy. She drives an expensive car, has a gorgeous home—everything Terri wants but can't have. She would love to be able to go on European vacations, eat in nice restaurants, and shop the pricier stores in the mall. Terri struggles with being grateful, and is seriously considering going back to work. "I'm tired of living within such a tight budget," she says. "There are things I want in life!"

Terri is caught up in materialism, a form of idolatry we're all familiar with. Oftentimes, if we don't have a lot of material blessings, we think we're immune to materialism. However, it is when we *don't* have the things we want that we are most vulnerable. Satan tempted Eve to lust after something she didn't have (Genesis 3:6), and deceived her into thinking something as temporal as a piece of fruit was the key to happiness.

It's difficult to live in America and not get sucked up into wanting more, better, nicer. The *"deceitfulness of riches"* (Mark 4:19) says that wealth can satisfy our deepest heart's desires. But Jesus reminded us that we can't be divided in our devotion. *"No one can serve two masters; for either he will hate the one and love the other, or he will be devoted to one and despise the other. You cannot serve God and wealth"* (Matthew 6:24).

Materialism is a sin that destroys contentment, interrupts our worship of God, and hinders us from being effective in Kingdom work (1 Timothy 6:10-17, Deuteronomy 8:10-14). It's not wrong to have nice things you can afford, as long as they don't prevent you from being generous toward Kingdom work. The question is, do you spend more time and energy "storing up treasures on earth" than you do serving your Creator? Or perhaps you can afford to buy whatever you want. How much of your wealth is going to God's work, and how much toward your own comfort and affluence?

Application

Take a few minutes right now to make a list of any material things you've been longing for or spending a great deal of time or energy trying to obtain.

How easy was it to come up with your list? If items came to mind quickly, it is likely that you are worshiping the idol of materialism. If so, ask God to release you from your desire to accumulate things which rust, decay, or can be stolen (Matthew 6:19), and to help you keep your eyes on Him as the only object of your worship.

"Do not weary yourself to gain wealth, cease from your consideration of it. When you set your eyes on it, it is gone. For wealth certainly makes itself wings; like an eagle that flies toward the heavens" (Proverbs 23:4-5).

Week 35, Day 1

But now you also, put them all aside: anger, wrath, malice, slander, and abusive speech from your mouth.
COLOSSIANS 3:8

Application

When you are with your family and closest friends, how do you talk about your husband? All wrong speech—including gossip and slander—comes from wrong thoughts and attitudes. If you are constantly focused on how your husband has sinned against you, or the foolish decisions he's made, or the many ways he has failed you, then you are storing up a lot of garbage in your mind that is only going to spill out of your mouth in the form of slander and "abusive speech." God's desire is for you to keep your mind pure, to think about things that are true, honorable, right, and of "good repute" (those things which make for a good reputation—Philippians 4:8); and not to *"take into account a wrong suffered"* or *"rejoice in unrighteousness"* (1 Corinthians 13:5-6†).

ENCOURAGE EACH OTHER... EVEN WHEN THE OTHER ISN'T AROUND

I look around the room at all of the beautiful women who have gathered to study God's Word and learn how to be better wives. But before we get started, I have to tell them the "rules" for *The Excellent Wife* Study.

Rule #1: We NEVER talk bad about our husbands.

It's amazing the creative ways women circumvent this rule. Most often, it's in the form of a prayer request: "Please pray for my husband who is *such* an idiot." Or they'll tell a story that either starts with, "My husband is my best friend, but..." or ends with that Southern catch-all phrase, "Bless his heart."

Ephesians 4:31 says to *"let all bitterness and...slander be put away from you." Slander* is painting another person in a bad light, and I have found that most women find it very difficult *not* to slander their husbands. We want to share our lives with our friends, and that guy living in our home is a huge part of that. We want our closest friends to sympathize with our trials and justify our reactions by being just as appalled by his behavior as we are. Or, we want to identify with our friends' struggles. When a friend has spilled her guts about the bad things her husband has done, it's just not cool to say, "Really? My husband is great!" We want her to know we understand, so we chime in with what our husband has done that is just as bad.

No matter the reason, all slander is wrong. Even if you truly need guidance, you must be careful how and to whom you talk about your husband. Sometimes family members can be too close to the situation to give the best advice. On the other hand, some women wait too long to tell others about what they're going through. It's a delicate balance, finding the right people to talk to and getting the support you need, while still painting your husband in the best light and not poisoning other people's attitudes against him. Make sure, before you talk to anyone, that your attitude is right, that you have humbled yourself, and that you are truly seeking biblical counsel—not just sympathy.

Memorize It!

For what credit is it if, when you are beaten for your faults, you take it patiently? But when you do good and suffer, if you take it patiently, this is commendable before God.
(1 Peter 2:20, NKJV)

Fail-Proof Love

Love never fails.
1 Corinthians 13:8†

In the 1960s, when America was going through a cultural and sexual revolution, a popular catchphrase was, "Love is the answer." Anti-war activists, hippies, and the news media used that slogan to define what they thought was a revolutionary solution to all of mankind's problems.

While their definition of "love" may have differed vastly from God's, the point is that Love is the answer. In counseling women and teens, I have discovered that no matter what issue they're struggling with, I usually end up bringing them back to love. It seems there is no problem we cannot solve if we accurately apply God's truth about love to the situation. Hence, when Paul wrote 1 Corinthians 13, he ended his dissertation on love with this summary statement in verse 8: Love never fails.

Love never fails to win. Christ's love never fails to heal. Godly love never fails to correct, or set right, or renew. Unselfish love never fails the lover, or the one who is loved. Love never fails.

Throughout this book we've discussed several aspects of love, based on 1 Corinthians 13:4-7:

> *Love is patient, love is kind and is not jealous;*
>
> *Love does not brag and is not arrogant, does not act unbecomingly;*
>
> *It does not seek its own, is not provoked, does not take into account a wrong suffered,*
>
> *Does not rejoice in unrighteousness, but rejoices with the truth;*
>
> *Bears all things, believes all things, hopes all things, endures all things.*

When you "put on love," you choose to incorporate these aspects of love in your attitudes and actions toward your husband, rather than thinking and behaving selfishly. These qualities will become habits the more you practice them.

Application

Looking at each aspect of love from 1 Corinthians 13:4-7, write down specific, practical ways you can express love to your husband, incorporating those qualities. If you need help, refer back to the devotionals on love throughout the book. (See Index.) For example, you might say something like, "I am not going to keep thinking about what he did because 'love does not take into account a wrong suffered.'" Even if your efforts do not bring immediate results, remind yourself that, like God, "love never fails."

Memorize It!

For what credit is it if, when you are beaten for your faults, you take it patiently? But when you do good and suffer, if you take it patiently, this is commendable before God.
(1 Peter 2:20, NKJV)

Week 35, Day 3

He has told you, O man, what is good; and what does the LORD require of you but to do justice, to love kindness, and to walk humbly with your God?
MICAH 6:8

Application

Building humility into your life means learning to hate what God hates and love what God loves. God hates pride and loves humility, but our Godless society does just the opposite: it loves those who are proud and has contempt for the humble. *"For all that is in the world, the lust of the flesh and the lust of the eyes and the boastful pride of life, is not from the Father, but is from the world"* (1 John 2:16). One need only look as far as the TV show *American Idol* to see how the "pride of life" is praised in our society.

Take time today to meditate on the above verses. Then make a list of anything in your life that promotes pride and "my way" kind of thinking. Ask God to help you purify your life of anything which encourages pride in you.

PRIDE GOES BEFORE THE FALL

God HATES pride. Because everyone is guilty of it, we tend to think God understands and tolerates small amounts of pride. However, Proverbs 16:5 says, "*Everyone who is proud in heart is an abomination to the LORD; assuredly, he will not be unpunished.*" And why wouldn't God hate pride? It is the evil that brought sin into the world:

> *How you are fallen from heaven, O Lucifer, son of the morning! How you are cut down to the ground, you who weakened the nations! For you have said in your heart: "I will ascend into heaven, I will exalt my throne above the stars of God...I will ascend above the heights of the clouds, I will be like the Most High."* (Isaiah 14:12-14 NKJV)

Pride is the number one cause of strife in marriage (Proverbs 13:10). It is at the heart of every sin we can conceive, as in our pride we think we can live life separately from God. If you are guilty of thinking it's just a minor sin, consider these verses:

> *There are...things which the LORD hates...which are an abomination to Him: Haughty eyes...and one who spreads strife among brothers* (Proverbs 6:16-17, 19†).
>
> *Pride and arrogance and the evil way, and the perverted mouth, I hate* (Proverbs 8:13†).
>
> *The haughty He knows from afar* (Psalm 138:6†).
>
> *Pride goes before destruction, and a haughty spirit before stumbling* (Proverbs 16:18).
>
> *When pride comes, then comes dishonor.* (Proverbs 11:2†).

Contrast these verses to what God has to say about humility, which is His desire for us:

> *O LORD, You have heard the desire of the humble; You will strengthen their heart, You will incline Your ear* (Psalm 10:17).
>
> *To this one I will look, to him who is humble and contrite of spirit, and who trembles at My word* (Isaiah 66:2†).
>
> *A humble spirit will obtain honor* (Proverbs 29:23†).
>
> *God...gives grace to the humble* (James 4:6†).
>
> *But with the humble is wisdom.* (Proverbs 11:2†).
>
> *Humble yourselves in the presence of the LORD, and He will exalt you* (James 4:10).
>
> *Before honor comes humility* (Psalm 15:33†).

Memorize It!

For what credit is it if, when you are beaten for your faults, you take it patiently? But when you do good and suffer, if you take it patiently, this is commendable before God.
(1 Peter 2:20, NKJV)

Public Respect

Jeanette sat nervously on the couch, keeping an eye on her husband Mitch as he and Missy's husband Dave played a video game. As their digital cars racked up points, she could see the competitive spirit burning in Mitch's eyes, and feel his tension as palpably as her own. When the game ended, Mitch threw the remote control into the air and pointed at Dave. "Ha! In your face, dirt bag!" Jeanette cringed. Her husband's outburst in the heat of the moment was expected, but that didn't make it any less embarrassing. "Mitch, it's just a stupid game," she said. "It's not like you won at Daytona."

Jeanette is trying to control her husband's behavior by humiliating him. She believes that when he gets too full of himself, it is her job to prick the balloon of his ego and let out some of the hot air. What she doesn't understand is how painful her disrespect is to her husband. Rather than deflating his "ego," she is actually making him feel small and inadequate.

It's bad enough when we disrespect our husbands in private. But when we do it in front of others, the effects can be devastating. Many men are in constant competition with each other on every front, from their jobs to their cars to their athletic prowess. If your husband doesn't have your respect, to him that is like wearing a t-shirt with FAILURE printed across the chest. Others will see him as weak and feel sorry for him, and his estimation in his own eyes will be diminished.

"The wife must see to it that she respects her husband" (Ephesians 5:33†). You may think your husband doesn't need your respect, or that emotions don't play a part in his dealings with the world. If so, you could not be more wrong. By either showing or withholding respect, you can make him feel stronger, or cripple him and make him feel weaker. You have the ability to influence him for good and for God's glory, or to make it difficult for him to not react sinfully to you.

Memorize It!

For what credit is it if, when you are beaten for your faults, you take it patiently? But when you do good and suffer, if you take it patiently, this is commendable before God.
(1 Peter 2:20, NKJV)

Like an apple tree among the trees of the forest, so is my beloved among the young men... My beloved is dazzling and ruddy, outstanding among ten thousand...he is wholly desirable. This is my beloved and this is my friend, O daughters of Jerusalem.
Song of Solomon 2:3; 5:10, 16†

Application

Just as your husband will be hurt and humiliated if you publicly disrespect him, he will likely fall in love with you all over again if you praise him in front of others. Think carefully about how you treat your husband in public. Do you:

- Take every opportunity to praise and brag about him to others?
- Ask for his opinions or include him in group conversations?
- Laugh *with him* when he does something embarrassing, and let him know it's ok?
- Publicly show him affection, allowing others to "catch" you admiring him?
- Tell him, in front of others, how proud you are of him?

Week 35, Day 5

Make my joy complete by being of the same mind, maintaining the same love, united in spirit, intent on one purpose. Do nothing from selfishness or empty conceit, but with humility of mind regard one another as more important than yourselves; do not merely look out for your own personal interests, but also for the interests of others.
PHILIPPIANS 2:2-4

Application

It is important to allocate your time and resources so you have enough energy to devote to your husband when he needs it. Keeping him in mind and anticipating his needs throughout the day will help you reserve energy in your body, and space in your heart and mind for him at the end of the day. God understands that you have many responsibilities, but you need to be constantly aware, as you manage your day, that your *first* responsibility is to your husband. Otherwise, you may find yourself like the bride in the Song of Solomon, who wished she had responded to her man's desires sooner.

ENERGY ALLOCATION: ANTICIPATING HIS NEEDS

Brianna plopped onto the couch and let out a happy sigh. The kids were in bed, the house was clean—it had been a busy day, but now she could rest and maybe read a little before going to bed.

Her husband's voice shattered her reverie. "Hon, could you give me a hand?" Chip was a night owl and often worked on home projects after dinner. She walked into the bathroom where he was deeply involved in retiling the shower. "I need you to hold this grout," he instructed. "It hurts my back to keep bending over for it." Brianna took the grout and leaned against a wall, wondering how long this would take. Forty minutes later, just before she was sure she was going to pass out, he finally finished. He thanked her and gave her a kiss, but he had that *look*. Brianna knew what he was thinking. *Are you kidding me?* she thought. *He wants* that, *now?* She was so tired; did he not realize how hard she had worked all day?

Brianna is guilty of what many of us are guilty of: using up all of her energy during the day, with very little left over for her husband at night. The bride in the Song of Solomon had the same problem, feeling "inconvenienced" by her man's needs:

> *I was asleep, but my heart was awake. A voice! My beloved was knocking:*
>
> *"Open to me, my sister, my darling, My dove, my perfect one!"*
>
> *I have taken off my dress, how can I put it on again?*
>
> *I have washed my feet, how can I dirty them again?*
> (Song of Solomon 5:2-3†)

Can't you just picture it? She's sound asleep, and suddenly her husband is calling for her. She's thinking, "Ugh, I *just* got to sleep! What does he want? Now I have to get dressed, my feet are gonna get dirty...!" She repents of these feelings, but too late:

> *My beloved extended his hand through the opening, and my feelings were aroused for him.*
>
> *I opened to my beloved, but my beloved had turned away and had gone!*
>
> *My heart went out to him as he spoke. I searched for him but I did not find him;*
>
> *I called him but he did not answer me.*
> (Song of Solomon 5:4, 6)

The Power of Prayer

Everyone who meets Jodi can tell she's a take-charge kind of woman. She has an amazing amount of energy, and tackles difficult projects with an enthusiasm and commitment that usually ensures success. So she was very frustrated when all of her efforts to "fix" her husband proved ineffective.

Jodi was a former student in *The Excellent Wife* Bible study, and when she and I caught up with each other over coffee, she shared her frustration with me. "I'm studying God's Word and trying to live by it, and I am definitely a more submissive wife than I used to be. Gavin has even noticed how hard I'm trying. But we just seem to lack something in our marriage. I don't feel any unity or intimacy with him, and we are both still very spiritually immature."

After further questioning, I couldn't see anything she was doing wrong, and was just about to tell her to keep persevering, when suddenly I realized we'd missed something important. "How much do you pray for Gavin?" I asked. She got a sheepish look on her face. "Honestly," she admitted, "that is pretty hit-and-miss. I pray for his health and safety every day, but my life is so rushed. Rarely do I take the time to pray for his walk with God."

If you are not consistently praying for your husband and your marriage, you are like the athlete who tries to compete after a fast. You will lack the power to sustain your efforts. It is by obedience and praying in faith that we appropriate the power of the Holy Spirit for our lives. Through prayer, we acknowledge and remind ourselves that we are not doing any ministry or good works out of our own strength, but that *"it is God who is at work in you, both to will and to work for His good pleasure"* (Philippians 2:13†).

Richard Trench (1807-1886), said that "Prayer is not getting man's will done in heaven, but getting God's will done on earth. It is not overcoming God's reluctance but laying hold of God's willingness." It is God's will that your marriage glorifies Him; you lay hold of His will through prayer.

Memorize It!

Therefore I urge you, brethren, by the mercies of God, to present your bodies a living and holy sacrifice, acceptable to God, which is your spiritual service of worship. And do not be conformed to this world, but be transformed by the renewing of your mind, so that you may prove what the will of God is, that which is good and acceptable and perfect.
(Romans 12:1-2)

Devote yourselves to prayer, keeping alert in it with an attitude of thanksgiving.
Colossians 4:2

Application

How faithful are you at praying for your marriage, your husband, his spiritual growth, and maturity? In order for you and your husband to achieve the kind of loving unity that glorifies God, you must make your marriage a matter of faithful prayer. If prayer is difficult for you, here are some easy ways you can improve your prayer life:

- Pray out loud whenever you're alone. (I often pray during walks, or while I'm in the car.) This keeps your mind from wandering while you pray.
- Pray for your husband first. After you have spent time praising God and confessing any known sins, your first petition should be for your husband.
- Pray every day. If you forget during the day, make it the last prayer before you fall asleep.

Week 36, Day 2

Every person is to be in subjection to the governing authorities. For there is no authority except from God, and those which exist are established by God. For (governing authorities are) a minister of God to you for good.
ROMANS 13:1, 4†

Application

Notice that 1 Peter 2:13 says, *"Submit yourselves **for the LORD's sake** to every human institution."* The purpose of submitting to human authority is not *primarily* for our protection, but "for the LORD's sake"—that God might be glorified. No matter how much conflict you have in your marriage, the question is, are you biblically and properly responding to sin in your life and the life of your husband?

Taking full advantage of the resources God has provided for your protection is the right thing to do, and is the most spiritually mature course of action. The more you submit to God and your husband, the more likely your husband is to repent and turn to God. However, even if he does not repent, you will have honored the LORD and shown love to your husband.

A Safe Place

The first time Clay hit her, Brandi was so scared she called the police. After spending the night in jail, Clay was ordered to take an anger management course, which helped for awhile. But Clay is not a believer and has had no real change in his heart. He still thinks his wife is partly to blame for his anger.

He doesn't hit her every day; in fact, he does it infrequently. But chances are very great that Clay will grow increasingly violent, and Brandi is in real danger. She loves her husband, but loving him does not mean protecting him from the consequences of his behavior.

If your husband is physically abusing you, he is breaking the law, and you must protect yourself and your children. *"Submit yourselves for the LORD's sake to every human institution, whether to a king as the one in authority, or to governors as sent by him for the punishment of evildoers"* (1 Peter 2:13-14†). Calling the police is one of the resources God has given to protect you. You would be foolish not to take advantage of it and to see how God might use it for good, even in your husband's life.

If you are *not* being abused by your husband, you may be tempted to rush through this lesson. But don't miss the main point: ***sin is serious, and must be seriously dealt with***. If your husband is breaking the law, your protection comes from those divinely appointed authorities who deal with lawbreakers. If your husband is sinning against God, you are commanded to address his sin, even if that means appealing to your church for protection and help in bringing him to Christ.

The temptation for many of us is just to go along and not "make waves." As long as we're relatively undisturbed, we don't seek holiness and a pure devotion to God in our marriages. We tolerate sin in ourselves and in our husbands. The reason the Bible gives such specific instructions on how to deal with sin in your marriage is not so that you can have a good marriage that is conflict-free. The purpose is to have a holy marriage that glorifies Christ.

Memorize It!

Therefore I urge you, brethren, by the mercies of God, to present your bodies a living and holy sacrifice, acceptable to God, which is your spiritual service of worship. And do not be conformed to this world, but be transformed by the renewing of your mind, so that you may prove what the will of God is, that which is good and acceptable and perfect.
(Romans 12:1-2)

The Idol of Another

Do not be deceived:
"Bad company corrupts good morals."
1 Corinthians 15:33

Shortly after Danae and Lee were married, Lee's job moved them to a city far from their friends and family, and Danae took a job at a large company. They found a good church, but Danae found it difficult to make friends there. Making friends at her job was easier; Danae was outgoing, and people naturally gravitated to her, especially Brandon, a young man in her department. They had a lot in common, and Danae enjoyed his company. He often came to their house for dinner, and while he and Lee were friendly, the real bond was with Danae. Since she wasn't sexually attracted to him, she thought he was "safe."

That is, until the day Brandon confessed he was in love with her. "I know you love your husband," he said. "But I can't keep quiet about this." Danae had known all along that it was wrong to have a close relationship with another man, but even after his confession it was hard to sever the emotional ties.

Danae's friendship with Brandon was an idol in her heart. She knew it was wrong, but keeping him in her life was more important to her than pleasing her husband or glorifying Christ. Remember that an idol is anything that you will sin to attain, or that tempts you to sin if you're denied it. In Danae's case, she would become angry or depressed whenever her friendship with Brandon was threatened.

Perhaps you have a friendship that is not honoring to your husband or to Christ. It might be a girlfriend who does not build you up in Christ, or that you tend to "get into trouble" with. She might even be a Christian, but your friendship is far from godly. Or it might be a male friend you are inappropriately close to.

I'm not saying you can't have unsaved or guy friends, because we are called to love and build relationships with people who need Christ. But your best friends, the ones with whom you share your heart, should be first of all your husband and then other women who encourage you to "love your husband" (Titus 2:4) and love Christ.

Memorize It!

Therefore I urge you, brethren, by the mercies of God, to present your bodies a living and holy sacrifice, acceptable to God, which is your spiritual service of worship. And do not be conformed to this world, but be transformed by the renewing of your mind, so that you may prove what the will of God is, that which is good and acceptable and perfect.
(Romans 12:1-2)

Application

If the Holy Spirit has convicted you about a friendship that is tearing you down, write the name of that person(s) here:

If you have not been willing to sever those ties, you need to begin the process of ending that relationship *today*. Start by telling your husband what you intend to do, and enlisting his help. I've had to do this in my own life, so I understand how difficult it will be. But it is very necessary for your life, your spiritual health, and your marriage. Most of all, it is critical if Christ is going to be Lord of your life and your number one passion. Remember that your God *"**will** supply all your needs according to His riches in glory in Christ Jesus"* (Philippians 4:19†).

Week 36, Day 4

Lay aside the old self, which is being corrupted in accordance with the lusts of deceit... Be renewed in the spirit of your mind, and put on the new self, which in the likeness of God has been created in righteousness and holiness of the truth.
EPHESIANS 4:22-24†

Application

If you've fallen into the trap of worldly thinking, the solution is for you to bring your beliefs and values in line with Scripture. Look up the Scriptures listed below and write out the values described. Then ask yourself if your values line up with God's. If not, memorize those verses so that you can renew (change) your mind according to God's Word.

1 Corinthians 13:4-5
Philippians 2:3-4
2 Corinthians 4:8-18
Colossians 3:12-18
Galatians 5:13-26
Titus 2:3-5
Ephesians 4:1-3, 30-32
James 3:13-18
Ephesians 5:1-24
1 Peter 3:1-14

RENEWING YOUR MIND

When David and Claire were married, David had a growing career as a consultant, and Claire had just completed her degree in physical therapy. They put off having kids while she established herself in her career and he built up his client base. Claire's plan was to stop working after their first child was born. By then, David's consulting business would be established enough for them to handle the loss of her income.

That was the plan. The reality was that after their second child was born, David's business was still not where it should have been, while Claire's job more than paid the bills. By the time their third child arrived, Claire was firmly entrenched as head of the house—supporting the family financially and making most of the major decisions. When David tried to lead, Claire held veto power. It's not surprising, therefore, that resentment and bitterness took root in their marriage.

Many wives believe they should aggressively pursue equality in the marriage and that their careers are just as important as their husband's. They get so wrapped up in materialism that making money becomes a greater priority than having a Christ-honoring marriage. Have you fallen for this worldly philosophy? Do you have a negative reaction to the concept that you should regard your husband's career as more important than your own? If so, your values are unbiblical. Your job is to be your husband's helper, committed to meeting *his* goals, not your own.

As Christians, our standard is Christ, who sacrificed Himself for the sake of those He loves. We are called to be a "living sacrifice" (Romans 12:1)—to sacrifice our desires and goals for the sake of Christ and for our husbands. That's what you signed up for when you asked Christ to be your LORD and Savior. "*You have died, and **your** life is hidden with Christ in God*" (Colossians 3:3†). Your intellect, gifts, and strengths are still important and useful to God, but they should be directed toward fulfilling God's higher purposes for your life.

Memorize It!

Therefore I urge you, brethren, by the mercies of God, to present your bodies a living and holy sacrifice, acceptable to God, which is your spiritual service of worship. And do not be conformed to this world, but be transformed by the renewing of your mind, so that you may prove what the will of God is, that which is good and acceptable and perfect.
(Romans 12:1-2)

A Prescription For Anger

In her book *The Excellent Wife*, Martha Peace demonstrates how to use God's Word to tackle sin issues in your life. Today we're going to talk about using Scripture to "put away" anger, as commanded in Ephesians 4:31. But remember that these methods can be applied to any sin you're struggling with, such as bitterness, gossip, fear, etc.

Second Timothy 3:16 says that *"All Scripture is inspired by God and profitable for teaching, for reproof, for correction, for training in righteousness."* Using those four ideas as a guide, let's examine how you can put away anger from your life.

Teaching—What does the Bible teach about anger? Carefully study the passages in Scripture that deal with anger, such as James 1:19-20, 1 Corinthians 13:4-7, Proverbs 16:32, and Proverbs 15:28. Choose several verses that seem especially relevant to you and memorize them until you can say them automatically without a great deal of thought. Study these principles so well that you could explain them to someone else.

Reproof—A biblical reproof is pointing out how someone is violating Scripture. Ask others, including your husband, to point out to you when you seem angry or even a little too harsh. Whenever you feel angry or frustrated, write out your angry thoughts, then examine those thoughts closely to see where you are wrong or have deviated from Scripture. Once you've done this, it is very important to move on to the next stage:

Correction—Biblically analyze each thought you wrote down, then write out a kind, biblically corrected thought. If you spoke to someone or did something in anger, write that down. Then record what you should have said or done. Even if you don't write these things out, it is still important to analyze what you said or did wrong, and ask yourself, "If I could rewind time, what would I do differently so that I could be pleasing to Christ?"

Now for this very reason also, applying all diligence, in your faith supply moral excellence, and in your moral excellence, knowledge, and in your knowledge, self-control, and in your self-control, perseverance, and in your perseverance, godliness, and in your godliness, brotherly kindness, and in your brotherly kindness, love.
2 Peter 1:5-7

Application

Training in Righteousness—This last part is where you *practice* thinking and acting according to God's Word until the *godly* response is your *natural* response. While you are practicing, keep praying and asking God to change your heart and your character. If you are diligent in this training phase, the results will be life-changing.

Perhaps you have been angry for years. In Christ, you can change for life—not just improve a little, but truly live out Ephesians 4:31-32†: *"Let all bitterness...wrath...anger...clamor and slander be put away from you... [and] be kind to one another."* If your character truly changes, you will be able to go through very difficult times without sinning against God and others.

Week 37, Day 1

Having a reputation for good works; and if she has brought up children, if she has shown hospitality to strangers, if she has washed the saints' feet, if she has assisted those in distress, and if she has devoted herself to every good work.
1 TIMOTHY 5:10

Application

Take a quick inventory of your home right now and see where you need to make improvements.

My Home:

- ☑ is fairly clean and free of clutter.
- ☑ has a nice smell to it.
- ☑ is decorated as tastefully as my budget will allow.
- ☑ has a sense of warmth and calm.

If you are the type who has trouble organizing or is not particularly skilled at decorating, remember that this is your job, and like any job, when skills are needed training may be necessary. Ask a friend who is good at these things to help you, or look for books or magazines that can help supply the tools you need to do your work well.

CREATING A PEACEFUL ENVIRONMENT

Several years ago I heard an interview on a Christian radio station with a woman whose ministry was teaching other women how to decorate and create a calming environment in their homes. When I tuned in, she was talking about using candles and potpourri to create a pleasant scent in the home, and soothing music to promote a calm atmosphere.

I have to be honest—I thought it was the most ridiculous thing I had ever heard. When she started talking about how to use baskets, I went on a self-righteous rant about how she should be telling lost people about Christ, not talking to Christians about which colors are more peaceful than others.

Here's the thing: I was so wrong in my attitude. God gave this woman a gift He obviously did not give to me. The only thing I know about decorating is the strategic placement of silk ficus trees! But just because I'm not a decorator doesn't mean God doesn't care about how my home looks. He does care, because He is concerned about the environment I am creating for my family and how that promotes godliness and contentment in their lives.

As your home's keeper, it is part of your ministry to create an atmosphere that is peaceful, relaxing, comfortable, and inviting for both your family and for guests. In this way, you are living out Romans 12:10-13†: *"Give preference to one another in honor; not lagging behind in* ***diligence****, fervent in spirit, serving the LORD; rejoicing in hope... devoted to prayer, contributing to the needs of the saints,* ***practicing hospitality****."*

Even if your skills, like mine, don't run in that vein, there are simple things you can do to make your home calm and welcoming. At a minimum, your home should be clean and mess-free. But on top of that, you can make it a pleasant environment by learning to decorate (within your budget, of course) and by being sensitive to the effect that sounds and scents have on the *ambiance* of the home.

Memorize It!

That, in reference to your former manner of life, you lay aside the old self, which is being corrupted in accordance with the lusts of deceit, and that you be renewed in the spirit of your mind.
(Ephesians 4:22-23)

Monkey See, Monkey Do

Her children rise up and bless her; her husband also, and he praises her, saying: "Many daughters have done nobly, but you excel them all."
Proverbs 31:28-29

Grace stood at the stove scrambling eggs as she listened carefully to the commotion coming from the family room. Suddenly her daughter stormed into the kitchen, tears of exasperation leaking down her cheeks. "Mom!" she cried, "Dad is being ridiculous!"

"What's going on?" Grace asked. Emma explained: "I have two papers to write and a huge test to study for. IF I get all of that done, Jason and I had plans tonight. But *Dad* wants me to work in the yard *all day*! Why does he need me all day?!" Grace could feel her irritation rising. She knew the only reason Joe wanted Emma to work in the yard was to keep her from seeing her boyfriend. In his efforts to keep Emma busy, he frequently interfered with her ability to keep up with her schoolwork.

"I have no idea why your father does the things he does," Grace said. "But don't worry, I'll take care of it." Grace knew it would cause a problem with her husband, but she could not let him affect Emma's grades. Her scholarship was at stake; did he even think about that?

It's obvious where Emma gets her lack of respect for her father: straight from the heart of her mom. You can be sure that in any home where the wife does not respect her husband, the children won't either. The result is chaos, where everyone is walking in rebellion to God's plan for the family. The wife who does this is growing a spirit of insubordination in her children—a very serious offense. *"For rebellion is as the sin of witchcraft and stubbornness is as iniquity and idolatry"* (1 Samuel 15:23 NKJV).

You may think that your children need to be protected from their dad's poor decisions. However, it is paramount that no matter how good a parent he is, you must give him unfailing respect, especially in front of the kids. They will respect their father only to the degree that you respect him. If your respect is intermittent or lacking, your children will not learn to respect authority—including *your* authority and, ultimately, God's authority.

Memorize It!

That, in reference to your former manner of life, you lay aside the old self, which is being corrupted in accordance with the lusts of deceit, and that you be renewed in the spirit of your mind.
(Ephesians 4:22-23)

Application

If your children are young, it's not too late to begin undoing any damage you may have caused by disrespecting your husband. If your children are older, your task is more difficult, but still doable.

- Purpose that, with God's help, you will be wise and respectful, even if it is necessary to question your husband's decisions or actions in front of his children.
- Ask your husband to hold you accountable for any disrespectful behavior.
- Apologize to your children (if age appropriate) for not showing their father respect.
- Emphasize the importance of respect, that their relationship with God will mirror their obedience to and respect for their father.
- Continue to work on cultivating respect in your heart, which will spill over to your kids.

Week 37, Day 3

For we have become partakers of Christ, if we hold fast the beginning of our assurance firm until the end.
HEBREWS 3:14

Application

We live in a culture that rejects pain and suffering. If we are called to suffer, we think something is wrong. But the only time something is wrong is when we fail to do what is right. Going back to your own sinful ways because God's way didn't seem to "work" is not an option for the woman who is truly committed to pleasing Christ, no matter what. God calls us to endure: *"But My righteous one shall live by faith; and if he shrinks back, my soul has no pleasure in him"* (Hebrews 10:38).

What about you? Are you "trying" God's way, seeing if it will work? Or are you committed to following Christ for life, no matter what happens here on earth?

STAYING POWER

On the day Grant announced he was leaving her, Morgan fell on her knees and begged God to keep her marriage together. Even though Grant had his faults, she knew she had not always been the best wife she could be. She also came to me for help, and for months I counseled her on submitting to her husband. I especially encouraged them to engage in the process of mutual sanctification: helping each other to see their faults and working together to purify sin from their lives.

For about two years, things improved and Grant stopped threatening to leave her. But then all of a sudden, she moved out and took the kids with her. Incredulous, I asked what happened. "I tried it God's way, but nothing has really changed," she said. "He has only stayed because I've been doing everything 'right.' But he hasn't changed a bit, and I'm tired of being the only one putting in any effort."

It was apparent Morgan was only obeying God in order to get something in return. But she was not able to persevere in doing what was right because she was doing it for herself and not for Christ. Despite my encouragements, she never fully "bought in" to the concept of mutual sanctification. She was afraid that pointing out Grant's sin would only drive him away. As long as things were "calm," she didn't want to rock the boat.

Many of us try God's way for a season, hoping that our efforts will be rewarded. When nothing happens in our timeframe, or if the result is more suffering and testing, we give up and go back to our old sinful habits. It's just too difficult to endure hardship with no reward in sight. But God promises that if we *"do good...expecting nothing in return,"* our *"reward will be great"* (Luke 6:35). Not only that, but the Bible is clear that those who turn back from following Christ were never His to begin with. *"If you continue in My word, then you are truly disciples of Mine"* (John 8:31†).

Memorize It!

That, in reference to your former manner of life, you lay aside the old self, which is being corrupted in accordance with the lusts of deceit, and that you be renewed in the spirit of your mind.
(Ephesians 4:22-23)

Saying All The Right Things

Kim opened up her email and found one from her husband, Phillip. He had forwarded an off-color joke, and when she read it, she couldn't help but laugh. Yes, it was a little raunchy, but it was hilarious! She sent it on to her friend, knowing Lacey would appreciate it.

After she finished checking her email, Kim opened her Bible and found herself in Ephesians, chapters 4 and 5. As she read, the Holy Spirit began working on her about "walking as the Gentiles [unbelievers] walk" (4:17). She knew that because her "new self" was created "in righteousness and holiness" (4:24), there was no place in her life for "sensuality (and) impurity" (4:19) or "unwholesome words" (4:29). But when she got to Ephesians 5:3-4, she had to stop and ask God's forgiveness: *"But immorality or any impurity...must not even be named among you, as is proper among saints; and there must be no filthiness and silly talk, or coarse jesting, which are not fitting..."* Kim knew that forwarding that joke was "not fitting" for someone who was made "in the likeness of God" (4:24).

Ephesians 5:25-27 goes on to explain the husband's role in this purification of the wife; but even if your husband is not leading you spiritually or is not a willing participant in your sanctification, your goal should be to present yourself "holy and blameless" before God. This means, among other things, that you purify your speech of such things as cursing, racial jokes, crude or sexualized humor, obscenities, or any other kind of speech that is not honoring to God or to His creation.

Most of our modern entertainment is saturated with crude or sexualized language, and we are surrounded by it in our culture, so it's difficult for this kind of talk not to work its way into our heads. If you've ever worked or gone to school in a secular environment, you know how impure speech can become second nature. But God calls us to reflect His Son. Do you think Christ would ever talk this way? Of course He wouldn't! So then why would you?

Memorize It!

That, in reference to your former manner of life, you lay aside the old self, which is being corrupted in accordance with the lusts of deceit, and that you be renewed in the spirit of your mind.
(Ephesians 4:22-23)

And there must be no filthiness and silly talk, or coarse jesting, which are not fitting, but rather giving of thanks.
Ephesians 5:4

Application

I'll be honest with you: the hardest thing for me in purifying my speech is when other people talk this way to me. If they're not a believer, I don't want to appear prudish or make them uncomfortable; and if they are a believer, I don't want to come off as self-righteous, so I just laugh it off. But as I have become more convicted about this and cleaned up my own mouth, I have found that people talk this way to me less and less.

If this kind of speech is a normal part of your marriage, you may need to sit down with your husband and share Ephesians 4-5 with him, and ask him to cooperate with you in purifying your speech to reflect the fact that you are "made in the likeness of God."

Week 37, Day 5

For you were called to freedom, brethren; only do not turn your freedom into an opportunity for the flesh, but through love serve one another.
GALATIANS 5:13

Application

One of the most powerful tools God uses to keep me walking in the Spirit is worship music. Music has great influence on your spirit, and the right kind of music will keep your thoughts focused and give you energy to obey God and love your husband more. It's no wonder, then, that when the Bible gives instruction on being filled by the Spirit, it often references music. *"Be filled with the Spirit, speaking to one another in psalms and hymns and spiritual songs, singing and making melody with your heart to the LORD"* (Ephesians 5:18-19†). Take a look at your iPod, radio station presets, or CDs. Are you surrounding yourself with music that encourages the filling of the Holy Spirit, to help you serve and love your husband as God desires?

LOVE IS NOT AN EMOTION

It's difficult for me to do something I should do if I don't want to do it or if I think not doing it is an option. For instance, I should have a turkey sandwich on whole wheat bread for lunch, but chips and a hot dog are so much easier and tastier! When I'm disciplined, I make good choices. But on those days when I'm not so disciplined, I waste time, eat popcorn and brownies for lunch, and scramble to get the house clean at zero hour.

Any productivity I have is a result of how disciplined I am at yielding to the Holy Spirit. My flesh says, "Here is the path to happiness," then lifts the curtain on things that are probably the worst choices for me. But the Spirit says, *"discipline yourself for the purpose of godliness"* (1 Timothy 4:7). And so it goes with my marriage. My flesh does not always feel love for my husband, and often leads me to react to him in anger or selfishness. But my spirit desires God's best, which is gained through obeying His Word and loving my husband, no matter how I'm feeling.

If you feel you're not in love with your husband, the good news is you can get that back. The first step is to stop viewing love as a romantic emotion and start seeing it as a set of actions you take that result in loving emotions. Secondly, you have to stop making "provision for the flesh" (Romans 13:14) and start being obedient to Scripture even when you don't feel like it.

How do we make provision for the flesh? By choosing those things that reinforce a worldly view of love (such as fleshly music, soap operas, adult films, romance books, etc.) as well as sensual activities that work against godly intimacy, such as masturbation or fantasizing. Anytime you give in to your flesh rather than to what you know is right—even it's something as harmless as a candy bar—you are providing for your flesh.

God understands how powerful the flesh is and how weak you are. As you admit your weakness, He will give you grace to yield to the Spirit and do what is right.

Why We Won't Reprove

I was talking to my friend Eliza about an ongoing problem in her marriage, and for the 90th time I was encouraging her to reprove her husband for his drinking habit. Even though Bronn claimed to be a Christian, he regularly consumed alcohol to excess. He clearly had a problem, and was no longer able to his sin from their children.

However, Eliza did not feel she was "good enough" to reprove her husband. "How am I supposed to make him accountable for his sin?" she asked. "I have so much sin in my own life!" So because she was stuck in that place, she put up with Bronn's drinking for years.

When your husband is not living righteously, you have an obligation to reprove him biblically for his sin. That biblical reproof always starts with you being "spiritual" and "looking to yourself" (Galatians 6:1), making sure you've taken care of the "log that is in your own eye" (Luke 6:42).

This does not mean you have to be perfect before you can reprove your husband. Sinless perfection is not what our LORD was getting at when He instructed us to take care of those logs first. What He wanted us to avoid was accusing our husbands of sins that we ourselves are guilty of. *"For in the way you judge, you will be judged; and by your standard of measure, it will be measured to you"* (Matthew 7:2). In other words, if you expect your husband to stop getting angry, you must stop getting angry. You have to hold up the standard you want him to live by, not being "the pot calling the kettle black."

Your job is not only to reprove your husband of sin, but also to set an example for him to follow. That's tough to do, day in and day out. I've heard more than one weary wife confess to not feeling "good enough" to reprove her husband. That defeated attitude is a scheme of the devil (Ephesians 6:11) that you are to stand firm against! You stand firm against this attitude by making sure your conscience is clean before God and that you are actively pursuing holiness in your life.

Memorize It!

And put on the new self, which in the likeness of God has been created in righteousness and holiness of the truth.
(Ephesians 4:24)

But like the Holy One who called you, be holy yourselves also in all your behavior; because it is written, "You shall be holy, for I am holy."
1 PETER 1:15-16

Application

Most women do not reprove their husbands biblically. We usually have no trouble telling our husbands when they've messed up. But doing it biblically means taking care of those "logs" first—those sins in our own life that are weighing us down and keeping us from being obedient to Christ.

Usually I ask you to "take a moment" to reflect on a given truth. But the principle of holiness is so important, it requires much more careful consideration than just a moment's worth. Make a special effort this week to spend at least an hour talking to God about your personal holiness, and what would be required for you to have a completely clean conscience before Him.

Week 38, Day 2

Therefore I, the prisoner of the LORD, implore you to walk in a manner worthy of the calling with which you have been called, with all humility and gentleness, with patience, showing tolerance for one another in love, being diligent to preserve the unity of the Spirit in the bond of peace.
EPHESIANS 4:1-3

Application

You can't control what your husband does, but *"so far as it depends on you, be at peace with all men"* (Romans 12:18), including your husband. You do this by putting on *"a heart of compassion, kindness, humility, gentleness and patience"* (Colossians 3:12). If you have complaints against your husband, you are to forgive him, *"just as the LORD forgave you"* (vs. 13).

This section is where you find practical advice, but nothing is more practical than God's Word: *"Beyond all these things put on love…Let the peace of Christ rule in your hearts…and be thankful"* (Colossians 3:14-15†). *"To sum up, all of you be harmonious, sympathetic…kindhearted, and humble in spirit; not returning… insult for insult, but giving a blessing instead"* (1 Peter 3:8-9†).

HUMILITY CREATES PEACE

As Noelle looked at her husband and three sons, tears welled up in her eyes. "Honey, what's wrong?" Jared reached for her hand, concerned. "Nothing." She smiled. "I am just…*so happy*."

Noelle is filled with gratitude when she sees how God's joy and peace permeate her family—especially when she considers where they were just a year ago. At that time they were fighting almost constantly, the boys were doing poorly in school and rebelling against their parents, and Noelle had already contacted an attorney to begin the divorce process. But then godly friends sat down with them and showed them through the Bible how pride was causing most of the problems in their marriage. Neither Noelle nor Jared believed they were proud people, but after studying James 4, they came face-to-face with the central issue in their marriage:

> *What is the source of quarrels and conflicts among you? Is not the source your pleasures that wage war in your members? You lust and do not have…you are envious and cannot obtain; so you fight and quarrel… But He gives a greater grace. Therefore it says, 'God is opposed to the proud, but gives grace to the humble.' Submit therefore to God…Humble yourselves in the presence of the LORD, and He will exalt you* (James 4:1-10†).

Proverbs 13:10 says *"By pride comes nothing but strife"* (NKJV). If you have strife in your home, no matter what the issues are, pride is driving all of your problems. The solution is simple: "*walk by the Spirit, and you will not carry out the desire of the flesh*"(Galatians 5:16). When we humbly submit to God, we will manifest the "*fruit of the Spirit [which] is love, joy, peace, patience, kindness, goodness, faithfulness, gentleness, self-control*"(vss. 22-23†). But when we resist God in our pride, our homes and marriages are characterized by the "*deeds of the flesh…enmities, strife, jealousy, outbursts of anger,*"etc. (vss. 19-20†). How much better would it be for your family to live in peace, loving and treating each other with kindness?

Memorize It!

And put on the new self, which in the likeness of God has been created in righteousness and holiness of the truth.
(Ephesians 4:24)

The Idol of Ideals

The devil and his friends were discussing how to step up their efforts to trip up Christians. "The key," Satan said, "is to keep them from loving Jesus too much. Any thoughts?" Several ideas were tossed out which elicited a *been there, done that* response from everyone: drugs, sex, entertainment, materialism. "What about ministry?" one demon asked.

Everyone looked dumbfounded. "Uh, I think ministry is what we're trying to keep them *from*," another demon said. "Yes, but ministry for ministry's sake—busy work that looks like ministry but really just makes them feel good about themselves." A murmur of approval went around the meeting, then another one spoke up. "What about *movements*?" he said. "Or ideals!" another one said. They were all excited about this new line of thinking. Finally, the devil spoke: "OK, you know what to do. Get them to care about *anything*—church programs, abortion, politics, recycling, ending famine, I don't care what—as long as they care more about their *cause* than they care about God!"

That's kind of a ridiculous scenario, because we know that the enemy is much more organic than that. He *"prowls around like a roaring lion, seeking someone to devour"* (1 Peter 5:8); looking to turn anything that is good in your life into something ugly and vain. Because we're sinners, *everything* has the potential to become an idol—including your ministries, ideals and passions.

Matthew 6:33 says that we are to seek His kingdom (the exclusive rule of Christ in our lives) and His righteousness (His character). Sometimes while trying to obey that verse, we can become very passionate about a ministry, to the point that we care more about our ministry than about submitting ourselves to the rule of Christ in our hearts. Our mission becomes an idol that is separate from a pure love and devotion to Christ and to people.

But whatever things were gain to me, those things I have counted as loss for the sake of Christ. More than that, I count all things to be loss in view of the surpassing value of knowing Christ Jesus my Lord, for whom I have suffered the loss of all things, and count them but rubbish so that I may gain Christ.
Philippians 3:7-8

Application

While serving in a ministry, have you ever been frustrated that things weren't going as you'd envisioned? Or have you ever ended up in a personal conflict with another believer? These are both signs that the ministry may have become an idol.

Even if you're serving Christ, your church and your community, you still have to keep reminding yourself to pursue the exclusive rule of Christ in your heart and His character above all other concerns. CHRIST, not the ministry itself, should be your passion. "*But grow in the grace and knowledge of our Lord and Savior Jesus Christ. To Him be the glory, both now and to the day of eternity*"(2 Peter 3:18†).

Memorize It!

And put on the new self, which in the likeness of God has been created in righteousness and holiness of the truth.
(Ephesians 4:24)

Week 38, Day 4

(Love) does not rejoice in unrighteousness, but rejoices with the truth; bears all things, believes all things, hopes all things, endures all things.
1 CORINTHIANS 13:6-7

Application

It's easy to assume the worst when jobs around the house go undone for weeks on end. But even then, you can *respectfully* encourage your husband to get stuff done around the home without nagging:

1. Make sure you have actually asked him to do the things you need done. If necessary, make a "Honey Do" list. Post it in a place of his choosing, then forget about it.
2. Ask God to help you think the best of your husband, and to help you stop worrying about when the items on the list will be accomplished.
3. Look for signs your husband is overworked or emotionally exhausted. If he's got a lot on his plate, ask what you can do to make his load lighter.
4. Remember, his days off are his down time. Let him enjoy the rest and have some fun.

RESPECT IN YOUR ASSUMPTIONS

Molly was on the phone with her friend Erica when she pulled into the driveway, the trunk of her car loaded with groceries. As soon as she got out of the car, she saw her husband's landscaping project still in its beginning stages. "Good heavens," she said to Erica, "What has he been doing this whole time!?" She walked over to inspect the plants still in their pots and holes in the ground where the young plants should be. "He promised he would get this done today!" she complained. As she unloaded the groceries, she continued to whine about her husband's lack of follow-through. "I should have done this myself—I'd have had it done weeks ago."

It was only after the groceries were unloaded that she found the note on the counter: Randy's dad had suffered a heart attack, and Randy was at the hospital. She knew he had tried to call while she was on the phone with Erica, but she had ignored the call, thinking it probably wasn't important. Molly felt immediate remorse for how she had assumed Randy was just being lazy by not finishing the landscaping.

One way our lack of respect for our husbands shows itself is when we jump to the wrong conclusions about our husband's behavior, or assume the worst rather than giving him the benefit of the doubt. When our husbands fail to meet our expectations in some way, the temptation is to chalk it up to poor character or less-than-honorable motives. This is just another form of disrespect.

The proper, respectful response when your husband fails to meet your expectations is to think the best. Instead of assuming that he's being stubborn or lazy, remind yourself that his priorities are not the same as your priorities, and he may have a good reason for his inaction. Remember that love *"believes all things"* (1 Corinthians 13:7). If, when all of the facts are known, it turns out that your husband is indeed sinning, then it may be time for you to reprove him biblically. But until all the truth is uncovered, you should always assume the best.

Memorize It!

And put on the new self, which in the likeness of God has been created in righteousness and holiness of the truth.
(Ephesians 4:24)

The Beauty Within

Your adornment must not be merely external—braiding the hair, and wearing gold jewelry, or putting on dresses; but let it be the hidden person of the heart, with the imperishable quality of a gentle and quiet spirit, which is precious in the sight of God. For in this way in former times the holy women also, who hoped in God, used to adorn themselves, being submissive to their own husbands.
1 Peter 3:3-5

Remember your wedding day? If you're like most women, you probably were never more beautiful. You spent hours getting ready: finding the perfect dress, getting your makeup just right, trying several different hairstyles, having your nails done.

Now, if you've ever seen the reality TV series *Bridezillas*, you've witnessed a classic example of *What Not to Wear* to a wedding. The women on that show demonstrate the antithesis of what we call "inner beauty." All of the primping, makeup, and hairspray in the world cannot fix the ugliness in these women. They are vicious, selfish, spiteful, bitter and hateful. I'm not easily shocked, but the first time I saw that show I about fell out of my chair with horror at the way these women talk to their future husbands. I was completely astonished that these guys still want to go through with the wedding after being subjected to a "sneak preview" of what living with this chick will be like!

From Scripture, life, and literature, we know that true beauty comes from within. (Not to overdo the entertainment references, but just think *Beauty and the Beast* or *Cinderella*.) If God is our ultimate Judge, then His opinion of our beauty should be the one that holds the most weight. He very closely links *beauty* to submission to our husbands:

It's OK to try to look your best. In fact, it's an important part of staying attractive to your husband. But your first concern should be to dress yourself with a "gentle and quiet spirit" (1 Peter 3:4) by humbly trusting God while being submissive to your husband. Your motivation comes from placing your hope and trust in God, not in physical beauty. Just like Sarah (who was a real beauty—see Genesis 12:14), you'll have a beauty that not only does not fade, but grows with age and is eternal. Inner beauty is not only pleasing to God, but other people (especially your husband) can actually *see* it and appreciate it.

Application

Think about how much time you spend getting ready in the morning—showering, putting on your makeup and doing your hair. Now think about how much time you devote to worshiping Christ or learning to be submissive to your husband. If you're spending more time in front of the bathroom mirror than in front of the mirror of God's Word, commit today to changing that ratio. Make sure you're spending more time working on your inner beauty, that doesn't fade with age.

Week 39, Day 1

Therefore, laying aside falsehood, speak truth each one of you with his neighbor, for we are members of one another.
EPHESIANS 4:25

Application

Sarcasm is a BIG problem in marriages today. It is never constructive, yet many wives are so used to speaking sarcastically they're not even aware they're doing it. Our speech should always be *"good for edification according to the need of the moment, so that it will give grace to those who hear"* (Ephesians 4:29). To "edify" means to "improve by instruction"—the opposite of what sarcasm does.

Now that you are aware of the problem of sarcasm, ask God to show you whenever you use it to communicate with your husband, your children, or with anyone. If you do "slip up" and speak sarcastically, immediately ask forgiveness from the person you were speaking to, then reword what you were saying *without* the sarcasm.

Sarcastically Speaking

Picture this: King David is bringing the Ark of the Covenant back to Jerusalem. He is so excited that he strips down to his skivvies, puts on a priestly apron, and leads the parade, singing and dancing all the way home. But Michal, his wife (and the daughter of his predecessor, King Saul) looks down from her ivory tower and scoffs. *"How the king of Israel distinguished himself today!"* she says sarcastically. *"He uncovered himself today in the eyes of his servants' maids as one of the foolish ones shamelessly uncovers himself!"* (2 Samuel 6:20†).

I love David's response to his wife's sarcasm. *"[My celebrating] was before the LORD, who chose me above your father...to appoint me ruler...over Israel; therefore I will celebrate before the LORD"* (verse 21†). David was saying "Hey, *I'm* king, not your dad, and I will worship God the way I want." He then says, *"I will be...humble in my own eyes, but with the maids of whom you have spoken, with them I will be distinguished"* (verse 22†). In other words, David was saying, "You don't like who I am? Well, I can always find someone who does!" This was no empty threat: David had seven wives and many more concubines. The "maids" were essentially Michal's competition for David's love and attention. I don't think David was normally a spiteful person, but he reacted to his wife's disrespect in a way that put her in her place.

I'm not defending David's rash response or even his polygamy. But Michal was completely out of line in speaking to David—who was both her husband and the king—in such a sarcastic and disrespectful way.

Sarcasm comes from a Latin word which means "to tear the flesh," and it's easy to see why. Sarcasm tears at the one-flesh unity God wants for your marriage. For example, a wife cleans the yard all by herself then says to her husband, "Thanks for your help." Rather than addressing his possible laziness or selfishness in a constructive way, she has shown him disrespect and cut off any possibility of godly communication.

Memorize It!

And without faith it is impossible to please Him, for he who comes to God must believe that He is and that He is a rewarder of those who seek Him.
(Hebrews 11:6)

Godly Love vs. Romantic Love

Beloved, let us love one another, for love is from God; and everyone who loves is born of God and knows God. The one who does not love does not know God, for God is love.
1 John 4:7-8

Janelle sat in her dorm room, working through a quiz in her devotional book for engaged couples. The quiz was titled, "Godly Love or Infatuation?" and Janelle was scoring her love for Luke very highly on the "love" scale. She was sure they would have a wonderful life together—they were graduating from a Christian college, and they'd taken several marriage classes together. They seemed to be so in-sync with each other and had passed the infatuation stage months ago. Yes, she was in love with Luke, but what they had was real. Even the quiz said so!

I used to be Janelle. And every girl I grew up with—we were all Janelles, certain that when we got married our love would last forever. The key to our misunderstanding is just in that phrase: our love. At its best, human love is weak, fleeting and based more on romance and feelings than anything else. When we expect romantic love to keep our marriage afloat, we set ourselves up for disappointment. If you're basing your marriage on feeling romantic, your expectations are unrealistic and immature.

The key to a good marriage is not our love, but God's love. Human love is self-centered, loving only when it gets what it wants. But God's love is righteous and unselfish. *"But God demonstrates His own love toward us, in that while we were yet sinners, Christ died for us"* (Romans 5:8). Like God, we should demonstrate love, no matter what we get in return. Every day of our lives, we should be asking, "How can I show love?" rather than, "How can I get love?"

You might be thinking, "How can you say good marriages are possible only through God's love? What about unsaved couples who have good marriages?" That's true; unsaved people can have good marriages, but only by following godly principles such as patience, kindness, and self-sacrifice. However, *"what does it profit a man to gain the whole world [or a good marriage] and forfeit his soul?"* (Mark 8:36†). They may have a great marriage, but they are still lost and hopeless without Christ.

Application

Someone once said, "It's not love that keeps your marriage together; it's your marriage that keeps love together." This is true, but God's love can keep your marriage and your love safe. If you have adopted the world's view that love is all about romance and having your needs met, you need to re-train your mind toward a scriptural view of love; that no matter what your husband does, you will be patient, kind, and self-sacrificial.

The way to keep love alive is to give it freely. When you express godly, biblical love to your husband, the resulting tender feelings will help pull you and your man together in a bond more intimate and lasting than all of those intense feelings of your early days of infatuation put together.

Memorize It!

And without faith it is impossible to please Him, for he who comes to God must believe that He is and that He is a rewarder of those who seek Him.
(Hebrews 11:6)

Week 39, Day 3

Let love be without hypocrisy. Abhor what is evil; cling to what is good. Be devoted to one another in brotherly love; give preference to one another in honor.
ROMANS 12:9-10

Application

What does it mean to put your husband first in all things? Romans 12:10 gives us a clue: *"Give preference to one another in honor."* Giving preference to your husband means that you:

- Prefer your husband's company to friends, family, even your children. Rearrange your schedule, if necessary, to be with him.
- Prefer his goals to your own. When you make decisions for your family, ask yourself how you can meet your husband's goals first. For instance, prefer his goal to save money over your need to remodel that bathroom.
- Prefer his choices when deciding what to make for dinner, what to watch on TV, or where to go for recreation.

CHECK YOUR PREFERENCES

Romans 12 is an amazing passage that takes on a whole new meaning when you read it with your husband and your marriage in mind. Take time right now to read over this chapter, thinking specifically about this concept: How does God want me to act toward my husband?

Time Out: Read Romans 12

Verse 1 says we are to present our bodies as *living sacrifices*. Just as a corpse has no needs and does not respond to any desire, so you must be dead to your own desires. As you love, you will not selfishly seek your own way (1 Corinthians 13:5), but in all things look to do what is good, helpful and pleasing to God and to your husband first.

Dying to self goes against our human nature. People are born selfish; we naturally seek to have our own needs met before we consider the needs of others. And our pleasure-seeking culture only reinforces our naturally selfish bent. But being a godly wife means going against your natural self-centeredness and reprogramming your mind to consider your husband's needs first, before your own. Remember that *"the natural man does not receive the things of the Spirit of God"* (1 Corinthians 2:14, NKJV). If you want God's blessing on your life and marriage, you'll have to behave *un*naturally and put your husband and his needs first, before your own.

The best marriage is one where the husband puts his wife's needs before his own, and where the wife puts her husband's needs before her needs. Can you imagine what your marriage would be like if both of you did this consistently? Even if your husband is not putting you first, you can set a good example for him, and show him your greatest love, by putting him first.

Dying to yourself doesn't mean you ignore your needs completely, because being able to perform your tasks well requires physical and emotional energy. And that means you have to take care of yourself. But even taking care of yourself should have as its ultimate goal being the best you can be for God and for your husband.

Memorize It!

And without faith it is impossible to please Him, for he who comes to God must believe that He is and that He is a rewarder of those who seek Him.
(Hebrews 11:6)

Getting Up After Falling Down

As far as the east is from the west, so far has He removed our transgressions from us.
Psalm 103:12

Alexis was saved as a child, walked the narrow path all of her childhood, and married a Christian man. But then something happened. Her husband, Tanner, started his own construction business, working long hours six or seven days a week. Lonely and bored, Alexis spent a lot of time with their best friends Evan and Lisa...and was undeniably attracted to Evan.

She knew she was vulnerable, but underestimated just how much. Then one day Evan stopped by to drop something off, one thing led to another, and before long they found themselves in a passionate embrace, confessing their desire for one another.

Evan and Alexis concealed their relationship for years before everything finally came out and they ended their affair. But for years afterwards, Alexis struggled with trying to regain her spiritual footing. She could not believe she had actually cheated on her husband, and that she had ignored God for so long. She felt completely unworthy of salvation, her husband, and God's grace. She knew that both Tanner and God had forgiven her, but she couldn't forget what she had done.

It's difficult to get back on your feet after a failure. Satan is the great accuser (Revelation 12:10), and he loves to remind us of our past. You may not have fallen as far as Alexis did, but perhaps you are discouraged because you keep doing the same sins over and over, and you believe you'll never "get it right."

I want to encourage you that change comes in baby steps. There was a time in my life where I was very far from God, and my journey back to Him took ten to fifteen years. It would have taken a lot less time if I had just believed that I was already forgiven and holy (1 Corinthians 6:11). God was ready for me to get "back on the horse" long before I actually did!

You're going to fail. That's not an excuse, because failure is still a sin. But that doesn't mean you should give up. *"Forgetting what lies behind"* (Philippians 3:13-14†) you must keep pressing on for Christ.

Application

I wish we could just choose the path of obedience and from that day forward, stay obedient. But that's not even possible. Pursuing spiritual growth and maturity means that you continually keep choosing His rule and His character (Matthew 6:33) even after you've sinned. In time it will get easier because the more you obey, the more of Christ's character you will model.

It won't be complete until Christ returns and *"we will be like Him, because we will see Him just as He is"* (1 John 3:2). But while you're here on earth, you must keep moving in that direction. If you fail, don't give up! Like a runner who falls in a race, you must get up, keep your eyes on the goal, and *"run with endurance the race that is set before"* you (Hebrews 12:1).

Memorize It!

And without faith it is impossible to please Him, for he who comes to God must believe that He is and that He is a rewarder of those who seek Him.
(Hebrews 11:6)

Week 39, Day 5

Whom have you reproached and blasphemed? And against whom have you raised your voice, and haughtily lifted up your eyes? Against the Holy One of Israel!
2 KINGS 19:22

Application

Imagine how you would feel if you were to hear your child, or someone you love very much, talking about you in a way that disparaged you or brought you down in the eyes of the hearer. You would not like it very much, would you? Neither does God like it when we reduce Him with our words.

Our job is to know God and to make Him known, which we can't do if we talk about Him blasphemously. Even when you're talking to your husband, you must be careful to always refer to God in a way that shows reverential fear and deep gratitude for all He has done for you. He created you, loved you, saved you, and sealed you by His Holy Spirit for an "imperishable inheritance" (1 Peter 1:4†). Your job is to glorify Him, not disrespect Him.

DOWNPLAYING GOD'S HOLINESS

Samuel and Lucy were remodeling their kitchen and Samuel was having a terrible time with the new cabinets. They just didn't seem to fit, and he was getting very frustrated. Lucy watched him struggle, then said to him, "Well, you know that's why Jesus went into the ministry. Anything is better than being a carpenter!"

In her attempt to get Samuel to laugh and relax a little, Lucy has allowed her speech to slip into blasphemy. Sometimes we are so comfortable and unguarded talking to our husbands that we say things we would never say to anyone else. That's fine, as long as what we say is "reverent, pure, kind and beyond reproach" (Titus 2:3-8). But letting your guard down can often lead to speech that is not honoring to Christ. Between husbands and wives, we can often talk blasphemously about God and not think a thing about it.

Blasphemy is talking about God in an untruthful, careless way that downplays His holiness, or misinterprets His character. It's assuming God won't mind if we make a joke at His expense or treat Him like He's one of us. Any kind of speech that portrays Him as less than perfect, holy, omnipotent, beautiful, majestic, and God Most High is blasphemy and is displeasing to God.

The cure for blasphemy is to consistently think about and meditate on God's character and His attributes. He is not anything like us (Psalm 50:21; Isaiah 55:8-9). He is Almighty God! By meditating on Who He is, we gain a healthy fear and respect for Him. Speaking about God in a blasphemous way shows that you don't fear Him, for if you did, you would be afraid to disparage or belittle Him in any way. *"But I will warn you whom to fear: fear the One who, after He has killed, has authority to cast into hell"* (Luke 12:5†). It's not that God doesn't have a sense of humor, but He does not tolerate disrespect from anyone—least of all, from His people.

Walking By Sight

Week 40, Day 1

For we walk by faith,
not by sight.
2 Corinthians 5:7

Adrienne answered her cell phone and heard her son's excited voice. "*Mom!*" Ryan cried, "I got accepted to YALE!" Her heart rose and sank, all at the same time. She knew it was his dream to go to Yale Law School, but it was so expensive. She had no idea how they were going to pay for it.

Days later she sat down with her husband. She'd been scrambling to find a way to make up the difference between Ryan's scholarship and the cost of Yale, and she finally had a plan—including a loan her husband would have to co-sign. "Nope," Chuck said flatly, looking at her proposal. "Not gonna do it." Adrienne was incredulous. "Are you serious? You're going to let your son miss this opportunity?" Chuck just shrugged. "He's the one who wants to go to Yale, not me. He'll have to figure it out."

Many times we have to accept decisions from our husbands that are completely opposed to what we want. The temptation is to lean on our own understanding (Proverbs 3:5), which can cause us to be upset, angry, or afraid. We might then turn to nagging or manipulation to get our way. The consequence is that we lose a close, loving relationship with our husbands, peace in the home, and fellowship with Christ.

The other alternative is to view every situation through God's sovereignty and goodness. God has purpose in every circumstance, including your husband's decisions. Even when something "bad" happens, you can trust that God is always in control, and He is always good—no matter what your husband does. Consider these verses in light of that reality:

> *We are afflicted in every way, but not crushed; perplexed, but not despairing; ...But having the same spirit of faith...we also believe...Therefore we do not lose heart...For momentary, light affliction is producing for us an eternal weight of glory far beyond all comparison, while we look not at the things which are seen, but at the things which are not seen; for the things which are seen are temporal, but the things which are not seen are eternal* (2 Corinthians 4:8, 13, 16-18†).

Application

It's easy to focus on "the things which are seen," the realities of life staring us in the face every day. But the things that *really* matter are "the things which are NOT seen." This requires faith and a consistent attention to God's Word. When your husband makes a decision you don't agree with, meditate on 2 Corinthians 4, then take a moment to pray a prayer like this: *"Lord, help me to have enough faith to see this situation in light of eternity. Help me to see what matters to You, looking at what is eternal, not temporal. You are good, and You do all things well. Thank you for my husband's answer."* As you view your life through God's sovereignty and goodness, you will be continuously aware of God's purpose and grace in your life.

Memorize It!

See to it that no one comes short of the grace of God; that no root of bitterness springing up causes trouble, and by it many be defiled.
(Hebrews 12:15)

Week 40, Day 2

Wives, be subject to your husbands, as is fitting in the LORD. Whatever you do, do your work heartily, as for the LORD rather than for men.
COLOSSIANS 3:18, 23

Application

As important as *respect* is to the health of a marriage, it's hard to believe that it's rarely mentioned in the average wedding ceremony. If it was not mentioned in yours, today might be a good day to repeat your vows and this time, include the word *respect*. If you don't have access to or can't remember your wedding vows, here's a sample of a traditional vow. Write your names in the blanks, and either say it aloud now or, better yet, say it to your husband the next time you're alone together.

I ___________ take thee ___________ to be my lawfully wedded husband. I promise to love, honor, obey and **respect** *you consistently; in sickness and in health, for richer, for poorer, for better or worse, in sadness and in joy, as long as we both shall live.*

Respect Him Consistently

Jim and Judi were having a great time at the couples' retreat. They'd heard some great sermons on marriage, and had a blast canoeing and hiking in the mountains. However, the whole weekend threatened to crash and burn when, during a workshop, the couples were asked to evaluate how they were doing in different areas of their marriage. Judi scored herself very highly—an eight out of ten—on how well she communicated respect to her husband. But Jim only gave her a five on that question.

Judi was flabbergasted. She suddenly felt like one of those wives on *The Newlywed Game*, who didn't have a clue her husband's answer would vary so widely from hers. As soon as they were alone, she burst out, "A five!? Why just a five? You know I respect you!" Jim gave his wife a hug. "Yes, sweetheart, I know you respect me. But you don't always show it very well. I would say your respect lacks...consistency."

Judi immediately thought back to a week earlier, when she'd been upset with him for buying a new cell phone that had a ton of features he would probably never use. She thought his behavior was irresponsible—and that disrespectful thought probably came out in the way she talked to him that day. *But most of the time*, she argued to herself, *I'm very respectful!*

The problem with "most of the time" is that it betrays an ongoing attitude of disrespect. Remember that as *"a little leaven leavens the whole lump of dough"* (Galatians 5:9), so a little bit of disrespect can color your whole attitude toward your husband. It's like leaving some of the weeds in a garden; eventually, they'll take over. They have to be removed completely—just as you have to remove from your heart all traces of disrespect toward your husband.

I know that sounds like a tall order, and it would be impossible if not for the Holy Spirit working in you. Once you commit to the necessity of respecting your husband, respect becomes a fruit of the Spirit which will grow in you as you mature in Christ, through His Word.

Memorize It!

See to it that no one comes short of the grace of God; that no root of bitterness springing up causes trouble, and by it many be defiled. (Hebrews 12:15)

Pride Results In Anger

Kerry sped down the highway, her hands gripping the wheel tightly and tears streaming down her face. She was so angry—not about anything her husband had done recently, but about their life in general. He wasn't the man he said he would be; he didn't provide for their family, and her children often went to bed hungry because they had no money to buy food and Mark refused to go on food stamps. Her car was probably not insured, so if in her rage she hit and hurt someone… well, life is tough.

You might find it hard to believe that Kerry's problem is her pride. She is reacting to her situation with sinful anger because she thinks she deserves more than what she has. She is angry with her husband *and* God, and blames both of them for her unhappiness. God could intervene; why hasn't He?

While we may not be in Kerry's situation, we still tend to get angry with God when bad things happen—as though God owes us a tranquil existence where all our desires are fulfilled. "*By pride comes nothing but strife*" (Proverbs 13:10, NKJV†). Pride produces strife when we hold onto our right to have life go the way we would like. If you are suffering and angry, God knows what you're thinking, and you cannot hide your thoughts from Him. However, it is never right to vent anger at God over your circumstances. It is blasphemy to doubt God's character by questioning His care and provision for you.

Instead, you need to change your thinking and humbly submit to God's sovereign control over every detail of your life. Jesus *is* Lord; you have to decide if you are going to cooperate with Him, or if you're going to resist Him in sinful anger. Obviously the wisest course is for you to *"submit to God"* (James 4:7). If you graciously submit, you are responding in humility and God will give you grace to endure every trial that comes your way. Even when you are suffering for the Lord's sake (1 Peter 3:17), you can be grateful to God for how He is using you to glorify Him.

Memorize It!

See to it that no one comes short of the grace of God; that no root of bitterness springing up causes trouble, and by it many be defiled. (Hebrews 12:15)

By pride comes nothing but strife, but with the well-advised is wisdom.
Proverbs 13:10, NKJV

Application

While He was on earth, Jesus gave us an example of humility to follow. *"For you have been called for this purpose, since Christ also suffered for you, leaving you an example for you to follow in His steps"* (1 Peter 2:21). Jesus had *no* pride, and willingly suffered *"to the point of death, even death on a cross"* (Philippians 2:8). We should be willing to do the same for Him.

"For this reason also, God highly exalted Him, and bestowed on Him the name which is above every name" (Philippians 2:9). This is always God's response to suffering and humiliation: He will lift you up (James 4:10). It may not be on earth, but God is faithful. And His exaltation will be so much greater than anything you in your pride can produce for yourself.

Week 40, Day 4

It is better to live in a corner of a roof, than in a house shared with a contentious woman.
PROVERBS 21:9

Application

If you really need to persuade your husband to your point of view, you can do so without arguing:

- Make sure you're right in what you're saying. Are you giving an opinion, or do you have facts to support your position? If you have facts, make them available for your husband to look at.
- Use sweet words in a calm voice, rather than arguing harshly and stubbornly. *"Sweetness of speech increases persuasiveness"* (Proverbs 16:21†).
- Seriously consider his opinions; don't just pretend to listen, waiting for your turn to speak.
- Pick the right time to have the discussion, and be patient with him. He may need time to consider what you're saying. Accept that, in most cases, he doesn't have to and probably won't be persuaded right away.

For the Sake of Argument

So what would you like to talk about today? Sanctification? Conflict resolution? Free will versus the Sovereignty of God? I'm open to anything except… except what I'm *supposed* to be talking about today, which is "argumentativeness."

If you knew me even a little bit, you would understand why I might run from this topic. I'm the type of person who can argue a thing to death; one who argues just for the sake of arguing. I can't tell you how many times my kids have said, after listening to me and their dad talk, "You're arguing about *that*?" I like the challenge of the debate, and I like to think of it as an "iron sharpens iron" kind of thing (Proverbs 27:17)—that when Scott and I argue, he's keeping me on my toes and making me think.

The problem, however, is that sometimes arguing can be a sin. Many times when we argue, what we're really saying is, "I'm smart, you're dumb, and you need to change your thinking to be more in line with mine." It's thinking "more highly" of yourself than you ought to think (Romans 12:3), as though your opinion is the only one that matters. Even if you know for a fact that you're right and your husband is wrong, it is still wrong to argue. There are always better ways to discuss something without arguing or being contentious or contradictory.

The Bible says that a *"constant dripping on a day of steady rain and a contentious woman are alike"* (Proverbs 27:15). In other words, a contentious, argumentative woman is annoying, like a drippy faucet. If you're constantly contradicting your husband or wanting to argue, then he's not going to hear what you have to say. He's most likely thinking, "Can we just turn her *off?*"

If you're like me and you just like to argue, ask God to stop you before you head down that path. I have learned over the years to just let some things go, particularly if it's not important. If it is critical for your husband to be persuaded to your point of view, then ask God for the grace to present your case without being confrontational.

Memorize It!

See to it that no one comes short of the grace of God; that no root of bitterness springing up causes trouble, and by it many be defiled.
(Hebrews 12:15)

A Quiet Spirit

It is impossible to biblically work through conflict if you have a fearful, anxious, or "disturbed" spirit. Therefore, when you are dealing with conflict in your marriage, it is important to take the time to pray and quiet your heart before God. Spend time in His Word, reading through passages which are meaningful to you, that promise peace.

Some of these peace passages are listed below. Each of these verses has a command for you to obey, and a promise that results. Look up each verse, and then fill in the command and the promise. (The first one is done for you.)

Command	Promise
Philippians 4:6 *Let God know what my concerns are*	Philippians 4:7 *God's peace will guard my heart.*
Romans 12:18, 20	Romans 12:19
Psalm 45:7	Psalm 45:7
Isaiah 41:10	Isaiah 41:10
Jeremiah 29:13	Jeremiah 29:13
James 4:10	James 4:10

Many of us demand the promises (the right column) without ever doing our part (the left column). It's not that we must "work" for God's blessings, but His blessings are the natural results of our obedience.

Be anxious for nothing, but in everything by prayer and supplication with thanksgiving let your requests be made known to God. And the peace of God, which surpasses all comprehension, will guard your hearts and your minds in Christ Jesus.
Philippians 4:6-7

Application

If you are struggling in your marriage; if you have reached a point of conflict with your husband that seems to be insurmountable or to have no solution, then it is probably true that your heart is disturbed and distressed. Even in the midst of conflict, a godly wife can have perfect peace and a "quiet spirit," if she is placing all of her hope and trust in God. "Fixing" your husband is not your responsibility, and working yourself up into a froth is not going to accomplish anything. You are here to be your husband's helper, but not his healer. Only God can make true, permanent changes in your husband's heart. It's time for you to *rest*. It's time for you to trust God, *"for it is God who is at work in you, both to will and to work for His good pleasure"* (Philippians 2:13).

Week 41, Day 1

Let us also lay aside every encumbrance and the sin which so easily entangles us, and let us run with endurance the race that is set before us, fixing our eyes on Jesus, the author and perfecter of faith, who for the joy set before Him endured the cross, despising the shame, and has sat down at the right hand of the throne of God.
HEBREWS 12:1-2†

Application

People who are really into something use the "life" phrase to describe anything that consumes most of their time, thoughts and energies: "Music is my life." "Skiing is my life." "Chocolate is my life." My friend, the really good skater, has a T-shirt that says, "Skating is my life."

Rarely do you hear Christians say, "Christ is my life." But I love that very simple phrase in Colossians 3:4—*"When Christ, who is our life. . . ."* I would like to be able to say that Christ is my life; that He consumes most of my time, thoughts and energies; that He is my greatest passion. Remind yourself throughout the day of the preeminence of Christ in your life by repeating Colossians 3:4: *"Christ, who is our life."*

SET YOUR MIND ON THINGS ABOVE

Back when in-line skating was all the rage, I bought a pair of skates and learned to skate. Every Saturday I was out on the trail, working on my form and speed. As a beginning skater, I would constantly be watching the edge of the trail, fearful of falling off the edge. Finally, my friend, who is a much better skater, told me, "Keep your eyes straight ahead. Wherever your eyes go, that's where your body will go."

It's interesting how God has designed the universe so that the laws of physics often reflect spiritual truth. Nowhere is this more true than in that statement, "Wherever your eyes go, that's where your body will go." This is why God commands us in Colossians 3:1-2, *"Therefore if you have been raised up with Christ, keep seeking the things above, where Christ is, seated at the right hand of God. Set your mind on the things above, not on the things that are on earth."* Wherever your heart is, that's the direction your life will go.

We've talked throughout this devotional about how anything that distracts us from a wholehearted devotion to Christ is an idol. Often, when we're aware of the idols that trip us up, we become so focused on avoiding them that we end up going right back to them. But God never tells us to set our minds on avoiding idols. Always, His cure for resisting idolatry is to set our thoughts and hearts on the LORD Jesus.

In verse 3, we see the basis for this new affection: *"For you have died and your life is hidden with Christ in God."* A dead person has no appetite. If your old nature is dead, then the appetites and lusts of your old nature should also be dead. But this is not an automatic or permanent result of our salvation; we must still make a conscious effort to continually keep our body in the grave. We do this by focusing on Christ, and keeping our eyes on Him. Our reward for keeping our "eyes on the prize" is not only a loving, conversational relationship with Christ, but being *"revealed with Him in glory"* someday (verse 4).

Memorize It!

Every man's way is right in his own eyes, but the LORD weighs the hearts. To do righteousness and justice is desired by the LORD more than sacrifice.
(Proverbs 21:2-3)

A Conscious Act of the Will

Katie and her mom, Donna, were in the kitchen, preparing dinner and catching up on the week's events. The men were outside, supposedly tending to the grill, but in actuality, they had picked up a basketball and were heavily engaged in a game of one-on-one. As Katie watched the flames lick higher and higher, she opened the window and yelled at her husband, "JAKE! The steaks??" Jake flipped the ball to his father-in-law and sprinted over to the grill, rescuing the steaks from incineration. Katie rolled her eyes as she closed the window, shaking her head.

Donna's heart fell when she saw her daughter's disrespect for her husband. "Sweetie," she began, "remember when we talked about how important it is to show Jake respect?" Katie frowned. "I know," she said, "and I've been praying about it. I just have a hard time with some of the dumb stuff he does." Donna smiled at her daughter. "Respect is like love: it's a choice you make, not something you do only when you feel like it." Donna went on: "I love you *and* Jake, and it hurts to see how you disrespect him sometimes. I can imagine how it must grieve the heart of God!"

Like Katie, many of us struggle with consistently showing respect to our husbands. It's easy to respect a guy who is always on his game and meeting your every expectation. But that kind of husband is rare. Most of our husbands are flawed humans, and they don't always act in a way that earns respect. It helps to remember that we *"all have sinned and fall short of the glory of God"* (Romans 3:23). To act as if we are more worthy of honor than our husbands is nothing but pride. And pride is a hateful attitude: *"Everyone who is proud in heart is an abomination to the Lord… he will not be unpunished"* (Proverbs 16:5†).

Just as our husbands choose to love us despite our flaws, we too must choose to always demonstrate respect toward our husbands. Sometimes this comes easily, but often we have to make a conscious effort to show respect, out of obedience to God and love for our husbands.

Memorize It!

Every man's way is right in his own eyes, but the Lord weighs the hearts. To do righteousness and justice is desired by the Lord more than sacrifice.
(Proverbs 21:2-3)

Now accept the one who is weak in faith, but not for the purpose of passing judgment on his opinions... Why do you judge your brother? Or you again, why do you regard your brother with contempt? For we will all stand before the judgment seat of God.
Romans 14:1, 10†

Application

If God has convicted you today of not consistently showing respect to your husband, you might want to pray a prayer of faith and confession to Him, similar to this one:

Father, please forgive me for not choosing to respect my husband the way I should. Help me to live dependent on You for my actions and my attitudes. May Your Holy Spirit convict me if I ever begin feeling or showing disrespect to my husband. I choose today to give you my pride and all of my expectations for how my husband should act and think. Help me show respect to my husband at all times, no matter how he is acting, as You give me grace and strength and as I walk in the path you've put before me. Thank you for my husband and for the life you've given us together.

Week 41, Day 3

She looks for wool and flax, and works with her hands in delight. She is like merchant ships; she brings her food from afar. She rises also while it is still night, and gives food to her household and portions to her maidens. She is not afraid of the snow for her household, for all her household are clothed with scarlet. She makes coverings for herself; her clothing is fine linen and purple. She looks well to the ways of her household, and does not eat the bread of idleness.
PROVERBS 31:13-15, 21-22, 27

Application

Often, simple tips can revolutionize your house-keeping skills. You can pick up these tips from magazine articles and self-help books on organization and time management. Some of the simple solutions I follow are:

- Make your bed every morning, before you leave the bedroom.
- Set aside time for daily "cleaning bursts"—fifteen minutes of full-on cleaning fury, in whatever room needs it most.
- Never leave a kitchen dirty!
- Use timers to remind yourself when it's time to start dinner, stop goofing off, turn off the computer, walk the dog, or whatever.
- Christians should have a "sanctifying" influence on their environment. I always try to leave a room looking better than how I found it, even if it's just a very quick and simple tidy.

CHAOS THEORY

Have you ever seen those television reality programs about "hoarders": people who seem to have a complete inability to throw anything away? I know a woman who once struggled in this way, and I cannot tell you the pain it caused her and her family. Mounds of clothes, toys, trash, and "supplies" covered every square inch of her house. Every surface was heaped high with stuff, most of which just needed to be pitched. Her hoarding was based on her fear and lack of trust in God, but knowing this did not help. The mess overwhelmed her, and she had no hope she could ever clean her way out of it.

Most of us do not struggle with this problem, but many of us do need a little help in the area of housekeeping. We are so busy, and life sometimes gets out of control—and when it does, a neat house is often the first thing to go. If your home is messy and chaotic, your family will feel stressed and tense. The guilt of not keeping up with things will drain you of the energy you need to keep up with things! (Yes, it's a vicious cycle.) A dirty or messy house can deprive you and your family of joy and peace. Failure to plan ahead with regards to grocery shopping and meal preparation usually results in poor nutrition or overextending the budget by eating out too often.

As the keeper of the home (1 Timothy 5:14), you must make it your business to learn *how* to keep an orderly and clean home and stay organized with shopping and cooking. If any of these areas in your life are out of control, you should seek the resources to change, and through prayer, have the discipline to follow through with your plan.

Memorize It!

Every man's way is right in his own eyes, but the LORD weighs the hearts. To do righteousness and justice is desired by the LORD more than sacrifice.
(Proverbs 21:2-3)

Learning Through Conflict

The little mouse ran through the maze, sniffing out the cheese he knew was hidden somewhere inside. *I turn here, smell gets stronger*, he thinks. He rounds the corner and suddenly *ZAP!* An electric shock zings his little mouse feet. *OK, bad idea*. The mouse turns back, but now the cheese smell is going away. Confused, little mouse turns around and tries again. *ZAP!*

Eventually, our little mouse will learn that every time he takes that route, he's going to get zapped.

It would be nice if every time we sinned against God, we were instantly zapped. Our training in righteousness might take a lot less time! But God is kind, loving and patient (Romans 2:4). He gives us time to learn; but as we're learning, we're going to get "zapped" with the consequences of trying to go our own way.

Have you ever said, "God will keep bringing this situation into my life until I learn what He wants me to learn"? Many people say something like that after they've gone through a difficult trial that seems to be a repeat of a previous difficult trial. You want to blame the repetition on God, but the truth is that the trial keeps recurring because you keep going your own way. God doesn't have to providentially alter your circumstances to bring this trial to you; you keep doing it to yourself! You and your husband keep having that same difficulty because you still have not learned to submit graciously. You keep getting zapped because of your own sin.

However, the question, "What is God trying to teach me through this?" is a good one, and I'll tell you what the answer is, every time. God is always trying to teach you about Himself.

All of the Bible is about Him. It's not primarily a manual about your life. It is *primarily* about God and His son Jesus Christ, whom God has *"highly exalted"* and given *"the name which is above every name, so that at the name of Jesus every knee will bow... (and) every tongue will confess that Jesus Christ is Lord, to the glory of God the Father"* (Philippians 2:9-11†).

Memorize It!

Every man's way is right in his own eyes, but the Lord weighs the hearts. To do righteousness and justice is desired by the Lord more than sacrifice.
(Proverbs 21:2-3)

Turn to Me and be saved, all the ends of the earth; For I am God, and there is no other. I have sworn by Myself, The word has gone forth from My mouth in righteousness and will not turn back, that to Me every knee will bow, every tongue will swear allegiance.
Isaiah 45:22-23

Application

Why does God want to teach you about Himself?

1) So you will fear Him. (Psalm 111:10)
2) So you will love Him. (Luke 10:27)
3) So you will keep His commandments. (Joshua 22:5)
4) So you will be like His Son. (Romans 8:29)

If you feared God and were conformed to the image of His Son, if you loved God and kept His commandments, do you think you would have the conflict in your marriage that you do now? Yes, you may still have trials, but your trials would all be "for righteousness sake" (1 Peter 3:14).

Week 41, Day 5

I am the vine, you are the branches; he who abides in Me and I in him, he bears much fruit, for apart from Me you can do nothing.
JOHN 15:5

Application

Jesus didn't die so that you could be a better wife, mother, sister and friend. He didn't die so that you could go to a nice church and have a nice life. He died to redeem you to a dynamic life and love relationship with Himself. It is out of this conversational love relationship that you learn to be like Him and do what He would do.

Yes, read your Bible. Yes, go to church. But do not neglect spending time with Him. Reading His Word, praying and singing praises to Him, and listening to His voice all takes time. You can't fit it into fifteen minutes a day. If you try, you won't be "abiding" in Him. *"As the branch cannot bear fruit of itself unless it abides in the vine, so neither can you unless you abide in Me"* (John 15:4).

Chameleons For Christ

Several years ago, film director Woody Allen made a film called *Zelig* about a man who was the ultimate "chameleon." Whenever he stood next to someone, he would take on not just their personality, but their actual appearance. Standing next to a Native American, his skin got darker and his clothing changed to match. He even grew a feathered headdress!

We're all aware of the human tendency to take on some of the attitudes, idioms, and mannerisms of the people we spend time with. This is most noticeable in teenagers, who adopt their own unique language when they're together and participate heavily in "group think." As much as we like to talk about individuality, we still tend to conform to others in our social group. What God requires, however, is that we conform to the image of His Son.

I think it's interesting when I see someone wearing a WWJD ("What Would Jesus Do?") bracelet, and I know they either don't have a relationship with Christ, or they don't spend any time in His Word. There is no way you can be conformed to His image (Romans 8:29), or know what Jesus would do or how He would react, if you don't spend a LOT of time with Him. Going to church and listening to sermons is necessary, but it cannot be the sum total of the time you spend with Jesus Christ. Your relationship with God needs to be interactive and conversational, where you are talking to *and* listening to Him.

God commands us to love Him (Luke 10:27), obey Him (John 3:36), seek after Him (Jeremiah 29:13), worship Him (Psalm 99:9), pray to Him (Matthew 26:41), hear Him (Hebrews 3:15), pay attention to Him (2 Peter 1:19), bring our requests to Him (Philippians 4:6), fear and serve Him (1 Samuel 12:24), and praise Him (Psalm 22:23). As for His Word, we are to study it (2 Timothy 2:15), memorize it (Psalm 119:11), and let it indwell us (John 15:7).

Now, how are you going to do all that if you're just spending a few minutes a day with Christ?

Bad Habits

But now you also, put them all aside: anger, wrath, malice, slander, and abusive speech from your mouth.
Colossians 3:8

Gus and Darla were a cute couple with a not-too-cute problem: they loved to entertain others by putting each other down. One night we were at a restaurant, and the perpetually moody Darla was looking at the menu. She said to Gus (who is somewhat "vertically challenged"): "Oh look, Honey, we're on the menu. Shrimp and crab!"

Most of their friends got a big kick out of the way they would jab and make fun of the other, but it always made me sad. I worked with Darla and often heard her berate her husband on the phone in a way that wasn't part of the act. I knew their comedy routine was just a cover for a troubled marriage. And much of the trouble was that Darla did not respect her husband. Gus went along with the "fun," but I know it hurt him deeply when his wife made fun of him in front of his friends.

Very early in their relationship, Gus and Darla developed a habit of speaking disrespectfully to and about each other. While we may not be as obvious about it as my friends, we can also develop habits of disrespect that are hurtful to our husbands and not honoring to God. These habits include sarcasm, name-calling, put-downs, or using humor as a way to belittle your husband or disguise complaining. If you are guilty of any of these sinful habits, you need to recognize that you're not being funny or cute, you're being disrespectful. Even if your husband seems to join in the fun, that kind of disrespectful speech will tear both of you down in the end.

Ephesians 5 describes how we should model our speech: *"Therefore be imitators of God, as beloved children; and walk in love, just as Christ also loved you…and there must be no filthiness and silly talk, or coarse jesting, which are not fitting, but rather giving of thanks"* (Ephesians 5:1-4†). Could you imagine God using the kind of language we typically use with our husbands? If we are "imitators of God" and walking "in love," we will always speak respectfully to our husbands.

Memorize It!

It is better to live in a desert land than with a contentious and vexing woman.
(Proverbs 21:19)

Application

Does your speech demonstrate respect for your husband, or do you make jokes at his expense, making him look stupid or foolish? If so, you are not respecting your husband the way God commands. Your *attitude* toward your husband needs to change; once your attitude changes, your speech will follow.

You can work on your attitude by breaking any habits of disrespect you've fallen into. It's been said that it takes three weeks to break a habit, so for the next three weeks, ask God daily to help you identify disrespectful habits, and replace them with actions and speech that show your husband respect. If you're the type who just needs to entertain others, work on finding a *shtick* that doesn't make fun of your husband.

Week 42, Day 2

Let all bitterness and wrath and anger and clamor and slander be put away from you, along with all malice. Be kind to one another, tender-hearted, forgiving each other, just as God in Christ also has forgiven you.
EPHESIANS 4:31-32

Application

The key to overcoming anger is to humble yourself, and to stop loving *things*—possessions, dreams, goals, or any fleshly desire—more than you love Christ or others. (See 1 John 2:15-16.) Nothing you have, and nothing you desire, is more important than your relationship with your husband and with Christ.

Whenever something happens that frustrates, annoys or angers you, you can please yourself by clinging to your right to be angry, or you can be patient and loving and therefore pleasing to God. To help you choose wisely, stop and ask yourself these questions: Am I getting angry because of my pride? Is what I am angry about more important than loving my husband and pleasing Christ?

ANGER & PRIDE

When my husband does something foolish, I can get a little angry, but years of practice have taught me to convert my angry thoughts to forgiving thoughts fairly quickly. For instance, recently he was helping me in the kitchen, and he threw a steak knife into my new non-stick skillet and put a big ol' scratch in the finish. My instant angry thought was, *I cannot believe he just did that! How many times have I TOLD him to be careful with that!!* But my follow-up forgiving thought was, *He probably wasn't paying attention; I need to be grateful he's even in here helping me.*

It is difficult to come up with those forgiving thoughts if I'm thinking "more highly" of myself than I ought to think (Romans 12:3). In other words, if my heart is full of pride, I will continue to feed the angry part of me and will not be able to be understanding or forgiving.

Pride is one of the biggest contributors to anger. If you think your husband is less intelligent, competent, or mature than you are, you will become frustrated, impatient or annoyed with him when he doesn't behave as you would like him to. Pride says, "I would never act that way!" and makes it nearly impossible to forgive. But humility reminds that we are all sinners, we all do stupid things, and we all *"come short of the glory of God"*(Romans 3:23). When you stop to consider how forgiving God is toward you, it is much easier to forgive your husband, which will keep you from anger.

The other major contributor to anger is frustrated idol worship. In other words, when we don't get what we want, or when our idols are taken from us, we can get very angry. The Bible makes this connection between anger and our fleshly lusts very clear: *"What is the source of quarrels and conflicts among you? Is not the source of your pleasures that wage war in your members?"* (James 4:1). If I had made an idol of my new skillet, taking more pleasure in it than in my husband, then it would have been very easy for me to react to him in a sinful way.

Memorize It!

It is better to live in a desert land than with a contentious and vexing woman.
(Proverbs 21:19)

Training for Submission

Tammy was having one of those days where nothing was going her way. By the time dinner rolled around, she was not in a good mood, and the dinner she'd planned was not coming together well. She was tired, in a bad mood, and just wanted to go out to eat. When Jerry came home, she was lying on the couch, trying to get rid of a headache. "Can we please go out to dinner tonight?" she asked. Jerry sighed. "We've eaten out twice this week already. You know that's our limit. Come on, I'll help you make dinner," he offered. "Never mind!" she said, storming off to the kitchen. She'd figure something out, even if it was soup and sandwiches. But she was annoyed—did he not get how stressful her life is?

As she reached to open the refrigerator, she saw the Scripture she'd put up that morning: *"Love does not act unbecomingly, it does not seek its own"* (1 Corinthians 13:5†). She had acted rudely and was seeking her own way, rather than submitting to Jerry's decision. Rebuked, Tammy quickly asked God to forgive her, then went to Jerry. "I'm sorry," she apologized. "I have a huge headache, but that's no excuse. I was more committed to making things easy for myself than to your decision." Jerry smiled. "It's okay, sweetheart." "No, it isn't," she said, "I didn't submit and that is just wrong. The next time you make a decision I don't like, I need to accept it without complaining."

What Tammy is doing is training or disciplining herself *"for the purpose of godliness"* (1 Timothy 4:7). The Greek word translated "discipline" in this verse is *gymnazo,* from which we get our word *gymnasium*. It implies doing something over and over until you get it right. Learning to submit to your husband does not happen automatically as a reward for you "sticking it out." You must discipline yourself to build godly principles into every aspect of your life. God will help you with this process, but even with His help, it does not happen overnight.

Memorize It!

It is better to live in a desert land than with a contentious and vexing woman.
(Proverbs 21:19)

Discipline yourself for the purpose of godliness; for bodily discipline is only of little profit, but godliness is profitable for all things, since it holds promise for the present life and also for the life to come.
1 Timothy 4:7-8†

Application

Learning godliness is God's plan for you. It requires your disciplined effort, and often involves struggle. It would be great if it were easy, but our struggle to learn obedience makes us stronger, and keeps us dependent upon the Father. *"The testing of your faith produces endurance. And let endurance have its perfect result, so that you may be perfect and complete, lacking in nothing"* (James 1:3-4†).

When you fail to submit as you should, go through the process Tammy did: Confess your sin to God and to your husband, then replace your sinful thoughts (the ones that led to failure) with God-honoring thoughts. Do this every time, until it becomes automatic, until you are "lacking in nothing" in the area of submission.

Week 42, Day 4

To sum up, all of you be harmonious, sympathetic, brotherly, kindhearted, and humble in spirit; not returning evil for evil or insult for insult, but giving a blessing instead; for you were called for the very purpose that you might inherit a blessing.
1 Peter 3:8-9

Application

The quicker you react to trying circumstances, the less likely you are to react biblically. When the temptation comes to return evil instead of blessing to your husband, that is the time to STP: Stop, Think and Pray (see p. 89). Think about how you should react, then pray for God to give you the grace to follow through.

God promises to give *"grace to help in time of need"* (Hebrews 4:16). He will help you respond righteously, even in difficult circumstances. But you have to trust that He will give you strength to do what is right, and will reward your obedience with far greater blessing than if you react in the flesh. Remember: you are responsible for your actions, and your husband is responsible for his. Let your actions always be righteous.

A Blessing Instead

Even though my dad lived in a tiny single-wide trailer, he loved having people over for dinner. One hot June day, about twenty of us were packed into Dad's trailer—including my husband, who hates crowds and thus was complaining, and directing many of his complaints at me. I wanted to tell him to knock it off, but I was reminded not to return "evil for evil," but to give "a blessing instead" (1 Peter 3:9). When he finished his rant, I said, "Let me get you something to eat." I went to the kitchen, filled up a plate and got him a large glass of iced tea. Fifteen minutes later, he and his blood sugar had returned to normal, and he was apologizing for what he said.

Sadly, I can tell you many more stories where I returned "evil for evil," rather than blessing my husband. What I learned from doing it God's way was how much peace and joy comes from obedience. I contrast how happy Scott and I were at the end of that evening, to the many times I've defended myself, reacted in anger, or failed to respond in love as God would have me respond. Every time I've responded sinfully I have felt much worse afterward, Scott and I were no closer, and God was not glorified.

When your husband does something unloving, the natural response is to return "evil for evil." The flesh says, "Stand up for yourself! If you let him get away with that, he'll just keep doing it!" We think that if we "even the score," we'll protect ourselves, and this will bring us some benefit. But the Bible says, *"The anger of man does not achieve the righteousness of God"* (James 1:20).

God's prescription for standing up to your husband's unkindness is this: *"Do not be overcome by evil, but overcome evil with good"* (Romans 12:21). God does want you to fight back, but with loving thoughts, words, and actions. If you've ever done this, or had someone do it to you, you know how completely disarming it can be. The more intense your hurt, the greater the need for you to return blessings instead of evil.

Memorize It!

It is better to live in a desert land than with a contentious and vexing woman.
(Proverbs 21:19)

People Pleaser

Imagine you had a badge representing every idol in your life, and you wore those badges on a sash like a girl scout. You could have a little $ badge for the idol of wealth, a ♥ representing the idol of an intimate marriage, etc. Each of us would have our own unique set of badges representing the idols we worship, but almost all of us would have one particular badge. Answer the following True/False questions and see if you can figure out what it is:

___ I often make decisions based on what people will think of me
___ Being well-liked is important to me
___ I am easily embarrassed
___ I don't share the gospel very often
___ I think about the impression I'm making on others when I talk to them
___ I rarely go out in public without my makeup
___ I have never led anyone to the Lord

If you answered *True* to any of these, it is likely that one of your idols is the approval of others. The more of these you answered in the affirmative, the bigger the idol is in your life. If you answered True to all of them, you have a genuine fear of man.

Matthew 10:28 says, *"Do not fear those who kill the body but are unable to kill the soul; but rather fear Him who is able to destroy both soul and body in hell."* The fear of man is a crippling idol that keeps us from living under the Lordship of Jesus Christ. If you lust after approval from others, you've set other people up as idols in your heart. *They* are ruling you, not Christ.

The biggest reason the gospel is not moving forward is because we live in fear of what people will think of us. They'll think we're weird, fanatics, or just not very cool. Compare that to the apostles who, when they were commanded to stop preaching the gospel, said, "*We must obey God rather than men*" (Acts 5:29). When they were beaten for proclaiming Christ, they went away *"rejoicing that they had been considered worthy to suffer shame for His name"* (Acts 5:41). We need to be joyfully willing to suffer shame for Christ, if that's what He calls us to.

The fear of man brings a snare,
but he who trusts in the
Lord will be exalted.
Proverbs 29:25

Application

In Acts 4-5 we see ordinary men doing extraordinary things. The key to their courage is found in Acts 4:31. *"And when they had prayed, the place where they had gathered together was shaken, and they were all filled with the Holy Spirit and began to speak the word of God with boldness."* The apostles joined with other disciples who desired the same thing and prayed for strength.

Write the names of other believers you can ask to come alongside you in rejecting the idol of the fear of man and pursuing His kingdom. Then sometime in the next week, make an appointment to get together and pray with each other for boldness in sharing the gospel.

Week 43, Day 1

Only fear the LORD *and serve Him in truth with all your heart; for consider what great things He has done for you.*
1 SAMUEL 12:24

Application

One of our problems with a lack of spiritual growth is our tendency to spend a small amount of time with God during our "quiet time." Then we consider the rest of the day to be ours. If that's your attitude, then I don't know who you're spending your quiet time with, but it's not *"the God of gods and the* LORD *of* LORDS*, the great, the mighty, and the awesome God"* (Deuteronomy 10:17†). Everyone who sees God for Who He truly is fears Him and loves Him. Your attitude about God is the most important ingredient in your spiritual growth and maturity.

If you do not fear or love God as you should, consider increasing the amount of time you spend with Him each day. Use the extra time to really focus on the LORD your God and worshiping Him.

FEAR AND LOVE

For almost three years, Tori suffered severe depression which almost ended her marriage. She had no joy in any of her relationships, and at times felt suicidal, yet she wasn't entirely sure why. She took antidepressants, but could tell they were just masking her symptoms. Finally, her husband, Brent, insisted they go talk to their pastor. Pastor Don helped them see that Tori's depression could be traced back to unresolved sin issues.

Tori had prayed a salvation prayer as a child, but had never matured as a Christian. She set aside small amounts of time for God: going to church on Sunday morning, and having fifteen minutes of "devotions" every morning. But once her "minimum requirement" was met, she rarely thought about God. She regularly consumed alcohol to take the edge off of her anxiety, she was inexplicably angry toward her husband, and the only fun she ever had was going clubbing with her girlfriends. God's Word had virtually no impact on her life.

Tori is an extreme example of what can happen to us if we do not fear or love God. She only reads God's Word to fulfill an obligation; she doesn't do it out of love for Him and a sincere desire to learn and obey His truth. As a result, she never grows in her faith.

Many of us do the same thing. Many of you are reading this book today because it is part of your routine, but once the book is closed and your "quiet time" is over, you take control of your day, with very little thought of serving Christ.

A true disciple of Christ follows the pattern set for us in Deuteronomy 10:12-13†: *"What does the* LORD *your God require from you, but to fear the* LORD *your God, to walk in all His ways and love Him, and to serve the* LORD *your God with all your heart and with all your soul, and to keep the* LORD'S *commandments and His statutes which I am commanding you today for your good?"* If you fear God, you will be afraid to sin. If you love Him, you will want to spend time with Him, and you will seek to obey His commands.

Memorize It!

Truly, truly, I say to you, unless a grain of wheat falls into the earth and dies, it remains alone; but if it dies, it bears much fruit. He who loves his life loses it, and he who hates his life in this world will keep it to life eternal.
(John 12:24-25)

More Important Than You

Kathy smiled as her dad kissed her cheek then sat down on the front pew. Her wedding dress whispered across the carpet as she turned toward Rick. *He's so handsome,* she thought. She barely heard her pastor as he addressed the audience, but moments later it was time to say their vows. Kathy repeated each line, eagerly promising to love Rick "in sickness and in health, for better or worse, till death do us part."

But suddenly, the pastor said something she didn't remember being part of their vows. "I promise to consider your ministry, career, and goals as more important than my own." Pastor waited for her to repeat the words, which she did. "When we have a disagreement, I will cheerfully defer to your opinions; when we have important decisions to make, you will have the final say." *Is this some kind of joke? Who wrote these vows?* she thought. "In all things, you are the leader and I joyfully put myself under your authority, even when your decisions seem stupid to me." Kathy repeated the words, but the smile on her face had given way to confusion. "I will die to myself and put you first, as long as we both shall live."

Chances are, you've never been to a wedding where the wedding vows were as pointed as those. Wedding vows usually reflect the flowery fog that most of us live in during the time of our engagement, blissfully ignoring the realities of married life and the sacrifices that are required.

The truth is, most of us get married for selfish reasons. We want a man to take care of us, meet our needs, and fulfill us, without considering how much we'll have to give up to meet his needs. As you mature in your relationship and in your walk with Christ, you should be growing past a self-centered view of marriage, and learning to give rather than expect love. One of the best ways to practice this selfless love is to actively set your husband's needs and goals above your own. (See Philippians 2:3-4.)

Memorize It!

Truly, truly, I say to you, unless a grain of wheat falls into the earth and dies, it remains alone; but if it dies, it bears much fruit. He who loves his life loses it, and he who hates his life in this world will keep it to life eternal.
(John 12:24-25)

(Love) is not self seeking.
1 Corinthians 13:5, NIV†

Application

When two people have completely different objectives, the result is conflict. Look at the areas in your marriage where you have conflict, and try to ascertain what your goals are versus your husband's. Write down these conflicting goals, then ask God to change your mind about which goal is more important. Unless your husband's goal is sinful, then it automatically should become more important to you than your own. If you aren't sure what your husband's ultimate goal is, then discuss it with him and try to determine exactly what he is trying to achieve. You may be able to suggest a compromise, but if not, remember that his goals take priority, not yours.

Week 43, Day 3

For this reason a man shall leave his father and mother and be joined to his wife, and the two shall become one flesh. So they are no longer two, but one flesh. What therefore God has joined together, let no man separate.
MATTHEW 19:5-6†

Application

Most theologians, pastors, and counselors teach that divorce is justified in the case of infidelity, based on Matthew 19:9. However, even if your husband has been unfaithful, his sin is ultimately against God (2 Samuel 12:13, Psalm 51:4). If God can forgive him, then by God's grace so can you. There is *nothing* your husband has done that you, through the power of the Holy Spirit, cannot forgive.

If your husband has not repented of his sin, knowing he will have to suffer God's wrath should help you have mercy on him and to return his evil (1 Peter 3:9) with the blessing of forgiveness. Divorce may still be unavoidable, but *you* will have done all you can to pursue peace and righteousness (2 Timothy 2:22).

HARD HEARTS

Bridget and Cole sat in Pastor Dave's office, both of them crying. That very morning, Cole had confessed to an affair with a woman in their church. "Pastor, I have been so miserable," he said, "and I've ended that relationship. But I know I've done irreparable damage to my wife."

Bridget listened but couldn't look at him. She wasn't feeling his sorrow, just her own anger and pain. "I know what the Bible says," she said to the pastor. "Isn't infidelity grounds for divorce?" Pastor Dave looked at her thoughtfully, and said, "Yes. However, it is also grounds for *forgiveness*."

When the Pharisees came to Jesus and asked about this issue of divorce, Jesus answered them: *"Because of your hardness of heart Moses permitted you to divorce"* (Matthew 19:8). The LORD was not *just* talking about the hardness of heart that leads to sin, but also the hard heart that is unable to forgive the sinning spouse.

If your marriage has reached the point where you are considering divorce, examine yourself first to see if your heart has been hardened, and if your own inability to forgive is contributing as much to the breakup as your husband's sin. It is certainly understandable to be hurt, confused, and angry. However, those emotions should not be given more weight than God's desires for your life. God *hates* divorce (Malachi 2:13-17); He sees you and your husband as one flesh (Matthew 19:6) and His desire is for you to seek reconciliation. Divorce should always be the option of last resort.

If your heart is hardened because of how your husband has sinned against you, pray for a heart of mercy before making any decisions about the future of your marriage. This is especially difficult if he has sinned against you for a long time and your heart has grown harder over the years. But God can change your heart, if you are willing. *"Moreover, I will give you a new heart and put a new spirit within you; and I will remove the heart of stone from your flesh and give you a heart of flesh"* (Ezekiel 36:26).

Memorize It!

Truly, truly, I say to you, unless a grain of wheat falls into the earth and dies, it remains alone; but if it dies, it bears much fruit. He who loves his life loses it, and he who hates his life in this world will keep it to life eternal.
(John 12:24-25)

The End of the Rope

Yesterday, we said that divorce should always be the option of last resort, and that even infidelity can be forgiven. Some of the sweetest marriages I know are those that have reconciled after an extremely difficult trial.

However, there is one circumstance where God not only allows divorce, but He acknowledges that divorce might be your only option.

> *If...a woman has an unbelieving husband, and he consents to live with her, she must not send her husband away. Yet if the unbelieving one leaves, let him leave; the brother or the sister is not under bondage in such cases, but God has called us to peace* (1 Corinthians 7:12-13, 15†).

In other words, if your husband is not a believer and he has abandoned the marriage, God releases you from the union and calls you to find your peace in Him.

But what if he says he is a believer? Let's say your husband has been unfaithful, and you reprove him privately (Matthew 18:15). If he repents and turns from his sin, "you have won your brother" and you should forgive him. If he doesn't repent, you should bring two or three witnesses to rebuke him for his sin, as we have discussed previously (Matthew 18:16; see pages 166-167). If he still does not repent, it may be necessary to bring him before the church (verse 17) for the purpose of putting congregate pressure on him to repent.

If after all of this he still does not repent, you are to consider him to be an unbeliever (verse 18). If he is an unbeliever, you still don't *have* to divorce, as long as he wants to stay in the marriage (1 Corinthians 7:12). If he wants to stay married to you, you should have mercy toward him and forgive him (Matthew 18:21-22). But if he wants to leave, you are "not under bondage"—i.e., you are no longer bound to your husband.

Memorize It!

Truly, truly, I say to you, unless a grain of wheat falls into the earth and dies, it remains alone; but if it dies, it bears much fruit. He who loves his life loses it, and he who hates his life in this world will keep it to life eternal.
(John 12:24-25)

But from the beginning of creation, God made them male and female. For this reason a man shall leave his father and mother, and the two shall become one flesh; so they are no longer two, but one flesh. What therefore God has joined together, let no man separate.
Mark 10:6-9

Application

Even if you have freedom in the Lord (in some circumstances) to divorce your husband, you also have freedom in the Lord to forgive and reconcile. If your husband is repentant and wants to stay in the marriage, pray for wisdom, and seek guidance from godly, biblical counselors.

For some people and in some situations, divorce is unavoidable. *"But God has called us to peace"* (1 Corinthians 7:15). What God wants for us is peace in our hearts and our homes. Genuine peace only comes by obeying God, and sometimes, obeying God means forgiving your husband. It is, at the very least, the best place to start.

Week 43, Day 5

A constant dripping on a day of steady rain and a contentious woman are alike; he who restrains her restrains the wind, and grasps oil with his right hand.
PROVERBS 27:15-16

Application

A good check-list for avoiding nagging your husband about his responsibilities can be found in the lesson on page 189. Our focus here is on communication: how do you communicate your expectations to your husband without nagging? If he repeatedly fails in some way, how do you get him to change his behavior without nagging him?

The key to all good, godly communication is found in Colossians 3:8-17. Read this passage right now, taking special note of the many places where our speech is referenced. No matter how much or how little you tend to nag your husband, today is a good day for you to focus on this passage, and ask God to help you make *"compassion, kindness, humility, gentleness and patience"* (verse 12) a normal part of your speech.

NAG, NAG, NAG!

Krista learned about giving a biblical appeal in her Excellent Wife Bible study, but evidently she missed the part about giving the appeal only once. Ever since Ray told her that his job would be moving them to Phoenix within the year, she has been appealing to him over and over again to change his mind.

She has also begun to nag him about other things as well. She stopped picking up after him and now constantly reminds him to pick up his clothes or put his tools away in the garage. With the impending move, she has made a list of repairs needed to make their house more saleable, and Ray wishes she would just leave it at that. But she feels the need to bring up the list several times a week, asking him when he's going to get to them. "I have a lot to do to get ready for this move," she says. "He created this, so he has to live with the fallout."

What is clear is that Krista is very unhappy with her husband and has not submitted to his decision to move. Her unhappiness is spilling over into the way she communicates with him. Instead of lovingly helping him with his responsibilities, she just nags him. Her nagging is so constant that even when she is just asking a simple question, it comes across as nagging.

Nagging is a bad habit we wives get into, as we become dissatisfied with our life and our husbands' behavior. We nag when we put ourselves in the driver's seat, rather than submitting to our husbands and letting *them* decide when and how things should be done. Nagging never accomplishes anything. In fact, it often has the opposite effect: the more we nag, the less our husbands want to please us.

If you have a tendency to nag or "remind" your husband about his responsibilities, you need to recognize that *"the **husband** is the head of the wife, as Christ also is the head of the church"* (Ephesians 5:23). You are not the head of the family; he is. All of your speech directed at him should reflect that you are following him and his leadership, not the other way around.

Suffering for the Right Reasons

For the one who desires life, to love and see good days, must keep his tongue from evil and his lips from speaking deceit. He must turn away from evil and do good; he must seek peace and pursue it. For the eyes of the Lord are toward the righteous, and his ears attend to their prayer, but the face of the Lord is against those who do evil.
1 Peter 3:10-12

For years, Joelle suffered through a miserable marriage. Her husband was harsh and demanding, and whatever love they had during the honeymoon was nowhere to be found once the newness wore off. Joelle fought against Drake's hostility the only way she knew how: by arguing, retaliating, standing up for her rights, or confronting him angrily. By the time their children were in their early teens, Joelle could see the effect their unhappy marriage was having. What hurt Joelle deeply was knowing that *she* was the injured party, yet her kids directed their anger and disrespect toward her. "Drake is the guilty one in this marriage" she thought. "If those kids only knew how much their dad has hurt me, they would always come to my defense."

But God was merciful and led Joelle to attend a women's retreat, where she learned about *"suffering for the sake of righteousness"* (1 Peter 3:14). She could see how most of the suffering she had in her life was due to her own sin. So she committed herself to giving her husband a blessing whenever he mistreated her.

At first, her efforts not only went unrewarded, but they seemed to make Drake angrier. When she apologized to him for years of unrighteous living, he laughed. "Yeah, right, like you're going to change?" He seemed intent on testing her resolve, reacting disdainfully whenever she did something nice. He even made fun of her in front of the kids, which backfired on him. "Dad's a jerk," their daughter Mandy said one day. "No, sweetheart, your dad is not a jerk, and you should not talk about him that way," Joelle answered. Mandy looked surprised, but that day seemed to be a turning point. As Joelle's children began reacting to their mom's sweet nature, Drake could see that he was alone in his attitude. Finally he came to church with Joelle and eventually accepted Christ as his Lord and Savior. Today their marriage glorifies God, as Drake is now committed to loving Joelle as *"Christ loved the church"* (Ephesians 5:25).

Memorize It!

Let love be without hypocrisy. Abhor what is evil; cling to what is good. Be devoted to one another in brotherly love; give preference to one another in honor.
(Romans 12:9-10)

Application

God has not promised you a good life. Did you know that? We often rebel against hardship in our life because we think we're entitled to a certain kind of life. We would rather not experience hard things for the kingdom of God, and we compromise our walk with Christ as needed in order to avoid suffering.

But God has called us to suffer, not to live the good life, and often, that suffering is done within the context of marriage as we suffer for the sake of righteousness. Look up the following passages, and record in your prayer journal the richness of the blessings that come with suffering for Christ:

Romans 8:12-18
1 Peter 2:18-25
2 Corinthians 1:1-7
1 Peter 3:13-17
Philippians 1:27-29
1 Peter 4:12-19
2 Timothy 1:7-12
1 Peter 5:6-10

Week 44, Day 2

Do not regard lightly the discipline of the Lord*, nor faint when you are reproved by Him; for those whom the* Lord *loves He disciplines, and He scourges every son whom He receives.*
Hebrews 12:5-6†

Application

How do you respond when your husband reproves or corrects you? Do you get angry and defensive? Or do you humbly consider what he has to say? I have a friend who, whenever someone points out an area of her life where she could be doing better, she says, "I can receive that." That might be a good phrase for you to practice in humbly receiving correction from your husband.

You should always respond in humility—with tender, gentle, gracious obedience—to God and to your husband. If you know you have failed, take a few minutes to confess your sins to the Lord and then to your husband. Be specific and give examples, with a humble attitude that focuses only on what you have done wrong, not in how your husband chose to reprove you.

A Humble Response

Dee jumped when Jim walked into the room. She had planned to get up early and get started on her weekend chores, but first she wanted to check her email. Then her mom called, and while they were talking, Dee opened up the Solitaire game on her laptop. An hour later, she was on her 23rd game when Jim walked into the room.

"What are you doing?" he asked. He looked at the screen and sighed. "Dee, seriously? I thought we had plans for today." "Well, you were still in bed!" she countered. Immediately, she felt the Holy Spirit rebuking her for her reaction, and she stopped. "I'm sorry," she said. "You're absolutely right. This is irresponsible behavior on my part." She got up and kissed him. "Are you ready for breakfast?"

Dee's initial reaction was to get angry and argumentative. But Dee has been praying for the Lord to humble her and help her respond with gentleness whenever she and Jim have a disagreement or if he reproves her.

It's never a good feeling to realize that others see you as less than perfect. Any reproof can be humiliating, and our natural, sinful response is to react defensively, which only compounds our sin. *"All discipline for the moment seems not to be joyful, but sorrowful"* (Hebrews 12:11a). But discipline and correction are necessary if you're going to become the woman God wants you to be. *"Yet to those who have been trained by it, afterwards it yields the peaceful fruit of righteousness"* (Hebrews 12:11b).

Even if your husband reproves you in an angry and unkind manner, you are still responsible before God for how you respond back. You may think you're protecting yourself when you defend your sinful actions, but in reality, you are opening yourself up to continued pain and humiliation by not following God's plans for your life and your progressive sanctification. God says, *"Whoever loves discipline loves knowledge, but he who hates reproof is stupid"* (Proverbs 12:1). In other words, not responding properly and humbly to correction is just *dumb*.

Memorize It!

Let love be without hypocrisy. Abhor what is evil; cling to what is good. Be devoted to one another in brotherly love; give preference to one another in honor.
(Romans 12:9-10)

HANGING AROUND THE GOSSIP FENCE

When Heather and Jaimie met at a Thursday morning Bible study, they hit it off instantly. They had a lot in common, and it seemed everything Heather was going through in her marriage, Jaimie was going through as well. They often said their husbands must have been twins separated at birth; they were so similar in every way. In each other, Heather and Jaimie found comfort, support, and sympathy.

However, what should have been a friendship of godly encouragement turned into a relationship forged on mutual disrespect for their husbands. The women fed off each other, using the other's opinions as validation of their own. When they felt afflicted, they complained to each other endlessly; and when they were feeling light-hearted they had a great amount of fun at their husbands' expense. They often spent hours on the phone, gossiping about their husbands.

If you are having a difficult time respecting your husband, it is likely that you're not keeping your feelings to yourself. Women love to share—it's part of being female and being relational. Think about your best friends and the things you talk about. Do you encourage each other to respect your husbands and to be obedient to Christ? Or have you gotten into a bad habit of gossiping and complaining to them about your marriage?

In Matthew 18, Jesus said that if you have something in your life causing you to sin, even if it's very important to you—like a good friend—it is better to cut it off and throw it away than allow it to deprive you of a life of obedience. *"If your eye causes you to stumble, pluck it out and throw it from you. It is better for you to enter life with one eye, than to have two eyes and be cast into the fiery hell"* (Matthew 18:9). How much better would it be to begin turning those friendships into godly friendships, before something so drastic must be done?

Women must likewise be dignified, not malicious gossips, but temperate, faithful in all things.
1 TIMOTHY 3:11

Application

If you have a friend who is a godly influence, thank God for her today. But if you have a friend, or even a family member, who encourages you to gossip or laughs at your disrespect to your husband, you need to correct your attitude of disrespect first, then go to that person and ask their forgiveness. You not only sin against your husband when you disrespect him that way, but you're sinning against your friend (See Hebrews 12:15).

Memorize It!

Let love be without hypocrisy. Abhor what is evil; cling to what is good. Be devoted to one another in brotherly love; give preference to one another in honor.
(Romans 12:9-10)

Week 44, Day 4

Let us not lose heart in doing good, for in due time we will reap if we do not grow weary.
GALATIANS 6:9

Application

The prospect of "patiently enduring" does not always sound very appealing. It sounds difficult, whereas the world promises fun, happiness and freedom if you would just take care of yourself. But that is a lie of the enemy that never delivers. It is only through Christ that you can find joy, peace and freedom.

The following passages all talk about the rewards of endurance. Pick one and take the next ten minutes to meditate on it. You can journal your thoughts or use this time to pray the Scripture back to God, asking Him to make you willing to endure:

1 Peter 2:13-25
James 1:2-12
Hebrews 11
2 Timothy 2:1-13
Matthew 5:1-12
Romans 15:1-13
Galatians 5:13-25

ALWAYS REWARDED

Crystal rolled her eyes and sighed deeply. "I know what you're going to say," she said. "I did the Excellent Wife thing, and I know what the Bible says to do. But it doesn't work. Doug is never going to change, and I'm just...done." Crystal and her husband had been having problems for years, and she had just recently learned how to respond to her husband biblically. I understood her frustration; many times when we study the Scriptures, we get excited about God's promises to reward our obedience. Then when it doesn't happen the way we thought it should, we get discouraged.

I thought about an earlier incident, when I had reminded my daughter Ciara not to repay her sister's unkindness with more unkindness. "You want her to stop, don't you?" I asked. "Yes," Ciara replied, "but being nice to her will not make her stop." We talked about how she needed to be obedient to Christ no matter what. "You don't obey Christ to get the reward of Brittan's changed behavior. Your reward is that you glorify God and please Him. In time, Brittan will probably be nicer to you as you are nice to her. But even if she doesn't, *you* are doing what is right." I found myself having that identical conversation with Crystal, as she struggled with being obedient in her marriage—no matter what.

The difficulty for us is continuing to obey over the long term, even when it doesn't yield the results we want. Submission is always rewarded, but not always in the way we had hoped. Sometimes our husbands respond properly, change their behavior, and become better husbands. Sometimes our reward is simply that our character changes to be more like Christ. We become more patient, loving, and selfless, and we gain the character quality of endurance. *"And let endurance have its perfect result, so that you may be perfect and complete, lacking in nothing"* (James 1:4).

The question is, are you willing to patiently endure? Are you willing to be obedient, even if your husband never changes?

Memorize It!

Let love be without hypocrisy. Abhor what is evil; cling to what is good. Be devoted to one another in brotherly love; give preference to one another in honor.
(Romans 12:9-10)

The Very Best Way to Show That You Believe

Yesterday we talked about doing what is right, no matter what, and trusting God with the results. The **only** way submission (or any obedience) fails to have a good result is when *we* fail to keep doing it. God's way is always perfect, and *"He is a rewarder of those who diligently seek Him"* (Hebrews 11:6†, NKJV).

When we give up on God's way, we demonstrate that we don't trust Him. By our actions, we are saying one of three things:

- God's ways don't work; therefore, God is a liar.
- God's ways are pretty good, but they don't work for me. My way is better.
- God's ways work in some situations, but not in mine. God just doesn't understand my situation.

Of course none of these things are true, but we act as though they are true when we give up on God's ways and turn back to our old sinful ways of doing things. If you "try" obedience and give up because it doesn't produce the desired results, then your husband may give up as well. Moreover, you will not be made more like Christ, and God will not be glorified.

You can't control your husband's behavior by doing what is right, and I don't want to make empty promises. But the truth is that the more you submit to your husband, the more likely he will be to step up to the plate and try to live up to what you've freely given. If you treat him with disrespect, he will think that nothing he does is good enough, and he may stop trying to please you altogether. But even the promise of having a good influence on your husband should not be your motivation to submit to him. Your motivation should always be to obey God's commands and do what is right, no matter what.

Week 44, Day 5

Consider it all joy, my brethren, when you encounter various trials, knowing that the testing of your faith produces endurance. And let endurance have its perfect result, so that you may be perfect and complete, lacking in nothing
James 1:2-4

Application

The next time you're tempted to give up on obedience, ask yourself which of the following you are choosing in that moment to believe:

- God is a liar (Romans 3:4).
- My way is better than God's way (Isaiah 55:8).
- God doesn't understand my situation (Hebrews 4:15).

The godly wife will realize, instead, that God's ways are perfect: *"As for God, His way is perfect; The word of the Lord is proven; He is a shield to all who trust in Him"* (Psalm 18:30, NKJV). Meaning, God's ways are right and will always have a God-honoring result. You can always trust God to reward you for your obedience in submitting to your husband.

Week 45, Day 1

Let all bitterness and wrath and anger and clamor and slander be put away from you, along with all malice.
EPHESIANS 4:31

Application

Because the problem of bitterness is so pervasive, and so important, we're going to take two days to fully address it. For today, concentrate on identifying whether or not you are harboring bitterness or resentment against your husband. Read and pray aloud the following prayer from Psalm 139, then wait on God to identify any bitterness in your heart. Tomorrow, we'll talk about how to deal with what you find there.

Search me, O God, and know my heart; try me and know my anxious thoughts; and see if there be any hurtful way in me, and lead me in the everlasting way (Psalm 139:23-24).

BITTERNESS DESTROYS LOVE (PART 1)

Meredith sat across from me at the restaurant, devouring a stack of chocolate-chip pancakes. "So, you're off your diet?" I observed. "Oh yeah!" she laughed. "I'm done starving myself for him." Meredith had struggled with her weight for years, but had been doing well on her latest diet. I was surprised to see her come off it so...voraciously. However, she had recently discovered her husband (a soldier serving overseas) had committed adultery, and she was giving up.

Ian had confessed the affair and seemed to be truly repentant, but Meredith was not about to let him off that easy. While it's true that Ian had grievously sinned against her, she was adding her own sin of bitterness to the problem. "I go back and forth between feeling really sad and really angry," she said. "I know this sounds terrible, but honestly? I'd much rather have been told he was killed in action than to find out he slept with another woman!"

Maybe your husband has never had an affair; his sins may be many or few, big or small. Perhaps he has simply failed to meet your expectations. The question is, are you bitter toward him? If you answered a quick *No*, ask yourself if you ever participate in any of the following:

- *Gossip/Slander:* You talk to your friends about the things your husband has done that have hurt you.
- *Ingratitude:* It's been a long time since you felt truly thankful for the things he does for you. (If you just thought, "It's been so long since he's done anything for me!" you can stop right there. No matter how true that statement, you are definitely bitter!)
- *Judgmental/Critical:* In your mind, you criticize almost everything he does. You assume he is lying or has ulterior motives behind many of his actions.
- *Vengeful/Brooding:* You spend considerable amounts of time thinking about ways to even the score. You fantasize about leaving him, or wonder how much better your life would be if he were to die.
- *Self-centered*: You believe he is more to blame for the problems in your marriage than you are.

Memorize It!

Not lagging behind in diligence, fervent in spirit, serving the LORD; rejoicing in hope, persevering in tribulation, devoted to prayer, contributing to the needs of the saints, practicing hospitality. (Romans 12:11-13)

Bitterness Destroys Love (Part 2)

Yesterday we talked about identifying bitterness in your heart. Today, we're going to talk about what to do with bitterness, and develop a godly plan for responding to any pain your husband may have caused you.

STEPS FOR DESTROYING BITTERNESS

1. ***Understand what bitterness is.***

Bitterness grows when you "take into account a wrong suffered"—in other words, when you continue to keep charges of wrongdoing on your husband's account rather than forgiving him. When you do this, you're not showing the mercy God showed to you when He saved you. (See Matthew 18:23-35.) The truth is, there is nothing that your husband has done that God cannot forgive and you cannot forgive.

2. ***Clear your conscience.***

One reason we get so incensed when our husbands hurt us is because we believe too much in our own righteousness. "I would never do what he did to me!" However, if you're going to remove bitterness from your heart, you must be honest about your own sin and take 100% responsibility for your share of any problems in your marriage. (See Matthew 7:3-5 and Galatians 6:1-3.) This means identifying your sin and confessing it to God and to your husband.

3. ***Convert bitter thoughts to loving thoughts.***

Identify thoughts that are unloving, vengeful, or in any way unbiblical. If it helps, write them down (just make sure you destroy the written copy afterwards). Then take time to convert each thought to a kind, tender-hearted, or forgiving thought. For instance, instead of thinking, "He's never loved me!" you can think, "He doesn't demonstrate love as well as he should, but I know he loves me." Instead of getting angry when he comes home from work in a bad mood, choose instead to focus on the pressures he has to deal with in his job. Instead of thinking, "He's stupid and incapable of understanding me," ask yourself, "What can I do to communicate better to him?" You demonstrate love when you take *"every thought captive to the obedience of Christ"* (2 Corinthians 10:5).

Memorize It!

Not lagging behind in diligence, fervent in spirit, serving the Lord; rejoicing in hope, persevering in tribulation, devoted to prayer, contributing to the needs of the saints, practicing hospitality.
(Romans 12:11-13)

Be kind to one another, tender-hearted, forgiving each other, just as God in Christ also has forgiven you.
Ephesians 4:32

Application

Step 4 in overcoming bitterness is to **Begin making "second mile" investments**—going above and beyond the call of duty to be kind to your husband. It comes from Matthew 5:41, "*Whoever forces you to go one mile, go with him two.*" This is your homework today. If your husband asks you to do something, do what he asks and then some. Or do something nice for him without being asked. You could make his favorite meal, give him a massage, or (most men's favorite) initiate sex when he least expects it. Your guy may not deserve any of these things, but you do them because you love him and it pleases God. As you clear your conscience, change your thinking, and invest in your husband, bitterness will disappear and peace will take its place in your heart.

Week 45, Day 3

An excellent wife, who can find? For her worth is far above jewels.
PROVERBS 31:10

Application

The reason the excellent wife's worth is far above jewels is because, honestly, what good is a diamond? It's pretty, and it's costly, but it isn't very useful. Your worth comes not just because you are God's child, but because you are useful for God's kingdom—particularly in how you support and help your husband. The description of the Excellent Wife in Proverbs 31 is of a woman who works, who has godly actions and attitudes.

Don't rest on your laurels thinking that just because you're a woman, you're "all that." Because you're human, God loves you. But your *value* comes in your service to Him and to your husband. The wife who is worthless (Titus 1:16) and has no good deeds proves by her disservice not to be God's child at all (James 2:14-20).

BETTER THAN DIAMONDS

I used to work at a large jewelry store, and some days it was difficult to concentrate on my job. I just wanted to walk around and look at the beautiful diamond tennis bracelets, four carat diamond rings, sapphire earrings, diamond and ruby-studded watches, etc. It was a feast for the eyes, and I was often envious of the women who could afford to walk out of our store with several thousand dollar's worth of gold and diamonds.

If someone gave you a box full of diamond jewelry, you would probably cry, once you fully grasped how beautiful and priceless the gift was. Yet in Proverbs 31:10, God says that the worth of an excellent wife is "far above jewels."

One of the challenges of being an excellent wife is to see ourselves as God sees us and then to rest in that vision. You might be tempted to believe that others, such as your husband, children, family or friends, see you as less than valuable. Perhaps you come from a background where people used passages such as 1 Timothy 2:13 (*"For it was Adam who was first created, and then Eve"*) to teach that men are more important or valuable than women. But if the order of creation is an indication of value, then plants and cows would be more important than humans!

God made both man and woman in His image. In role and function they are different, yet still equal in value and personhood. As you seek more and more to become the wife God wants you to be, it is important to remember that God sees you as beautiful and priceless, equally as treasured as your husband.

Think about this: where else in the Bible does God spend almost an entire chapter praising the qualities of a godly man, apart from the LORD Jesus? Nowhere! But in Proverbs 31, God moved the author to spend twenty-one consecutive verses discussing the admirable qualities of a godly woman—and you can plug your name into that passage as you truly seek to be the wife God has called you to be.

Memorize It!

Be of the same mind toward one another; do not be haughty in mind, but associate with the lowly. Do not be wise in your own estimation. (Romans 12:16)

If You Must Work

In a previous lesson (see pg. 11) I told you about a Bible study my husband and I attended where one Sunday's lesson was all about how women should not work outside the home. A friend of mine was part of that Bible study...until that Sunday, when she was so offended by some of the attitudes of the people in the class, she no longer felt comfortable being part of that group. She shared with me later why she had quit the class: "I don't have a choice. I *have* to work. Yet some of these women have this attitude like they're better than me because they can stay home with their kids."

I've never forgotten that conversation, because it stressed to me the importance of not judging others based on their life choices. We don't know everyone's situation, or why people make the decisions they do. In the absence of credible information that they are actually sinning, it is up to us to assume the best of our brothers and sisters in Christ.

If you are able to stay home with your children and don't have to work outside of the home, you need to praise God that He has provided the means for you to do so. But *"do not think more highly of yourself than you ought to think"* (Romans 12:3) by judging women who have to work. This means, if your friend is working outside the home, please do not assume that she is in sin. (See Romans 14:10.) Love her, pray for her, and as long as she is submitted to her husband, support her decision.

If you do work outside the home, you need to closely examine both your budget (to see if it is really paying you to work) and your motives for having an outside job. Some sinful motives would be to avoid becoming a "non-person," to have more material possessions, or to get away from the kids or the house. Remember, too, that working outside the home does not relieve you of your responsibility to be the keeper of the home or primary caregiver of your children. That is still your top priority.

Memorize It!

Not lagging behind in diligence, fervent in spirit, serving the Lord; rejoicing in hope, persevering in tribulation, devoted to prayer, contributing to the needs of the saints, practicing hospitality.
(Romans 12:11-13)

Therefore, I want younger widows to get married, bear children, keep house, and give the enemy no occasion for reproach; for some have already turned aside to follow Satan.
1 Timothy 5:14-15

Application

I know several women who work outside the home, yet are better at keeping up with their household responsibilities than some stay-at-home moms I know. The question is not, do you work outside the home, but how are you doing in living up to God's command to be your home's keeper? Whether you work inside or outside the home, the following things should characterize your home and family. Which of these are true for you?

- ☐ My house is consistently clean and tidy.
- ☐ My family eats home-cooked meals together regularly.
- ☐ Our home atmosphere is calm, not chaotic.
- ☐ Other than when they are in school, I am my child's primary caregiver.
- ☐ I regularly spend time in God's Word and prayer with my husband and children.

Week 45, Day 5

But no one can tame the tongue; it is a restless evil and full of deadly poison. With it we bless our L*ORD and Father, and with it we curse men, who have been made in the likeness of God*
JAMES 3:8-9

Application

Immaturity might not be your husband's issue, but there are a vast number of other ways you could speak disrespectfully to or about him. Colossians 3:12-13† says that we are to *"put on a heart of compassion, kindness, humility, gentleness and patience; bearing with one another, and forgiving each other."* If you're putting your husband down, you are not showing compassion, kindness or humility toward him.

Pay special attention to how you talk to and about your husband. Do you ever say things like, "He couldn't ________ if his life depended on it"? Or how about "Yeah, that'll be the day!" or "He just doesn't get it"? Any speech that puts him down, is belittling or condescending is wrong and needs to be stopped.

WORDS THAT WOUND

Josh and Hillary were having dinner with her parents and younger siblings one Sunday afternoon when Hillary's 14-year-old sister began telling them about a boy at her school. "He asked me out during second period," Hannah said. "But then at lunch, he just walked right past me and didn't say a word!"

Hillary looked at her sister sympathetically. "Boys are stupid," she said. "It takes them a long time before they're mature enough for a relationship." "Like, in their 20s?" Hannah asked. Hillary glanced at Josh and rolled her eyes. "At least!" she said.

How do you think Josh feels after hearing his wife tell her entire family that he is immature? She didn't come right out and say it, but that's what she implied, and her implications were disrespectful. Even if her husband sometimes acts childishly, she should not be sharing that information with others. She's being condescending, acting as though she is more mature than he is.

The accusation of immaturity is a very common way wives belittle their husbands. For some reason, we think it's funny, but our guys don't. Most of them go to work, provide for their families, and shoulder a lot of very mature and sometimes overwhelming responsibility—more than we will ever have to bear. For men, goofing off or doing stuff which seems childish to us is a way to compensate for the burden of their responsibilities. It's how they "blow off steam" and burn physical energy, and it is extremely disrespectful for a wife to be condescending toward her husband because of it.

1 Timothy 4:12 says *"Let no one look down on your youthfulness."* If your husband is "youthful" or sometimes acts childishly, you are not to look down on that. If he's still young and active, remember that he won't always be like this. Someday, God willing, he will be older and unable to do many of the crazy things he might be able to do today. You should treasure these days when he still has the energy to be a little immature!

Submission Honors God's Word

Week 46, Day 1

...being subject to their own husbands, so that the word of God will not be dishonored.
Titus 2:5†

Our adult Sunday school class was going through a study on child rearing, and Mason, our teacher, was giving us time to discuss the concepts and ask questions. As we were sharing some of the struggles with our kids, Mason's wife, Katrina, piped up, "Well, I'm the one who handles all the discipline in our house. Mason is a wimp when it comes to that stuff!"

I think it took awhile for all of us to recover from the shock of Katrina's words. How could we respect Mason as a teacher if his wife demonstrated so little respect? I wish I could say this was out of the ordinary, but unfortunately I had come to expect it from her. Mason seemed unaffected by Katrina's blatant disrespect, but many of us in the class were extremely embarrassed for him. Not only did she disrespect her husband, but it was clear to everyone that she was not submissive to him either.

If a child misbehaves in public, our natural response is to wonder why the parents don't have better control. We tend to look at the parents of a misbehaving child negatively. In the same way, your behavior reflects either positively or negatively on both your husband and on the God you say you serve. You cause people to look at your guy negatively when you disrespect him in public. And you put your Heavenly Father in a negative light when you sin in any way, but especially when you are not submitted to your husband. The woman who disrespects or does not submit to her husband not only dishonors him, but she brings shame to God and to His Word by her behavior.

The Apostle Paul expressed it this way: "*Wives, be subject to your husbands, as is fitting in the Lord*" (Colossians 3:18). Anything other than godly submission is not fitting (proper) for a Christian wife since it dishonors God and His Word.

Application

Think about how you respect and submit to your husband in front of your children, family and friends. Then answer *True* or *False* to the following statements:

___ It is clear to everyone that I am submissive to my husband.

___ Other people respect my husband because of the way I treat him.

___ I defend my husband's honor if it is ever questioned.

___ Based on how our marriage is perceived by others, I would not be ashamed to share the gospel with my friends and neighbors.

If you cannot answer *True* to each one of those questions, it's possible you are dishonoring God's Word by not being biblically submitted to your husband. Recommit yourself today to making each one of those a True statement in your life.

Memorize It!

Bless those who persecute you; bless and do not curse. Rejoice with those who rejoice, and weep with those who weep.
(Romans 12:14-15)

Week 46, Day 2

Therefore be imitators of God, as beloved children; and walk in love, just as Christ also loved you and gave Himself up for us, an offering and a sacrifice to God as a fragrant aroma. But immorality or any impurity or greed must not even be named among you, as is proper among saints; and there must be no filthiness and silly talk, or coarse jesting, which are not fitting, but rather giving of thanks.
EPHESIANS 5:1-4

Judging Him Unfavorably

My good friend, Sue, and I were watching a movie together that featured an actor who was, in a word, *gorgeous*. When he first appeared on the screen, he was shot in such a way that he looked very attractive—all perfect hair and teeth, and the muscles of a well-toned athlete. I leaned over to Sue and whispered, "My husband looks like that. How about yours?" Then we both burst into laughter!

OK, so we're not married to Hollywood heartthrobs. Not many of us are. Sue knows I love my husband dearly; however, I shouldn't have said what I did. If he had been there, I'm sure he would have been fairly humiliated. It's a bad habit to get into when we start comparing our husbands unfavorably to other men around us.

It's not just physically that we're tempted to compare our husbands with other men. For women who desire to serve Christ, there is a great temptation to look at other men in the church who are more faithful servants, have higher positions of ministry, or have different gifts than our husbands, and wish that our husbands were more like *that* guy. The woman whose marriage is troubled may look at men who appear to be fantastic husbands or great fathers and say, "I wish my husband were more like him."

If you're comparing your husband unfavorably with other men, you are coveting something that doesn't belong to you (Romans 13:9). You may justify it by saying, "I don't want that other man. I want my husband to be more like him!" But the bottom line is that you're disrespecting your husband and his gifts, and being discontent and ungrateful to God for the man He has given you.

Application

It is helpful to remember that every man comes with his own set of troubles. I have a friend who is married to a guy who looks like a Hollywood leading man, and I know many women look at her with envy. However, I know the pain she has had to deal with in her marriage, and believe me, looks only go so far! The same is true for men who appear to have other great qualities that your husband does not. Your husband has great qualities *they* don't have. Take time right now to list in your prayer journal several things you love about your husband. When you're done, stop and thank God for him!

Memorize It!

Bless those who persecute you; bless and do not curse. Rejoice with those who rejoice, and weep with those who weep.
(Romans 12:14-15)

All Things Work Together For Good

When I think of suffering, I think of my friend Ellen.

Ellen was a new believer with three young children, including a baby girl. One night I got a call from her sister. "Please pray for Ellen," she said. "Her three-year-old, Cody, was killed tonight in a car accident." Her husband had been driving and suffered minor injuries, but their son was gone.

Of course we all held her up in prayer, but we questioned how God could allow something so terrible to happen to a new Christian. Little did we know that was not the end of it; just a few weeks later, Ellen's baby was found in her crib, not breathing. They called the paramedics but it was too late: their baby had died from SIDS. In less than a month, they buried two of their three children.

It's hard to imagine going through something like that, and harder still to imagine what good could possibly come from it. Romans 8:28 says that *"God causes all things to work together for good to those who love God, to those who are called according to His purpose."* God is sovereign over life and death, and nothing happens to us without flowing first through the fingers of God. He knew Ellen's children were going to die, and in His goodness, He prepared her to endure her trial. He saved her and surrounded her with godly women who prayed her through it. Through that experience, she learned more about God: that He was a great comforter to us when we are hurting. In the end, her character was changed to make her more like Christ Jesus.

The secret to having a good result in every trial is being *"called according to His purpose."* If you are committed to God's purposes in your life, then you will view everything that happens as an opportunity to glorify God by how you react to it. You can doubt Him and demonstrate your lack of trust in His care, or you can *"give thanks to the LORD, for He is good! For His mercy endures forever!"* (Psalm 136:1, NKJV).

Memorize It!

Bless those who persecute you; bless and do not curse. Rejoice with those who rejoice, and weep with those who weep.
(Romans 12:14-15)

Week 46, Day 3

But Joseph said to them, "Do not be afraid, for am I in God's place? As for you, you meant evil against me, but God meant it for good in order to bring about this present result, to preserve many people alive."
GENESIS 50:19-20

Application

You may never have suffered as much as my friend, but you've probably gone through some things that caused you to wonder how God could possibly turn it into good. In our marriages, we often go through conflict that we just want to be over. We don't really look at how God might use it for good.

The good He brings out of trials and tribulations is found in James 1:2-4: *"My brethren, count it all joy when you fall into various trials, knowing that the testing of your faith produces patience. But let patience have its perfect work, that you may be perfect and complete, lacking nothing"* (NKJV). No one wants to go through trials, but we can always praise God that those trials will make us "perfect and complete, lacking nothing."

Week 46, Day 4

The words of the wise heard in quietness are better than the shouting of a ruler among fools.
ECCLESIASTES 9:17

Application

How do you sprinkle your words with grace so that you can have a sanctifying influence on others? First, memorize God's Word so that you can work it into everyday conversation. If you make God's Word a normal part of the way your family talks, His grace will be sprinkled throughout each conversation. Secondly, be sure whenever you speak, that your voice is gentle and kind.

Only God's grace, flowing through us and out to others, is capable of improving the lives of the people we speak to. You can give a lot of worldly or fleshly advice, but permanent change that improves a person's faith comes only *"from hearing, and hearing by the word of Christ"* (Romans 10:17).

SWEET SPEECH

When I was in college, one of my professors told us, "A Christian should always have a sanctifying influence on his environment." By that, he meant we should improve every place where we live and move. "That house or restaurant or world should be better or cleaner because a follower of Christ was there," he would say. That means we should be good stewards of the ecosystem in which we live and not pollute or be wasteful. On a more local level, whenever we leave a room, it should be neater than when we found it, not messier—even if that room is at Target or Starbucks or Red Lobster.

We can also have this same kind of sanctifying influence on people. When we talk to others, the words we speak should improve the conversation, not bring it down. The Holy Spirit calls this sanctifying influence "edification," which means "to improve by building up" *"Let no unwholesome word proceed from your mouth, but only such a word as is good for edification...so that it will give grace to those who hear"* (Ephesians 4:29†). We improve conversations and edify others when we share God's grace, *"speaking the truth in love"* (Ephesians 4:15).

Colossians 4:6 tells us that our speech should *"always be with grace, as though seasoned with salt, so that you will know how you should respond to each person."* Have you ever heard the expression, "His speech was peppered with obscenities"? That's a picture of how the words we speak can be "seasoned"—but for the Christian, our speech is sprinkled with God's grace, just as we season our food with salt. You can serve up a dish of words that are missing this vital ingredient, and it will not do any good for the Kingdom. It will just be words. But sprinkling your words with God's grace is how we make *"the most of the opportunity"* (Colossians 4:5) of every conversation, to have a sanctifying influence on the people to whom we speak. This includes your husband, who is in need of your grace more than anyone, since he is your most important ministry.

Memorize It!

Bless those who persecute you; bless and do not curse. Rejoice with those who rejoice, and weep with those who weep.
(Romans 12:14-15)

A Radar for Needs

Week 46, Day 5

Neither was man created on account of or for the benefit of woman, but woman on account of and for the benefit of man.
1 Corinthians 11:9
(The Amplified Bible)

Remember Corporal "Radar" O'Reilly from the old TV series *M*A*S*H*? Radar was the clerk who kept the army medical base running smoothly. He earned the moniker "Radar" because of his ability to anticipate the Colonel's needs even before the Colonel was aware of them. Radar was good at his job, and the Colonel would have been lost without him.

That level of needs anticipation is only possible by someone who keeps vigilant attention to the needs, desires, and goals of their boss. In my "other" life (before working full-time as a writer), I was the assistant to the president of a company, and my job was to be that kind of "Radar" assistant, actively thinking about what my boss wanted to achieve and how I could help him achieve it.

Since you are called to be your husband's helper, you should be just as serious about your job as assistant to the chief executive officer of your home. Doing that job well means that you are always mindful of your husband, seeking to daily accomplish something that meets his needs or helps him achieve his goals.

This is impossible to do if you're focusing only on what you want and not what your husband wants. Some wives can go days without even considering what their husband might need. If you aren't always thinking about what your husband wants or needs, you will tend to make decisions based on your desires, not his. *"Do not merely look out for your own personal interests, but also for the interests of others"* (Philippians 2:4). We tend to dismiss that verse, as long as we're thinking about his needs at some point in time or including his needs in with our own. But the context makes it clear that you are to put his cares ABOVE your own: *"with humility of mind regard one another as more important than yourselves"* (vs. 3—see also verse 7). It's your job to think of his needs, and it brings glory to God and peace to your marriage when you seek to be the best you can be at your job.

Application

Think of your position as wife as the executive assistant to your CEO husband. What would your performance review look like? Rate yourself in the following areas using E = Excellent; G = Good; A = Adequate; N = Needs Improvement; F = Fails miserably:

___ ***Work Quality:*** Is consistent with management's expectations. Strives to increase productivity.

___ ***Judgment:*** Exercises self-control; appropriate appearance; shows commitment to goals.

___ ***Initiative:*** Is a self-starter, actively pursuing tasks rather than waiting to be asked.

___ ***Communication:*** Expresses self in a clear and calm manner. Listens attentively.

___ ***Professional Conduct:*** Cooperates, gets along with others. Brings enthusiasm and optimism to the workplace.

Week 47, Day 1

Be kind to one another, tender-hearted, forgiving each other, just as God in Christ also has forgiven you.
EPHESIANS 4:32

Application

Paul reminded the Corinthians they used to be *"drunkards, adulterers, homosexuals, fornicators, thieves,"* etc., but that they had been *"washed...sanctified... justified [made righteous] in the name of the LORD Jesus Christ"* (1 Corinthians 6:9-11†). Forgiving your husband begins when you remember how much God has forgiven you.

Examine your heart today to see if there is anything you are still holding your husband accountable for, that you have not yet forgiven. If so, you must recognize that your spirit of unforgiveness is killing love in your marriage. Through God's grace, there is absolutely nothing that you cannot forgive. Even if your husband still needs to correct his behavior, that is his responsibility. Your responsibility is to forgive.

LOVE FORGIVES

I wish we could get a statement from God that shows exactly how much we owe Him. Such a bill might list all of our sins and what each one cost. Something like this:

Date	*Qty*	*Item*	*Price (Loss of)*
3/1/04	4	Lies told	Trust
3/1/04	3	Hours wasted	Eternal riches
3/2/04	9	Unkind words	Respect, harmony
3/2/04	2	Angry outbursts	Peace...

I know my statement would be so long, they would have to bind it and put it in volumes by year! But because I have accepted Christ's payment for my sins, PAID IN FULL would be stamped on each page.

If we had a statement like that, we would see just how much God has forgiven us. It would be like borrowing $12 billion from your dad and then having him say, "Don't worry about paying me back. Your brother took care of it." Would you not deeply love your dad and your brother after that?

Our sin debt cannot be measured in dollars, but if it could, it would be much larger than $12 billion. Yet when our husband sins against us, we feel entitled to hold him responsible for that debt and expect him to make up for it somehow. Our many payment options include suffering our wrath, living with our indifference, giving us something we want, or giving up something they want. We expect them to undo any damage done by their sin, as well as change their personality and character so that we are ensured their sin never happens again. And even then, we remember the debt for years and feel free to remind ourselves of it at will. Wives can be pretty unmerciful when it comes to dealing with their husbands' sin. (Read the account of the Unmerciful Slave in Matthew 18:21-35 for a picture of what this ugliness looks like.)

Nothing destroys love faster than unforgiveness. Your husband's sins against you are not nearly as many as your sins against God, yet God has forgiven you without expecting any payment in return. We, too, should forgive as we have been forgiven. Even the most hurtful sins can be forgiven, when we remember how much God has forgiven us.

Memorize It!

Be of the same mind toward one another; do not be haughty in mind, but associate with the lowly. Do not be wise in your own estimation.
(Romans 12:16)

HIS BURDEN IS LIGHT

Week 47, Day 2

Aimee rested her head against the wall at the restaurant where we sat nursing cups of hot chocolate. No makeup, hair a mess...she just looked *tired*. I asked if she had done any of the things we talked about two weeks ago. "I can't," she said. "It's just too much for me right now. Anthony is so demanding. If I do one little thing wrong, he's all over it. I can't open myself up to *more* pain."

Aimee's husband was harsh, and he set very high standards for her. When I encouraged her to reprove her husband's lack of love as part of the process of mutual sanctification, she felt I was adding to her burden, not making it go away. Because she feared her husband more than God, she was not willing to reprove him of his sin.

If you've ever felt like God is putting just one more layer of responsibility on you, requiring more of you than you have to give, then today's lesson is for you. Jesus said, *"My yoke is easy, and my burden is light"* (Matthew 11:30). Even though God requires your obedience, He is not giving you a set of legalistic rules to follow. Instead, He is giving you the opportunity to have a relationship with Himself that results in loving obedience. Through this relationship, Jesus Christ takes on all the burdens (1 Peter 5:7)—***even the burden of obeying God***.

You are not bound to a bunch of rules, but to Christ. You *"were made to die to the Law through the body of Christ, so that you might be joined to...Him who was raised from the dead, in order that [you] might bear fruit for God"* (Romans 7:4†). Christ's burden is "light" because He is the one who is carrying it. He's doing all the work, and any fruit you have, all of the good you do, comes from Him. The only time you should feel overwhelmed by any responsibility is if it is totally up to you. But obedience to God is NOT totally up to you. "*It is no longer I who live, but Christ lives in me*"(Galatians 2:20). He enables you to obey, causes your efforts to have a good result, then rewards you with peace and joy. What a fantastic arrangement!

Come to Me, all who are weary and heavy-laden, and I will give you rest. Take My yoke upon you and learn from Me, for I am gentle and humble in heart, and you will find rest for your souls.
MATTHEW 11:28-29

Application

Working on your mutual sanctification with your husband is a command from God that you must obey, and if you're not working on it, it's only because you're not trusting Christ to enable you and take care of the results. You are likely afraid of confronting your husband. If so, you can be liberated from this fear by realizing the only person you have to please is Christ! One of the burdens Christ lifts from your shoulders is the need to please others (Galatians 1:10), including your husband.

Of course you should try to please your husband, but sometimes you may have to confront him instead. If he is ungrateful or responds to you sinfully, you can still have peace, knowing you have done what is right (1 Peter 3:14), which pleases God.

Memorize It!

Not lagging behind in diligence, fervent in spirit, serving the LORD; rejoicing in hope, persevering in tribulation, devoted to prayer, contributing to the needs of the saints, practicing hospitality.
(Romans 12:11-13)

Week 47, Day 3

For by these He has granted to us His precious and magnificent promises, so that by them you may become partakers of the divine nature, having escaped the corruption that is in the world by lust.
2 PETER 1:4

Application

What is stopping you from being fruitful for Christ? Think about that for a moment, then write it here or in your prayer journal:

Look at the things you wrote down: are any of them too big for God? Of course not! *"I can do all things through Christ who strengthens me"*(Philippians 4:13).

ALL THE FULLNESS

Think about this verse: *"For in Him all the fullness of the Deity dwells in bodily form"* (Colossians 2:9). In other words, every power, ability, attribute, authority, character quality, and characteristic of God is resident in Christ—and it's not just a sampling of God's power, but the full maximum capacity.

Now think about this: Christ lives in *you*. Isn't that fact completely mind-blowing? We certainly don't deserve that, and it is such a praiseworthy grace that He gave us this privilege!

Many of us think we're lacking something—knowledge, wisdom, experience, power, a "gifting," whatever—that keeps us from being effective for God. But that is not true. The only thing that limits the power of God in you is sin, which is why God wants you to work on getting sin out of your life. He gave you your husband to help you with the process of sanctification (even if your husband is unsaved), and He gave you the power of Christ to enable you to do it. But even before you had the opportunity to purify your life from sin, at the moment of your salvation, God gave you everything you need in Christ (2 Peter 1:3). *"In Him you have been made complete"* (Colossians 2:10). You don't need to work up to some level to begin living the power of Christ in your life.

The requirements of the law—those things that determine your guilt—were nailed to the cross and you "bear them no more."[11] Because your guilt of sin is gone, you lack nothing. And because Christ is *"the head over all rule and authority"* (Colossians 2:10), everything falls under and is subject to Him, so *nothing* can stop you from doing what God calls you to do. You *can* obey, you *can* be fruitful for Him.

How is this fruit produced? Through Christ, "the LORD of the harvest" (Luke 10:2). He takes the seeds of our pitiful efforts and produces an entire crop. We always get back so much more than what we put into the ground, because *"all the fullness of the Deity dwells"* in Him.

Memorize It!

Be of the same mind toward one another; do not be haughty in mind, but associate with the lowly. Do not be wise in your own estimation. (Romans 12:16)

Body Language

Logan was on a rant and it was really getting on Holly's nerves. They had a great day of hiking planned, but chores had to be done first. When Logan discovered one of the kids left a gate open and some cows had wandered out, he gathered everyone together to remind them about the responsibilities of living on a farm. Holly had heard the speech before and was tired of it. She just wanted it to end so they could finish their chores and get to their fun time. She sat at the kitchen table with the rest of the family, resting her chin on her hand and looking bored.

"You kids are old enough to know better," Logan was saying…and that's when Holly rolled her eyes and let out a sigh. Logan shot her a glance; she could see by the narrowing of his eyes that he was not pleased with her. *What!?* She thought. *I didn't say a word! Why is he giving me that look?*

Holly knows exactly why her husband is unhappy with her: even though she isn't *saying* anything disrespectful, her non-verbal communication is speaking volumes. If "a picture is worth a thousand words," the picture of Holly right now is of a woman who has little respect for her husband.

Sometimes, when a wife realizes she needs to speak respectfully to her husband, she is successful in biting her tongue, but her facial expressions and body language still communicate her disrespect loudly. Some women are fortunate, in this respect, to have a naturally non-expressive demeanor; but most women are very expressive with their bodies, completely unable to hide their looks of disgust, impatience, or disrespect.

If you're not so good at hiding your emotions, you need to be very conscious of your non-verbal communication, especially when you are in a disagreement with your husband. But even if you have a handle on this, hiding your true emotions is not the end game. The ultimate goal is to change what's going on inside, so there is nothing to hide.

Memorize It!

Be of the same mind toward one another; do not be haughty in mind, but associate with the lowly. Do not be wise in your own estimation.
(Romans 12:16)

God sees not as man sees, for man looks at the outward appearance, but the Lord looks at the heart.
1 Samuel 16:7†

Application

When Christ was on the earth, he was surrounded by people who were good at hiding their true emotions. On the outside, they looked very religious. But on the inside, they were *"full of hypocrisy and lawlessness"* (Matthew 23:28). They couldn't hide anything from Jesus, and neither can you.

You can, and should, be conscious of your body language and facial expressions, that they never convey disrespect to your husband. But don't let it stop there. *"Your adornment must not be merely external…but let it be the hidden person of the heart, with the imperishable quality of a gentle and quiet spirit"* (1 Peter 3:3-4†). Make sure that both "inside" and "outside," you truly respect your husband as you should.

Week 47, Day 5

He who is faithful in a very little thing is faithful also in much; and he who is unrighteous in a very little thing is unrighteous also in much. Therefore if you have not been faithful in the use of unrighteous wealth, who will entrust the true riches to you?"
LUKE 16:10-11

Application

Take a serious look at how faithful you are in managing your personal finances by answering the following questions:

- Are you paying a regular tithe from your household income? Are you giving an offering over and above your tithe?
- Do you have a budget? Are you living by it?
- Does your husband know how much money you have in the bank, generally speaking?
- Does your husband feel financial pressure? If so, what can you do to turn down some of that pressure?

If money pressures are weighing down your marriage, see if your church can recommend any resources, such as a Bible study or Christian financial seminar, which can give you a biblical perspective on managing your finances.

MONEY MATTERS

A young couple I know were having their dream home built when, unexpectedly, the husband lost his job. Soon after that, they found out the wife was pregnant. With twins.

Can you imagine the stress in that marriage? Well, I can, because that young couple was actually me and my husband! It was a very tough time for us, but God was faithful and we survived. In the process, I learned that if I want a happy marriage, I have to do everything within my power to keep my husband feeling good about our financial situation. Not that I could have done anything about his job, or about the twins, but I learned to sacrifice in other ways to help keep his emotions steady.

Since financial stress is a leading cause of divorce, you need to be diligent about your finances if you want to protect your marriage. As the keeper of the home, you have a major role in managing your family's financial health. It doesn't matter which one of you actually makes the money, writes the checks, or pays the bills. As the wife, you (hopefully) do most of the discretionary spending on groceries, clothing, supplies, etc. and you have a responsibility to make sure you are spending wisely. This is one of the best ways you can be your husband's *suitable helper*—by keeping financial pressure to a minimum to the best of your ability.

If you actually keep the checkbook and pay the bills, then you must not only spend wisely, but you must also communicate honestly with your husband about your financial status. Many wives get in the habit of hiding their true financial status from their husbands, hoping things will get better. This is not only deceitful, but when he does find out the truth, he will have trouble trusting you in the future. *"Therefore, laying aside falsehood, speak truth each one of you with his neighbor, for we are members of one another"* (Ephesians 4:25). As one-flesh partners, you and your husband are "members of one another." He is the *last* person you should ever hide the truth from.

Shaking Your Fist at God

For rebellion is as the sin of divination, and insubordination is as iniquity and idolatry.
1 Samuel 15:23

Maggie is trying to decide how she should be involved in ministry. She loves singing in the choir, but the Tuesday night Bible study needs a facilitator. Unfortunately, she can't do both, because choir rehearsals are also on Tuesday nights. "What does your husband think?" her friend Susan asked. "Oh, I haven't asked. If it were up to him, I wouldn't do either one. He doesn't like me being away from the house in the evenings, but it's just one night a week."

Susan looked at Maggie thoughtfully, then said, "Come outside for a minute." Puzzled, Maggie followed Susan out onto the back patio. The stars were out in full force. "Can't you just imagine God's presence when you look at these stars?" Susan asked. "Oh yes!" Maggie agreed. "OK, now pretend you're talking directly to God. Hold up your fist, like this..." Susan held her fist up and began shaking it angrily. "And look up to God and say, 'God, I don't care what You want! I'm going to do what *I* want!'" Maggie looked at her friend in horror. "What? No! I'm not going to do that!" Susan smiled and replied, "Oh, but that's exactly what you *are* doing."

By not submitting to her husband's desire that she stay home in the evenings, Maggie was rebelling against God's will for her life. The truth was she liked getting away a couple of nights a week. It really had nothing to do with serving Christ.

If you are not submitted to your husband, God will cause your conscience to accuse you of sin. The temptation is to salve that guilty conscience by over-compensating in another area of obedience, hoping God will be satisfied and ignore your rebellion toward your husband. However, God is not fooled. If you are sinning against your husband, God is not be pleased with any of your works of righteousness. *"If you are presenting your offering at the altar, and...remember that your brother has something against you, leave your offering there before the altar and...be reconciled to your brother, and then come and present your offering"* (Matthew 5:23-24†).

Memorize It!

No temptation has overtaken you but such as is common to man; and God is faithful, who will not allow you to be tempted beyond what you are able, but with the temptation will provide the way of escape also, so that you will be able to endure it.
(1 Corinthians 10:13)

Application

Are you active in ministry and faithful to your Bible study, but still disobedient to your husband in some way? This is rebellion, and rebellion is a very serious sin. If you fail to submit to your husband or ignore his desires, you are indirectly shaking your fist at God. You are saying in your heart, "God, I don't care what You say. I'm going to do this *my way*!"

You can repent of your rebellion at any time by confessing your sin to God, asking your husband to forgive you, and submitting to your husband's authority in all things from that moment forward. When you're tempted to rebel, imagine shaking your fist at God and challenging Him, "No, I won't do it!" That frightening picture should be a powerful motivation for you to be submissive.

Week 48, Day 2

But as for you, brethren, do not grow weary of doing good.
2 THESSALONIANS 3:13

Application

What God calls us to is *endurance*, to "keep on keeping on." We are better able to endure when we remember Christ, and what He endured for us. *"For consider Him who has endured...so that you will not grow weary and lose heart"* (Hebrews 12:3).

Trying to do the right thing all the time gets very tiring. I understand that; struggling is wearying to the mind and the body. I can promise that if you will commit to obeying Christ every day; if you will die to yourself and your desires and *"stand firm...be strong [and] let all that you do be done in love"* (1 Corinthians 16:13-14), it does get easier. Life itself may not get easier, and your biggest battles may be yet to come. But if you endure, you will be better equipped to face whatever comes your way.

KEEP ON KEEPING ON

"I've tried that. It didn't work. And I'm tired of beating my head against a wall."

This is something I hear frequently from women who have tried God's way of resolving conflict yet have not seen the results He promises. Have you ever felt that way—that you just can't seem to get any real victory over conflict in your marriage? There are two reasons why you may "grow weary while doing good" (Galatians 6:9, NKJV). Either you're doing it right but not getting results, or you're fighting in your own flesh.

God's way of overcoming conflict in your marriage is for you to 1) *"be harmonious, sympathetic, brotherly, kindhearted, and humble in spirit; not returning evil for evil or insult for insult, but giving a blessing instead"* (1 Peter 3:8-9); and 2) deal biblically with sin in your own life and in your husband's (Matthew 7:5, Galatians 6:1).

If you're doing it God's way but not seeing any fruits, you need to be obedient anyway, with the understanding that this is how you are to live for the rest of your life. It's not a temporary life-change to be abandoned as soon as you get what you want. This is how God wants you to live at all times, whether you ever have conflict with your husband or not.

Many wives give up too soon because they don't see God's blessings, as promised. *"For you have need of endurance, so that when you have done the will of God, you may receive what was promised"* (Hebrews 10:36). But what has been promised? The promised blessing is eternal life that comes as a result of your salvation, and the change in your character as you become someone who is now more *"harmonious, sympathetic, brotherly, kindhearted, and humble in spirit"* (1 Peter 3:8). To give up because you're not getting what you want means that you are seeking the *blessing* more than you are seeking God, the blessing Giver.

To give up means you've decided the sacrifice is not worth it, because you can't see the benefit of living a life that is pleasing to God. Is that really the choice you want to make?

Memorize It!

No temptation has overtaken you but such as is common to man; and God is faithful, who will not allow you to be tempted beyond what you are able, but with the temptation will provide the way of escape also, so that you will be able to endure it.
(1 Corinthians 10:13)

Battle Weary

You need not fight in this battle; station yourselves, stand and see the salvation of the Lord on your behalf... Do not fear or be dismayed; tomorrow go out to face them, for the Lord is with you.
2 Chronicles 20:17

Yesterday we gave two reasons why you might "grow weary while doing good" (Galatians 6:9, NKJV). Either you're doing it right but getting no result, or you're fighting in your own flesh. Today we're going to talk about fighting in your own flesh.

Fighting a battle in your own flesh means you're trying to defeat sin in your life without the assistance of the Holy Spirit. It's assuming God will help you be victorious when you never ask Him for help or follow His commandments. It's neglecting His Word, yet presuming you'll have the defenses needed when temptation comes.

The other definition is thinking that it is all up to you and therefore becoming anxious or afraid. You can spend time in God's Word and try to be obedient, but when a trial or a conflict comes up in your marriage, do you spend a great deal of time anxiously looking for a solution? Do you feel the need to talk it out repeatedly with your friends, read various articles on the problem, journal about it, and in general just do a lot of worrying?

Or do you rest in God, knowing that He will fight this battle for you? You must learn to see conflict in your marriage from the same perspective Jehoshaphat had when a vast army threatened God's people. *"Thus says the Lord to you, 'Do not fear or be dismayed because of this great multitude, for the battle is not yours but God's... You need not fight in this battle; station yourselves, stand and see the salvation of the Lord on your behalf"* (2 Chronicles 20:15, 17†). God is ready and able to fight this battle for you. He doesn't ask you to enter the battle yourself, merely to take a stand.

It's not your job to fix your husband or save your marriage or resolve any conflicts that come your way. It's your job to stand firm in Christ, being obedient to Him and letting Him take care of the results. When you do that, you can be confident that *"He who began a good work in you will perfect it until the day of Christ Jesus"* (Philippians 1:6).

Application

Is there a conflict in your marriage right now that you are worried about? God will fight this battle for you, and He promises to give you a "way of escape" so that you can endure any trial that comes your way. He does this because He loves you, and because He is faithful to His people.

Even if God does not choose to remove the conflict from your life, He can rescue you from the dangers of fear, anxiety, anger, and despair—and turn every conflict into something good, for His glory.

Memorize It!

No temptation has overtaken you but such as is common to man; and God is faithful, who will not allow you to be tempted beyond what you are able, but with the temptation will provide the way of escape also, so that you will be able to endure it.
(1 Corinthians 10:13)

Week 48, Day 4

A man's discretion makes him slow to anger, and it is his glory to overlook a transgression.
Proverbs 19:11

Blame Shifting

Throughout the year we have revisited the subject of *anger*, because it is such a major issue for many people. Even if you don't have an explosive temper, you can still be guilty of having anger if you brood, yell, react harshly, or continuously replay in your mind the things your husband has done that have angered, frustrated or annoyed you.

It is important to understand the single cause of anger. Anger is always caused by sin: and not your husband's sin, but *your* sin.

When your husband upsets or irritates you, the natural response is to get angry and then to shift the blame for that anger onto something outside of yourself. The first place most of us look to lay the blame is on the person or circumstance that provoked us to irritation or anger. *"Of course I'm angry–look at what he did!"* After that, we blame stress, hormones, menopause, having our period, or other physiological factors. *"I'm sorry I got angry, but I have been really stressed lately."* We make excuses and try to justify our anger. Other common justifications are "I'm not as bad as I used to be" or "I'm just a passionate person."

All of our excuses and justifications do not square up with the reality that anger is sin, and we must take responsibility for our sins. Even if your husband has done something to exacerbate your anger, you made the conscious decision to be angry. God gave you a "way of escape" (1 Corinthians 10:13); *you* chose not to take it.

Your husband might do things that would naturally cause you to get angry, but remember that the *"natural man does not accept the things of the Spirit of God"* (1 Corinthians 2:14). Our goal is not to be natural—i.e., controlled by our old sinful nature. Rather, our goal is to have the mind of Christ and to be controlled by the Holy Spirit. When we are controlled by the Holy Spirit, we will always choose love over anger.

Memorize It!

No temptation has overtaken you but such as is common to man; and God is faithful, who will not allow you to be tempted beyond what you are able, but with the temptation will provide the way of escape also, so that you will be able to endure it.
(1 Corinthians 10:13)

Application

So what is this "way of escape" from anger that we keep talking about? Generally speaking, the way of escape is the grace of God, giving you the power of God to be obedient to the Word of God. But specifically, if you look at the context of 1 Corinthians 10, you will find the *many* ways God provides for you to escape sin:

- *Resist idolatry* (vss. 6, 14)–Frustrated idol worship is one of the biggest contributors to anger. If you give up your idols, you will be less angry.
- *Live righteously* (vs. 8)–Live by God's moral laws, keeping your conscience clean.
- *Trust God* (vs. 9)–Do not "test" God, but trust Him to provide.
- *Be grateful* (vs. 10)–It is impossible to be angry when you are truly grateful for how God meets all of your needs.

LITTLE FOXES

Wives, be subject to your own husbands, as to the LORD. For the husband is the head of the wife, as Christ also is the head of the church, He Himself being the Savior of the body. But as the church is subject to Christ, so also the wives ought to be to their husbands in everything.
EPHESIANS 5:22-24

Katherine sat in the pastor's office, exhausted from crying. Her marriage was over, and nothing anyone could say now would fix it. She appreciated her pastor and his wife—over the last six months, they had met with her weekly to try to help her reconcile to her husband. But Derek would not be moved. Whenever she thought of him, she couldn't help but replay in her mind the last words Derek said to her before he left: *You have never loved me.*

Through counseling, Katherine had come to realize that, even though she loved Derek, she had never learned to show him the respect he was due as her husband. She questioned every decision he made, and argued until she got her way. After her pastor's wife showed her how devastating disrespect was to a marriage, Katherine tried to change her ways, but it was difficult, too little and too late. Granted, Derek had his share of blame for the breakdown of their marriage, and her pastor reassured her that Derek's decision to leave was entirely his sin. But she often asked herself how different things would be if she had just learned to respect him sooner.

The wife who is disrespectful to her husband will experience a variety of negative consequences. Her husband can be hurt and embarrassed by her disrespect and lose motivation to be her spiritual leader. Disrespect tears him down in front of his children and can paralyze him as the leader of his home. Proverbs 12:4 says that the *"wife who shames [her husband] is as rottenness to his bones."* Disrespect is so debilitating, it can actually cause a man to experience physical symptoms of depression and stress-related illness. He can also become bitter, angry, or abusive—emotions that affect the whole family.

You can't expect to disobey God's commands and not pay for it, and sometimes, the price is high. If left unchecked, disrespect can so weaken a marriage that divorce could be the end result. There have been few marriages dissolved where the spouses respected each other as God commands.

Application

With so many negative consequences of disrespect, it is hard to understand why any wife would want to treat her husband disrespectfully. However, we are too often guilty of believing we can get away with small amounts of disrespect, forgetting that it's the *"little foxes that are ruining the vineyards"* (Song of Solomon 2:15). Look over the negative consequences mentioned in this lesson and examine whether any of these are already starting to manifest themselves in your marriage. If so, it's time for you to get serious about learning to properly respect your husband.

Week 49, Day 1

Do not turn your freedom into an opportunity for the flesh, but through love serve one another. For the whole Law is fulfilled in one word, in the statement, 'You shall love your neighbor as yourself.' . . . Walk by the Spirit, and you will not carry out the desire of the flesh.
GALATIANS 5:13-14, 16†

Application

You put on love when you meditate on Scripture and live by its principles. But you must discipline yourself to continually focus on those principles. For example, if your husband is being difficult you can choose to react sinfully and get huffy with him, or you can remember that "love is kind" and show him kindness. But you will be unable to pull kindness out of your toolbox if you have strayed from the Word and are not walking in the Spirit.

Where are you today, this week, this past month? Have you been drifting in your walk with Christ, and thus failing to put on love? You are free to spend this day however you choose. *"Only do not turn your freedom into an opportunity for the flesh, but through love serve one another"* (Galatians 5:13†).

PUT ON LOVE

On December 7, 2009, Starbucks hosted an on-line event called the "Starbucks Love Project" to raise money for the fight against AIDS in Africa. They invited people to log onto the internet at exactly 1:30 EST and sing the song, "All You Need is Love" by John Lennon. Thousands of people from all over the world sang with seemingly one voice, "All you need is love!" and "it's easy!"

Watching that broadcast, one might think that love is easy. All we have to do is sing about love and, magically, it will happen. AIDS will be eradicated, warring neighbors will stop fighting, peace will reign on earth. It's a beautiful thing.

The truth is, love doesn't just happen. The Bible tells us to "put on love"—meaning, you have to work at it. You especially have to work on loving your husband, because he likely has the most potential for getting on your nerves. You work on loving your husband by "renewing your mind" (Romans 12:2, Ephesians 4:23) through prayer, study and meditating on the Word of God. Like love, this is not natural. It takes God's grace, self-control and discipline to be faithful at renewing your mind.

Most of us spend our life on a roller coaster of obedience. We go for awhile being faithful to Christ, but then we get busy and start choosing other things rather than choosing "God" things. D.A. Carson puts it this way: "People do not drift toward holiness. Apart from grace-driven effort, people do not gravitate toward godliness, prayer, obedience to Scripture, faith and delight in the LORD."[12] If you're not disciplining yourself to pray and read God's Word daily, it will be next to impossible for you to love your husband biblically.

When your love is tested, you will either react in the flesh or in the Spirit. It will be much easier for you to react in love if your mind is renewed through the Scriptures and you are walking in the Spirit. But if you consistently neglect the Word, you will end up carrying out "the desire of the flesh" (Galatians 5:16).

Memorize It!

Do not fear, for I am with you; do not anxiously look about you, for I am your God. I will strengthen you, surely I will help you, surely I will uphold you with My righteous right hand.
(Isaiah 41:10)

Helping, Not Enabling

Brethren, even if anyone is caught in any trespass, you who are spiritual, restore such a one in a spirit of gentleness; each one looking to yourself, so that you too will not be tempted.
Galatians 6:1

Kelsey was just finishing up the dishes when Mike walked in with a stack of papers. "I need your help," he said. She steeled herself against what she knew was coming; the paperwork was their tax return, and Mike's business had done well last year. "I need about $2,000 more deductions. Can you make up some more of your 'receipts' for business expenses?" In the past, Kelsey had been a willing accomplice in Mike's tax cheating, but since she rededicated her life to Christ, she knew what they'd done was dishonest.

Mike had also recommitted himself to Christ, but at times he reverted back to his old ways. She certainly didn't want to pay any more tax than necessary, and wasn't she supposed to submit and be his helper? But then she remembered that the purpose of being her husband's helper was to help him become more Christ-like.

For the next two weeks, Kelsey pored over their receipts, talked to an accountant, went on websites and did exhaustive research. In the end, she found not only the deductions Mike asked for, but an additional $1,200 he'd missed—and all of it completely above-board. When she gave her findings to Mike, she gently reminded him that God always provides for them, and they did not have to lie to make it financially.

At times, you may be unsure if you should resist or go along with what he wants. But keep in mind the *reason* you're helping him. It's not to give him whatever he wants, but to bring him closer to Christ and help him be more obedient. Therefore, be careful how you are helping. If you're helping him sin or enabling him to continue a destructive lifestyle, you're not helping him. Love *"does not rejoice in unrighteousness, but rejoices with the truth"* (1 Corinthians 13:6). Also, if you're helping him so that you can get what *you* want, your motives are selfish, and that also is not helping him (or you) become more Christ-like (Romans 8:29). The end goal of your help is to glorify God and to move your husband toward sanctification.

Application

Does your husband ever ask you to go along with something sinful? Remember that helping is not enabling, and submitting never requires sinning. Yes, you are to submit in all things *unless he asks you to sin*; beyond that, you are to help your husband grow in his love for Christ and in obedience to God's commands.

Throughout *The Excellent Wife* and in this book, you will find steps you need to take to reprove your husband when he is in sin. (See Index for a complete list of lessons on Biblical Reproof.) Reproving your husband is just as much helping him as doing his laundry or keeping him well-fed. It's your God-given privilege to help in this way, and while it is not always easy, all obedience brings joy.

Memorize It!

Do not fear, for I am with you; do not anxiously look about you, for I am your God. I will strengthen you, surely I will help you, surely I will uphold you with My righteous right hand.
(Isaiah 41:10)

Week 49, Day 3

Every tree that does not bear good fruit is cut down and thrown into the fire. So then, you will know them by their fruits. Not everyone who says to Me, 'Lord, Lord,' will enter the kingdom of heaven, but he who does the will of My Father who is in heaven will enter.
Matthew 7:19-21

Application

Submitting to your husband might be a new concept to you, or something you've been working on for years. The question is, are you farther along in your obedience to this truth than when you first learned about it, or do you find that you have made little progress in this area? Are you "bearing fruit in every good work" (Colossians 1:10) or are you like the women of 2 Timothy 3:7 who are "*always learning and never able to come to the knowledge of the truth*"? If this latter describes you, then you need to seriously consider whether or not you are truly God's child. If you are a Christ-follower, then allow that fact to motivate you to continue submitting yourself to your husband, in obedience to the God you love and serve.

The Proof is in the Fruit

I look at the list of women who have taken our Excellent Wife Bible study over the years, pausing to pray for each of them. Some of them have remained faithful and are producing fruit for the Kingdom of Christ. But some are a continual burden on my heart. One name in particular stands out. I remember hearing Abby say how much she had learned through our Bible study. "Honestly, Karen, I don't know if I was even saved before I came to this study! I have learned so much. It's really exciting!"

Recall Matthew 13, where Christ talks about a farmer who scattered seed in a field. The seed fell all over the place: on the road, among the thorn bushes, and on soil. Christ explains that the seed represents the Word of God, and we are the soil. Unfortunately, I fear that Abby proved to be "rocky soil": *"This is the [one] who hears the word and immediately receives it with joy; yet he has no firm root in himself, but is only temporary, and when affliction or persecution arises because of the word, immediately he falls away"* (vs. 20-21†). Abby had seemed to be growing and receiving the truth about her marriage "with joy," but less than a year after completing our study, she was divorced and no longer walking in the Word.

If you say you are a Christian but are not following Christ, you are deceived. If you are a Christ-follower, then you will have a desire to please Him. Each act of obedience to God's Word is part of the fruit Jesus said we would bear. "*By this is My Father glorified, that you bear much fruit, and so prove to be my disciples*" (John 15:8). Godly fruit is the evidence that someone has become a Christ-follower.

A person who is truly saved will not always be perfectly obedient, but they will be growing. Submission to your husband is an act of obedience, and therefore evidence of your salvation. It is one of the ways you "*work out your salvation with fear and trembling*" (Philippians 2:12). It is how you prove to yourself, your husband and the world that you are truly God's child.

Memorize It!

Do not fear, for I am with you; do not anxiously look about you, for I am your God. I will strengthen you, surely I will help you, surely I will uphold you with My righteous right hand.
(Isaiah 41:10)

Sharing Your Heart

Rejoice with those who rejoice, and weep with those who weep. Be of the same mind toward one another.
Romans 12:15-16†

A husband reading the newspaper came across an article that said women use twice as many words per day as men. He read the article to his wife. "See? That's what I've been saying!" he said. The wife thought for a moment, then said, "Well, that's because we have to repeat everything we say." The husband looked up from his newspaper and said, "What?"

OK, that was a joke. But you've probably heard similar claims that women use anywhere from 5,000 to 50,000 words per day, as opposed to men who use half that many. I hate to be a "myth buster," but clinical research doesn't support those numbers. Some studies have shown that men actually use more words than women, although most research shows the differences are insignificant. What is important, however, is *how* you communicate. Not every woman is good at expressing herself, and many marital problems can be solved if both partners would work on their communication skills.

I have a friend who is not nearly as expressive as her husband, and when they sit down to dinner, she can go through the entire meal without saying a word. She has to remind herself to share her thoughts and feelings with her husband. But she does it, because she knows it's important.

It's critical for the health of your marriage that you and your husband talk frequently, openly sharing your stories, thoughts, feelings, and concerns. Like my friend, some wives get protective and don't communicate as much or as often as they should. If that describes you, it will be difficult for you to have an intimate marriage. On the other hand, if you're naturally expressive, you need to be careful not to overload your husband with words, and make sure you give him plenty of opportunity to share his thoughts. You may have to pull conversation out of him, but eventually he will feel comfortable opening up if you keep at it.

When you and your husband communicate openly, you knit your hearts together and develop the unity and intimacy within marriage that God desires for each of us.

Application

1 Corinthians 7:3 says, *"The husband must fulfill his duty to his wife, and likewise also the wife to her husband."* While that verse specifically applies to sexual intimacy, making an emotional connection is part of intimacy and thus is one of the duties husbands and wives have to each other.

The challenge for today is to analyze how much and how well you and your husband communicate. You should spend several hours every week in meaningful conversation. If you watch television every night instead of communicating, it's time to turn off the TV and focus on each other. If he's a Christian, spend time praying and reading God's Word together; if not, you can and should still have heart-to-heart discussions on a regular basis.

Memorize It!

Do not fear, for I am with you; do not anxiously look about you, for I am your God. I will strengthen you, surely I will help you, surely I will uphold you with My righteous right hand.
(Isaiah 41:10)

Week 49, Day 5

Therefore repent and return, so that your sins may be wiped away, in order that times of refreshing may come from the presence of the Lord.
Acts 3:19

Application

Most of the time, we sin because we are living for ourselves and not sacrificing our desires—desires for revenge, honor, self-justification, the lusts of our flesh, etc.—for our husbands' sake and for God's glory. But God wants you to stop living for yourself and start living for Him. And that means continually confessing your sins and turning from them, which is repentance.

Your sins are not minor inconveniences, but relationship destroyers. *"When sin is accomplished, it brings forth death"* (James 1:15). Repentance from sin is absolutely indispensable for any healthy marriage that honors God.

Continuous Confession

Before Annie and Bryan were saved, their marriage was on the brink of disaster. Annie was in an emotional affair headed toward physical infidelity, and Bryan had checked out emotionally. When Christ saved them, they immediately went into biblical counseling to turn their marriage around.

Although she ended the relationship, Annie continued to struggle with many of the things that led her to that sin in the first place. Bryan was a "workaholic" who traveled frequently, and still did not give her the attention she craved. Annie always blamed him for her wandering heart. Even though she stayed faithful for years, many of her old bitter attitudes remained.

Not all sin is as devastating to a marriage as unfaithfulness, but any sin will erode the love and harmony that God intends us to have. We all bring into marriage sinful patterns of thinking and responding that hurt our spouses and grieve the Lord. Annie's anger continued to fuel unhappiness in her home, until one day she realized that her bitterness was just as much a sin as immorality.

John the Baptist preached, *"Repent, for the kingdom of heaven is at hand"* (Matthew 3:2). He wasn't saying "confess your sins," but rather, to turn from sin. And that is what we are to do: *turn* from our sins toward the Lord Jesus. This takes time and hard work. *"A cord of three strands is not quickly torn apart"* (Ecclesiastes 4:12) and our sins are wrapped much more thickly than that. That's why we are instructed to *"discipline [ourselves] for the purpose of godliness"* (1 Timothy 4:7†).

The Greek word for *discipline* means "to exercise or train." In other words, do it over and over until you get it right. How godly you become depends on how hard you work at it. Old habits of sinful thinking and responding do not just disappear. They must be replaced with godly thoughts and responses. You have to be *"transformed by the renewing of your mind"* (Romans 12:2). As you work at it, the Holy Spirit enables you until, eventually, the godly response becomes the automatic response.

Creating a Godly Atmosphere

Jeremy put his key in the front door lock, then hesitated. He had not been looking forward to coming home this evening. When he left for work that morning, Mandy had been in one of her "moods," and he knew it would only get worse.

But when he stepped inside, he was taken aback by what he saw. The house was clean, and something smelled really good coming from the kitchen. Soft music was coming from the stereo, and none of the kids were screaming or crying. He walked into the kitchen and found Mandy preparing a salad. A smile lit up her face when she saw him. "Hi, Sweetheart!" she said, and then laughed when she saw the puzzled look on his face. "You're wondering what happened here," she said. "Well, this morning after you left, I was reading Proverbs 31, and I realized, none of those things about the 'excellent wife' describe me." She shared how God had convicted her of how her unrighteous attitudes were affecting their family. "I want to do better," she said. "I'm not saying I'm going to be perfect every day. But with God's help, I'm going to start being a more cheerful, positive person."

We've talked previously about creating an atmosphere of calm in the home and about being sensitive to the sights, sounds, and smells that are part of the home environment. All of these things are good, but creating a *godly* atmosphere in your family should be your top priority. Anyone can create a calm environment; women's magazines are filled with pictures of homes that look gorgeous, peaceful and all *feng shui*. It doesn't take a Christ-follower to put together a home that looks good. But since you are the "keeper" of the home, and you set the tone for the family, it is up to you to make sure that your attitudes promote the "joy of the Lord" in your home and in your family (Nehemiah 8:10). The Proverbs 31 woman is clothed with "strength and dignity," and her strength comes from her joy in Christ and in her family.

Memorize It!

To sum up, all of you be harmonious, sympathetic, brotherly, kindhearted, and humble in spirit; not returning evil for evil or insult for insult, but giving a blessing instead; for you were called for the very purpose that you might inherit a blessing.
(1 Peter 3:8-9)

Week 50, Day 1

Strength and dignity are her clothing, and she smiles at the future.
Proverbs 31:25

Application

What are some specific things you can do to promote a godly atmosphere in your home?

- Memorize Scripture and work God's Word into everyday conversation.
- Keep praise music or hymns on the family stereo.
- Talk to your family about God's goodness to you and to them.
- Be cheerful and optimistic. Smile frequently!
- Set a good example to your husband and children by being patient and loving no matter what is going on.

Above all else, *"Love the Lord your God with all your heart, and with all your soul, and with all your strength, and with all your mind"* (Luke 10:27). When you love God with everything that is in you, the godliness that results will pour out into your home.

Week 50, Day 2

Therefore encourage one another and build up one another.
1 THESSALONIANS 5:11†

Application

You can probably agree with the necessity of being your husband's "steroids," but if it's not normal for you to act this way, you may be at a loss as to *how*. As you learn more about respect, you will naturally become more of a help to your husband in this way. But you can begin changing your ways immediately by doing the following:

- Pray for the Holy Spirit's help in making you a more positive and encouraging wife.
- Look for something to praise your husband about today, then just say it!
- Hold your tongue when he does or says something you might normally criticize.
- Praise him to someone else—your children, your parents, a friend—in his hearing.

BUILDING HIM UP

In 2003, the world of sports was jolted when San Francisco Giants' outfielder Barry Bonds was accused of taking anabolic steroids to enhance his performance in professional baseball. Fans everywhere were disappointed to learn that Bonds may have cheated when he broke the homerun records of Babe Ruth and Hank Aaron.

Steroids have a number of uses, but we're most familiar with how they help athletes artificially excel in their sport. Something about the drug builds up muscle mass, delays fatigue and creates a feeling of euphoria—making it possible for the user to run faster, hit harder, and last longer than they would without it.

Did you know *you* are a steroid? When you praise, encourage, and build your husband up, you are like a performance-enhancing drug, giving him an "unfair" advantage over his competition in the world. That edge helps him in his job, his ministry, and his relationships. It helps him emotionally, intellectually, even physically. Generally speaking, men who are loved and honored by their wives are healthier, happier and more successful than men whose wives tear them down or make them feel inferior. Building your husband up helps him become a better husband.

American novelist John Steinbeck said, "It is the nature of man to rise to greatness if greatness is expected of him." Sometimes we get in the extremely bad habit of criticizing our husbands because we believe he needs to hear what he's doing wrong so he can fix it. But criticizing and tearing a man down drains him of the strength he needs to live well. You may think you're "helping" your husband, when, in fact, you're doing quite the opposite. No woman ever nagged her husband to greatness.

Proverbs 12:4 says, *"An excellent wife is the crown of her husband, but she who shames him is like rottenness in his bones."* How much better to be the performance-enhancing "drug" God means you to be!

Memorize It!

To sum up, all of you be harmonious, sympathetic, brotherly, kindhearted, and humble in spirit; not returning evil for evil or insult for insult, but giving a blessing instead; for you were called for the very purpose that you might inherit a blessing.
(1 Peter 3:8-9)

The Boss of Me

Nicole's husband died unexpectedly when her children were very young, leaving her alone and devastated. Thankfully, Richard had provided for his family financially, and Nicole was able to stay home with the kids for a while. Once they were in middle school, Nicole took a part-time job, giving her a little extra money and a feeling of independence and control.

A few months into her job Nicole met and fell in love with a man who loved the Lord as much as she did. When Jonathan asked her to marry him, she didn't hesitate. What she didn't anticipate, however, was how difficult it was to give up the control over her life that she had enjoyed for so many years. She was used to answering only to herself for how she spent her days. Now when Jonathan asked her to do something or kept her from doing what she wanted, she could feel frustration welling up inside.

You don't need to live Nicole's story to understand the lust for autonomy. The idol of self-determination is the most basic, universal idol of the heart. It's the idol Satan used to deceive Eve in the garden and is at the root of almost every other idol we have. When the serpent said to Eve, *"God knows that in the day you eat from it your eyes will be opened, and you will be like God, knowing good and evil"* (Genesis 3:5†), what he was saying was, "Wouldn't you rather decide things for yourself? Eat this, and you'll be able to make your own life decisions, instead of having to come to God for everything."

The temptation to be our own god is a temptation we struggle with at almost every moment of the day, and our husbands frequently frustrate our idol of self-rule. God uses them to remind us that, as the "bride of Christ," we are not our own, but have been "bought with a price" (1 Corinthians 6:20). Much of our stress and anxiety actually comes from our habit of being our own boss and pursuing a plethora of fleshly goals, rather than the singular goal of Jesus Christ.

You felt secure in your wickedness and said, 'No one sees me.' Your wisdom and your knowledge, they have deluded you; for you have said in your heart, 'I am, and there is no one besides me.'
Isaiah 47:10

Application

Pursuing His kingdom and His righteousness is not easy. It is like a mountain each of us must climb, and we're all at different places on that mountain. But you don't make progress if you keep hopping off to climb other mountains. What most of us do is try to climb a whole mountain range. We have so many goals for our life, so many pleasures we are seeking, and in our lust for self-rule, *we* decide which mountain we're going to climb today, which goal we're going to pursue, rather than continuing on the one mountain that pleases God.

What makes climbing the Kingdom mountain easier is to keep your eyes on Jesus Christ. If you truly love Him, you will set your heart wholly on Him and not be easily distracted by the lusts of the flesh.

Memorize It!

To sum up, all of you be harmonious, sympathetic, brotherly, kindhearted, and humble in spirit; not returning evil for evil or insult for insult, but giving a blessing instead; for you were called for the very purpose that you might inherit a blessing.
(1 Peter 3:8-9)

Week 50, Day 4

Who is there to harm you if you prove zealous for what is good? But even if you should suffer for the sake of righteousness, you are blessed.
1 Peter 3:13-14†

Application

You can endure righteous suffering when you remember that your affliction is "momentary and light" (2 Corinthians 4:17) compared to the:

- Persecution many Christians have suffered throughout history and are continuing to suffer today. But *"**you** have not yet resisted to the point of shedding blood in your striving against sin"* (Hebrews 12:4†).
- Sacrifice Christ made for you (Hebrews 12:3).
- Blessing that comes from obedience (1 Peter 3:14).
- Peace knowing that God is working to accomplish His purposes even in trying circumstances (Romans 8:28, 1 Peter 4:19).
- Joy that results from following the example of the Lord Jesus (Hebrews 12:2; Colossians 1:10-12; 1 Thessalonians 1:6).
- Glory that awaits you (Romans 8:18, Colossians 3:4).

Light Affliction

The last time Cheryl and Marty went to Nick and Josie's, Nick offered her marijuana, so she was reluctant to go back. Unlike her husband and his friends, Cheryl was a born-again believer. She had very little in common with Nick and Josie and did not feel comfortable in their home. She suggested they go out to dinner, but Marty dismissed her concerns. "Don't worry, there won't be any pot," he assured her.

True, there wasn't any pot—but there was plenty of beer, and it didn't take long for all propriety to go out the window. "Strip poker!" Josie laughed as she took out a deck of cards. Nick grinned, "Sounds good!" and pulled Cheryl over to the kitchen table. Marty looked with bleary eyes at his wife. "Relax," he said. "If it gets too crazy for you, we'll stop."

Cheryl is in a difficult situation. No matter which path she chooses, she's going to suffer consequences. If she stands up for what is right, she will suffer their scorn and possibly embarrass her husband. But if she goes along with the party, she will suffer in her spirit by doing something she knows is sinful. What's worse, she will be disobeying Christ.

Cheryl's responsibility is to continue submitting to Marty, but without sinning. She must refuse to participate in their "fun," but she can still do so in a way that is respectful to her husband. If she returns "evil for evil" (1 Peter 3:9), she will suffer, but not for "doing what is right" (1 Peter 3:17). Returning evil for evil would be to sulk, get angry, talk down to her husband or his friends, or lie about her reasons for not participating. ("I'm not wearing enough layers, I would be at a disadvantage!") Instead, she should remain polite and respectful, but firmly refuse to go along with the game. She can suggest they go for a walk, watch a movie, or play a different game. She can even "return a blessing" by helping Josie clean up or making everyone something to eat. In almost every test of our faith, God will provide opportunities to serve others.

Memorize It!

To sum up, all of you be harmonious, sympathetic, brotherly, kindhearted, and humble in spirit; not returning evil for evil or insult for insult, but giving a blessing instead; for you were called for the very purpose that you might inherit a blessing.
(1 Peter 3:8-9)

THE WINTER OF OUR DISCONTENT

Not that I speak from want; for I have learned to be content in whatever circumstances I am. I know how to get along with humble means, and I also know how to live in prosperity; in any and every circumstance I have learned the secret of being filled and going hungry, both of having abundance and suffering need.
PHILIPPIANS 4:11-12

One night I dreamed a friend of mine was standing at an ATM machine with seven children in tow. The next day I told her about my dream. "I wonder what that means?" she laughed. "Maybe you're going to come into some money," I said, "and have four more kids?" Nancy smiled. "More kids I can take. But I don't need more money. I'm perfectly content with what we have."

When Nancy said that, I thought she was nuts. Who in the world doesn't want more money? The next year, however, would show me clearly the Source and depth of Nancy's contentment.

Nancy's husband Rod was a policeman, and shortly after my dream he was killed in the line of duty. In the midst of her sorrow, she leaned fully on her Savior. Nancy was a humble woman who trusted God to *"supply all [her] needs according to His riches in glory in Christ Jesus"* (Philippians 4:19). I never heard her complain about her circumstances, even when she didn't know what she would face in the future. She loved and missed her husband, but refused to be bitter.

My dream turned out to be tragically, yet beautifully, prophetic. Even though her trust was not in riches, God saw fit to take care of her financially as she received a large monetary settlement. Then, a year later she met a widower who had two small children. They married and had two children of their own—bringing the total to seven!

I contrast Nancy to other women who have endured similar tragedies but did not fare nearly as well. I truly believe the difference is in the pride or humility of the sufferers. The proud heart rebels against hardship and doesn't trust God to work (Proverbs 19:3). But people like Nancy, who humbly submit to trials from the LORD (1 Peter 1:6-7, James 1:12) find that He is a good God who faithfully *"causes all things to work together for good to those who love God [and] are called according to His purpose"* (Romans 8:28†).

Application

Nancy's story turned out well in this life, but God does not promise a similar outcome for every believer. In Hebrews 11, we see how God deals differently with each of us. Some of His servants "received back their dead by resurrection" (Hebrews 11:35) but others were "stoned...sawn in two... put to death with the sword" (vs. 37). Only God knows how we can best glorify Him with our lives.

You don't know how God is going to use you, but clinging to your right to have life go smoothly will not guarantee that it will. Pride demands a certain kind of life and a certain level of comfort. What God requires is that we respond with humility to whatever happens to us, being ready to "suffer for the sake of righteousness" (1 Peter 3:14) if that is what He asks.

Week 51, Day 1

But have nothing to do with worldly fables fit only for old women. On the other hand, discipline yourself for the purpose of godliness; for bodily discipline is only of little profit, but godliness is profitable for all things, since it holds promise for the present life and also for the life to come.
1 Timothy 4:7-8

Application

In Christ, you can change—not just improve a little, but truly repent and turn from your sin. If your character changes to be conformed to Christ, you will be able to go through times of testing without sinning against God and offending others.

While you are working on changing, keep praying and asking God to change your heart and your character. Perhaps you have been angry and bitter for years. Maybe you're naturally sarcastic, or heavily involved in some sinful habit that is difficult to change. Remember that He always *"provides a way of escape"* (1 Corinthians 10:13); you *always* have the option of practicing righteousness.

Practice Makes Perfect

I'm one of those people who never quite mastered the art of doing cartwheels. Even as a child, my cartwheels were absolutely pathetic, and this was always a source of embarrassment to me, because as far as I could tell, I was the only girl in the state of Indiana who was incapable of making her body move like that. So when I had daughters, I was determined that they were going to learn to do cartwheels. I signed the twins up for gymnastics when they were four years old, and after several weeks, their cartwheels looked...well, terrible. But eventually, they got it down. It took several months, but they learned to do them perfectly.

Brittan and Ciara did not learn to do cartwheels overnight. It took practice and bodily discipline. They had to train their little hands to get in the right position, their little legs to...do whatever it is little legs do in a cartwheel. (Like I said, I never figured it out!) After they got cartwheels down, they learned to do more difficult stuff, like round-offs and back handsprings. At times they were frustrated, and they fell, and got hurt a few times, but they kept at it. They knew in their heads how to do these stunts, but it took lots of practice to get good at it.

Being a godly wife is no different. You can learn all about how to be a submissive wife, but if you don't practice it, you won't get good at it. You're close to the end of this book, so you've learned much about being a godly wife. Now comes the hard part, doing it, which takes discipline and plain old practice. You must repeatedly think and act according to God's Word until gentle, loving responses are your first thoughts instead of afterthoughts. The results will be life-changing if you work long and hard on disciplining yourself *"for the purpose of godliness"* (1 Timothy 4:7).

Remember that God has given you everything you need. *"His divine power has granted to us everything pertaining to life and godliness"* (2 Peter 1:3†). Every tool you need is only a prayer away. Your part is to humble yourself, cry out to God for help, grab those tools, and get to work!

Memorize It!

Do not worry then, saying, "What will we eat?" or "What will we drink?" or "What will we wear for clothing?" For the Gentiles eagerly seek all these things; for your heavenly Father knows that you need all these things.
(Matthew 6:31-32)

A Path to Harmony

You husbands in the same way, live with your wives in an understanding way, as with someone weaker, since she is a woman; and show her honor as a fellow heir of the grace of life, so that your prayers will not be hindered.
1 Peter 3:7

Many of us have some odd ideas about the order of events in the fall of Man. (See Genesis 1-3.) Everything about the earth was good and perfect, but God observed, *"It is not good for the man to be alone; I will make him a helper suitable for him"* (Genesis 2:18). Notice that God created Eve to be Adam's helper *before* sin entered into the world. This was part of God's perfect creation: a husband-wife team living in perfect harmony, cultivating and populating the earth. Being your husband's helper is God's perfect will for you—it is not part of the curse! What *is* part of the curse is your desire to rebel against and dominate your husband.

After Adam and Eve sinned, God pronounced a curse on married couples from that day forward: *"Your desire will be for your husband, and he will rule over you"* (Genesis 3:16). That word *desire* implies the desire to control or overtake the husband's authority. The husband, under the same curse, would from that day forward desire not to guide his wife lovingly, but to "rule over" and dominate her.

The good news is that Christ came to redeem us from this curse. He can bring you and your husband to a restored, intimate relationship with God and with each other. If you are "in Christ," you and your husband have the potential to regain much of the harmony that was lost at the fall of man. But this is only possible as you willingly submit to God's command to be your husband's suitable helper.

One of Satan's schemes in getting you to be disobedient is to make you discontent with your role as your husband's helper. Not helping your husband brings many consequences: it plays into Satan's hands to subvert the purposes of God in your life; reinforces the painful effects of the curse brought about by sin; sets a poor example for your children, teaching them to rebel against their father and against God; shames your husband, creating bitterness and disunity; and creates conflict and turmoil, disrupting the efficient operation of the family.

Application

It will help you to be more obedient when you "renew your mind" and remind yourself of the benefits of helping your husband. Helping your husband:

- restores the harmony that God originally intended in marriage
- gives your husband strength for the work God has called him to do
- sets a good example of submission to authority for your children; brings peace to your spirit and your home
- allows the family to operate most efficiently
- glorifies God

If you have been failing lately at helping your husband, today is a good day to confess that sin and turn from it. As you confess, read the preceding lists to God, agreeing with Him about the benefits of being your husband's helper and the consequences of rebellion in this area.

Memorize It!

Do not worry then, saying, "What will we eat?" or "What will we drink?" or "What will we wear for clothing?" For the Gentiles eagerly seek all these things; for your heavenly Father knows that you need all these things. (Matthew 6:31-32)

Week 51, Day 3

Let the peace of Christ rule in your hearts, to which indeed you were called in one body; and be thankful.
Colossians 3:15

Application

How grateful are you for the life God has provided through your husband? Even if you don't have a lot by the world's standards, remember that your treasure is in heaven (Luke 18:22). Tomorrow's lesson will focus on specific Scripture and how to apply it to renew your thinking to become a more thankful person. For today, focus on discovering any unconfessed ingratitude in your heart. Write down your ungrateful thoughts, and tomorrow we will talk about replacing them with grateful thoughts.

Next, write down all you have to be thankful for. "Count your blessings" as the old hymn goes. Your blessings list should be much longer than your ingratitude list. If not, we have a lot of work to do tomorrow!

Love is Grateful (Part 1)

Charlotte sat staring out the window, tears falling from her eyes onto her bulging stomach. It helped her to look outside; when she looked inside the apartment, all she saw were two tiny bedrooms, very little furniture, and a stack of bills on the kitchen table which would go unpaid for probably several more months. She felt the baby move inside her womb, and wondered what life would be like for their child. Corey promised they would have a house by the time the baby came, but this morning they had argued about it, and he finally admitted there was no way they would have a house by then. In fact, he didn't know when they would be able to get out of this apartment.

Charlotte was so angry, she wondered why she had married Corey in the first place. She had seen signs even while they were dating, and she should have known he would not live up to his promises. She turned and looked at the mess in the apartment. *I should clean,* she thought. *But Corey would like that, wouldn't he! No way am I going to do anything nice for him right now!*

Charlotte's love for her husband is being destroyed by her ungrateful attitude and her lust for things she doesn't have. She is willing to sacrifice obedience to Christ and intimacy with her husband for what—a house? Nice things? It's interesting, the things we think are worth that kind of sacrifice. How much better to sacrifice what we want for what Christ wants?

If you have a heart of gratitude, you will want to express love to your husband. But if you're discontent and ungrateful, you will be unable to love your husband biblically and instead will become self-pitying and self-focused. You might be somewhat successful at hiding your attitude, but it will come out eventually. The only real way to glorify Jesus Christ and love your husband is to think according to God's Word (Romans 12:2) and to be grateful for all God has given you—including your husband.

Memorize It!

Do not worry then, saying, "What will we eat?" or "What will we drink?" or "What will we wear for clothing?" For the Gentiles eagerly seek all these things; for your heavenly Father knows that you need all these things.
(Matthew 6:31-32)

Love is Grateful (Part 2)

Always giving thanks for all things in the name of our Lord Jesus Christ to God, even the Father.
Ephesians 5:20

Yesterday we talked about thankfulness, and how ingratitude is a love killer in marriage. Today we're going to talk about how to "put on love" (Colossians 3:14) by learning to be continually grateful for your husband, and expressing that gratitude to him, to God, and to yourself. How grateful you are determines, in part, how you talk to yourself—but you can also become more grateful by talking to yourself differently. By focusing your inner conversation on things that are good and true, and by reflecting on the many things you have for which you can be grateful, you can change your way of thinking and become a more thankful person.

The following are examples of how a wife might think sinful, ungrateful thoughts; after each one is a corresponding godly thought that expresses love and gratitude to God and her husband. As you read these, see if you have been guilty of similar thinking. You may not think these exact thoughts, but after yesterday's exercise you may be aware of other destructive thinking. Write down your own ungrateful thoughts. Then cross them out, and after each one, write a godly thought to replace it with. This exercise will help you get into the habit of replacing sinful thoughts with God-honoring thoughts.

"My husband is not as loving (smart, kind, spiritual, sexy, etc.) as I would like him to be."

- *Thank you, Lord, for my husband. He's not perfect, but he's a work in progress, just as I am!* (Philippians 1:6)

"I wish he would just go away and leave me alone."

- *So many wives feel neglected and ignored; I'm grateful I have a husband who wants to spend time with me.* (Philippians 4:11)

"I wish I had married someone more like my friend's husband. He is so good to her."

- *I have no idea what life with that man is really like. There's no such thing as a perfect husband, but I know that God sees my husband as the perfect man for me.* (Genesis 2:22-24)

"I wish my husband made more money, so I can have more of the things that I want."

- *I have much to be thankful for, and need to be content with the things God has given me. I am thankful for a husband who provides for me as well as he does.* (Hebrews 13:5)

"I made a mistake in marrying my husband. He is not the man I thought he was."

- *I thank God for the grace He gives me to die to myself and love sacrificially, the way Christ loves me. "Forgetting what lies behind and reaching forward to what lies ahead, I press on toward the goal for the prize of the upward call of God in Christ Jesus"* (Philippians 3:13-14†).

Memorize It!

Do not worry then, saying, "What will we eat?" or "What will we drink?" or "What will we wear for clothing?" For the Gentiles eagerly seek all these things; for your heavenly Father knows that you need all these things.
(Matthew 6:31-32)

Week 51, Day 5

Let your light shine before men in such a way that they may see your good works, and glorify your Father who is in heaven.
MATTHEW 5:16

Application

If your husband is unsaved, or if there is any doubt as to his salvation, then nothing is more important in your marriage than seeing your husband come to follow Christ. Your respectful behavior is one of the most powerful tools God has to bring your husband to Christ. It's not that we never use words to speak truth to our husbands, but "actions speak louder than words."

If at any time you are tempted to show disrespect to your husband, ask yourself, "Is the *reason* I am disrespecting my husband right now *more important* than him coming to know Christ?"

WITHOUT A WORD

Bruce and his brother Steve worked their way down the buffet line at his niece's wedding, loading their plates with chicken wings and jello salad. Suddenly, Steve asked, "So, what's with your wife?" "What do you mean?" Bruce replied. Steve shrugged. "You know, we've talked about how she's always in a bad mood. But I haven't heard her say one negative thing all day, and she's been really nice!"

Bruce smiled as they took a seat. "She found religion." Steve looked dumbfounded. "Seriously?" Bruce continued, "Yeah. She went to this retreat, and when she came home she said she was a born-again Christian." Steve put his hand on his brother's shoulder in mock sympathy. "Dude, I'm sorry! So, has she been all preachy at you?" Bruce laughed, "Not at all! In fact, I feel like I have a brand new wife. She's more respectful, more concerned about my needs for once." He leaned in close and lowered his voice, "And the sex has never been better!" Steve's jaw dropped and he stared at Bruce. "I'm telling you," Bruce laughed, "I think there may actually be something to all of this church stuff!"

When Bruce's wife was saved, she very quickly learned—through the Scriptures and the faithful mentoring of a friend—that she needed to respect and obey her husband, not manipulate him. She realized that if her husband was ever going to come alongside her in this faith journey, she would have to make Christ more attractive to him. The best way to do that was to glorify God by obeying His Word.

Being under the authority of Christ means respecting your husband even if he is not a believer. The reason God does not exempt you from that command is because respect is critical to a healthy marriage, even if one of the partners is unsaved. In fact, He goes on to apply this command further in 1 Peter: "*You wives, be submissive to your own husbands so that* ***even if any of them are disobedient to the word****, they may be won without a word by the behavior of their wives*" (1 Peter 3:1-2†).

PAIN AVOIDANCE

Whenever I talk to women about being the excellent wives God has called them to be, I share God's command to submit to their husbands. Many will counter with some kind of scenario as to why they are unable to do so. "You don't know my husband." "But what if he…?" "I tried that and it didn't work!"

What each of these objections boils down to is this: if I submit to my husband, something bad will happen to me. In other words, they are afraid to be obedient for fear of suffering uncomfortable or unbearable consequences.

What is your greatest fear if you were to totally submit to your husband in all things? Think about that for a moment, and then either write it here or write it in your prayer journal, as a prayer to God for help:

There are a number of reasons why you do not need to fear submitting to your husband. First of all, you know that God rewards obedience, and that He is faithful to His people never to desert them or forsake them (Hebrews 13:5). Secondly, you need to recognize the many ways God is providing for your protection. One of the main reasons God establishes any authority—whether that's your husband, the police, the church, or the government—is for protection. He has given you the right and the responsibility to biblically reprove your husband for sin, which protects you from the consequences of his sin if he responds properly. If he doesn't respond well, you can seek the help of the church or governmental authorities, who are all on standby and charged by God with protecting you.

Even though God has put these institutions into place for your protection, the truth is that even these may fail you. God's system works well when everyone does what they're supposed to do, but you and I know that doesn't always happen. Your response when the system fails should not be to take matters into your own hands. You can still *"do what is right without being frightened by any fear"* (1 Peter 3:6), because, ultimately, your protection comes from God.

Memorize It!

But seek first His kingdom and His righteousness, and all these things will be added to you. So do not worry about tomorrow; for tomorrow will care for itself. Each day has enough trouble of its own.
(Matthew 6:33-34)

For this reason I also suffer these things, but I am not ashamed; for I know whom I have believed and I am convinced that He is able to guard what I have entrusted to Him until that day.
2 TIMOTHY 1:12

Application

Does obedience to God mean that nothing bad will ever happen to you? Of course not. It is common for Western Christians to expect protection from all harm, and to avoid pain. But look at the thousands throughout history who have been martyred for Christ. Go to www.persecution.com and read about the many Christians today who are suffering and dying for Christ. Like Paul, these people rejoice that they have been *"considered worthy to suffer…for His name"* (Acts 5:41†).

You, too, may have to suffer in order to do what is right. The standard for obedience should never be, "What will bring me the most benefit and the least amount of pain?" The standard should always be, "What is the right thing to do, no matter how dire the consequences?"

Week 52, Day 2

I do all things for the sake of the gospel, so that I may become a fellow partaker of it.
1 Corinthians 9:23

Application

Many of us are involved in ministry, but our service lacks one key component: we never share the gospel. You can be very sacrificial at home and in your church, but if you're not making Him known—if you're not sharing the gospel with lost people, you're still missing the boat.

You may want to share the gospel but not know where to begin. Like anything else, it starts with planning. Take two days this week, and for 30 minutes on each of those days, devote yourself to pursuing a way to share the gospel with others. Even if you're involved in ministry at your church already, find a ministry where you actively tell others about Christ.

The Whole Point

If you've read this entire book up to this point, you've learned much about being an excellent wife. Now let me ask you a question: Why should you be an excellent wife? So you can be happy? So your marriage will be peaceful, your relationship with your husband satisfying, your home free of conflict?

No. ***The reason you should be an excellent wife is to share the gospel.*** Your main objective in everything you do should be to glorify God. The purpose of glorifying God is to share the gospel. The gospel of Jesus Christ is the ultimate goal of all that we do.

When your marriage honors God, He is glorified, His Word is glorified, and people are attracted to Him. One of the problems in modern Christianity is that the gospel is hindered by the condition of our marriages. The national divorce rate is about 43%, and Christian marriages fail at about the same rate. How are lost people going to be attracted to the God who designed marriage, if His people are no better at keeping their marriages together than anyone else?

On the flip side, some believing couples are successful in staying together, yet they never let the secret out that Christ is the reason for the joy and harmony in their marriage. They don't leverage their marriage for the Kingdom. They selfishly consume all of the benefits of their marriage on themselves, enjoying the intimacy and unity that God gives, yet never giving God the glory so that others may be saved as a result.

Jesus said the greatest commandment was to *"love the Lord your God with all your heart, and with all your soul, and with all your strength, and with all your mind; and your neighbor as yourself"* (Luke 10:27). The purpose of being an excellent, godly wife is so you can fulfill the greatest commandment: to love God and to love others. You cannot love God without loving others. And you cannot love others without sharing the gospel.

Memorize It!

But seek first His kingdom and His righteousness, and all these things will be added to you. So do not worry about tomorrow; for tomorrow will care for itself. Each day has enough trouble of its own. (Matthew 6:33-34)

SUBMISSION HONORS GOD'S WORD

We've talked a lot this year about submission. In summary, you bring honor to your husband, the LORD Jesus Christ, and God's Word when:

- **Obeying God is more important to you than having your own way.** When you obey rather than contend for your own way, you are being a "living sacrifice" (Romans 12:1-2), sacrificing what you want for what the LORD wants for you.
- **You have a reverential fear of the LORD.** God is a Holy, Almighty God that you are here to serve. Proverbs 3:7 warns, *"Do not be wise in your own eyes. Fear the LORD and turn away from evil."* I know it sounds harsh, but when you rebel against God's Word and your husband, you are doing evil. An appropriate fear of the LORD puts all things into proper perspective (Matthew 10:28).
- **You let the Word of Christ direct your life.** *"Let the Word of Christ richly dwell within you"* (Colossians 3:16†). When you respond in *grateful* submission to God as well as *gracious* submission to your husband, you give evidence that the Word of Christ (the Scriptures) is dwelling within you and directing your life.
- **Your life is not an affront to the pattern for marriage given in Ephesians 5.** *"But as the church is subject to Christ, so also the wives ought to be to their husbands in everything"* (Ephesians 5:24†). Marriage is a beautiful picture of the church's submissive relationship to Christ. As you submit to your husband, you live out the pattern God has appointed for you.
- **You are submissive whether you feel like it or not.** Just before His crucifixion, Jesus prayed, *"My Father, if it is possible, let this cup pass from Me; yet not as I will, but as You will"* (Matthew 26:39). The suffering and humiliation He endured were not enjoyable, but He did it in order to carry out the Father's plan of redemption. He did it *"for the joy set before Him"* (Hebrews 12:2). Likewise, you will not always feel like being submissive, but with God's grace and power you can be submissive with a godly motive and for the glory of the LORD Jesus.

Memorize It!

But seek first His kingdom and His righteousness, and all these things will be added to you. So do not worry about tomorrow; for tomorrow will care for itself. Each day has enough trouble of its own.
(Matthew 6:33-34)

Older women likewise are to be reverent in their behavior...so that they may encourage the young women to love their husbands, to love their children, to be sensible, pure, workers at home, kind, being subject to their own husbands, so that the word of God will not be dishonored.
TITUS 2:3-5†

Application

The challenge for today is to go back to Week 1, Day 1 and read what you wrote, either on that page or in your prayer journal, about submission. You were asked to record your thoughts and what you hoped to accomplish over the year with regard to becoming more submitted to God and to your husband.

Compare what you wrote then with where you are now. Is there definite growth in the area of submission? Can you say, to the praise and glory of God, that you are farther along in this journey than you were when you began? Hopefully you are growing and yielding fruits of righteousness in your life. If not, it's never too late to begin again!

Week 52, Day 4

If we have food and covering,
with these we shall be content.
1 Timothy 6:8

Application

Discontentment limits your view of God's provision; it says to God that you don't trust Him to meet your needs, and it betrays a lack of appreciation for His care of you. The way to build contentment back into your life is to be grateful to God and to express that gratitude frequently.

We serve a good God, who has blessed us with so much. Therefore, you should always be *"content with what you have, for He has said, 'I will never leave you nor forsake you'"* (Hebrews 13:5 ESV).

The Cure for Idolatry

Latrell Sprewell was an incredible basketball player with a promising career in the NBA. In 2000, the New York Knicks gave Sprewell a five-year, $62-million dollar contract. However, he was known for having a violent temper, and coaches were wary of him. He was eventually traded to the Minnesota Timberwolves, who offered him only $21-million over three years.

Sprewell was outraged. His agent declined this and other offers, claiming his client "would not stoop or kneel" to such a small salary. Publicly, Sprewell railed against the Timberwolves, spewing out the infamous complaint: "I have a *family* to feed!"

We are not all that different from Sprewell. Americans have so much, we've lost our perspective of abundance. It seems the more affluent the culture, the less contented its people. This truth, if nothing else, should be a blinding reminder of how wealth can never satisfy our hearts.

No matter where you are on the socio-economic scale, you will be surrounded by people who have more than you, which can seriously erode your contentment. It's not that we're trying to be discontent, but we are literally drowning in options, which makes contentment difficult. Often, what guides our decision-making in the midst of these options is the "lust of the eyes" (1 John 2:16). We think we're okay with our body type, but then a woman walks into the room who is skinnier or prettier, and suddenly we're discontent. We think we're okay with our house, until we see a nicer home, and *poof!* There goes our contentment. We think we're okay with our husband until we see someone better looking, wealthier, more affectionate, or godlier than our husband and we become discontent. We think we're okay with God's provision until we see someone who has something we don't have, and then we lust. We covet what other people have, and we set our hearts to pursuing *those* goals rather than pursuing Christ.

Memorize It!

But seek first His kingdom and His righteousness, and all these things will be added to you. So do not worry about tomorrow; for tomorrow will care for itself. Each day has enough trouble of its own.
(Matthew 6:33-34)

The Dance

Tatiana Navka and Roman Kostomarov take the ice. As Georges Bizet's *Carmen* fills the Olympic arena, the ice skaters glide together in a beautiful, poetic dance. One wrong move could spell disaster as they perform graceful, yet complicated, spins, lifts, and dance steps on skates. It's easy to see why Tatiana and Roman are Olympic champions: in both technical and artistic ability, they are perfect and a thrill to watch.

The beauty of ice dancing is that the dancers move closely together in a gorgeous display of art and physical expression. But the dance only works because the man *leads* and the woman *follows*. It would be awkward and lose much of its grace if the woman were to try lifting the man or guide him across the ice. One of the beautiful things about couple's figure skating is seeing how the man leads, guides, and protects the woman on the ice. He pushes her out for a moment so she can execute a jump or spin, but very quickly draws her back to himself so they can continue their dance together.

What a magnificent picture of submission! God has a vision of you and your husband moving gracefully and purposefully through life as a one-flesh unit. But this partnership only works if you both understand your roles in the dance. If both try to lead, at best you will look ridiculous, and at worse you'll get tangled up and hurt. If neither of you leads, you may as well stay off the dance floor. But when you submit to your husband's loving leadership, the dance begins to work.

You will have to practice to get as good at your dance of submission as Roman and Tatiana are at ice dancing, but as you keep working on your marriage dance, in time you will find that it has become beautiful. When your husband leads and you submit in love, together you produce this beautiful, symmetrical dance that displays God's glory. This is God's purpose in marriage: to bring glory to Himself, to attract lost people to Himself, and to entice His children to love Him more.

Be filled with the Spirit, speaking to one another in psalms and hymns and spiritual songs, singing and making melody with your heart to the Lord; always giving thanks for all things in the name of our Lord Jesus Christ to God, even the Father.
Ephesians 5:18-20†

Application

Every dance has a rhythm, and in the dance of submission, God has already prepared a soundtrack for you to dance to. You'll find this in Ephesians 5:19—*"Be filled with the Spirit, speaking to one another in psalms and hymns and spiritual songs."* This is our soundtrack: as we are filled with the Spirit through the Word of Christ, we will express ourselves to each other in psalms, hymns, and spiritual songs, and we will be thankful. I don't think it's an accident those verses come right before Paul's instructions about marriage. Submission becomes easier as we follow the Spirit's leading with thankfulness in our hearts.

Appendix

How to Know If You Are a True Believer

I am assuming that most women who pick up this book already know the basics of the gospel of Jesus Christ: that our sins have separated us from a just and holy God (Isaiah 59:2); yet God loved us so much that He provided His Son, Jesus Christ, as the only way to bridge that gap (Romans 5:8); Jesus died as a payment for the debt that our sin created (1 Corinthians 15:3); He was buried in a tomb, where He remained for three days (1 Corinthians 15:4); and that He "raised Himself up" as the first of those who would later be resurrected to eternal life in Christ (1 Corinthians 15:20). Those who trust in Christ's sacrifice for their sins, rather than trusting in their own good works (Titus 3:5), are adopted into God's family, and at that moment become a "new creation," (2 Corinthians 5:17, Ephesians 1:5), destined to live forever with God in the place He is preparing for His children (John 14:1-3).

James 2:19 (NKJV) says, "You believe that there is one God. You do well. Even the demons believe—and tremble!" In other words, they know about God, but they do not *know* God. They know about God, but they do "not honor Him as God" (Romans 1:21). They don't accept His authority over their lives, but instead have rebelled against Him and His authority.

Many people know the truths of the gospel and can even tell others how to be saved. But like the demons, they haven't accepted His authority over their lives. The question is, how do you know if you are truly saved, that you have received Christ into your heart and life, and not just acknowledged intellectually that certain things are true, just as the demons do?

The Bible gives many "tests" of whether or not a person is a true child of God:

- ☐ You believe that Jesus Christ is God, come in the flesh (1 John 5:1, John 10:30).
- ☐ You are submitted to the authority of Christ, through His Word, to direct your life (2 Timothy 3:15-17, 2 Corinthians 10:5, 1 Timothy 4:6).
- ☐ You love God and His Son, Jesus Christ (1 Peter 1:8-9; 1 John 5:1).
- ☐ You love other believers (1 John 3:10, 14).
- ☐ You desire to spend time with God (Psalm 42:1).
- ☐ You have a conscious awareness that the Holy Spirit lives within you (1 John 4:13).
- ☐ You long more for God than for the things of this world (1 John 2:15).
- ☐ Your life shows a pattern of obedience to God (1 John 2:4; 1 John 3:10, 24).
- ☐ You are disciplined by God when you sin (Hebrews 12:5-8).
- ☐ There is evidence of growth in your life (Hebrews 5:12-14).
- ☐ You are producing good "fruit" (good works) for God (Colossians 1:10).
- ☐ You are exhibiting the fruit of the Spirit to some degree in your character (Galatians 5:22-23).

If these things are not true of you, then you must question whether you have truly trusted Christ as your LORD and Savior. Many people accept Jesus Christ as a sort of "fire insurance" to keep them from hell, but they are not at all interested in having God tell them how to run their lives. Their attitude is, "Thanks for the rescue, LORD, but I can take it from here."

James 2:17† says that "faith, if it has no works, is dead." And James 2:14† asks the question: "Can that faith save [you]?" The obvious answer is *no*: dead faith cannot save anyone. People who have that kind of faith will face God someday only to hear Him say, "I never knew you; depart from me" (Matthew 7:23†).

What about you? Is your faith alive? Or do you have the same kind of faith that demons have, knowing *about* God but not knowing God? As a preacher friend of mine says, "You know God's truth. The question is, do you *love* it?" The demons know the truth of God, but they clearly do not love it.

As you have worked through this book, I pray that God has shown you clearly whether or not you are truly "in the faith" (2 Corinthians 13:5). If you doubt your salvation, or are convicted of your need to trust Christ, not just as your Savior but as your LORD, and to truly become God's child, you can pray a prayer similar to this one:

> *Heavenly Father, God, I realize that until today I have only wanted you to rescue me from hell, but I haven't wanted* You, *LORD. I haven't wanted you to tell me what to do, and I haven't submitted myself to the authority of Christ in my life. I have loved myself more than I have loved you; I have loved the things you give more than I have loved you, the Giver; I have worshipped creation—myself, my goals, the things of this world—more than I have worshipped the Creator. I want that to change today, LORD. I want you more than anything, and I want to please you with my life. I trust in the sacrifice Your Son made on the cross on my behalf. Use me however you please for your glory, as from this day forward I purpose to live only for you, LORD. In Jesus' name I pray, Amen.*

Endnotes

[1] (pg. 12) 1 Corinthians 13:4-7

[2] (pg. 34) Joshua 24:19

[3] (pg. 46) James 1:20

[4] (pg. 46) Ephesians 6:4

[5] (pg. 51) 1 Timothy 5:14-15 is written specifically about young widows, but the inference is clear that they are to behave as all young wives should behave in raising children, keeping the house, etc.

[6] (pg. 80) Colossians 3:8

[7] (pg. 122) *Changed into His Image: God's Plan for Transforming Your Life*, BJU Press, Greenville, South Carolina, 1999, p. 69-70.

[8] (pg. 128) Jim Berg, *Changed into His Image: God's Plan for Transforming Your Life*, BJU Press, Greenville, South Carolina, 1999, p. 76.

[9] (pg. 142) Jim Kochenburger, *The Top 20 Messages for Youth Ministry*, Group Publishing, Inc.

[10] (pg. 159) www.NANC.org

[11] (pg. 233) From the hymn, "It is Well with My Soul" by Horatio Spafford.

[12] (pg. 241) *For the Love of God, Volume Two: A Daily Companion for Discovering the Riches of God's Word*, Crossway Books, Wheaton, Illinois, 1999, p. 23.

Topical Index